BOB DYLAN

BY GREIL MARCUS

ALSO BY GREIL MARCUS

Mystery Train: Images of America in Rock 'n' Roll Music
(1975, 2008)

Lipstick Traces: A Secret History of the 20th Century (1989, 2009)

Dead Elvis: A Chronicle of a Cultural Obsession (1991)

In the Fascist Bathroom: Punk in Pop Music, 1977–92
(1993, originally published as *Ranters & Crowd Pleasers*)

The Dustbin of History (1995)

The Old, Weird America: The World of Bob Dylan's Basement Tapes
(2000, 2011, originally published as *Invisible Republic*, 1997)

*Double Trouble: Bill Clinton and Elvis Presley
in a Land of No Alternatives* (2000)

"The Manchurian Candidate" (2002)

Like a Rolling Stone: Bob Dylan at the Crossroads (2005)

The Shape of Things to Come: Prophecy and the American Voice
(2006)

When That Rough God Goes Riding: Listening to Van Morrison
(2010)

As Editor

Stranded (1979, 2007)

Psychotic Reactions & Carburetor Dung, by Lester Bangs (1987)

*The Rose & the Briar: Death, Love and Liberty in the
American Ballad* (2004, with Sean Wilentz)

A New Literary History of America (2009, with Werner Sollors)

BOB DYLAN

BY GREIL MARCUS

WRITINGS 1968–2010

PUBLICAFFAIRS
NEW YORK

PublicAffairs books are available at special discounts for bulk purchases in
the U.S. by corporations, institutions, and other organizations. For more
information, please contact the Special Markets Department at the Perseus
Books Group, 2300 Chestnut Street, Suite 200, Philadelphia, PA 19103,
call (800) 810-4145, ext. 5000, or e-mail special.markets@perseusbooks.com.

Editorial production by *Marra*thon Production Services. www.marrathon.net

DESIGN BY JANE RAESE
Set in 12-point Apollo

Library of Congress Control Number: 2010934404

ISBN 978-1-58648-831-4

FIRST EDITION
10 9 8 7 6 5 4 3 2

FOR JENNY

CONTENTS

PART SEVEN
Find a Grave, 2001–2004

WHERE I CAME IN

In the summer of 1963, in a field in New Jersey, I'd gone to see Joan Baez, a familiar face in my hometown, in Menlo Park, California, and suddenly a familiar face everywhere else—she'd been on the cover of *Time*. This day she was appearing at one of those old theaters-in-a-round, set up under a tent. She sang, and after a bit she said, "I want to introduce a friend of mine," and out came a scruffy-looking guy with a guitar. He looked dusty. His shoulders were hunched and he seemed slightly embarrassed. He sang a couple of songs by himself, then he sang one or two with Joan Baez, and then he left.

I barely noticed the end of the show. I was transfixed. I was confused. This person had come onto someone else's stage, and while in some ways he seemed as ordinary as anyone in the audience, something in his demeanor dared you to pin him down, to sum him up and write him off, and you couldn't do it. From the way he sounded and the way he moved, you couldn't tell where he was from, where he'd been, or where he was going—though the way he moved and sang somehow made you want to know all of those things. "My name it is nothing, my age it means less," he sang that day, beginning his song "With God on Our Side," which would turn up the next year as the lynchpin of *The Times They Are A-Changin'*—and while the whole book of American history seemed to open up in that song, the country's story telling itself in a new way, the song also kept the singer's promise. As he sang, you couldn't tell his age. He might have been seventeen, he might have been twenty-seven—and to an eighteen-year-old like me, that was someone old enough.

When the show was over, I saw this person, whose name I hadn't caught, crouching behind the tent—there was no backstage, no guards, no protocol—and so I went up to him. He was trying to light a cigarette, it was windy, his hands were shaking; he wasn't paying attention to anything but the match. I was just dumbfounded enough to open my mouth. "You were terrific," I said, never at a loss for something original to say. He didn't look up. "I was shit," he said. "I was just shit." I didn't know what to say to that, so I walked off. I asked someone in the crowd who the person was who along with Joan Baez was getting into her black Jaguar XK-E, then the most glamorous car on the road. When I got back to California I went straight to a record store and bought *The Freewheelin' Bob Dylan,* his second album, the only one in the shop. I couldn't figure out why some of the songs—about the John Birch Society and a "ramblin' gamblin' Willie," something with a band I called "Make a Solid Road"—didn't fit the songs described in the liner notes. I took it back and told the store owner there was something wrong with it. "Oh, they're all like that," he said. "I've had a lot of complaints. Come back next week and I'll have some good copies." But I never did go back. I fell in love with "Don't Think Twice." I played it all day long. I figured if I exchanged my album it might not be on the next one.

For me, for a lot of other people, perhaps in ways for Bob Dylan himself, his life and work opened up from right about that time. Very quickly—with, say, "Blowin' in the Wind," "Masters of War," "A Hard Rain's A-Gonna Fall," "The Lonesome Death of Hattie Carroll," a score more songs about conflict and justice, truth and lie, that could be epic and commonplace in the same moment, songs orchestrated by nothing more than the singer's own bare guitar and harmonica—and then with the mid-sixties albums *Bringing It All Back Home, Highway 61 Revisited,* and *Blonde on Blonde,* filled with visionary performances, most with equally visionary rock 'n' roll not so much behind the songs as all through them—Bob Dylan became in the common imagination far more than a singer who had, by some happenstance, caught his moment. To do what he'd done, Dylan wrote years later, you had to be someone "who could see into things, the truth of things—not metaphorically, either—but really see, like seeing into metal and making it melt, see it for what it was and reveal it for what it was with hard words and vicious insight." In the early 1950s, kids like Bob Dylan watched someone seeing into metal and making it melt every week on *The Adventures of Superman;* in the next decade, as Paul Nelson puts it later in these pages, Dylan "evoked such an intense degree of personal participation from both his admirers and detractors that he could not be permitted so much as a random action. Hungry for a sign, the world used to follow him around, just waiting for him to drop a cigarette butt. When he did they'd sift through the remains, looking for significance. The scary part is they'd find it—and it really would be significant."

This is where I came in, as a writer—six years after the show in New Jersey, at the end of Dylan's adventure as an oracle on the run, just after he released his spare, cryptic album *John Wesley Harding,* an album of parables of the republic, riddles about its cops and robbers, and love songs that took the sting away.

Bobby Darin had three hit records under his belt when he announced his goal in life: "I want to be a legend by the time I'm twenty-five." He didn't make it, but Bob Dylan did.

Those are the first lines from a piece I wrote in 1969 that is not included in this collection of most of what, outside of two earlier books—one on "Like a Rolling Stone," one on the songs that travel under the name of the basement tapes—I've written about Bob Dylan over the years. In 1969 Bob Dylan was twenty-eight. He'd been a legend—a story people passed on as if it might even be true—at least since 1964. But time moved fast then—Bobby Darin, you can imagine, wanted to be a legend by the time he was twenty-five because after that it might be too late.

As a chronicle of events happening as they were written about—which this book, much of it a matter of reviews, reports, sightings, comment in monthly or bi-weekly magazines and weekly newspapers, to some degree is—that heroic period hangs over what I wrote. It's a given that I am writing about someone who has done signal work, has made music so rich that even as it appeared it suggested it might be untouchable, not merely by others but by Dylan himself. It was an enormous achievement: the rewriting, in all senses, of American vernacular music, from the fiddlers who took up "Springfield Mountain" at the end of the eighteenth century to Little Richard, at once a recapturing of the past and the opening of a door to what had never been heard and had never been said. All of that is in this book. But at least for its first half it is present as a shadow, a shadow cast by a performer who, as I began to write about him, had fallen under it himself.

The story I followed was, in its beginning, the story of Bob Dylan as he tried to transcend, match, avoid, deny, or escape what he'd already done. I was a fan; I looked for those dropped cigarettes. But if the achievement of the previous years was a given as I began to write, what was not a given was how the story unfolded, and how so far it has turned out. This chronicle really begins with Dylan's 1970 double album *Self Portrait;* by the end of the year, the Beatles would be defunct; Jimi Hendrix, a great Bob Dylan fan and perhaps his greatest interpreter, in time maybe a partner, would be dead; and the notion of Bob Dylan as someone who could not open his mouth without telling his own kind of truth would be gone, too. So I began as a disbeliever: Is that all there is? This *can't* be all that there is. One record, one show followed another as the seventies turned into the eighties, as Ford replaced Nixon and Carter Ford and Reagan Carter and all through those years Bob Dylan sang, "Even the president of the United States sometimes has to stand naked"; for a time, I tried to convince myself that whatever the record or the show, it was as good as I wanted it to be, until the falsity became just too clear.

If the decline, a kind of public disappearance, became a given in itself, what was not was the almost biblical story the music would tell: that it would take Bob Dylan more than twenty years to play his way out of the trap set for him by his own, once-upon-a-time triumph, that after all that time of wandering in the desert of his own fame—that time, as Dylan once put it, explaining the imperatives of folk music, by which he meant the Bible, by which he meant the mystery of plenty and famine, of "seven years of this and eight years of that"—that the old pop star, the antique icon, the dormant oracle, might then begin again as if from the beginning, with no limits to what he might say or how he might say it. There was no telling that this turn in the river would occur in 1992, with a quiet little album released on election day, carrying the cigarette-butt title *Good As I Been to You*, a collection of the kind of songs Bob Dylan was singing in coffeehouses, in friends' apartments, before he ever stepped into a recording studio. It was an event that passed almost unnoticed, and which opened up the next two decades as fields in which anything was possible, where any new song could be discovered and any old song could be, in itself, the oracle that, once, people had taken the singer to be.

From that point on there was a new story to follow—and it was so strong, so surprising, that it cast everything that had preceded it in a new light. That is the arc of this book.

Along with a lot of other things, becoming a Bob Dylan fan made me a writer. I was never interested in figuring out what the songs meant. I was interested in figuring out my response to them, and other people's responses. I wanted to get closer to the music than I could by listening to it—I wanted to get inside of it, behind it, and writing about it, through it, inside of it, behind it was my way of doing that.

The pieces collected here begin with a rumor and end with a presidential election. There are reactions in the moment and long looks back for undiscovered stories. But more than anything there is an attempt to remain part of the conversation that Bob Dylan's work has always created around itself: You have to hear this. Is he kidding? I can't believe this. *You* won't believe this—

A lot of the noise of that conversation is in the items scattered through the book from my column Real Life Rock Top 10, which I began writing in 1986 at the *Village Voice,* and has since migrated to *Artforum, Salon, City Pages* in Minneapolis, *Interview,* and the *Believer,* where it is as I write here. From any particular column it might be a 2) reconstructing an advertisement, a 7) quoting someone's letter or e-mail, along with a 1) for one song from an album and a 10) for another. But as much of that conversation is in longer pieces following the way a Bob Dylan song found its way into people's lives, real, as with "High Water" after the terrorist attacks of 2001, or fictional, as with the episode of *Homicide* that was not ripped from the headlines but from "The Lonesome Death of Hattie Carroll."

More than half of this book was written in the last thirteen years, both because that period in Bob Dylan's career and work is infinitely interesting in its own right, and because what he's done in those years has brought all of his previous work, heard and unheard, and all that lies behind it, back into play. There are pieces here I cannibalized in the course of writing other books, but that may have said more, or anyway something else, in their original and shorter form. There are any number of times when what I wrote was wrong—usually when I convinced myself something was better than it was—and in these pages I'm still wrong. I have edited to omit redundancies as best I could, but I haven't gone back to make myself look smarter than I was, or for that matter to make myself look like a better writer. There are a few early pieces that are not here because they're simply too puerile to see the light of day. But I stand behind everything that is here, even when it's wrong—in the midst of a conversation, especially one I think many somehow knew would last their whole lives, the heat can't always be separated from the light.

The conversation I'm speaking of ultimately goes back to Bob Dylan's voice—his conversation with his audience, his songs, other people's songs, and himself. It's a conversation that has enlisted Ma Rainey and Roy Orbison, John F. Kennedy and Brigitte Bardot, Charlie Chaplin and Blind Willie McTell, Medgar Evers and Stagger Lee, Tom Paine and the Fifth Daughter on the Twelfth Night, Gene Austin and Robert Burns, Georgia Sam and Martin

Luther King, Jr., Lyndon Johnson and Diamond Joe, Arthur McBride and Bill Clinton, Barack Obama and Jack-a-Roe. Finally, in that conversation, I think Bob Dylan has kept his promise. Heedlessly, haltingly, clumsily, with mastery, from Hibbing, Minnesota, to wherever he might be playing tonight, from the age of twenty, when his public life began in New York, to almost fifty years later, he has worked as if his age meant nothing and his name less. He has moved from state to state and decade to decade as if nothing was certain, as if everything was up for grabs. The conversation in and around his music has for many made life more interesting than it would have otherwise been, more fun, more frustrating, and it has raised the stakes of the lives of those who have taken part.

This is a constant, and it is a constant subject of this book, by the happenstance of pieces following one after the other over more than four decades, the left hand likely not remembering what the right hand did in any one moment, but ending up holding the same albums and singles and books and movies and letters. The constant is Bob Dylan's voice—I mean the physical thing, what you listen to. It's not the pitch, the tone. In the songs that come to life, whether in 1962 with "See That My Grave Is Kept Clean" or 2009 with "Forgetful Heart," it's the attack, the point of view, the way the voice enters a piece of music, what it does there, how it gets lost, how it gets out, how it remains the same, which is to say that voice remains unpredictable.

This is music as a game of three-card monte. It's what happens in the curls in the words in "As I Went Out One Morning," the heavy steps in the cadences of "Ain't Talkin'," when you are, suddenly, taken out of yourself, out of your house or your car or the street where you're walking, into a place that you recognize but can't name. It's this ability to unsettle, to unhand the conventions by which anyone lives a life—what one expects to hear, say, be told, learn, love, or hate—that defines Bob Dylan's voice, in the smallest and in the greatest sense. It's the ability to bring the whole world into focus with the dramatization of a single syllable—the way the word *care* drops off its line in "High Water" like someone quietly stepping out of a tenth-story window, or being pushed—and that I've tried to follow.

BOB DYLAN BY GREIL MARCUS

PROLOGUE

THE LEGEND OF BLIND STEAMER TRUNK

San Francisco Express Times
24 December 1968

Raised high above the audience were three paintings done in orange and red, somehow a confusion of the masks of comedy and tragedy, now in their own spotlights. The bass player, bending his instrument into circles, was bopping all over the stage, even in motion like a still photograph of the personality of movement which is the freedom of rock 'n' roll. The singer was flashing a red axe at the lead guitarist, sending out the last lines of "Baby Let Me Follow You Down" as he set up for the crash of notes that was sure to follow. They hit it; the two musicians whirled around the microphone, guitars only inches apart, fingers almost touching, the sounds climbing higher and up to the rafters, the roof getting in the way.

Moving out now, the singer twisted around with a grin for the crowd, the band on its own, building toward the final chorus, the singer framed by the tangles of his own hair, hands traveling fast over the red guitar:

> You can do anything that you want to baby
> That you want to baby
> Yes, if you want to baby if you
> Just don't make me *hurt!*

That was Bob Dylan in the fall of 1965, over three years ago. Bob Dylan and the Hawks onstage—there's been nothing like it before or since. Three years of memories, of waiting, scares of the end and false starts toward another chance. Will we remember the thrill of that last time? Memories turn inward and return with legends, images too big to hold.

Legends are out of sight but not quite out of mind; they never intrude, but only emerge out of the day, off the streets, out of the walls. Legends are supposed to represent the pomposity of death, but they can tell jokes, too. The legend of the sightless blues singer used to mean a lot in Berkeley; somehow that story brought people into contact with suffering and creation on the road, down the American highway, maybe to the mountain men before the beaver were trapped out of the high streams, back to Oedipus and Homer, the man who walked but couldn't see, the man carried by his own secret knowledge.

It got to be something of a cult, and cults don't tell jokes. People turned around and laughed at their legends, and lo, out of Blind Lemon Jefferson came Blind Joe Death and the immortal Blind Ebbets Field. New legends were appearing, though, some that at times seemed too grand to speak with, figures with an innocent grandeur that somehow made you nervous. Such was the mood one night in the old Jabberwock in Berkeley.

The place was filled and it was late, time for that ever-recurring Berkeley rumor. One guy turned to another and began it. "I heard . . . I heard that Dylan's in town." Two minutes, and everyone in the place had heard it as well. By itself, the process began to grow. "Somebody said he might show up here, don't know yet . . ." Every time the door opened or closed heads turned and eyes brightened and then turned away. Before half an hour had passed the tension was almost unbearable.

Backstage, eager minds were plotting. A man stepped onto the platform. Quiet came, and he began to speak. "Tonight a very wonderful thing has happened. As some of you may know, someone who has created much of our finest music has arrived in Berkeley—a singer, a musician, a songwriter. As a special favor, he has agreed to do a song for us, but because of complications in his contract—I just can't explain them right now—he cannot allow us to announce his name. But," he winked, "I'm sure you all know who

I mean." It was going to happen. Everybody beamed. The announcer retreated backstage, and returned. "I've just learned," he said, "that because of those complications I just mentioned, B—, I mean, *he,* cannot actually appear in person. But"—and there was a pause—"he *will* perform!"

There was a great scuffling noise. Backstage, a figure was being lowered into a huge box, harmonica in hand. Out front, the audience edged closer. The announcer moved in for the kill. "And now, since he cannot actually appear in person, since we cannot actually pronounce his name, we bring you—*Blind Steamer Trunk!*" The enormous box was carried onto the stage, the lid propped up, and out of the old timbers and rusty hinges came a tantalizingly brief harmonica solo in the best Dylan style. The lid plopped down and the great box was borne way into the night. Blind Steamer Trunk belonged to the ages.

Bob Dylan, "Baby Let Me Follow You Down," on *Long Distance Operator* (Wanted Man bootleg, recorded Berkeley Community Theatre, 4 December 1965). An even hotter version can be found on *the bootleg series volume 4: Live 1966—The "Royal Albert Hall" Concert* (Columbia, 1998, recorded Manchester Free Trade Hall, 17 May 1966).

PART ONE

Breath Control, 1970–1974

SELF PORTRAIT NO. 25

Rolling Stone
23 July 1970

Written and arranged by Greil Marcus
Chorus: Charles Perry, Jenny Marcus, Jann Wenner, Erik Bernstein,
Ed Ward, John Burks, Ralph J. Gleason, Langdon Winner, Bruce Miroff,
Richard Vaughn, and Mike Goodwin

(1)
What is this shit?

(1) Sung by a female chorus, "All the Tired Horses" is a gorgeous piece of music, perhaps the most memorable song on this album. In an older form it was "All the Pretty Horses in the Yard"; now it could serve as the theme song to any classic western. Can you hear the organ standing in between the strings and voices? *Shane* comes into view, and *The Magnificent Seven:* gunmen over the hill and out of time still got to ride. It sounds like Barbara Stanwyck in *Forty Guns* singing, as a matter of fact.

The beauty of this painted signpost promises what its words belie, and the song's question becomes the listener's: he can't ride when the horse is asleep in the meadow.

(2)
"I don't know if I should keep playing this," said the disc jockey, as the album made its debut on the radio. "Nobody's calling in and saying they want to hear it or anything . . . usually when something like this happens people say 'Hey, the new Dylan album,' but not tonight."

Later someone called and asked for a reprise of "Blue Moon." In the end it all came down to whether radioland really cared. The DJ kept apologizing: "If there is anyone who needs—or deserves to have his whole album played through it's Bob Dylan."

(2) After a false beginning comes "Alberta #1," an old song now claimed by Dylan. One line stands out: "I'll give you more gold than your apron can hold." We're still at the frontier. The harmonica lets you into the album by its nostalgia, and it's the song's promise that matters, not the song itself, which fades.

(3)

"What was it?" said a friend, after we'd heard thirty minutes of *Self Portrait* for the first time. "Were we really that impressionable back in '65, '66? Was it that the stuff really wasn't that good, that this is just as good? Was it some sort of accident that made those other records so powerful, or what?

"My life was really turned around, it affected me—I don't know if it was the records or the words or the sound or the noise—maybe the interview: 'What is there to believe in?' I doubt if he'd say that now, though."

We put on "Like a Rolling Stone" from *Highway 61 Revisited* and sat through it. "I was listening to that song five, ten times a day for the last few months, hustling my ass, getting my act together to get into school—but it's such a drag to hear what he's done with it . . ."

(3) Something like a mood collapses with the first Nashville offering, "I Forgot More Than You'll Ever Know," a slick exercise in vocal control that fills a bit of time. After getting closer and closer to the Country Music Capital of the World—and still keeping his distance with *Nashville Skyline,* one of the loveliest rock 'n' roll albums ever made—the visitor returns to pay his compliments by recording some of their songs. How does it sound? It sounds all right. He's sung himself into a corner. It sounds all right. Sign up the band.

(4)

GM: "It's such an unambitious album."

JW: "Maybe what we need most of all right now is an unambitious album from Bob Dylan."

GM: "What we need most of all is for Dylan to get ambitious."

JW: "It's such a . . ."

GM: ". . . though it is a really . . ."

GM & JW: ". . . *friendly* album."

(4) "Days of '49" is a fine old ballad. Dylan's beginning is utterly convincing, as he slips past the years of the song (listen to the vaguely bitter way he sings "But what cares I for praise?"). He fumbles as the song moves on, and the cut falls apart, despite the deep burr of the horns and the drama generated by the piano. It's a tentative performance, a warm-up, hardly more than a work-tape. The depths of the history the song creates—out of the history of pathos Johnny Cash gave "Hardin Wouldn't Run" (sounding like it was recorded in the shadows of an Arizona canyon) or "Sweet Betsy from Pike"—has been missed. The song is worth more effort than it was given.

(5)

"It's hard," he said. "It's hard for Dylan to do anything real, shut off the way he is, not interested in the world, maybe no reason why he should be. Maybe the weight of the days is too strong. Maybe withdrawal is a choice we'd all make if we could . . ." One's reminded that art doesn't come—perhaps it's that it can't be heard—in times of crisis and destruction; art comes in the period of decadence that precedes a revolution, or after the deluge. It's prelude to revolution; it's not contemporary with it save in terms of memory.

But in the midst of it all artists sometimes move to rewrite history. That takes ambition.

(5) When you consider how imaginative the backing on Dylan records has been, the extremely routine quality of most of the music on *Self Portrait* can become irritating. It is so uninteresting. "Early Morning Rain" is one of the most lifeless performances on the entire album; a rather mawkish song, a stiff, well-formed-vowel vocal and a vapid instrumental track that has all the flair of canned laughter.

(6)

The Four Questions. The four sons gazed at the painting on the museum wall. "It's a painting," said the first son. "It's art," said the second. "It's a frame," said the third son, and he said it rather coyly. The fourth son was usually considered somewhat stupid, but he at least figured out why they'd come all the way from home to look at the thing in the first place. "It's a signature," he said.

(6) "In Search of Little Sadie" is an old number called "Badman's Blunder" (or sometimes "Badman's Ballad" and sometimes "Little Sadie") that Dylan now claims as his own composition. As with "Days of '49," the song is superb—it's these kinds of songs that seem like the vague source of the music the Band makes—and what Dylan is doing with the tune, leading it on a switchback trail, has all sorts of possibilities. But again, the vocal hasn't been given time to develop and the song loses whatever power it might have had to offer, until the final chorus, when Bob takes off and does some real singing.

This bit about getting it all down in one or two takes only works if you get it all down. Otherwise it's alluding to a song without really making music.

(7)

Imagine a kid in his teens responding to *Self Portrait.* His older brothers and sisters have been living by Dylan for years. They come home with the album and he simply cannot figure out what it's all about. To him, *Self Portrait* sounds more like the stuff his parents listen to than what he wants to hear; in fact, his parents have just gone out and bought *Self Portrait* and given it to him for his birthday. He considers giving it back for Father's Day.

To this kid Dylan is a figure of myth; nothing less, but nothing more. Dylan is not real and the album carries no reality. He's never seen Bob Dylan; he doesn't expect to; he can't figure out why he wants to.

(7) The Everly Brothers version of "Let It Be Me" is enough to make you cry, and Bob Dylan's version is just about enough to

make you listen. For all of the emotion usually found in his singing, there is virtually none here. It is a very formal performance.

(8)
"Bob should go whole-hog and revive the Bing Crosby Look, with its emphasis on five-button, soft-shoulder, wide-collar, plaid country-club lounge jackets (Pendelton probably still makes them). And, like Der Bingle, it might do well for Dylan to work a long-stemmed briar pipe into his act, stopping every so often to light up, puff at it, raise some smoke and gaze, momentarily, toward the horizon, before launching into [this is John Burks in *Rags*, June 1970] the next phrase of 'Peggy Day.' Then, for his finale—the big 'Blue Moon' production number with the girls and the spotlights on the Mountains—he does a quick costume change into one of those high-collar 1920s formal shirts with the diamond-shaped bow tie, plus, of course, full length tails and the trousers with the satin stripe down the side, carnation in the buttonhole, like Dick Powell in *Gold Diggers of 1933*. Here comes Dylan in his tails, his briar in one hand, his megaphone in the other, strolling down the runway, smiling that toothpaste smile. 'Like a *roll*-ing stone' . . ."

(8) "Little Sadie" is an alternate take of "In Search of . . ." I bet we're going to hear a lot of alternate takes in the coming year, especially from bands short on material who want to maintain their commercial presence without working too hard. Ordinarily, when there are no striking musical questions at stake in the clash of various attempts, alternate takes have been used as a graveyard rip-off to squeeze more bread out of the art of dead men, or merely to fill up a side. "Little Sadie" fills up the side nicely.

(9)
"It's a high school yearbook. Color pictures this year, because there was a surplus left over from last year, more pages than usual too, a sentimental journey, 'what we did,' it's not all that interesting, it's a memento of something, there's a place for autographs, lots of white space, nobody's name was left out . . . It is June, after all."

(9) "Woogie Boogie" is fun. The band sounds like it's falling all over itself (or maybe slipping on its overdubs) but they hold on to the beat. There is as much of Dylan's feel for music here as anything else on *Self Portrait*. If you were a producer combing through a bunch of *Self Portrait* tapes for something to release, you might choose "Woogie Boogie" as a single—backing "All the Tired Horses."

(10)

Self Portrait most closely resembles the Dylan album that preceded it: *Great White Wonder*. The album is a two-record set masterfully assembled from an odd collection of mostly indifferent recordings made over the course of the last year, complete with alternate takes, chopped endings, loose beginnings, side comments, and all sorts of mistakes. Straight from the can to you, as it were. A bit from Nashville, a taste of the Isle of Wight since you missed it, some sessions from New York that mostly don't make it, but dig, it's Dylan, and if you wanted *Great White Wonder* and *Stealin'* and *John Birch* and *Isle of Wight* and *A Thousand Miles Behind*, *Self Portrait* will surely fill the need.

I don't think it will. It's true that all of the bootlegs came out in the absence of new music from Dylan, but I think their release was related not to the absence of his recordings but to the absence of the man himself. We are dealing with myth, after all, and the more Dylan stays away the greater the weight attached to anything he's done. When King Midas reached out his hand everything he touched turned to gold, it became valuable to everyone else, and Dylan still has the Midas touch even though he'd rather not reach out. It is only in the last two years that the collecting of old tapes by Dylan has become a national phenomenon, and there are many times more tapes in circulation than are represented on the bootlegs. It sometimes seems as if every public act Dylan ever made was recorded, and it is all coming together. Eventually, the bootleggers will get their hands on it. Legally, there is virtually nothing he can do to stop it.

He can head off the theft and sale of his first drafts, his secrets, and his memories only with his music. And it is the vitality of the music that is being bootlegged that is the basis of its appeal. The noise of it. *Self Por-*

trait, though it's a good imitation bootleg, isn't nearly the music that *Great White Wonder* is. "Copper Kettle" is a masterpiece but "Killing Me Alive" will blow it down. *Nashville Skyline* and *John Wesley Harding* are classic albums; but no matter how good they are they lack the power of the music Dylan made in the middle sixties. Unless he returns to the marketplace, with a sense of vocation and the ambition to keep up with his own gifts, the music of those years will continue to dominate his records, whether he releases them or not. If the music Dylan makes doesn't have the power to enter into the lives of his audience—and *Self Portrait* does not have that power—his audience will take over his past.

(10) Did Dylan write "Belle Isle"? Maybe he did. This is the first time I've felt cynical listening to a new Dylan album.

(11)
In the record industry, music is referred to as "product." "We got Beatle product." When the whirlwind courtship of Johnny Winter and Columbia was finally consummated everyone wanted to know when they would get product. They got product fast but it took them a while longer to get music. *Self Portrait*, which is already a triple gold record, the way "O Captain! My Captain!" is more famous than "When Lilacs Last in the Dooryard Bloom'd," is the closest thing to pure product in Dylan's career, even more so than *Greatest Hits*, because that had no pretensions. The purpose of *Self Portrait* is mainly product and the need it fills is for product—for "a Dylan album"—and make no mistake about it, the need for product is felt as deeply by those who buy it, myself included, as by those who sell it, and perhaps more so.

As a throw-together album it resembles *Flowers**; but it's totally unlike *Flowers* in that the album promises to be more than it is, not less. By its title alone *Self Portrait* makes claims for itself as the definitive Dylan album—which it may be, in a sad way—but it is still something like an

---

*The album the Rolling Stones cobbled together in 1967, during the Summer of Love ("Be Sure to Wear Flowers in Your Hair"), in order to have something on the market in the face of the Beatles' *Sgt. Pepper* juggernaut.

attempt to delude the public into thinking they are getting more than they are, or that *Self Portrait* is more than it is.

(11) "Living the Blues" is a marvelous recording. All sorts of flashes of all sorts of enthusiasms spin around it: the Dovells cheering for the Bristol Stomp, Dylan shadow-boxing with Cassius Clay, Elvis smiling and sneering in *Jailhouse Rock*. The singing is great—listen to the way Bob fades off "deep down insyyy-*hide,*" stepping back and slipping in that last syllable. For the first time on this album Dylan sounds excited by the music he's making. The rhythm section, led by the guitar and the piano that's rolling over the most delightful rock 'n' roll chord changes, is wonderful. The girls go through their routine and they sound—cute. Dylan shines. Give it 100.

(12)

". . . various times he thought of completing his baccalaureate so that he could teach in the college and oddly enough [this is from 'A Rimbaud Chronology']* of learning to play the piano. At last he went to Holland, where, in order to reach the Orient, he enlisted in the Dutch Army and sailed for Java in June of 1876. Three weeks after his arrival in Batavia [Charles Perry: 'We know Dylan was the Rimbaud of his generation; it seems he's found his Abyssinia'] he deserted, wandered among the natives of the jungle and soon signed on a British ship for Liverpool. After a winter at home he went to Hamburg, joined a circus as interpreter-manager to tour the northern countries, but the cold was too much for him and he was repatriated from Sweden, only to leave home again, this time for Alexandria. Again, illness interrupted his travels and he was put off the ship in Italy and spent a year recovering on the farm at Roche. In 1878 he was in Hamburg again, trying to reach Genoa to take a ship for the East. Once more he tried to cross the Alps on foot but in a snowstorm he almost perished. Saved by monks in a Hospice, he managed to reach Genoa and sail to Alexandria, where he worked as a farm laborer

---

*Included in Arthur Rimbaud, *A Season in Hell and The Drunken Boat*. New York: New Directions Press, 1946, 1961. xvi.

for a while. In Suez, where he was stopped on his way to Cyprus, he was employed as a ship-breaker to plunder a ship wrecked on the dangerous coast at Guardafui. Most of the first half of 1879 he worked as a foreman in a desert quarry on Cyprus, and went home in June to recover from typhoid fever."*

(12) "Like a Rolling Stone"—Dylan's greatest song. He knows it, and so do we. Not only that, but the greatest song of our era, on that single, on *Highway 61 Revisited,* on the tape of a British performance with the Hawks in 1966. If one version is better than the other it's like Robin Hood splitting his father's arrow.

1965: "Alright. We've done it. Dig it. If you can. If you can take it. Like a complete unknown, can you feel that?"

We could, and Bob Dylan took over. All that's come since goes back to the bid for power that was "Like a Rolling Stone."

"Can you keep up with this train?" The train no longer runs; I suppose it depends on where your feet are planted.

Playboy, March 1966: "PLAYBOY: Mistake or not, what made you decide to go the rock-'n'-roll route? DYLAN: Carelessness. I lost my one true love. I started drinking. The first thing I know, I'm in a card game. Then I'm in a crap game. I wake up in a pool hall. Then this big Mexican lady drags me off the table, takes me to Philadelphia. She leaves me alone in her house, and it burns down. I wind up in Phoenix. I get a job as a Chinaman. I start working in a dime store, and move in with a 13-year-old girl. Then this big Mexican lady from Philadelphia comes in and burns the house down. I go down to Dallas. I get a job as a "before" in a Charles Atlas "before and after" ad. I move in with a delivery boy who can cook fantastic chili and hot dogs. Then this 13-year-old girl from Phoenix comes and burns the house down. The delivery boy—he ain't so mild: He gives her the knife, and the next thing I know I'm in Omaha. It's so cold there, by this time I'm robbing my own bicycles and frying my own fish. I stumble onto some luck and get a job as a carburetor out at the hot-rod races every Thursday night. I move in with a high school teacher who also does a little plumbing on the side, who ain't much to look at, but who's built a special kind of refrigerator that can turn newspaper into lettuce. Everything's going good until that delivery boy shows up and tries to knife me. Needless to say, he burned the house down, and I hit the road. The first guy that picked me up asked me if I wanted to be a star. What could I say? PLAYBOY: And that's how you became a rock-'n'-roll singer? DYLAN: No, that's how I got tuberculosis." I couldn't resist.

Dylan from the Isle of Wight is blowing his lines, singing country flat, up and down, getting through the song somehow, almost losing the whole mess at the end of the second verse. You don't know whether he dropped the third verse because he didn't want to sing it or because he forgot it. It's enough to make your speakers wilt.

Self Portrait enforces or suggests a quiet sound. "Like a Rolling Stone" isn't "Blue Moon" but since most of *Self Portrait* is more like "Blue Moon" than "Like a Rolling Stone," and since it is a playable album that blends together, you set the volume low. But if you play this song loud—very loud, until it distorts and rumbles—you'll find the Band is still playing as hard as they can, for real. Their strength is cut in half by the man who recorded it, but volume will bring it back up.

Some of "Like a Rolling Stone" is still there. A splendid beginning, announcing a conquest: Levon Helm beating his drums over the Band's Motown March (ba-bump barrummmp, ba-bump barrummmp), smashing his cymbals like the glass-breaking finale of a car crash; and best of all, Garth Hudson finding the spirit of the song and holding it firm on every chorus. Near the end when the pallid vocalizing is done with, Dylan moves back to the song and he and the Band begin to stir a frenzy that ends with a crash of metal and Bob's shout: "JUST LIKE A ROLLING STONE!" There is something left.

1965: "BAM! Once upon a time . . ." The song assaults you with a deluge of experience and the song opens up the abyss. "And just how far would you like to go in?" "Not too far but just far enough so's we can say we've been there." That wasn't good enough. "When you gaze into the abyss, the abyss looks back at you." It peered out through "This Wheel's on Fire" and "All Along the Watchtower," but it seems Dylan has stepped back from its edge.

The abyss is hidden away now, like the lost mine of a dead prospector. "Like a Rolling Stone," as we hear it now, is like a fragment of a faded map leading back to that lost mine.

(13)
I once said I'd buy an album of Dylan breathing heavily. I still would. But not an album of Dylan breathing softly.

(13) Why does "Copper Kettle" shine (it even sounds like a hit record) when so many other cuts hide in their own dullness? Why does this performance evoke all kinds of experience when most of *Self Portrait* is so one-dimensional and restrictive? Why does "Copper Kettle" grow on you while the other songs disappear?

Like "All the Tired Horses," it's gorgeous. There are those tiny high notes punctuating the song in the mood of an old Buddy Holly ballad or "The Three Bells" by the Browns, and that slip-stream organ, so faint you can barely hear it—you don't hear it, really, but you are aware of it in the subtlest way. There is the power and the real depth of the song itself, that erases our Tennessee truck-stop postcard image of moonshining and moves in with a vision of nature, an ideal of repose, and a sense of rebellion that goes back to the founding of the country. "We ain't paid no whiskey tax since 1792," Bob sings, and that goes all the way back—they passed the whiskey tax in 1791. It's a song about revolt as a vocation, not revolution, merely refusal. Old men hiding out in mountain valleys, keeping their own peace. (The old moonshiners are sitting around a stove in *Thunder Road,* trying to come up with an answer to the mobsters that are muscling in on the valley they've held since the Revolution. "Blaf sprat muglmmph ruurrp ffft," says one. The audience stirs, realizing they can't understand his Appalachian dialect. "If you'd take that tobacco plug out of your mouth, Jed," says another whiskey man, "maybe we could understand what you said.")

What matters is Bob's singing. He's been the most inventive singer of the last ten years, creating his language of stress, fitting five words into a line of ten and ten into a line of five, shoving the words around and opening up spaces for noise and silence that through assault or seduction or the gift of good timing made room for expression and emotion. Every vocal was a surprise. You couldn't predict what it would sound like. The song itself, the structure of the song, was barely a clue. The limits were there to be evaded. On "Copper Kettle" that all happens, and it is noticeable because this is the only time on *Self Portrait* that it happens.

"Not all great poets—like Wallace Stevens—are great singers," Dylan said a year ago. "But a great singer—like Billie Holiday—is always a great poet." That sort of poetry—and it's that sort of poetry that made Dylan seem like a poet—is all there on "Copper Kettle," in the way Bob changes into the lines ". . . or ROTTEN wood . . ." fading into a quieted "they'll get you—by the smoke . . ." The fact that the rest of the album lacks the grace of "Copper Kettle" isn't a matter of the album being different or new. It's a matter of the music having power, or not having it.

(14, 15, 16)
". . . very successful in terms of money. Dylan's concerts in the past have been booked by his own firm, Ashes and Sand, rather than [this is from *Rolling Stone*, December 7, 1968] private promoters. Promoters are now talking about a ten-city tour with the possibility of adding more dates, according to *Variety*.

"Greta Garbo may also come out of retirement to do a series of personal appearances. The Swedish film star who wanted only 'to be alone' after continued press invasions of her life is rumored to be considering a series of lavish stage shows, possibly with Dylan . . ."

And we'd just sit there and *stare*.

(14) "Gotta Travel On." Dylan sings "Gotta Travel On."

(15) We take "Blue Moon" for a joke, a stylized apotheosis of corn, or further musical evidence of Dylan's retreat from the pop scene. But back on Elvis's first album, there is another version of "Blue Moon," a deep and moving performance that opens up the possibilities of the song and reveals the failure of Dylan's recording.

Hoofbeats, vaguely aided by a string bass and guitar, form the background to a vocal that blows a cemetery wind across the lines of the song. Elvis moves back and forth with a high phantom wail, singing the part that fiddler Doug Kershaw plays on Dylan's version, Elvis finally answering himself with a dark murmur that fades into silence. "It's a revelation," said a friend. "I can't believe it."

There is nothing banal about "Blue Moon." In formal musical terms, Dylan's performance is virtually a cover of Elvis's recording, but while one man sings toward the song, the other sings from behind it, from the other side.

(16) "The Boxer." Remember Paul Simon's "How I was Robert Mac-Namared into Submission," or whatever it was called, with that friendly line, "I forgot my harmonica, Albert"? Or Eric Anderson's "The Hustler"? Maybe this number means "no hard feelings." Jesus, is it awful.

(17)
Before going into the studio to set up the Weathermen, he wrote the Yippies' first position paper, although it took Abbie Hoffman a few years to find it and Jerry Rubin had trouble reading it. A quote:

"I'm gonna grow my hair down to my feet so strange till I look like a walking mountain range then I'm gonna ride into Omaha on a horse out to the country club and the golf course carrying a *New York Times* shoot a few holes blow their minds."

"Dylan's coming," said Lang.*

"Ah, you're full of shit" [said Abbie Hoffman in his *Woodstock Nation*], "he's gonna be in England tonight, don't pull that shit on me."

"Nah, I ain't kiddin', Abby-baby, he called up and said he might come . . ."

"You think he'd dig running for president?"

"Nah, that ain't his trip he's into something else."

"You met him, Mike? What he into?"

"I don't know for sure but it ain't exactly politics. You ever met him?"

"Yeah, once about seven years ago in Gertie's Folk City down in the West Village. I was trying to get him to do a benefit for civil rights or

---

*Michael Lang, one of the organizers of the 1969 Woodstock festival.

something . . . hey Mike will you introduce us? I only know about meetin' him through Happy Traum . . ."

"There's an easier way . . . Abbs . . . I'll introduce you. In fact he wants to meet you . . ."

Would *Self Portrait* make you want to meet Dylan? No? Perhaps it's there to keep you away?

(17) "The Mighty Quinn" sounds as if it was a gas to watch. It's pretty much of a mess on record, and the sound isn't all that much better than the bootleg. The Isle of Wight concert was originally planned as an album, and it's obvious why it wasn't released as such—on tape, it sounded bad. The performances were mostly clumsy or languid and all together would have made a lousy record. Two of the songs had something special about them, on the evidence of the bootleg, though neither of them made it onto *Self Portrait*. One was "Highway 61 Revisited," where Bob and the Band screamed like Mexican tour guides hustling customers for a run down the road: "OUT ON HIGHWAY SIXTY-ONE!" The other was "It Ain't Me Babe." Dylan sang solo, playing guitar like a lyric poet, transforming the song with a new identity, sweeping in and out of the phrases and the traces of memory. He sounded something like Billie Holiday.

(18)

It's certainly an odd self portrait: other people's songs and the songs of a few years ago. If the title is serious, Dylan no longer cares much about making music and would just as soon define himself on someone else's terms. There is a curious move toward self-effacement: Dylan removing himself from a position from which he is asked to exercise power. It's rather like the Duke of Windsor abdicating the throne. After it's over he merely goes away, and occasionally there'll be a picture of him getting on a plane somewhere.

(18) "Take Me as I Am or Let Me Go." The Nashville recordings of *Self Portrait,* taken together, may not be all that staggering but they

are pleasant—a sentimental little country melodrama. If the album had been cut to "Tired Horses" at the start and "Wigwam" at the end, with the Nashville tracks sleeping in between, we'd have a good record about which no one would have gotten very excited one way or the other, a kind of musical disappearing act. But the Artist must make a Statement, be he Bob Dylan, the Beach Boys, or Tommy James and the Shondells. He must enter the studio and come out with that masterpiece. If he doesn't, or hasn't bothered, there'll be at least an attempt to make it look as if he has. If Dylan were releasing more music than he's been—say, a single three times a year, an album every six months or so—then the weight that fixes itself on whatever he does release would be lessened. But the pattern is set now, for the biggest stars—one a year, if that. It's rather degrading for an artist to put out more than one album a year, as if he *has* to keep trying, you know? Well, three cheers for John Fogerty.

(19)
Because of what happened in the middle sixties, our fate is bound up with Dylan's whether he or we like it or not. Because *Highway 61 Revisited* changed the world, the albums that follow it must—but not in the same way.

(19) "Take a Message to Mary": the backing band didn't seem to care much about the song, but Dylan did. My ten-year-old nephew thought "It Hurts Me Too" sounded fake but he was sure this was for real.

(20)
Ralph J. Gleason: "There was this cat Max Kaminsky talks about in his autobiography who stole records. He stole one from Max. He *had* to have them, you know? Just had to have them. Once he got busted because he heard this record on a juke box and shoved his fist through the glass of the box trying to get the record out.

"We all have records we'd steal for, that we need that bad. But would you steal this record? You wouldn't steal this record."

You wouldn't steal *Self Portrait*? It wouldn't steal you either. Perhaps that's the real tragedy, because Dylan's last two albums were art breaking and entering into the house of the mind.

(20) Songwriting can hardly be much older than song-stealing. It's part of the tradition. It may even be more honorable than outright imitation; at least it's not as dull.

Early in his career, Bob Dylan, like every other musician on the street with a chance to get off it, copped one or two old blues or folk songs, changed a word or two, and copyrighted them (weirdest of all was claiming "That's All Right," which was Elvis's first record, and written—or at least written down—by Arthur Crudup). Dylan also used older ballads for the skeletons of his own songs: "Bob Dylan's Dream" is a recasting of "Lord Franklin's Dream"; "I Dreamed I Saw St. Augustine" finds its way back to "I Dreamed I Saw Joe Hill." "Pledging My Time" has the structure, the spirit, and a line from Robert Johnson's "Come on in My Kitchen"; "Don't the moon look lonesome, shining through the trees," is a quote from an old Jimmy Rushing blues. "Subterranean Homesick Blues" comes off of Chuck Berry's "Too Much Monkey Business." This is a lovely way to write, and to invite, history, and it is part of the beauty and inevitability of American music. But while Dylan may have added a few words to "It Hurts Me Too," from where he sits, it's simply wrong to claim this old blues, recorded by Elmore James for one, as his own. That *Self Portrait* is characterized by borrowing, lifting, and plagiarism simply means Bob will get a little more money and thousands of people will get a phony view of their own history.

(21, 22)

That splendid frenzy, the strength of new values in the midst of some sort of musical behemoth of destruction, the noise, the power—the *totality* of it! So you said, well, all right, there it is . . .

The mythical immediacy of everything Dylan does and the relevance of that force to the way we live our lives is rooted in the three albums and the two unforgettable singles he released in 1965 and 1966: *Bringing It All Back Home, Highway 61 Revisited,* and *Blonde on Blonde,* "Like a Rolling Stone," and "Subterranean Homesick Blues." Those records defined and structured a crucial year—no one has ever caught up with them and most likely no one ever will. What happened then is what we always look for. The power of those recordings and of the music Dylan was making on stage, together with his retreat at the height of his career, made Dylan into a legend and virtually changed his name into a noun. Out of that Dylan gained the freedom to step back and get away with anything he chose to do, commercially and artistically. The fact that more than a year now separates one album from another heightens their impact, regardless of how much less they have to offer than the older albums which established this matrix of power in the first place. In a real way, Dylan is trading on the treasure of myth, fame, and awe he gathered in '65 and '66. In mythical terms, he doesn't have to do good, because he has done good. One wonders, in mythical terms of course, how long he can get away with it.

(21) "Minstrel Boy" is the best of the Isle of Wight cuts; it rides easy.

(22) The Band plays pretty on "She Belongs to Me" and Dylan runs through the vocal the way he used to hurry through the first half of a concert, getting the crowd-pleasers out of the way so that he could play the music that mattered. Garth Hudson has the best moment of the song.

(23)
Vocation as a Vocation. Dylan is, if he wants to be, an American with a vocation. It might almost be a calling—the old Puritan idea of a gift one should live up to—but it's not, and vocation is strong enough.

There is no theme richer for an American artist than the spirit and the themes of the country and the country's history. We have never figured out what this place is about or what it is for, and the only way to even begin to answer those questions is to watch our movies, read our poets, our novelists, and listen to our music. Robert Johnson and Melville, Hank Williams and Hawthorne, Bob Dylan and Mark Twain, Jimmie Rodgers and John Wayne. America is the life's work of the American artist because he is doomed to be an American. Dylan has a feel for it; his impulses seem to take him back into the forgotten parts of our history, and even on *Self Portrait* there is a sense of this—he's almost on the verge of writing a western. But it's an ambitious vocation and there is not enough of that, only an impulse without the determination to follow it up.

Dylan has a vocation if he wants it; his audience may refuse to accept *his* refusal unless he simply goes away. In the midst of that vocation there might be something like Hamlet asking questions, old questions, with a bit of magic to them; but hardly a prophet, merely a man with good vision.

(23) "Wigwam" slowly leads the album to its end. Campfire music, or "3 A.M., After the Bullfight." It's a great job of arranging, and the B-side of the album's second natural single, backing "Living the Blues." "Wigwam" puts you to bed, and by that I don't mean it puts you to sleep.

(24)

Self Portrait, *the Auteur, and Home Movies.* "Auteur" means, literally, author, and in America the word has come to signify a formula about films: movies (like books), are made by authors, i.e., directors. This has led to a dictum which tends to affirm the following: movies are about the personality of the director. We should judge a movie in terms of how well the auteur has developed his personality in relation to previous films. His best film is that which most fully presents the flowering of his personality. Needless to say such an approach requires a devotion to mannerism, quirk, and self-indulgence. It also turns out that the greatest auteurs are those with the most consistent, obvious, and recognizable mannerisms, quirks, and self-indulgences. By this approach *Stolen Kisses* is a better film than *Jules and Jim* because in *Stolen Kisses* there is nothing to look for but Truffaut while in *Jules and Jim* there was this story and those actors who kept getting in the way. The spirit of the auteur approach can be transferred to other arts, and by its dictum *Self Portrait* is a better album than *Highway 61 Revisited,* because *Self Portrait* is about the auteur, that is, Dylan, and *Highway 61 Revisited* takes on the world, which tends to get in the way. (*Highway 61 Revisited* might well be about Dylan too, but it's more *obvious* on *Self Portrait,* and therefore more relevant to Art, and . . . please don't ask about the music, really . . .)

Now, Dylan has been approached this way for years, whether or not the word was used, and while in the end it may be the least interesting way to listen to his music it's occasionally a lot of fun and a game that many of us have played (for example, on "Days of '49" Dylan sings the line "just like a roving sign" and I just can't help almost hearing him say "just like a rolling stone" and wondering if he avoided that on purpose). One writer, named Alan Weberman, has devoted his life to unraveling Dylan's songs in order to examine the man himself; just as every artist once had his patron, now it seems every auteur has his critic.

(24) *Self Portrait* is a concept album from the cutting room floor. It has been constructed so artfully, but as a cover-up, not a revelation. Thus "Alberta #2" is the end, after a false ending, just as "Alberta #1" was the beginning, after a false beginning. The song moves quickly, and ends abruptly. These alternate takes don't just fill up a side, they set up the whole album, and it works, in a way, because I think it's mainly the four songs fitted in at the edges that make the album a playable record. With a circle you tend to see the line that defines it, rather than the hole in the middle.

(25)
Self Portrait, *the Auteur, and Home Movies, con't.* We all play the auteur game: we went out and bought *Self Portrait* not because we knew it was great music—it might have been but that's not the first question we'd ask—but because it was a Dylan album. What we *want,* though, is a different matter—and that's what separates most people from auteurists— we *want* great music, and because of those three albums back in '65 and '66, we expect it, or hope for it.

I wouldn't be dwelling on this but for my suspicion that it is exactly a perception of this approach that is the justification for the release of *Self Portrait,* to the degree that it is justified artistically (the commercial justification is something else—self-justification). The auteur approach allows the great artist to limit his ambition, and turn it inward. To be crude, it begins to seem as if it is his habits that matter, rather than his vision. If *we* approach art in this fashion, we degrade it. Take that second song on *John Wesley Harding*, "As I Went Out One Morning," and two ways of hearing it.

Weberman has determined a fixed meaning for the song: it relates to a dinner given years ago by the Emergency Civil Liberties Committee at which they awarded Bob Dylan their Thomas Paine prize. Dylan showed up, said a few words about how it was possible to understand how Lee Harvey Oswald felt, and got booed. "As I Went Out One Morning," according to Weberman, is Dylan's way of saying he didn't dig getting booed.

I sometimes hear the song as a brief journey into American history; the singer out for a walk in the park, finding himself next to a statue of Tom Paine, and stumbling across an allegory: Tom Paine, symbol of freedom and revolt, co-opted into the role of Patriot by textbooks and statue committees, and now playing, as befits his role as Patriot, enforcer to a girl who runs for freedom—in chains, to the *south*, the source of vitality in America, in America's music—*away* from Tom Paine. We have turned our history on its head; we have perverted our own myths.

Now it would be astonishing if what I've just described were on Dylan's mind when he wrote the song. That's not the point. The point is that Dylan's songs can serve as metaphors, enriching our lives, giving us random insight into the myths we carry and the present we live, intensifying what we've known and leading us toward what we never looked for, while at the same time enforcing an emotional strength upon those perceptions by the power of the music that moves with the words. Weberman's way of hearing, or rather seeing, is more logical, more linear, and perhaps even more correct, but it's sterile. Mine is not an answer but a possibility, and I think Dylan's music is about possibilities rather than facts, like a statue that is not an expenditure of city funds but a gateway to a vision.

If we are to be satisfied with *Self Portrait* we may have to see it in the sterile terms of the auteur, which in our language would be translated as "Hey, far out, Dylan singing Simon and Garfunkel, Rodgers and Hart, and

Gordon Lightfoot . . ." Well, it is far out, in a sad sort of way, but it is also vapid, and if our own untaught perception of the auteur allows us to be satisfied with it, we degrade our own sensibilities and Dylan's capabilities as an American artist as well. Dylan did not become a force whose every movement carries the force of myth by presenting desultory images of his own career as if that was the only movie that mattered—he did it by taking on the world with assault, and by seduction.

In an attack on the auteur approach, as it relates to film, the actress Louise Brooks quotes an old dictionary, and the quote reveals the problem: "The novel [the film]"—the song—"is a subjective epic composition in which the author begs leave to treat the world according to his own point of view. It is only a question, therefore, whether he has a point of view. The rest will take care of itself."

Bob Dylan, *Self Portrait* (Columbia, 1970).

————. *Great White Wonder* (1969). The first Dylan bootleg: a two-record set comprised of songs taped in Minnesota in 1961, radio shows from the early 1960s, basement tape numbers, and even a TV performance of "Living the Blues."

Elvis Presley, "Blue Moon" (1955, first issued on *Elvis Presley,* RCA, 1956), collected on *Sunrise* (RCA, 1999).

Louise Brooks, in Kevin Brownlow, *The Parade's Gone By* . . . New York: Knopf, 1969, 364.

NEW MORNING

New York Times

15 November 1970

Bob Dylan's *New Morning* is his best album in years, a set of twelve new songs that hide their real power to move the listener within the bright pop flash of entertainment.

Many of the songs seem to have been made up on the spot, with confidence in the ability of first-rate musicians to move in any direction at any time. "I know you're gonna think this song is just a riff," Bob sang five years ago, being careful to add, "unless you've been inside a tunnel and fell down sixty-nine, seventy feet over a barbed wire fence." The riffs, inventions, and studio jams of *New Morning* have their own personality—not the repose of *Nashville Skyline* or the seeming indifference of much of *Self Portrait,* but the full joy of anticipating the right move and the exhilaration of hitting it square and bouncing off a chord into a new lyric.

The more carefully worked out songs—"Went to See the Gypsy" and "Sign in the Window" in particular—are deceptive, because they, too, maintain the listener's sense of the album as a work of effortless music. These songs appear obvious, and while they are not, one is still quite free to hear them as if they were.

New Morning is fun to listen to. Dylan has never sung with such flair. The record has its own sound, a rich, open rock 'n' roll combination of Dylan's piano, Al Kooper's organ, girl singers, two or three snappy guitars, and some fine hotshot drumming.

The musicians as a group are at their best on the title song, playing hard rock. The surprising toughness of the cut—which in other hands might have been (and probably will be) just another bland hymn to optimism—results not from dump-truck heaviness but from perfect timing, a jolt of pure excitement near the end of the number, and from Bob's singing. As the lyrics give us a pretty picture, Dylan sings out the last word or two with a hard-edged vengeance, not submitting to the obvious way to sing the song, but intensifying the simple enthusiasm of the number with such firm determination that a whole conversation of emotions comes into play.

One aspect of this album's distinction is its masterful organization. The songs speak to each other, sometimes working partly as cues for or comments on numbers that precede or follow. The first cut, "If Not for You," acts like the hook line of a single, breaking the ice with its gaiety. Dylan's harmonica moves in, just this once, like Alfred Hitchcock in a walk-on, offering a bit of familiarity. The frolic of the song disarms the listener's inevitably apprehensive stance ("Hmmmmm, what's this one going to be?") and creates a space of easy freedom for both Dylan and his fans.

In this kind of mood, you can either tune in on all the neat comments Bob is making about his honorary degree in the second song, "Day of the Locusts," or simply enjoy the fact that he's singing his head off.

The cut ends with an escape to the Black Hills of Dakota and the next opens up with the singer quietly celebrating the slow-passing time up in the mountains. This sort of correspondence, or the two casual references to catching fish, or the various place names that appear throughout the album (Utah, Las Vegas, Minnesota, Montana, California) give the album its own reality without forcing the songs into a logical pattern.

When the album ends, with two religious inventions—the first a spoken paragraph of what sounds like a TV preacher's sermon, the second a ghostly Calvinistic rumble—one finds that, again, the songs comment on each other, as the Oral Roberts corn of the last strains of "Three Angels" ("But does anyone hear the music they play? Does anyone even try?") is undercut by the stern testament of "Father of Night." After a bit, the two songs begin to fade into each other, each gains in interest, and the joke of "Three Angels" takes on a little of the force of "Father of Night." *New Morning,* as an album, has a context from which each song grows but to which no song submits.

This is an American album with a western impulse ("Movin' west," as we used to say), and "Sign on the Window" may lie at the heart of *New Morning.* "Sign on the Window" is the richest of the twelve songs and perhaps the best recording Dylan has ever made. His versatile piano work lies beneath much of the album; here, he's playing mostly by himself. The band and the girls move in briefly between verses, but it's Dylan's performance:

> Her and her boyfriend went to California
> Her and her boyfriend done change their tune
> My best friend said now didn't I warn ya . . .

"Sign on the Window" is the other side of "Sweet Betsy from Pike," in a way, the tale of the man who didn't get to make the trip. One can see the singer, drunk in a town somewhere east of the Mississippi, as his isolation deepens into exclusion. "Sure gonna be wet tonight on Main Street," goes a line, and the power of Dylan's singing and of his piano makes that feel like the best line he ever wrote. Gonna be wet tonight on Main Street, but you know, there's nowhere else to be.

Dylan plays out the emotion of the song on his piano. "Build me a cabin in Utah," he sings as it ends. "Marry me a wife, catch rainbow trout . . . That must be what it's all about." It's certain that these last lines will be hailed as Bob Dylan's new message to us all, but they're hardly that. When a wife and a trout stream settle easily on the same plane, that's not a way of life but the ease of a dream. A cabin in Utah is the sort of dream one needs when it's gonna be wet tonight on Main Street, when fantasy is set against experience.

Rather than "What it's all about" or even what this one song is all about, it's that old American urge, that old half-question: "There must be a place that's open, yet . . ." How far west do you have to go to be free? It's a very great song, a love song moving west on the first American dream.

This fine album comes only a few months after Dylan's mostly unsuccessful *Self Portrait*. Not only does *New Morning* rock with the vitality that *Self Portrait* lacks, but Dylan's decision to release a new record without the usual year's wait is in itself an act of vitality. One of the functions of rock 'n' roll is the disruption of cultural patterns, and, by extension, of rock 'n' roll patterns. Dylan has, to some degree, broken the rule of reserve that seems to have been governing his career, and in doing so he has brought some life back to the rock 'n' roll scene.

In the last year or so, the rock 'n' roll audience has become fragmented, as the music lost that public character that comes out of our common participation in the event on which the music of the '60s was founded—the Beatles. One man's meat may be another man's poison, but we gave that line the lie back in 1965, when the Beatles, the Stones, and Bob Dylan revealed the making of a common imagination accessible to each of us. Now that Captain Beefheart fans sneer at the legions of Led Zeppelin, who sneer right back, Dylan is offering an album of humor and depth, and it may well be accepted as a gift by almost all of the audience, as something to be held in common and as something to be shared.

As the lines and phrases of *New Morning* pass into our speech, we may find that Bob Dylan's remarkable new songs not only speak to us, but give us the means by which we can, for a time, speak among ourselves.

Bob Dylan, *New Morning* (Columbia, 1970).

WATCHING THE RIVER FLOW
Creem
October 1971

Lately it's been difficult to tell the commercials from the hits, and it's not because the commercials are getting any better. The summer charts are ghastly and almost every slot in the top ten is filled by some hokey Hollywood production number with a trick chorus line.

But now Bob Dylan, the Who, and Creedence all have new singles: "Watching the River Flow," "Won't Get Fooled Again," and "Sweet Hitch-Hiker."

Dylan's seems like the best.

It's getting the least airplay.

I'm not sure why this is so—it may be simply because it doesn't have that creepy Hollywood sound—but I have the feeling Dylan outsmarted himself on this one. "Watching the River Flow" is nothing fancy, good beat, good humor, good AM noise. But as with most of Dylan's records, there's more here than there seems to be—and the first impression turns out to be a joke on the listener.

But that only works if the listener is forced to hear the record often enough to get beyond the first impression. In this case, the first impression is that Bob Dylan is setting up the usual private scene: "I'll sit here and watch the river flow." Well, that's certainly a boring idea. It's the implicit message of just about everything James Taylor has ever written, whole bands are being built around the basic sentiment, and people are eating it up when they can get it cheap—that is, implicitly—but maybe they don't want it when they have to pay for it, in a confrontation with an explicit statement of withdrawal that can be so easily reversed into the mirror image of their own.

Then there's the probability that one of the reasons people listen to Dylan is that he usually seems to be ahead of the game in some way, and to hear his music and his songs is to get some idea of what's going on and what's going to happen, in music and in musical communication. And there are those hopes for a more obscure and tantalizing sort of intelligence that never seem to go away. But if Dylan is merely riding a trend, even if he started it, a good part of his charisma automatically cancels itself out.

And then, in a completely general sort of context, there are the curious rumors about Dylan's private life, which are, yes, a matter of his own business, and also public property—if you know about them you can't very well lobotomize yourself into forgetting them: support for the Jewish Defense League, trips to Israel, putting up office buildings with Dick Cavett. None of this stuff may be true, but it's all in the air, and like those stories about a young Bob Dylan running away from home every month or so, it doesn't much matter if they're true or not. You don't make a rational separation between True and False when you hear a record, you just hear it, and its sound combines with the grapevine into pop. And in this case that adds up to Dylan as this strange one-man model of how to make up for one's wild and odious youth. Sort of missing the point, as Stu Cook of Creedence Clearwater put it, that we all get to be thirty someday, *we're* going to be thirty, not the people who were thirty when people first began to worry about such things. Or, as someone put it to a friend of mine when he took over a fancy magazine: "*You* are them." Don't we remember how we were all supposed to stop liking rock 'n' roll when we turned eighteen?

We don't have to believe this stuff anymore; we have to learn how to act out its negation. We have to make being thirty in the seventies and eighties as different as being twenty in the sixties was from being twenty in the fifties. So I wonder about Bob Dylan, who seems to be working in the opposite direction. Can we trust this guy?

The first impression one gets from "Watching the River Flow" doesn't even raise this question, because that first impression is so *bland*. "I'll just sit here and watch the river flow." The music is really quite nice but it sounds like the cut that was left off the first Leon Russell album because it was too pat. The guitar playing is good but you can hear it coming, and when it comes it sounds just like you expected it would. As a musical composition the song is an extension of "One More Weekend," which came out of "Leopard-Skin Pill-Box Hat." Everything about the music is well done, all of it is familiar, and none of it is very exciting. It's as deeply a part of a trend as anything could be. I can't recall another Dylan record that had music with such a complete absence of *his* musical personality. Even on *Self Portrait,* maybe especially there, one was part of a certain realm of *Dylan* music, inimitable and un-repeatable, and this is Russell music, and not even because he plays on the record. The lack of Dylan's presence in the sound or the style of the band here is another element in the record's bland-ness—one of the things that's exciting about a Dylan record is that it's a *Dylan record!* and there's no Dylan in this music. I think that's another reason why it isn't getting played much, why people don't seem to care whether they hear it or not.

Contrasted to the good Leon Russell music, though, is another new Dylan voice—humorous, in its manner paternal, wise as hell, and very hip. Not only is Dylan contrasting his vocal sound to Russell's sound, it's a sound we haven't heard before. You don't hear it right away, not the DJs giving the record those first few ten-tative plays to see if anyone calls in in response and then dropping it when nobody does, and not the Dylan fans who wouldn't dream of calling up a Top 40 station and talking to one of those platter-chattering squares they hire.

The song itself has nervous words that are turned into a joke by the way Dylan sings them. People are fighting and breaking down right in the street and the singer is pacing back and forth trying to find some way to deal with it all. "Daylight's sneakin' through the window and I'm still in this all-night café" (and that's songwrit-ing—look at how much he gets into one line). He's bored out of his mind by this river bank that for some reason holds him with its own obscure inertia.

You thought I hadn't noticed, huh? You thought while I was learning Hebrew I forgot how to speak English?

> People disagreein' on just about everything, yep
> Makes ya stop and, wonduh why

Or this way:

> People disagreein' everywhere ya look
> Makes ya wanna stop and, uh, read a book!

Wow, says the voice, I rhymed it!

Hmmm. Rock 'n' roll is fun. I'd almost forgotten.

Dylan is still working on his myth of retirement and with-drawal, which from a different perspective is simply the problem of the private artist and art that seeks to make itself completely public. There's very little slack in his songs these days; they are perfectly controlled little statements, not so much about where Bob Dylan's head is at as about where he thinks the possibilities of staking out your own ground lie; how you deal with the world without being captured by it. The leitmotif of *New Morning* was that "12th Avenue bus moving west," and again and again the songs addressed the same problem: escape. The whole album moves west, but it never really gets there. That, in the end, is what makes it so American. The only way to keep the West from turning into what you left it for is not to go. Then the dream still means something.

Good humor turns sour. If one scene comes down too strong you can split back to the place where you were born and see what it looks like, but it's not only that you can't go home again—who would want to? Then dreams take over. You can always get away for a weekend—assuming the babysitter's free—but "Sign on the Window" isn't about a second honeymoon, it's about a second life. Does the smelly 12th Avenue bus pull up at a trout stream in Utah? But that cabin, wife and kids, fish and a big sky—that's a powerful dream. Its power, rather than its irrelevance, was most likely the thing that made so many of us critics deny it so quickly, as if we were overjoyed that the bus never really left New York. Nothing was resolved, but plenty was revealed.

Now Dylan is looking at it all from the other side, rocking a lit-tle harder, singing a little louder, playing the fading image of the country gentleman against the older one of the city boy, the mem-ory of the flaming youth against the puzzled father. His songs, it seems, are about growing up without growing away—from his au-dience as well as from his own past—the possibilities of change without betrayal. Dylan is smart enough to have always been aware that there are real questions as to whether or not those things are possible. There's little question that he lacks the answer and even less that he's interested in looking for one.

But Dylan's manipulation of his own themes—themes that he has appropriated and made his own—brings up strange problems that even he may have missed, like how to make a hit record. I think the most interesting thing about "Watching the River Flow" is that it isn't a hit, and why not. In this case, my guess is that the time has passed when people are interested in hearing Bob Dylan say he'll just sit there and watch the river flow, and even though that's not quite what he's saying, it is what people hear. If they are too impatient to hear him contradict himself, it may be because Dylan is becoming a victim of his own subtlety. I think the time has come when Dylan has to conquer the audience all over again, if he wants to have one. And I hope he's interested in trying *that*.

Bob Dylan, "Watching the River Flow" (Columbia, 1971).

BANGLA DESH
Creem
March 1972

The whole Bangla Desh set was premiered over the radio a few nights ago, neatly coinciding with the Indian Army's rout of the West Pakistani forces and the liberation of the East, thus putting the sweet seal of history on the cause that launched this record in the first place. Three of us sat listening for an hour or more, though admittedly we weren't as polite as the audience at George Harrison's Concert for Bangla Desh at Madison Square Garden last August: we turned off the first half-hour of Ravi Shankar. Then the Harrison-Leon Russell-Mad Dogs & So On part began.

I found most of it dull, and after a bit the whole show began to bother me immensely. Admittedly the huge band was tight and well-rehearsed. Harrison sang with conviction and Eric Clapton was spectacular. OK, it was well-produced. Well-produced oatmeal.

Every other song seemed to be about one of three things: 1) God saving us. 2) This is the way God planned it. 3) Chant the name of the Lord and you'll be free. (Nick Tosches has suggested that this course of action did not seem to be getting the people of Bangla Desh very far; nasty of him to bring that up.)

All of the devout rockers on Harrison's stage seemed to be missing their own point. If this gibberish had any relation to reality, or even any internal consistency—perils of pantheism—then the same god that allowed this wonderful concert to take place was also raining hot death on the other side of the globe. To achieve some kind of spiritual balance, perhaps.

Well, it reminded *me* of Joseph Heller's God, the Vicious Practical Joker. The songs chosen made a mockery of what the event was supposedly about—raising funds and world awareness for the plight of refugees from the war in East Pakistan and the fight for Bangladeshi independence—and I imagine this comes across much more blatantly on record than it did at the concert itself, since the electric presence of the stars doesn't blank out any doubts in a mindless glow of *being there* with George, Ringo, and Bob Dylan. Which is nothing to sneeze at: I'd have liked to have been there too. But I wasn't, and I have to take what I can get, along with the rest of the audience that wasn't there either, and what I get is a feeling of being sold down the river, smothered by some of the silliest ideals of western civilization, and flattered by a superstar glitter that fails to hide the almost total emptiness of the production.

There's a line in Harrison's "Beware of Darkness" where he warns, "Beware of maya," maya being an Indian word for "veil of illusion"—and without even going into the fact that the avoidance of darkness is a perfect definition of illusion, it has to be said that a veil of illusion is precisely what this concert has to offer.

There are some exceptions to the bland sound, the horrible fake gospel shouts, and the silly songs. Leon Russell makes a valiant attempt to erase the pompous mood of the event, delivering a wild version of "Jumping Jack Flash," braking into a long jive story that resolves itself into the Coasters' "Youngblood" and finally edges out and roars back to where it began. That's exciting, and as anomalous to the general drift of the concert as two other high points, Ringo's "It Don't Come Easy" and Dylan's last number, "Just Like a Woman." If the genius of this man seems occasional now, when it comes it is staggering, and nothing can touch it. Ah, Bob Dylan!

One of the best things about Dylan's side of the set is that it can make you feel like a fan again. A Bob Dylan fan. It's moving to hear George Harrison say, "I'd like to bring out a friend to us all, Mr. Bob Dylan," and implicitly join in the cheers; to recognize, in yourself, the thrill the audience is experiencing; to delight in the applause that breaks in on the choruses they and you have publicly celebrated and privately cherished for years. In spite of the fact that the movie promises to be uniquely boring, I'll be there to see how Ringo looks playing tambourine with Bob Dylan.

Dylan's performance is steady, but most of his material seems just out of his reach, as if he couldn't quite catch the emotional rhythm of the songs. But from the first notes of "Just Like a Woman," it's clear that something else is happening. Here he rises to one of the great performances of his career. He sings the song the way Hank Williams would sing it if he were still alive, with the ghostly chill of "Lost Highway." It may well be the equal of anything he has ever done, and if it took him five years to regain the power he once had, then what matters is not how long it took, but that he has regained it. What began, some years ago, as a change in attitude, seems finally to have grown into a changed point of view, and an authentic, as opposed to a contrived, maturity.

His performance reveals nuances of emotion and commitment that do not even seem to be implied in the recording we know from *Blonde on Blonde*. What is absent from the song, now, is the sense of bitterness that emerged both as a complaint and contempt five years ago, and the performance here imposes an enormous agony on the simple matter of living through the day, until finally, in the last verse, it increases in intensity and Dylan's voice is acting out a resistance to the calamity of life that stops a long way short of forgiveness.

There are words in this song that Dylan sings with such an unholy intensity that they vibrate, like the arms of a tuning fork. There is that moment when he sings,

I just don't fit

and the first word echoes off the rafters of the hall. The song has the impact that is really what's been missing in Dylan's work of the last few years, a force that makes you drop your jaw with amazement and recognition. He has reached it in moments, as with the first line of "All Along the Watchtower"—"There must be some way out of here"—and in the long, last choruses of "George Jackson," but here it merges in a sustained performance: you can't get out of the way.

Dylan's impact is a simultaneous clarifying and deepening of our lives, never in a facile celebration of his life *or* ours, but a challenge to the very sensibility that looks for such a celebration. And it is not all that complicated to define it. When Dylan has this force, it is risky to listen.

As the last song of the set, there is "Bangla Desh," which flopped when Harrison released it as a single. The performance here has such fire it might well hit now if released a second time. The lyrics still fall miles short of their subject ("It sure seems like a mess") but Clapton especially reveals all the power that previously lay dormant in the song. The sound, inevitably calling up images of carnage and horror, is inspiring and scary. Harrison beats his fists against that veil of illusion as he sings, and his words are helpless to pierce the velvet curtain this concert has thrown over itself—in a sense, to protect the event from the terror of its own subject—but this time the music breaks through and you get some idea of

40   GREIL MARCUS

why it was Harrison called all these people together in the first place.

Still, that's not much out of three LPs. I can't honestly recommend that anyone buy it for musical reasons, but I can encourage you to keep the radio on and listen to some of it. The recorded concert is a ponderous document of some of the worst foibles of the counter culture, but buried within it is a hint of what power that culture still retains.

Finally, though, the most pathetic thing about the event is its almost total lack of risk, be it artistic or political. Bangla Desh was a safe issue. It's always easier to turn to the troubles of a distant land than to enter into situations that directly threaten yourself, and, if you are a musician, your audience. The music, for the most part, could not have been less adventurous. Though many have implied that the soul of Woodstock, having been sold to the devil that day at Altamont, was bought back with this concert, they ought to know that not only can't you buy it back, you have to recreate it, on terms that recognize the fall implicit in the original deal. You can't redeem yourself by the spectacle of someone else's suffering, you have to come to terms with your own. That's why no matter what George thinks about my sweet Lord or Billy Preston about the way God planned it, Ringo deserves the last word. It don't come easy.

The Concert for Bangla Desh (Apple, 1972, #2). Featuring George Harrison, Ringo Starr, Bob Dylan, Eric Clapton, Billy Preston, Leon Russell, Ravi Shankar, Ustad Ali Akbar Khan, Ustad Alla Rakha, and Kamala Chakavarty; with band composed of Jesse Ed Davis, Tom Evans, Pete Ham, Mike Gibbins, Jim Keltner, Joey Molland, Don Preston, Carl Radle, and Klaus Voorman; with hornmen Jim Horn, Alan Beutler, Chuck Findley, Jackie Kelso, Lou McCreary, and Ollie Mitchell; and backing singers Don Nix, Jo Green, Jeanie Greene, Marlin Greene, Dolores Hall, and Claudia Linnear.

DOUG SAHM AND BAND

Creem

April 1973

Hi, welcome to 1973! (You're probably used to it by now, but this was written in January.) It's going to be a banner year for rackkanrill (heavy reggae influence on the horizon), starting out with the release of a whole batch of great new album covers. Grin's *All Out* is just stunning, the Guess Who goes down in history, and Claudia Linnear's *Phew*—well, she must be the most gorgeous woman who ever cut a record (best picture is on the inside—makes Freda Payne look like Mrs. Miller—a sure winner on the *Vogue* charts). Best of all may be Gilbert Shelton's cartoon on the front of the new Doug Sahm extravaganza. Check out that high-steppin' hillbilly in the purple shirt—yes sir, that's *Bob Dylan*, just a-pickin' and a-grinnin', getting his chops down in preparation for session work (they'll say "he just dropped in," but don't you believe it) with Rita Coolidge, Delaney Bramlett, Marjoe, and the Rowan Brothers.

As I said, the cover is fine (pic of Bob on the back, too). The album may be Sir Doug's dullest, but let's not push these guys too hard. Music is its own reward. The people who made this platter had a fine time doing it, and that's all that really matters, right?

Oh, we might get picky and say that David "Demon" Bromberg (a beatnik Mickey Dolenz, 'cept he don't sing as good) infects every cut he touches with his emotionless, mindless, pointless dobro-doodle, and that not only is his music a perfect example of not knowing what to leave out, *he* ought to be locked out. We could fret that the sound of the album is as homogenized as that city-slick peanut butter *The Greening of America* came down so hard on, which means that Charles Reich wouldn't like it—something to consider, these days—but then, Charles is a *nice* guy, and this is a *nice* record. We might be caught fessin' up that the only tracks to rise out of the sink are standard Texas blues, and only because their form, not their execution, is distinctive—nothing here to compare to the barroom funk of *The Return of Doug Saldaña*. I wouldn't want to be the one to say it, but the disc does feature the worst harp and the least expressive and least audible singing Bob Dylan has ever recorded. And when the lights are low, we might cop to the likelihood that Bob's original contribution to the LP, "Wallflowers," shows that he has absorbed his John Prine influences very well, and has succeeded in writing and whining a tune that could by no stretch of the imagination have the slightest effect on anybody.

But there's no sense to any of this. These guys have given us a lot, more than we can ever repay. It's up to us to give it back. Because wherever music is, spring can't be far behind.

Doug Sahm, *Doug Sahm and Band* (Atlantic, 1973).

HEAVY BREATHING
Creem
May 1974

Last January, writing from the Netherlands, Langdon Winner had this to say:

> I've gotten back into rock and roll, at least that part of it which shows up on Dutch, British, French or American Armed Forces stations. It's difficult for me to know which of the songs (other than soul group hits) are European and which are U.S. origin. Anybody can learn to sing like Mick Jagger so I suspect that some of the big tunes here are Dutch rock and not heard back there. One thing is entirely evident, however, as this year begins, and it may have been evident to you for some time. The radio is filled to overflowing with songs which are super-self-consciously about the business of making rock and roll and living on its terms. Two which come to mind: "Rock and Roll Baby" and "Rock and Roll I

Gave You the Best Years of My Life." I remember how precious a thing it used to be to hear any song make reference to its own medium. Now it seems to be the only thing going!

But perhaps this period of heightened but ultimately ridiculous self-consciousness is a prelude to what we've been waiting for— the appearance of something genuinely new. I don't mean just music either. There are good signs that the whole atmosphere, political and cultural, in both the U.S. and the rest of the world is about to undergo a transformation. Too many things remain unsettled after having been settled, e.g., the "end" of the Vietnam war, the "full disclosure" of Watergate and a host of submerged themes bequeathed to us by the last dozen years. There is a very great tension and it runs very deep. I don't see how it can do anything other than create tremendous forces to push our center of gravity into one direction or another. Like a tumbler in a lock falling into place when a key is inserted, there will be, I think, a convergence of new voices, styles, and interests headed in a particular direction. I don't know, perhaps something like Dylan's tour with the Band will be one sign. Maybe George Wallace will come out at half-time at the Super Bowl, throw off his crutches and lead a Bastille-type march and coup on Washington. The need is there. And I think, now, very, very definitely it is becoming a collective need. The tone of the time and the range of possibilities available to anybody at all are set by the coming together, often by coincidence, of a peculiarly matched set of human elements. There's no counting on logic any longer. But neither is there any denying that what is possible for us to do in any important way outside our personal lives does depend on a certain climate accompanied by a set of open doors which makes that climate visible. Unfortunately, I think that the working of these forces right now can only take the form of a Leader to personify what people are feeling. If it is proven that the Wallace assassination is connected to Watergate, we are in real trouble. Whatever the personification, we probably won't like it. There is too much evil in the air, too much that Agnew and Nixon did not satisfy in the tormented American soul.

But, as I am always heard to say, there may be some room to move in the cracks. The hard thing will be to avoid interpreting what's truly new in terms of what'd be old and familiar. It's easy to get locked in. What's interesting about the New York Dolls are some new bumps and crevasses—a strong sense of guilt, unfocused moral outrage, the missing sense of humor. It is, indeed, a lot like some very old stuff. But I get the feeling that for part of what we are about to see happening, the key may have gone about one click in the lock.

I had read a lot about Bob Dylan's tour with the Band before it arrived at the Oakland Coliseum Arena February 11, just before the close-out in Los Angeles; on paper, I knew all about it. I knew precisely how the show was structured: Dylan & Band, Band, Dylan & Band, intermission, Dylan solo, Dylan & Band, "Like a Rolling Stone," encore. With a few trivial variations, I knew what songs were to be played and in what order. I knew how the crowd would react and to what: they'd go wild for "Even the president of the United States must sometimes have to stand naked"; a few jerks would yell "We Want Dylan" when the Band played. I knew well-timed lights would cue the audience response for "Like a Rolling Stone," and that the song would be referred to as "an anthem" in the papers the next day; I knew that matches would be lit to solicit the encore. It seemed like a set-up. I was looking forward to giving Bob Dylan a standing ovation when he walked out, but I was damned if I was going to light any matches.

What the press did not prepare me for was the sound, the singing, the playing, and the impact. I wasn't prepared to hear "Rainy Day Women" come store-porching off the stage as a big, brawling Chicago blues; for the black usher dancing down the steps of the hall, waving his flashlight and singing "Knock, knock, knocking on heaven's door"; for the delight I felt when Robbie Robertson and Rick Danko rushed a single mike for a chorus just like Paul and George in *A Hard Day's Night*. I wasn't prepared for one bit of what mattered about the show, and I doubt if anyone else was either.

Never—not in 1965 when they were the Hawks, not at their 1969 debut at Winterland, or at half a dozen other concerts—have I heard the Band play with the fire Dylan got from them this time around. I've seen reports that barely mentioned their presence, let alone the music they made, but between sets, or the next day, the Band was what people wanted to talk about first. Robbie's guitar playing was unmatched—he drove through two shows with a pointed frenzy most of his performances only hint at—but the difference was the beat.

It was a massive, intensely syncopated THUMP that at first overwhelmed everything else. Everyone knows Levon Helm is a great drummer, but this time he played like a star. He was working right at the heart of rock 'n' roll—sometimes Richard Manuel joined him on a second set of drums, and while it was fun to watch, musically I couldn't tell the difference. It was the authority of Levon's beat that let Dylan, Robbie, and Garth Hudson sing and play with a freedom that with any less of a foundation would have seemed merely personal; with Levon there it was still personal, and also shared, sympathetic, dependent—on stage, and out in front of it.

Nothing the Band did on their own touched what they did with Dylan. Against the Band's comradeship he presents a physical image of utter self-reliance (though he cannot get where he wants to go without them and his new songs are about the poverty of going it alone); against their careful intelligence he pits genius, erratic and eager for rules to break (the Band at their worst have never been as embarrassing as Dylan at his, and at their best they write history while he makes it); against the Band's pleasure in music (they smile, he frowns), Dylan sets a nervous fury, an impulse to drama.

There is a side to the Band that is uncertain and a bit scared of the crowd, a side that takes refuge in a sort of rational craftsmanship. It's an emotional limit that only Garth Hudson always escapes, and it may be the source of both the spare elegance of Robbie's best lines and of the precise, even constricted arrangements the Band uses on stage and on record. There's also a side that is wild, mad, and chaotic, and it comes out, in *their* music, only in snatches: an occasional guitar solo, Garth's crazy piano on "The Weight," on "Don't Do It."

But this is a side of the Band that Bob Dylan almost always breaks wide open. He takes the spotlight, and they are free to follow their hearts. They get a certain energy playing with him they don't get from each other—and in any case they can't handle his twisting vocals with neat arrangements. They have to set the beat, play for it and against it, even risk collapsing the song for the chance to touch the emotions of anyone who listens. They have to give Dylan the momentum he so obviously wants and play for themselves.

The music, then, was not neat, it was not orderly, it was not elegant. It was fierce: riding that beat, full of hard-won arrogance, love, and anger. At first the music hit in explosions, and then resolved itself into textures—Garth's organ flowing delicately over a solo from Robbie that was pure anarchy while Dylan's howls cut across both. Then, when you thought you had a grip on the music, that you'd heard what they had to say, they came back with something tougher—like "All Along the Watchtower."

It was a jagged, growling blast; the Band reached roughly for the melody and Dylan shouted past it. They made the recorded version—likely the best thing Dylan has done since *Highway 61 Revisited*—seem tentative and weak, as if, down in Nashville in 1967, Dylan had hedged his bets. In fact, seven years later, he was raising the stakes.

As I write, I hear James and Carly singing "Ride with the tide, go with the flow," and while I'm gratified the two of them are limiting their goals to their talents, such a credo strikes me as the very opposite of what Bob Dylan—or any artist—is all about. The music Dylan made with the Band was not easy to relate to. If, in the past, you had only seen the Band, a group that sometimes spends more time on the soundcheck than they do playing, you might have written the edges off their music by assuming they were just a bit rusty after so much time off the road. As for Dylan's singing, it was a shock no simple excuse—he's tired, *he's* rusty, he's aloof—could

contain. Some writers have spoken respectfully about Dylan's experiments with melisma—that sounds classy, doesn't it?—but
melisma has to do with bending words, and Dylan was breaking
them. He came down on the last word of every line with all he had,
regardless, it seemed, of what they might have meant—like a gunfighter without a target, and Bob Dylan without a target is only
shooting blanks. But he did have a target, or several: music; his
songs; the audience; himself.

Music today—especially the polished, lifeless Elektra-Asylum
folk rock that is aimed at the audience that came to hear Dylan—
has a lot of well-defined, surface melody (in real rock 'n' roll, the
melody is inseparable from the rhythm and the beat). Such music
substitutes professionalism for inspiration. Dylan wailed out his
songs, attacking melody as if it were an obstacle, not a means, to
feeling; in place of professionalism he offered a crude expressiveness, breaking through the limits of phrasing and technique.
When he missed, he missed; when he scored, he drove his songs
past themselves. Often he was aiming not his words, but himself—
not as a persona, but as physical presence, as flesh and blood—at
the audience, and instead of the messages and meanings of his
songs there was something much more elemental: commitment and
force.

If these shows were not to be merely a live greatest hits package, Dylan had to find a way to get an authentically new kind of
life into the songs. This music doesn't wear out any more than
Robert Johnson, the Carter Family, or Little Richard, Dylan must
feel, but proving it is another matter. Only when he could liberate
the songs from his past and ours, yet without denying that past,
could the songs continue to liberate the musicians and the audience. The music had to feel right to the singer, and come across to
the crowd.

Dylan was shouting, chanting, partly, I'm sure, to be heard over
the noise, but if that was all he cared about he could have turned
down the amps. The noise was part of the shout. To simply present
the songs in a marginally new way—difference in phrasing here,

change in emphasis there, transposed intros, altered tempos, they did all that—would, by itself, have seemed contrived, to the singer even more than to the audience. So in one sense, Dylan chose not to really sing the songs at all. It seemed to me that more than anything else Dylan was reaching for an equivalent, though nothing like a copy, of his original sound: something very rough, disturbing, disorienting, not easy to like. It didn't always work. But the ambition was clear, and the songs that fit best with the hard chant, those with a beat strong enough to force Dylan to deal with the rhythm, grew as songs: "Ballad of a Thin Man," "Highway 61 Revisited," and "Maggie's Farm." On the last two, Dylan was flat out the ultimate rock 'n' roll singer; the Band was the final band. Any comparison between this combination and an earnest, talented group like the Allman Brothers Band—forget the lyrics—would be a joke. This was rock 'n' roll at its limits.

Other numbers were less songs than incidents in a struggle rock 'n' roll—or the blues, or country music—embodies but hardly contains: staying alive, keeping the faith, building and fighting for a life where humor, anger, and love are not only the means, but the ends. What hit me, so many times, was the strength of the man at the center of this struggle; I felt more alive being in the same room with such strength. This passed into the songs: they were stronger, as signs of life as well as comments on it. "He loves these songs as much as we do," said the woman next to me.

When Dylan first walked out on stage with Hudson, Manuel, Danko, Robertson, and Helm, the applause died away even before they cut into "When You Go Your Way and I Go Mine." ("No bullshit," that fast start said.) The crowd (and who can say who was in the crowd? I saw professors I'd had when I was a sophomore in college, students I'd taught when they were sophomores) seemed caught between reverence and celebration, between worship and caution.

It was only when Dylan came out alone that genuflection and nostalgia took over the night. If the response to Dylan's first electric numbers had been uncertain, the applause for the Band's first familiar set loud and passionate, here the cheers dwarfed all that had come before and all that followed. Part of the crowd didn't want to share their hero with backup musicians (not unless that was all they were, and it wasn't); some people wanted to hear the words; a lot of people still hate rock 'n' roll, especially the impolite version the Band was serving up. They wanted that old-time harmonica religion, and they cheered harmonica solos the way the rest of rock 'n' roll America cheers drum solos. They wanted noble sentiments and enemies to hate; they wanted the ambiguity the last few years have enforced on life washed away, and Dylan, on his own, had such things to offer. Here he was submitting to the worst desires of his audience, and raising the most tired ghosts of his past. That's all it seemed like—most of the acoustic numbers had none of the aggressive novelty, really a new sense of time, that was so striking in the electric sets. It's not a matter of genre: "Wedding Song" sounds as if it could have come from *The Freewheelin' Bob Dylan,* but that doesn't make it a throwback.

Here was "The Times They Are A-Changin'," even more lifeless and impersonal in 1974 than in 1964; "The Gates of Eden," which was ridiculous in 1965 and still is; and "The Lonesome Death of Hattie Carroll."

The title of that last song implies that the singer wants to reach out to a friendless woman, but the song is morally closed exactly where "George Jackson" is morally open, and a true attempt at friendship. I think Dylan would recognize, today, that Hattie Carroll's death was more important than William Zantzinger's six-month sentence. But while I thought how much better it would have been for Dylan to have sung "George Jackson," and tried to understand why that song seems both more modest and more important than "Hattie Carroll," I got a sense of why it would have been wrong for Dylan to sing the newer song. It had to do, as in so much of what's at the heart of Dylan's recent songs, with privacy. Jackson was a human being to Dylan—a man, not a principle—and while the record Dylan made when Jackson was killed expressed that, there is a way in which singing the song in front of

16,000 people would have been a shameful invasion of the privacy even dead men deserve: a man's right not to be made into a symbol. Hattie Carroll was a symbol, and she remains a symbol, as if she was never alive. She didn't die so Dylan could sing about her, and so we could applaud our own rejection of her killer's punishment, but that's all the song can do for her. Well, much of the crowd cheered and even stood up for morality, for justice, for better times, for when the world was black and white. It's said that Huey Newton and Bobby Seale founded Oakland's Black Panther Party for Self-Defense after listening to "Mr. Tambourine Man" over and over, but this night, likely in the same town, perhaps only a few miles from the place where Bob Dylan was playing, you could have found the Symbionese Liberation Army and Patty Hearst—if you knew where to look.

The songs that hit had new meanings—as events. With barely an exception they seemed to be sent out to every member of the audience, to roll out and change us and then bounce back to change the way we saw the singer on the stage. "When You Go Your Way and I Go Mine" was presented as Dylan's declaration of independence, and we cheered it as such (again, it was exhilarating to hear someone make so strong a statement), but the performance had room for us, too. "Ballad of a Thin Man"—I used to see Dylan sing that song, and I knew who Mr. Jones was: everyone who wasn't cool enough to buy a ticket to a Bob Dylan concert, the folkies who booed, the *others*. This night I had no doubt at all that I was Mr. Jones, that the image did not have to stretch to take in those around me, that Dylan meant much of the rage and contempt of the song for himself. Here the new style made it home—Dylan screaming "MISTER JO-*HONES!*" and flipping Jerry Lee Lewis riffs off his piano—and if the song condemned anyone, it wasn't those who didn't know, but those who wouldn't learn. When he sang "Wedding Song," it seemed not merely a tribute to his wife (if that's all it is, why bother to sing to anyone else?), but a challenge to live with the kind of extremes that must be communicated with words like "blood," "sacrifice," "knife," and "kill." Even with the context of Dylan's private life, the song seemed less a victory to claim than a goal to reach for, and that mood was perhaps at the heart of the show. When I borrowed binoculars and looked at Dylan's face, it was clear that his work is not easy for him to do, and the intensity in his face was staggering.

It no longer makes much sense for me to see Dylan's career in terms of progression; to look for a point of view refining or growing or slipping from year to year; to see a style at work in and against a changing world. All that is there, but somehow it's not very interesting. What sticks in my mind are a handful of songs—"All Along the Watchtower," "Down the Highway," "Bob Dylan's Dream," "Highway 61 Revisited"—and a feeling for how tough they are. For the moment, the rest slips away, just as it did at the shows. There is much that does not and may never reach me on *Planet Waves,* but "Wedding Song," for one, sounds more to me like the real ending of *John Wesley Harding* than it sounds like anything else. If the question what does it all mean? is worth asking about Dylan's performance—it's usually worth asking about anything—this might be part of it.

A man goes out into the world; he is bedeviled by its traps, seduced by its delights. If he is a fool he is determined not to remain one; he tries to read the signs God and the devil have scattered in the world, and he builds slowly toward a moral stance. He makes choices, and suffers by them, and grows both stronger and more wary. He tries to get across what he has learned to the crowd, but finds they don't listen too well; whether they do or not, he feels he has at least told the truth. Finally he returns home and meets his wife, down there at the cove, and the two of them take off to have a drink, to make love, to get some rest. He's worked hard, and he's earned his reward. That to me is the story told in *John Wesley Harding,* but there is one more tale to tell, the story Dylan has been working on since that time, a story he now seems to have focused on one tune.

"Wedding Song" says that all the struggles of the world are present in the reward as well; the struggle only shifts to another plane. I think Dylan was trying to get across such a sense of struggle and reward on *Planet Waves,* and that he didn't make it, because he has been out of the world too long, and the songs remain too personal. One verse of "Wedding Song" seems to claim that a man must reject the world to keep faith with his private struggle (typically, Dylan sings the line "But I love you more than all of that" with such grace he can make you believe the world must be abandoned); alongside of all the other love songs on *Planet Waves,* the last one can stay in that prison. But if the tune really does complete the story of *John Wesley Harding,* and if it's heard that way, you might learn that the struggle in the world only deepens the struggle at home; that in some mysterious way, each struggle justifies the other.

Since making *Planet Waves* Dylan has been all over the world. It is hard to believe the vital performances he gave are only a prelude to another effective retirement; it is impossible to believe that the vitality he must have received from the audience will not find its way into new songs as strong as those he shot off the stage. Elliot Murphy, who was there in the audience with everybody else, tells a story that I think makes sense out of the stakes of Bob Dylan's tour: "When I got together with Polydor, we went out to California to do an album with Leon Russell on piano, Jim Gordon on drums, and Dr. John on organ. I was out there and it just wasn't going right at all. One night I was eating dinner with my brother at a restaurant and really feeling down about the way the album would end up and thinking I wouldn't know who I was. Suddenly my brother starts pointing across the table and his face is turning white. These booths were arranged so you were almost sitting back to back with people. I turned around and looked at what he was pointing at, and that second the guy in back of me turns around and I'm nose to nose with Bob Dylan. For some reason that gave me strength and I went into the studio and told the producer to forget it. I came back to New York and we did it right."

Bob Dylan, like Murphy or the rest of us, needs other people from whom he can draw strength, who can inspire him and with whom he can struggle. This time, Dylan went to us, and it should make a difference.

Planet Waves (Asylum, 1974).

HIGHWAY 61 REVISITED REVISITED
Creem
June 1974

Since I wrote the report on the Oakland Dylan-Band concerts that appeared in the last issue, my crafty brother Steve has come up with a good, rough tape of one of the shows, which suggests a foot-note both on the concerts and the live album that is presumably set to follow.

The tape makes clear that nearly everything good I had to say about the performances ought to be raised to the tenth power. The music was wilder than I remembered, and Dylan's singing more exciting. Though musically very different, I haven't the slightest doubt that what Dylan and the Band did in 1974 was as memorable as what Dylan and the Hawks did in 1965 and '66, or that a live al-bum drawn from the tour should burn with all the force of the classic *Live at Albert Hall* bootleg, and carry with it an altogether new kind of humor and confidence. I wasn't sure, writing about the concerts, if the music would come across on record—Dylan's presence, and the Band's, was part of it all, perhaps an essential part. The tape proves that I was wrong. The music is potent in ways I haven't even hinted at. It may be that Dylan's presence, though part of the music, also overshadowed it.

It's possible that none of this will survive on official vinyl—not if Dylan, Robertson, or whoever else will be involved in producing the live album give in to the natural temptation to tone down and refine what was in fact a brash and unruly performance. If you insist on getting perfect stereo separation when you record an earthquake, you may produce a more professional product, but it won't sound like an earthquake. Too much precision, too much balance, mixing down the Band and mixing up Dylan—as Bob Johnston did on the Isle of Wight cuts on *Self Portrait*—will take the life out of the music. So, a plea: go for the total sound, even if it means you have to leak tracks all over the studio. Try and keep the momentum of the music. Let some distortion and confusion bleed through the songs, as it did when they were played. If you have to put anything in front, make it the drums.

And don't wait until Christmas.

A MOMENT OF PANIC

City
24 July–6 Aug 1974
with
Dylan/Band
Village Voice
15 August 1974

Before the Flood (and what does that mean? A natural correlate to *Planet Waves?* Après moi le déluge?), the live album from the grand tour Bob Dylan and the Band made last winter, taped almost entirely on the last night, in Los Angeles, may turn out to be the least played Dylan record since *Self Portrait*. The press is that Dylan's singing is mannered and emotionless; that the music is sloppy and perfunctory; that the use of old songs is both a failed attempt to recreate a glorious past and an admission that Dylan cannot create in the present; that he no longer has any real relationship to the generation he helped recognize itself. It is said that at best the album is a substitution of physical energy for the imagination and innovation of better days.

Dylan's generation dissolved as its members grew up. Dylan, quite some time ago, turned his back on his putative generation, just as he abandoned the strictures of his old styles, and joined a bigger, more complex America. These days, anyone who writes about Dylan's audience as us is using a very ambiguous word, or a very outdated one. Dylan now performs as an American artist, not a generational symbol. *John Wesley Harding* was a deeply intellectual exploration of what it meant to be an American artist, expressed in both words and music; *Before the Flood* offers not ideas but passions, and its ambitions are the same. The old context has crumbled—Paul Nelson is right when he says that in Dylan's new music the center will not hold, but the center is not in the music but in the country itself. The triumph of Dylan's new music is that Dylan seems to take the failure of the center—and, in terms of any our-generation, the failure of the edges—as an opportunity for freedom. If the failure is a fact, it is an exhilarating fact.

This is what I hear. Since I saw Dylan and the Band on their tour, and since *Before the Flood* was released, I have had no interest in the new music as part of Dylan's history, or as a part of ours. Perhaps it's not the context that's shattered; perhaps it's the music itself that blows the context apart. But I care about this music as incident—I am intrigued by the simple aesthetic fact of six men on a stage saying their piece, and leaving.

When I listen to the radio today, I hear Paul McCartney, Elton John. At home I play Steely Dan's *Pretzel Logic,* Roxy Music's *Stranded,* and Roxy singer Bryan Ferry's strange new oldies album, *These Foolish Things* (he does "A Hard Rain's A-Gonna Fall"; he also does "It's My Party"). *Before the Flood* exposes the calculation of these records. They are so well-made, either in terms of simple production (Paul and Elton) or a whole vision of popular culture (Steely Dan, Roxy Music, Bryan Ferry) that they leave almost no room for the listener to create. The tension between musicians and audience is proscribed; your responses have been figured out, and if the artist is good at his job, you go where he wants you to go.

There's nothing wrong with this. You get to a lot of interesting places. On one level, such means and ends are the essence of popular art. Critics bowing to Alfred Hitchcock have been claiming for years that the perfection of manipulation is all there is to it. But great popular art, like great rock 'n' roll, takes an audience—and, since we are talking about popular art, ultimately the artist as well—to places the artist glimpsed only by instinct, if at all.

I feel many good things when I watch Hitchcock or listen to Bryan Ferry, but I never feel free. What I miss is the sense of open possibility, the exhilaration, one gets from *Jules and Jim, Blonde on Blonde,* or *Weekend*—the feeling that an artist is working over his head, that you are in over yours, that limits have been trashed. This kind of freedom—when you're in the presence of an artist liberating himself from his form, you feel free—makes *Jules and Jim* a much more dangerous movie than *Shadow of a Doubt,* just as *Before the Flood* is funnier and more painful than Ferry's *These Foolish Things,* which has had me laughing and misting up for months.

I miss the sense that there is more to music, or to an artist, to myself, than I'd guessed, that when a song comes on the radio or goes on the turntable I can't predict what it will do to me. I miss the feeling of musicians diving into a performance without much idea of what route they are traveling, let alone of where they are going to come out, but with the good-humored, nervous conviction that the trip will return in surprise whatever it costs in uncertainty.

Dylan and the Band's music on *Before the Flood* was made in this spirit—a particularly American spirit. The best of it is brawling, crude, not completely civilized, an old-fashioned, back-country, big-city attack on all things genteel. There's a lot of Whitman's YAWP in this music. "The European moderns," D. H. Lawrence wrote fifty years ago, "are all *trying* to be extreme. The great Americans I mention" (Hawthorne, Poe, Dana, Melville, Whitman) "just were it."

I listened seriously, carefully, and constantly to this album, not enjoying it particularly, feeling put off by what seemed to be a one-dimensional, overly straightforward performance, until in the middle of "Highway 61 Revisited," right where Dylan is singing "Do you know where I can get rid of these things?" I caught Robbie Robertson tossing off two little noises—Awk! Awk!—and then flipping back to the main drift of the song with a combination of notes unlike anything I had ever heard. I couldn't believe it—he made it obvious that every other guitar player in America has webbed fingers—or that he has twelve. So I called him up, to find out how this music was made, how the riff was worked into place, what its purpose was in the structure of the song, and so on. "Yes," he said. "A moment of panic."

That moment made the album for me, opened it up: panic perhaps, but no accident, because now I could cite dozens of moments like it. Those few notes cracked the textures of the music, provided a way into its density. Within those textures are a fabulous collection of nuances, phrases, lyric fragments, pieces that seem to matter more than finished songs. Pieces shoot out of a song you've heard dozens of times and make new claims on your ability to respond. The music may be all familiarity on the surface (old songs), or beneath the surface (bought the album, took it home, played it), but you never get to the bottom. The sound of the recording—rough, blurry, fast, dark—hides the action at first, and may even make some tunes sound bland. After a time, strange incidents begin to poke through, all the more powerful because you were sure they weren't there. Then everything falls into place. A few days later you hear something different; the performance shatters; it rebuilds itself around that moment, and shifts again.

This kind of freedom—six men running wild within a structure that still keeps its shape, that is never incoherent or arbitrary—seems to be what is authentically new about this music, as well as what is best about it. The density of the music creates new space; I hear Garth Hudson as the star of this record, just as I heard Levon Helm as the star of the show. Neither man would have played with the fire he did without Dylan driving him past himself; that Garth Hudson can overshadow Dylan here is the album's success, not its failure.

The Band didn't play this way with Dylan when they toured as the Hawks in 1965 and '66, nor have they played this way on their own since. In the past, they backed Dylan, and he sang as if that was just how he wanted it. The coverage of the recent tour fell into these expectations. Writers spoke often of the excellent "fills" Robbie, Garth, and Richard Manuel provided, or the fine rhythms Levon Helm and Rick Danko came up with. *Before the Flood* makes such commentary ridiculous. Garth handles the rhythm; sometimes Levon seizes the story. There are whole songs in what Garth does on "Highway 61 Revisited," in Levon's drumming on "Most Likely You Go Your Way (And I'll Go Mine)"—complete, crazily intricate versions of what these songs are all about.

The performance is so rough it makes the Rolling Stones' live music sound polite, and yet the music Dylan and the Band make together is more complex, in an emotional sense, than the lyrics of the songs that are being played. This freedom—the way that the singers and musicians have freed themselves from the songs as artifacts—has something to do with the fact that Dylan and the Band are older than they were when they first played this music; they have less to prove to each other and more to say for themselves. They can take their partnership for granted, and build on it. They can be thrilled by the crowd and forget it, all at once.

Listen to the original version of "Highway 61 Revisited," from the album of the same name, made back in 1965; you hear a very laconic Bob Dylan, a dandy, casually describing events of incredible strangeness, as if to say, *Well, what* else *would you expect from a place like the U.S.A.?* But on *Before the Flood* it's a different story. *You wouldn't* believe *what's happening on Highway 61,* the singer is saying—*and we're going to take you out and show you, whether you're ready or not.*

Once, Bob Dylan cruised the strip with a cool eye, keeping his distance. Now, he's right in the middle, and so are we. You hear Garth Hudson waltzing you down the road, making you feel as if it's going to be a pleasant, Tom Sawyer sort of trip, and then suddenly he's calling down from the mountain, Gabriel bent on Judgment Day, and yes, you'd better run, if only to keep up. That is the *burden* of joining a bigger, more mysterious America, of abandoning the comforts of my-generation. And to enter the center that will not hold, to affirm it, to do one's work there—that is not, I think, a harmless act.

Dylan's tour with the Band was not an event, regardless of what *Newsweek* and *Rolling Stone* said, regardless that whole books on the tour are in the stores; as an event, the tour vanished in its own smoke. Elton's John's *Caribou* and *Before the Flood* were released simultaneously; *Caribou* is already number one, while Dylan and the Band are not even in the top twenty. Apparently the 450,000 people who came to see the show do not even need a souvenir.* Asylum must have believed its own hype, because they put *Before the Flood* on the market without ads. Now, hysterically, they are adding more hype: "The greatest tour in rock and roll history . . ."

Nonsense. Unlike Dylan's tours in the mid-sixties, the Band's debut in the spring of 1969, the Rolling Stones' climactic dash across the continent later that year, or Elvis's first appearances on television in 1956, this tour did not draw in the desires and fears and symbols that changed and deepened the public life we share through performers who matter to us. Dylan's tour was an opportunity for music, a chance for six people to break through the limits with which they'd surrounded themselves. Together, they pulled that off, and within the music they made and left behind on record, there is a chance for any fan to break through some of his or her own limits. Most other music will sound careful, hedged, and a bit false after *Before the Flood*—that may be why I haven't heard a single cut from the album on the radio since it was released.

Bob Dylan, *Before the Flood* (Asylum, 1974).

———. *the bootleg series volume 4—Bob Dylan Live 1966—The "Royal Albert Hall" Concert* (Columbia, 1998).

---

*Before the Flood eventually reached #3 on the *Billboard* charts.

PART TWO

Seven Years of This,
1975–1981

AN ALBUM OF WOUNDS
City
5–18 February 1975*

Bob Dylan wasn't kidding when he called his new album *Blood on the Tracks*—the songs are covered with it. "Warn all gentle and fastidious people from so much as peeping into the book," Herman Melville wrote of *Moby-Dick,* full of delight at his work and full of worry at its reception; Dylan has a right to feel the same. *Blood on the Tracks* is an album of wounds: at once the tale of an adventurer's war with a woman and with himself, and a shattering attempt to force memory, fantasy, and the terrors of love and death to serve an artist's impulse to redeem disaster by making beauty out of it.

It is a great record: dark, pessimistic, and discomforting, roughly made, and filled with a deeper kind of pain than Dylan has ever revealed. And while there are echoes of Dylan's earlier work on *Blood on the Tracks* (for its themes, *Another Side of Bob Dylan;* for its unity, *John Wesley Harding;* for its singing, *Before the Flood*), the only thing about Bob Dylan that could have prepared his audience for this music is his refusal ever to be pinned down.

Dylan is offering a fiction here, but he assumes the central role, kicking off his story with "Tangled Up in Blue," a cracked narrative that introduces us to the hero of *Blood on the Tracks* and to the woman he will pursue, abandon, damn, lose and lose again, right through to the album's end, nearly an hour later. Save for "You're Gonna Make Me Miss You When You Go," the album's one certifiable stinker, the songs are as good as any Dylan has ever written—every one of them different, and all of a piece.

---

*With a last line from *Rolling Stone,* 13 March 1975.

In a little hilltop village
They gambled for my clothes

Little red wagon, little red bike
I ain't no monkey but I know what I like

They say I shot a man named Gray
And took his wife to Italy
She inherited a million bucks
And when she died it came to me
I can't help it
If I'm lucky

This is classic American songwriting, as plain and mysterious as twenties country music, thirties blues, or fifties rock 'n' roll—stuff like the Carter Family's "Worried Man Blues," Buell Kazee's "East Virginia," Jimmie Rodgers's blue yodels, Rabbit Brown's "James Alley Blues," Willie Brown's "Future Blues," Sonny Boy Williamson's "Eyesight to the Blind," Johnny Ace's "Pledging My Love." These songs are as obvious and unsettling as weather; no one can fail to understand them, and no one can get to the bottom of them, either. *Blood on the Tracks* is no different.

The backing on the album is merely functional, undistinguished save for Dylan's harmonica, and his guitar on "Buckets of Rain" (he does nothing Ry Cooder couldn't do, but Cooder couldn't play with so much soul if he practiced for a hundred years). The music on the best Dylan records has always been special (think of Charlie Mc-Coy's bass on *John Wesley Harding* or Kenny Buttrey's drumming on "Absolutely Sweet Marie"), and I miss that.

Because the music here doesn't grab you from across the room, you may have to sit down and listen before you find your way into the songs. The album isn't inaccessible, but it makes demands. You have to bring something to the music before you catch the way Dylan will lead with what might be his worst lines, and then put you away:

Time is a jet plane, it moves too fast
Oh, but what a shame, that all we shared can't last
I, I can change, *I swear!*
Oh, see what you can do
I can make it through
You can make it, too

One mask of the adventurer fades into another: the perennial innocent of "Tangled Up in Blue" becomes the accuser of "Idiot Wind," the boozy blues spirit of "Meet Me in the Morning" the fantasist of "Lily, Rosemary and the Jack of Hearts," the loser of "Shelter from the Storm" the wasted survivor of "Buckets of Rain." And if there is a story line running through these songs, and I think there is—the odyssey of a mythical lover possessed by an affair he can never resolve—then "Lily, Rosemary and the Jack of Hearts" is at the center of the album. The Jack of Hearts is the secret hero the narrator would be if he could: the dark stranger who sweeps into town, turns it upside down, and makes off with the love of its women and its money to boot before anyone can get a clear look at his face, or his heart. Before and after come the songs of the man as he is: the one who sought shelter from the storm, found it, and lost it.

As he has done before, Dylan has dismissed the whole pop scene by releasing an album that cuts right through it. *Blood on the Tracks* reveals the emptiness and the failure of nerve of the records that these days pass for genius; it stakes a claim to its own voice, and for as long as the album lasts, that voice is a whole world. *Blood on the Tracks* proves that Dylan is a pathfinder because in the middle of the city he can discover forgotten streets and make them new.

Most of all, though, I like the way he says "Delacroix."

Bob Dylan, *Blood on the Tracks* (Columbia, 1975).

from LINER NOTES
Bob Dylan & the Band
The Basement Tapes (Columbia)
1975

. . . with a certain kind of blues music, you can sit down and play it . . .
you may have to lean forward a little.
—Bob Dylan, 1966

In 1965 and 1966 Bob Dylan and the Hawks played their way across the country and then around the world. Those rough tours pushed Bob Dylan's music, and the Band's, to a certain limit, and they had made a stand-up, no-quarter-given-and-no-quarter-asked music if there ever was such a thing. In the summer of 1967 Dylan and the Band were after something else.

Neither *John Wesley Harding,* made later that year, nor *Music from Big Pink* (for which all of the Band's numbers here were at one time intended) sound much like *The Basement Tapes,* but there are two elements the three sessions do share: a feeling of age, a kind of classicism, and an absolute commitment by the singers and musicians to their material. Beneath the easy rolling surface of *The Basement Tapes,* there is some serious business going on. What was taking shape, as Dylan and the Band fiddled with the tunes, was less a style than a spirit—a spirit that had to do with a delight in friendship and invention.

As you first listen to the music they made, you'll be hard put to pin it down, and likely not too interested in doing so. What matters is Rick Danko's loping bass on "Yazoo Street Scandal"; Garth Hudson's omnipresent merry-go-round organ playing (never more evocative than it is on "Apple Sucking Tree"); the slow, uncoiling menace of "This Wheel's on Fire"; Bob Dylan's singing, as sly as Jerry Lee Lewis, and as knowing as the old man in the mountains.

There's the kind of love song only Richard Manuel can pull off, the irresistibly pretty "Katie's Been Gone"; there is the unassuming passion of the Band's magnificent "Ain't No More Cane," an old chain gang song that ought to be a revelation to anyone who has ever cared about the Band's music, because the performance seems to capture the essence of what they have always meant to be. There's the lovely idea of "Bessie Smith," written and sung by Robbie Robertson and Rick as the plaint of one of Bessie's lovers, who can't figure out if he's lost his heart to the woman herself or the way she sings. There is Levon Helm's patented mixture of carnal bewilderment and helpless delight in "Don't Ya Tell Henry" (and the solos he and Robbie stomp out on that tune)—and the tale he tells in "Yazoo Street Scandal," a comic horror story wherein the singer is introduced, by his girlfriend, to the local Dark Lady, who promptly seduces him, and then scares him half to death.

The Basement Tapes, more than any other music that has been heard from Bob Dylan and the Band, sound like the music of a partnership. As Dylan and the Band trade vocals across the discs, as they trade nuances and phrases within the songs, you can feel the warmth and the comradeship that must have been liberating for all six men. Language, for one thing, is completely unfettered. A good number of the songs seem as cryptic, or as nonsensical, as a misnumbered crossword puzzle—that is, if you listen only for words, and not for what the singing and the music say—but the open spirit of the songs is as straightforward as their unmatched vitality and spunk.

One hears a pure, naked emotion in some of Dylan's writing and singing—in "Tears of Rage," especially—that can't be found anywhere else, and I think it is the musical sympathy Dylan and the Band shared in these sessions that gives "Tears of Rage," and other numbers, their remarkable depth and power. There are rhythms in the music that literally sing with compliments tossed from one musician to another—listen to "Lo and Behold!" "Crash on the Levee (Down in the Flood)," "Ain't No More Cane." And there is another kind of openness, a flair for ribaldry that's as much a matter of Levon's mandolin as his, or Dylan's, singing—a spirit that shoots a good smile straight across this album.

More than a little crazy, at times flatly bizarre (take "Million Dollar Bash," "Yazoo Street Scandal," "Don't Ya Tell Henry," "Lo and Behold!"), moving easily from the confessional to the bawdy house, roaring with humor and good times, this music sounds to me at once like a testing and a discovery—of musical affinity, of nerve, of some very pointed themes; put up or shut up, obligation, escape, homecoming, owning up, the settling of accounts past due.

It sounds as well like a testing and a discovery of memory and roots. *The Basement Tapes* are a kaleidoscope like nothing I know, complete and no more dated than the mail, but they seem to leap out of a kaleidoscope of American music no less immediate for its venerability. Just below the surface of songs like "Lo and Behold!" or "Million Dollar Bash" are the strange adventures and poker-faced insanities chronicled in such standards as "Froggy Went A-Courtin'," "E-ri-e," Henry Thomas's "Fishing Blues," "Cock Robin," or "Five Nights Drunk"; the ghost of Rabbit Brown's sardonic "James Alley Blues" might lie just behind "Crash on the Levee (Down in the Flood)." *The Basement Tapes* summon sea chanteys, drinking songs, tall tales, and early rock and roll.

Alongside of such things—and often intertwined with them—is something very different.

Obviously, death is not very universally accepted. I mean, you'd think that the traditional music people could gather from their songs that mystery is a fact, a traditional fact.
—Bob Dylan, 1966

I think one can hear what Bob Dylan was talking about in the music of *The Basement Tapes,* in "Goin' to Acapulco," "Tears of Rage," "Too Much of Nothing," and "This Wheel's On Fire"—one can hardly avoid hearing it. It is a plain-talk mystery; it has nothing to do with mumbo-jumbo, charms or spells. The acceptance of death that Dylan found in traditional music—the ancient ballads of mountain music—is simply a singer's insistence on mystery as inseparable from any honest understanding of what life is all about;

it is the quiet terror of a man seeking salvation who stares into a void that stares back. It is the awesome, impenetrable fatalism that drives the timeless ballads first recorded in the twenties; songs like Buell Kazee's "East Virginia," Clarence Ashley's "Coo Coo Bird," Dock Boggs' "Country Blues"—or a song called "I Wish I Was a Mole in the Ground," put down by Bascom Lamar Lunsford in 1928. "I wish I was a mole in the ground—like a mole in the ground I would root that mountain down—And I wish I was a mole in the ground."

Now, what the singer wants is obvious, and almost impossible to really comprehend. He wants to be delivered from his life, and to be changed into a creature insignificant and despised; like a mole in the ground, he wants to see nothing and to be seen by no one; he wants to destroy the world, and to survive it.

Dylan and the Band came to terms with such feelings—came to terms with the void that looks back—in the summer of 1967; in the most powerful and unsettling songs on *The Basement Tapes,* they put an old, old sense of mystery across with an intensity that has not been heard in a long time. You can find it in Dylan's singing and in his lyrics on "This Wheel's on Fire"—and in every note Garth Hudson, Richard Manuel, Robbie Robertson, Levon Helm and Rick Danko play.

And it is in this way most of all that *The Basement Tapes* are a testing and a discovery of roots and memory; it might be why *The Basement Tapes* are, if anything, more compelling today than when they were first made, no more likely to fade than Elvis Presley's "Mystery Train" or Robert Johnson's "Love in Vain." The spirit of a song like "I Wish I Was a Mole in the Ground" matters here not as an influence, and not as a source. It is simply that one side of *The Basement Tapes* casts the shadow of such things, and in turn is shadowed by them.

DYLAN GETS NASTY

Village Voice
18 October 1976

There was a moment in Bob Dylan's recent *Hard Rain* TV special, filmed in Fort Collins, Colorado, at the end of the Rolling Thunder tour, that I hope I never forget: when Dylan turned "Idiot Wind" into the roughest outlaw ballad in the book. Just into the first verse he lowered his head; with a turn of a line, he seemed to take in the whole history of the place in which he was singing, to understand in an instant the lives of such Colorado killers as Kid Curry and the Sundance Kid. His face alive with evil and glee, Dylan was suddenly the lowest, dirtiest, meanest killer of them all. "I can't help it—if I'm *lucky*." His eyes snapped and I cringed.

The show was filmed without competence or imagination. The radical chic A-rab outfits were dumb, and it was obvious even while watching that Dylan's presence was overshadowing any questions of musical quality. But that presence was so strong, so nasty, that it cut through everything in its way. The man came across. I was shocked when the credits ran; nothing like an hour seemed to have elapsed. As far as I was concerned the show could have gone on all night.

But *Hard Rain,* the soundtrack (and then some, and less some) of the show, is Dylan's worst authorized album—without Dylan's visual presence the music dies on the turntable. I never saw the Rolling Thunder tour, and the Mad Dogs & Englishmen (Folkie Division) concept of the affair sounded less than thrilling, but it's hard to believe the jumbled, random, offensively casual mess on this album represents the best music the tour produced. The musicians don't play, they bump into each other. Dylan doesn't phrase, he bleats, and for the first time in his career, he sounds stupid. There is no musical attack, no rhythm, no craft. The arrangements are pointless—nearly nonexistent, as with "Memphis Blues Again," or philistine, as with "Maggie's Farm." (Are those long, ridiculously drawn-out pauses after every verse, in which Dylan sounds like a dying horse, meant to give the song impact, or draw applause, which is all they do?) Occasionally, the tunes generate an initial momentum; it's dissipated almost immediately by the indifference of the performers. They sound as if they could, you know, care less. As a document of a tour where almost every show was taped, this makes no sense (and where are the songs introduced *on* the tour, like the old ballad "Railroad Boy," "Going, Going, Gone," or "Where Did Vincent Van Gogh?").

The tour reportedly ended badly—wearing out, with audiences declining, money disappearing into ballooning expenses. You could think this album represents the resentment felt by the musicians toward a public that ultimately refused to salaam to them. Whether that's so or not, what I hear in this music, in its dogged lack of charm or groove, is utter contempt for the audience. And that contempt may well be the other, duller side of Dylan's nastiness, of that malicious intensity he exposed on television with "Idiot Wind." Focused and revealed, that nastiness is at the heart of Dylan's art. Unfocused—and disguised as camaraderie with busy, chattering music—it's merely irritating, and, worse, it is empty.

Bob Dylan, *Hard Rain* (Columbia, 1976).

THAT TRAIN DON'T STOP HERE ANYMORE

Rolling Stone
30 December 1976

The late Junior Parker made the original recording of "Mystery Train" in 1953, taking the first lines—

> Train I ride
> Sixteen
> Coaches long

—from the Carter Family's "Worried Man Blues," which dates from the twenties, though no one knows exactly where the Carter Family got it. It is a very old song. When the Band went after the tune an hour or so into their farewell concert at Winterland Thanksgiving night, the song sounded new. I had heard Parker sing it, and Elvis, and Paul Butterfield, and I had heard the Band's version, with new lyrics, on *Moondog Matinee,* their oldies album; this was something else entirely. Both Levon Helm, singing lead, and Richard Manuel played drums; Paul Butterfield played harp; and together they began a jumping beat that kicked with greater force each time the tune turned a corner. I have never heard Butterfield play with such strength: his harmonica was a hoodoo night call hovering over the crowd, cutting through the event of the Band's last performance to show why such a performance could have become an event in the first place. The Band held nothing back; they played with an intensity I've seen them attain only occasionally over the years—behind Dylan in 1965, on the second night of their debut performance at Winterland in 1969, with Dylan in 1974 on "Highway 61 Revisited" and "All Along the Watchtower"—an intensity I've never forgotten.

> Come down to the station meet my baby at the gate
> Ask the stationmaster if the train's runnin' late
> He said if you're a-waitin' on that 4.44
> I hate to tell you son that train don't stop here anymore

Levon sang as if he were pleading for mercy—from God or from the devil, you couldn't tell.

The concert was billed as the Last Waltz; the Band came up with a song of the same name, written mostly the day before the show and rehearsed backstage during the only break they took in their five-hour performance. As an event the affair was overblown, but the Band escaped the pretensions that surrounded it.

Over the years, the Band has become identified with a set of songs in a manner that distinguishes them, for good or ill, from all other rock groups: they are less their mystique, or their faces, than they are "The Night They Drove Old Dixie Down" and other tunes from *Music from Big Pink* and *The Band*. The Band opened the show with such songs and they played them with greater precision and flair than I have seen in a long time. They came out of themselves; Rick Danko bopped across the stage, Robbie Robertson took extravagant solos, Garth Hudson roamed his organ like a tracker, his hair flying, and both Richard Manuel and Levon Helm seemed to sing with a special conviction. As I listened to their first number, "Up on Cripple Creek," it struck me that I might never hear them play the song again; they had been playing it since that first night in San Francisco eight years ago, and I had never seem them play without it. I had carped that the Band never changed their stage material, but suddenly the song seemed permanent, rightfully unchanging, no more transitory than a personality. At that moment, it made no sense that they would not be playing the tune as long as they lived. I was caught up in the song; I couldn't deal with it as a last anything, because it was a long way from wearing out.

They moved through various tunes, bringing on Allen Toussaint, there to conduct a horn section, and a fiddler, peaking at the end of "This Wheel's on Fire," always one of their high points (with Howard Johnson, who looks a little like Louis Armstrong, a little like Flip Wilson, and a lot like Roy Campanella, singing along, puffing his cheeks to sing just as he does with his tuba). They sang their recent single, "Georgia on My Mind," recorded as their contribution to Jimmy Carter's campaign (he was sent the master, and liked it—"The Night They Drove Old Dixie Down" was the appropriate flip). Garth provided an intro straight out of "Song of the South," while Manuel sang as a crooner, away from the piano. But the Band's solo set broke open with "The Night They Drove Old Dixie Down." They simply bore down harder on this song than I have ever seen them do before; there was a lot of love in the performance, and a certain desperation as well. The set also included

"The Shape I'm In" (sluggish, as it's always been onstage), "It Makes No Difference," "Life Is a Carnival," "Ophelia" and "Stage Fright"; they closed with "Rag Mama Rag."

Damned if someone didn't yell for "Free Bird."

Then the Band brought Ronnie Hawkins, the Arkansas rockabilly singer who recruited them as the Hawks in Toronto in the early sixties, onto the stage. Hawkins is no bigger than any two members of the Band put together; he is the ultimate fantasy of the unreconstructed rocker. He wore a huge, straw snap-brim hat, a black suit, a big beard, flashing eyes, a scarred face and a grin. The Band hit as tough a Bo Diddley beat as you'd ever want to hear and Hawkins commenced to prowl the stage, aiming "Who Do You Love" at the Band ("Take it easy, Garth, dontcha gimme no lip"), who had backed him on his classic recording of the song back in 1963. Hawkins howled, wailed, screamed, storming across the boards to fan Robbie's guitar with his hat ("Cool it *down,* boy!"), a riff from the act the six men had shared thirteen years ago, and my favorite moment of the night.

Dr. John, dressed as a fifties hipster—gold shoes, sparkling jacket, beret pulled down over his head—followed, with "Such a Night." Bobby Charles, also from New Orleans, came on for a rewrite of "Liza Jane": Dr. John, Charles, Danko, Robertson, Manuel and Helm put across as modest and perfect a piece of New Orleans music as a place like Winterland could contain. Dr. John's own tune had broken the mood, as the songs of most guests, when unidentified with the Band, would subsequently do, but singing as part of the group he brought it back.

Then came "Mystery Train," and then, with Butterfield still on the stage, Muddy Waters, with his own guitarist and piano player. He sang a weak version of "Caldonia"; he is, after all, sixty-one. It was nice of the Band to invite him; most of them had played on his Woodstock album, and as Levon and the Hawks they had recorded Waters's "She's 19" back in '63. It made sense. One conceived apologies, and then heard the Band and Muddy tear into "Mannish Boy." Waters first cut it in 1955, when he was a mere forty, barely younger than Hawkins is now, and suddenly the idea of aging, of over-the-hill, was satirized. Butterfield seemed to hold one dark note throughout the entire performance; Waters danced, jumped up and down; the Band smoked. It went on and on: "I'm a man . . . I'm a rollin' stone . . ." They went for everything the song had to give, and when Waters left the stage, there was nothing left. The Last Waltz had been carefully worked out; there were two nights of rehearsals in San Francisco, weeks of rehearsals in L.A., and every number was literally scripted, line by line and shot by shot, for camera angles and setups. "Mannish Boy" might have been run through, but as Muddy and the Band played it, it could hardly have been rehearsed. It was a titanic performance.

Waters was followed by Eric Clapton, Neil Young, Joni Mitchell and Neil Diamond, and for me the show lost its shape with their performances. Clapton played poorly, if spectacularly; neither Young's tunes ("Helpless" and Ian Tyson's "Four Strong Winds") nor Mitchell's (three from a new album) nor Diamond's ("Dry Your Eyes") seemed to have anything to do with the Band musically; here the concert slipped towards more stargazing. It was at this point that speculation about additional guests began; one fan predicted that Buddy Holly would appear precisely at midnight, while another claimed to have seen the deceased Murry Wilson tuning up backstage.

As Diamond left Manuel turned the piano over to John Simon and began to sing "Tura Lura," a song about an Irish lullaby; just as Manuel finished the last verse, Van Morrison made his entrance—and he turned the show around. I had seen him not many minutes before, prowling the balconies, dressed nondescriptly in a raincoat and jeans, scowling; but there he was onstage, in an absurd purple suit and a green top, singing to the rafters. They cut into "Caravan"—with John Simon waving the Band's volume up and down, and the horns at their most effective—while Van burned holes in the floor. He was magic, and I thought, why didn't he join the Band years ago? More than any other singer, he fit in, his music and theirs made sense together. It was a triumph, and as the song ended Van began to kick one leg into the air out of sheer exuberance, and he kicked his way right off the stage like a Rockette. The crowd had given him a fine welcome and they cheered wildly when he left.

The Band headed into an intermission—during which poets, including Emmett Grogan, Michael McClure and Lawrence Ferlinghetti, read—with "Acadian Driftwood." Neil Young and Joni Mitchell were brought back to sing harmony, since they are Canadians, and it is a Canadian song. It did not really hold together. The concert began again, some forty minutes later, with Garth's long intro to "Chest Fever"—this time, it was more stately than playful—followed by the song itself, and then "The Last Waltz," which has something of the feel of "Long Black Veil" to it. The next tune was "The Weight." I have heard the Band perform this song a dozen times, and never, until this night, did it ever seem to come off. Garth plays piano on "The Weight," and there has always been something so crazed, so country-time about his notes, that has always made it impossible for the rest of the group to follow him. But here, he played with some semblance of order, and the song was shining.

Immediately, Bob Dylan came on, plugged in, and hit the first notes of "Baby Let Me Follow You Down." His rhythm guitar was turned up, or mixed up, so loudly that everyone else was drowned out; the sound was rougher, shriller, faster and harder than it had been all night. Dylan rocked out. He danced across the stage, striding off-mike after every verse. His guitar was ringing. He shouted into the mike, tearing off a song he and the Hawks had used as a centerpiece for their shows in 1965 and '66, slowed the pace with "Hazel," from *Planet Waves,* and cut back into "I Don't Believe You," also one of the finest numbers from the Dylan-Hawks shows of ten years ago. It was a powerful, lyrical piece then; it was this night as well. Dylan swaggered; there was a great urgency in his performance, and unlike those of some other singers, no solemnity and no reverence. He was noisy, and he never stood still. After "Forever Young" he segued without a break—in fact, there hadn't been a break in time of so much as a note between his songs—back into "Baby Let Me Follow You Down." He was on, some said, for twenty-five minutes; I would have bet on seven.

The concert reached a formal end with "I Shall Be Released" ("Well," said a friend, "at least they didn't do 'Will the Circle Be Unbroken'")—and predictably, everyone, plus Ringo Starr and Ronnie Wood, came back to sing the finale. That over and the stage cleared, Levon and Ringo laid down a vamp until more musicians—Dr. John, Clapton, Wood, Carl Radle, Neil Young, Steve Stills, and various members of the Band—came back for long and rather typical jams. After thirty minutes, the Band returned alone and punched out "Don't Do It." That done, they did. They left.

It was a long night, and until the appearance of Ringo-Woods-Stills (plus Jerry Brown, not dressed in a suit, who waved), there was no sense of super-session. In the main, the people who played together made music only they would have made together; they pushed each other past their limits, and they broke through the nostalgia that was built into the show.

Exactly what is over is not easy to tell. No one expects that the Band's farewell will turn out to be much like Smokey Robinson's goodbye or any of David Bowie's retirements. Perhaps what is over is simply a set of songs, those songs the Band has been playing, and not escaping, for so long. It may be that part of the reason they decided to end their time as a public band was that their own music had driven them into a corner; perhaps they needed to orchestrate an end in order to start over, as individuals, and as a group. Certainly there will be more solo projects; the official line is that the Band will continue to record as the Band, but save for the live album of the Last Waltz, I wonder how long it will be before their name appears on another LP.

The fact is that the Band has never been, to their fans or to their detractors, just another top-flight rock 'roll band; they have always been special, and it was the very idea of a group of men sticking together over the years that along with their music made them special—it was that, no doubt, that made them unique. I'm not truly ready to deal with the likelihood that the songs the Band put into the American tradition now exist only on record, nor am I able to lay to rest my doubts that the Band has, whatever their intentions, closed only one door.

Weeks ago, I asked Robbie Robertson if a last concert meant the Band was breaking up, and he seemed both surprised and amused at the idea. "The Band will never break up," he said. "It's too late to break up." Well, I hope so. But that line from "Mystery Train" stays in my mind, as does the performance the Band and Butterfield gave to the song, as does a thought from Emmett Grogan's autobiography, where he wrote that his encounters with the Band taught him that if anything really good were to happen, it would be a long time coming. A long time coming, and a long time gone.

The Band, *The Last Waltz* (Warner Bros./Rhino, 2002).

SAVE THE LAST WALTZ FOR ME
New West
22 May 1978

Martin Scorsese lives in the Hollywood hills. His house instantly announces itself as the home of a filmmaker; except for a small Catholic triptych, movie posters are the only form of visual art in the place. Dominating almost every room, they're of all sorts: arty German collages for Scorsese's *Mean Streets,* a placard for *Rebel Without a Cause,* a hilariously effete tableau from Stewart Granger's forgotten *Saraband for Dead Lovers,* a huge ad in which Gary Cooper demonstrates how to fire two pistols simultaneously without dropping Paulette Godard. But this night—just following the first major screening of *The Last Waltz,* the film Scorsese has made of the grand farewell concert the Band staged in San Francisco on Thanksgiving night, 1976—the talk is all rock 'n' roll.

The Last Waltz is, by a long way, the best concert movie I've ever seen; it is, in a way, far better than the concert itself. I have my complaints. As he has for so many years now, Garth Hudson remains nearly invisible, and the sound mix doesn't give his music the prominence it deserves. Richard Manuel doesn't get the space on the screen he deserves, and his piano is often hard to catch. Still, the impact of the film swallows such reservations, burns them out.

The movie is first a set of performances: the Band as the Band, and the Band with an all-star line-up of friends, mentors, and collaborators. Segued through the film are brief snatches of talk with the Band, a sort of casual meditation on the sixteen years the five men spent as on-the-road rockers, starting in Toronto in 1959 and on as Ronnie Hawkins's bar-band Hawks, finally emerging on their own, nearly ten years later, with *Music from Big Pink* and *The Band*—their first albums, which, no matter how many the group has made since, still define them.

It's a long story, and a good one, but in Scorsese's house little is said of *The Last Waltz*. I want to absorb it, and Scorsese and Robbie Robertson, who produced the picture, want to escape it. Scorsese has put on Van Morrison's *Astral Weeks,* and we're simply listening. It's an album of transcendence: transcendence of childhood fears, adult sins. "Madame George" comes on—"That's the song," Scorsese murmurs. I can't help telling him he's picked my favorite record of all time, but he's way ahead of me. "I based the first fifteen minutes of *Taxi Driver* on *Astral Weeks*," Scorsese says, "and that's a movie about a man who hates music." I mentally scurry to recover images of the film so I can figure out what Scorsese means; he must be talking about the sense of doom, or anyway fate, that Morrison insists on.

Scorsese pulls out a Ray Charles album; the song he wants us to hear is "What Would I Do Without You," from 1957. It's a slow, tragic blues ballad; there's the assumption of a happy ending, or at least of resolution, in the lyrics, but not in Ray Charles's singing. "Leave out a few Billie Holiday tunes, and there's more heroin in that music than in anything you'll ever hear," Robertson says. "Heroin does something to your throat. It makes the voice thicker. Listen." We do; the title of the song takes on a new, acrid meaning.

"We used to do it," Robertson says, "'What Would I Do Without You,' after we left Ronnie, when it was just the five of us, before Bob, before *Big Pink*. But we couldn't get away with it. The song was too down, it was death. That's what it is. People would just sit there, or they'd leave."

I'd never even heard of the song, and I asked Scorsese how he found it. "It's the flip of 'Hallelujah, I Love Her So,'" he says. "I heard Alan Freed play it." In 1957 Scorsese was growing up in New York's Little Italy, and Freed, the only disc jockey who can be called a founder of rock 'n' roll, was ruling the New York airwaves. The soundtrack Freed provided for Scorsese's life later turned up as the soundtrack of *Mean Streets*. "I bought 'Hallelujah, I Love Her So,' and fell in love with the other side; I bought the 78. I've still got it. Right here."

I mention *American Hot Wax,* the new movie about Alan Freed, but Scorsese and Robertson don't want to hear about it. To them—Robertson, living in Ontario, was picking up Freed's original Cleveland broadcasts before 1954, when Freed left for New York—Freed was a real person, a titan. To me, a Californian out of range of Freed's signal, he was, until well after his death in 1965, no more than a name in the papers from the time when the payola scandals broke. I don't mind seeing Freed's life turned into myth; Scorsese and Robertson do. In a crucial way, their own lives are up there on the *American Hot Wax* screen.

"Alan Freed *talked* to me," Robertson says, as if he can't quite believe it happened. "We played his shows. The only person who could follow Ronnie Hawkins and the Hawks was Jackie Wilson. Alan Freed *loved* Ronnie Hawkins." I'm stunned; I knew the Hawks, the Band, went a long way back, but I'd never thought of them as taking their first steps right at the center of rock 'n' roll history, which is what the shows Freed put on were. I try to picture Levon Helm and Robertson, the first of the Band to join Hawkins, sharing a stage with Jackie Wilson.

"You're a little kid," Freed said to Robertson in 1959. "How old are you?" "Sixteen," Robertson replied. "The hell you are," said Freed—surely worried that along with his indictment for inciting to riot in Boston ("The cops don't want you to have a good time," Freed had said from the stage after the police turned up the house lights), he'd soon be facing charges for violating child labor laws. If you've seen *American Hot Wax*, imagine Helm and Robertson—in suits, with narrow ties and short hair—huddling in the wings of the Brooklyn Paramount, psyching themselves up for an audience of New York kids like Martin Scorsese, unconsciously preparing themselves to write and sing "The Weight."

The premise of the Last Waltz concert—staged by Bill Graham at Winterland, where, seven-and-a-half years earlier, Graham had produced the Band's post–*Big Pink* debut—was inescapably senti-mental, and Scorsese attacks that sentimentality with his very first shots. *The Last Waltz* opens with Rick Danko at a pool table; Scors-ese has him in very tight close-up. The sudden violence of the im-age is a shock: Danko rams his cue right across the screen with a noise that seems as loud as any in the movie, and whatever mood one might have brought into the theater is broken. "You want to put the other guy's balls in the pocket, and keep yours on the table," Danko explains in answer to Scorsese's query about the game he's playing. "It's called Cutthroat."

Emotionally, Scorsese then cuts not to the warmth of the con-cert, but to the determination behind it: the concert footage of *The Last Waltz* begins with the concert's end, as the Band returns to the stage—well after the formal, predictable "I Shall Be Released" finale—for "Baby Don't You Do It," the Marvin Gaye tune that had for years stood as the hardest number in their repertoire. Settling into place behind mikes and instruments, the members of the Band look less like tired, satisfied men who've just presided over their wake than like the Earp brothers and Doc Holliday cleaning out the last pockets of resistance at the O.K. Corral. For a few seconds, until the film moves on, that's also what they sound like.

The Last Waltz is a surprise to the eye: It doesn't look like a rock 'n' roll movie. There's no handheld camera work; it's all smooth dolly shots, zooms and framed images, and, in the numbers shot after the concert on an MGM sound stage, elegant crane and tracking shots. Instead of simply watching people play music, we often get to see how the music is made. We pick up the cues one musician tosses to another, the moments of uncertainty and panicky improvisation.

There are historic performances and extraordinary film sequences: Ronnie Hawkins, huge and unbowed, a forty-one-year-old Mike Fink, railing out Bo Diddley's "Who Do You Love"; an almost black screen, lit only by a single blue-white spot on Paul Butterfield and Levon Helm (the other lights had failed) as they take "Mystery Train" around a cliff at eighty miles an hour, nearly raising Junior Parker and Elvis from the grave. Muddy Waters holds the screen for almost seven minutes in brutal close-up: he declaims "Mannish Boy" like a voodoo preacher arguing down Saint Peter for a seat in heaven, or maybe talking the devil out of a pit in hell. Muddy Waters first recorded before most of the men in the Band were born, and it's all they can do to keep up with him. Waters takes his place in the Band's story; they earn a place in his. Throughout, the sound (as opposed to the clean but often flat sound of the three-LP *Last Waltz* album) is raw, crackling, shaking; when, at that first screening, Van Morrison appeared in the film to sing "Caravan," he blew out two speakers in the theater.

The film does more than record the presence of the performers. Often, it gives them more presence than they have on stage. Joni Mitchell, swaying her hips for "Coyote," is mesmerizing; she acts out the role of a goddess on the make, an image only slightly undercut—or reinforced?—by the pack of cigarettes jammed into the waistband of her skirt. Neil Young, as usual, arrives as a refugee from the Dust Bowl, but the way he's shot roughly intensifies his persona: hunching his body over his guitar, as if he can't hide his face with his shoulders, Young looks like a child molester, a bad dream—and then he opens his mouth and sings "Helpless" in the voice of a little boy who's scared of the man we're watching.

The cameras stay very close to Bob Dylan: we see angles, a flash of face shielded by a blur of straggling curls. Scorsese cuts as if he wants most of all to reveal the mystery that still hangs on Dylan like a cloak; whatever Scorsese's intentions, that's the result. There's a split second when Dylan shrugs his shoulders—and it nearly brought me out of my seat. It was as if he'd said, Let it come, throw what you've got, I was here yesterday, I'll be here to-morrow—a trivial gesture (in truth, Dylan was merely answering Levon Helm's question about a change in tempo) that carries more drama than any other moment in the film. Who is this man? you ask. Where did he come from? He's a visitation, not a singer.

The cuts between Scorsese talking with the Band about their early years and the action on stage almost always have a certain point to make. They establish roots, bring out themes of experi-ence, comradeship, hard times, craziness: We hear about the Hawks' bewilderment at finding themselves booked into a night-club featuring a one-armed go-go dancer, and their even greater displacement when they discover the club once belonged to Jack Ruby. We then move right into "The Shape I'm In," a song about a man with his back to the wall.

There's the tale of a time when, as the Hawks, the Band hunted up the great blues harmonica player Sonny Boy Williamson II. In West Helena, Arkansas, Levon Helm's home ground, they spent the night jamming—Sonny Boy with a bucket between his knees to catch the blood from his raw lips. We go from there to "Mystery Train," and Paul Butterfield puts so much force into his harmonica you half look for *his* bucket. Levon speaks of how, when rock 'n' roll was not the name of a kind of music but just what one heard in the Deep South—a natural mix of blues, country, Cajun, gospel, folk songs and minstrelsy—it seemed grotesque to outsiders. What to Helm was simply local entertainment was to the rest of the coun-try something threatening, vulgar, devilish. The film immediately moves to confirm that such weirdness has yet to be co-opted: fol-lowing hard on Helm's words is Van Morrison, overweight, poured into an impossible stage suit, conceding nothing. Yes, he is grotesque, and for a second he reminds me of Rumpelstiltskin stamping his foot straight through the floor when he finds out he can't have the spinner's baby—midway through "Caravan," you're afraid Morrison will do just that. Like Little Richard from Macon, Georgia, or Jerry Lee Lewis from Ferriday, Louisiana, Van Morrison, from Belfast, splits the atom. He breaks *The Last Waltz* wide open, and by the time he kicks his way off stage, not an edge of his power or his strangeness has been smoothed, and every edge has cut.

"It was a punk thing, in the beginning," Robertson says of the music and the way of life the Band first started to work out on the road in the late fifties and early sixties. "We were like a lot of people. We thought most of what was on the radio was shit; we didn't care what anyone else thought. We began by rebelling against what there was around us, against what we heard.

"And so"—when the Band first stepped out from behind Bob Dylan with *Music from Big Pink*—"there we were, up in the mountains, in Woodstock, doing what we did, what we'd learned how to do, and we thought, if anyone likes it, fine, and if people hate it, fine. We've gone this far; we can keep going. We were still rebelling against what was there, against what we heard."

What the Band heard was San Francisco music, *Sgt. Pepper,* psychedelia—"chocolate subways," as Richard Manuel witheringly puts it in *The Last Waltz*—and they thought it was a fraud. What did it have to do with the grace of Johnny Ace, the depth of "What Would I Do Without You," or the nerve and intelligence of the songs they'd played around the world with Bob Dylan? The naysaying of the sound of the times seemed easy to the Band; the music seemed all artifice, empty of real emotion. So instead the Band offered music rooted in country and soul and gospel, a set of emblematic songs that did not wear out—affirmations of American life based firmly in an ambiguity that kept them honest, that made room for any listener.

"When those first two records got through like nothing we ever expected—suddenly there was *Time* magazine, *Look,* money, pressures from all sides—well," Robertson says, "everything was fine until we went out into the world. Then we started to become what we'd rebelled against: stars, heroes, people who paid too much attention to what other people told us to do. The only thing left to rebel against was ourselves. And we did that; that's what a lot of the music after *The Band* was about. But that can be very destructive. We found that out. The road was part of it: The road is responsible for a lot of madness, a lot of sickness. It's very dangerous."

So the Band put on the Last Waltz, and quit the road. It was no tragedy, nor, as some are claiming, any sort of event comparable to the Beatles' first appearance on *The Ed Sullivan Show* (if anything, the release of *Music from Big Pink* was that sort of event). Rather, the Last Waltz was one more confirmation of the Band's commitment to a sense of history as an essential part of one's life. Unlike most rock 'n' roll groups, which break up or wander on forever, changing members, replacing strays or corpses, pushing their hits, the Band wrote their own calendar, because they respected calendars. "You can," Robertson says in the film, calling up the early deaths of Hank Williams, Buddy Holly, Janis Joplin, and Elvis, "push your luck."

The question that remains, given *The Last Waltz,* is what that luck—the Band's career and their music—is worth.

We find out, I think, about a third of the way into the movie, when we see the Band and the Staples—originally a black gospel quartet, Roebuck "Pop" Staples, born in 1915, and his daughters Mavis, Cleotha, and Yvonne have worked as a secular group since the sixties—take their places on the MGM sound stage to sing "The Weight." "We used to spend more time listening to the Staple Singers' albums than to anything else," Robertson says. "We wanted to find out how the vocals worked, how they sang to each other." The Band did find out; as it was recorded on *Big Pink,* the singing on "The Weight" was about sympathy, obligation, friendship. The singing played against the lyrics, which told the story of a man who, arriving in a strange town with a mission the listener (and maybe the man himself) never fully understands, can find no sympathy. The only people willing to offer him a hand want something in return—his soul, say.

In the Band's original version, the song was hilarious, and also unsettling. In *The Last Waltz,* it's very different. It begins much more slowly—not in terms of tempo, but in terms of how fast the emotion comes out—with striking notes from Robertson's double-necked Gibson guitar, clear gospel piano from Garth Hudson and a weary, utterly accepting vocal from Levon Helm. He's seen it all, his voice says; nothing will surprise him. The slightly bemused tone of his singing on *Big Pink* is gone, replaced by something much less easy to pin down.

As the number moves on, with Scorsese's camera gliding around the ensemble, the whole meaning of the song changes. The series of weird, inexplicable, even horrific events the song's narrator goes through are given permanence; the song is no longer depicting a trap to break out of, but simply ordinary life. The religious images in the lyrics begin to expand, to take over; the joke of "The Weight" becomes an elegy.

Following the story—the man shows up to do a job and finally hightails it out of town, not knowing if he's come close to completing it, not knowing if, God help him, he'll have to come *back*—you begin to hear "The Weight" as a parable of the Band's career: a version of the eager adventurousness with which teenagers began eighteen years ago ("You won't make much money," Robertson remembers Hawkins telling him, "but you'll get more pussy than Frank Sinatra"), and of the fear, in the end, that they were playing on borrowed time.

Watching the Band and the Staples, you see "The Weight" as a statement of the pluralism that has always been at the heart of the Band's music. As Mavis Staples, then Roebuck Staples, trade verses with the Band, we see an explicit, completely intentional statement of the idea of community that was the most profound affirmation of *Big Pink* and *The Band.* We see men sing to women, women sing to men, blacks sing to whites, whites sing to blacks, northerners sing to southerners, southerners sing to northerners, the young sing to the old, the old sing to the young. There's no distance.

It's a vision of utopia, and, to keep the story honest, it demands at least a partial contradiction. *The Last Waltz* provides it. The film leaves the last high chorus of "The Weight" hanging in the air and cuts directly to the stage at Winterland for "The Night They Drove Old Dixie Down," the post–Civil War story of a Rebel soldier who is desperately trying to pick up the pieces of the old south. It was the strongest number the Band played that night in San Francisco; before the song was over the crowd exploded in cheers, something I'd never seen happen in the dozen times I'd watched the Band do the tune. "There was more anger coming out," Robertson says of the singing of Levon Helm, the southerner for whom Robertson wrote the song.

What this means, I think, is that even when one has touched or entered a utopia that transcends all limited experiences—be that utopia "The Weight" as we see it in *The Last Waltz,* or the panorama of *The Last Waltz* itself—one should not, cannot, give up the limited experience one brings to others, even if, finally, that experience forces others out, even if it can't be shared, not in full. In other words, when Levon Helm, as the Confederate veteran Virgil Cane, says that he remembers the night the South went down to defeat, he—Levon Helm—does remember it. In the South in the forties and fifties, when Helm was growing up, the War Between the States wasn't history, it was part of the present. It was the weight one carried, and people like Helm, and Roebuck Staples, born in Mississippi, hefted it every day. The Band's songs catch their common ground and define the space between them.

The conjunction in *The Last Waltz* of "The Weight" and "The Night They Drove Old Dixie Down" proves that we can no more blithely use history than we can ignore it—as with the Band's career, or a conversation that ranged from Van Morrison to Ray Charles to Alan Freed, we can simply try to find our place in it. That place isn't fixed: That's the truth of the Band and the Staples' version of "The Weight." But it isn't quite a question of will, of what one wants, either: That's the truth of "The Night They Drove Old Dixie Down." One acts, but one also inherits.

From the start, an understanding of the possibilities of adventure and the limits of freedom has been what the Band have had to talk to us about. In *The Last Waltz,* they still speak clearly; they pressed their luck, it seems, just far enough.

The Last Waltz, directed by Martin Scorsese (MGM DVD, 1978/2002).

American Hot Wax, directed by Floyd Mutrux, written by John Kaye (Paramount, 1978).

STREET LEGAL
Rolling Stone
24 August 1978

It saddens me that I can't find it in my heart to agree with my colleague Dave Marsh that Bob Dylan's new record is a joke, or anyway a good one. Most of the stuff here is dead air, or close to it. The novelty of the music—soul-chorus backup modeled on Bob Marley's I-Threes, funk riffs from the band, lots of laconic sax work—quickly fades as you realize how indifferent the playing is: "Señor (Tales of Yankee Power)," the most musically striking number here, is really just a pastiche of the best moments of the Eagles' *Hotel California.* Still, I believe some of the songs on *Street Legal:* those that are too bad to have been made with anything but complete seriousness. Dylan may have once needed a dumptruck to unload his head, but you'd need a Geiger counter to find irony in "Is Your Love in Vain?" or affection in "Baby Stop Crying."

Both are wretched performances, but "Is Your Love in Vain?" is particularly cruel: compared to Dylan's posture here, Mick Jagger in "Under My Thumb" is exploring the upper reaches of humility. Not that there's any bite in the song, as there is in "On the Road Again" or "Don't Think Twice," two other numbers in which a woman gets what the singer thinks she has coming to her. There's too much distance here for that—distance between an ego and its object. The man speaks to the woman like a sultan checking out a promising servant girl for VD, and his tone is enough to make her fake the pox if that's what it takes to get away clean. When, after a string of gulf-between-the-sexes insults (which pretty much come down to *Are you good enough for me? I'm hot stuff, you know*), the singer finally makes the big concession ("Alright, I'll take a chance, I will fall in love with you"—odd notion of how falling in love works), you can almost see the poor girl heading for the exit. "Can you cook and sew, make flowers grow," the man mouths, apparently making a dumb leap from housewife to earth mother, but in truth just rhyming. Then comes the kicker: "Can you understand my pain?" Women all over America must be saying what a friend of mine said: "Sure, Bob, give me a call sometime. If I'm not home, just leave a message on the answer-phone." As it happens, "Is Your Love in Vain?" is a high-point on *Street Legal*—or, at least, the most emotionally convincing track on the album. No joke.

Ah, but the singing! The singing, which on other records has redeemed lines nearly as terrible as those I've quoted—what about the singing? Well, Bob Dylan has sounded sillier than he does on *Street Legal* (who could forget "Big Yellow Taxi"), more uncomfortable ("The Boxer"), and as uninterested ("Let It Be Me"), but he has never sounded so utterly fake. Though this quality is sometimes cut with playfulness ("Changing of the Guards"), in "Baby Stop Crying" the vocal is so fey, so intolerably smug, that the only reference point is one of those endless spoken intros Barry White was using a few years ago: an imitation of caring that couldn't fool a stuffed dog. Dave Marsh is right when he says there are echoes of Elvis on *Street Legal*—"Is Your Love in Vain?" plays with the melody of "Can't Help Falling in Love" before it turns into "Here Comes the Bride"—but not even "(There's) No Room to Rhumba in a Sports Car" was quite this creepy.

While most of the singing on *Street Legal* (the pronunciamentos of "No Time to Think," for example: "Loyalty, unity / Epitome, rigidity") falls short of creepiness, it's impossible to pay attention to it for more than a couple of minutes at a time. Why should this be, when again and again—especially during those times, such as before the release of *Blood on the Tracks,* when both his fans and detractors had written him off—Dylan has proved himself as expressive and inventive as any singer in American music? I don't know the answer; merely not giving a damn whether his record is good enough for his audience might be a big part of the problem. But I also think that the near-constant touring Dylan has done since 1974 (all that raw chanting in big halls, all that gruff railing over the band) has at once produced a new vocal style, destroyed Dylan's timing, and dissolved his ability to bring emotional precision to a lyric. In the singing style Dylan is using now, emotion has been replaced by mannerism, subtlety by a straining to be heard.

His word-to-word emphasis, when it isn't pure hokum, is patently random, so the good lines come off no better than the bad. Dylan has always written throwaway lines as a necessary means to setting up the line he's put his heart into, but when he sang, he'd toss off the throwaways, bury them, and then rush back with everything he had. What he was really setting up was an ambush for the listener—that's a lot of what "Like a Rolling Stone" is about. There are no such dynamics here. With little or no sense of rhythm in the singing, you can't stay with the music. Either it becomes an irritant or you stop hearing anything at all.

There have been bad Dylan albums before—but *Self Portrait* had "Copper Kettle," *New Morning* "Sign on the Window" and "Went to See the Gypsy," *Planet Waves* "Wedding Song," and *Desire* "Sara." The collapse of Dylan's timing ensures there are no such odd gems on *Street Legal.* Timing can spark an ordinary lyric with genius or a pedestrian arrangement with magic; no one who has heard Dylan swing "Al*right*" in "Sitting on a Barbed Wire Fence" or push the Hawks through the 1966 Manchester version of "Baby Let Me Follow You Down" can doubt it. On "Get Your Rocks Off," an unreleased basement tapes performance, he even *laughs* in time—or makes the rhythm recreate itself around his laugh. Here the only hint of decent singing comes in the first four verses of

"New Pony"—and it's the sort of blues Dylan can sing in his sleep, and probably does.

The most interesting—if that's the word—aspect of *Street Legal* is in its lyrics, which often pretend to the supposed impenetrability of Dylan' mid-sixties albums, the albums on which his reputation still rests. But the return is false. You may not have known why Dylan was singing about a "Panamanian moon" in "Memphis Blues Again," but you knew what "Your debutante just knows what you need / But I know what you want" meant, and it meant a lot. In *Street Legal*'s "Señor (Tales of Yankee Power)"—the parenthetical part of the title is the most inspired thing on the record— "Well, the last thing I remember / Before I stripped and kneeled / Was that trainload of fools / Bogged down in a magnetic field" is just a gesture, just a wave at the fans. Not that the effect of the lines can't hurt: it's hard not to hear the older songs now in terms of the new numbers that appear to resemble them, and then conclude that at bottom "Absolutely Sweet Marie" and "Highway 61 Revisited" are as empty as "Where Are You Tonight? (Journey Through Dark Heat)," even if that's not remotely true.

I mean, if I want a joke, I'll listen to Steve Martin sing "King Tut." That line "He gave his life for tourism" is really funny.*

Street Legal (Columbia, 1978).

Steve Martin and the Toot Uncommons, "King Tut" (Warner Bros., 1978).

---

*Jann Wenner, the editor-in-chief and publisher of *Rolling Stone,* disagreed with my review and decided to write his own. When it appeared two issues later it was widely taken as an editor sandbagging his own reviewer, but nothing could have been further from the truth. I encouraged Jann to put his own words in his own paper (as we called it then); just as he edited me, I edited him.

MORE OR LESS LIKE
A MOVING STONE

New West

18 December 1978

Bob Dylan is onto something with his new show—the big band, the three women on backup vocals, the stagy singing, nightclub demeanor, and patently rehearsed gestures—and whatever it is it seems to have been brewing for a long time. In 1969, when Dylan had been off the road for more than three years (and would not return for another five), Jann Wenner of *Rolling Stone* asked him about his touring plans. Dylan, presumably eager to deflect the question, promised he'd be back in public straight off. Then this odd exchange took place:

WENNER: What thoughts do you have on what kind of backup you're going to use?

DYLAN: Well, we'll keep it real simple, you know . . . drums . . . bass . . . second guitar . . . organ . . . piano. Possibly some horns. Maybe some background voices.

WENNER (clearly amazed): Girls? Like the Raylettes?

DYLAN: We could use some girls.

Now, coming on the heels of *John Wesley Harding* and *Nashville Skyline,* which defined simple in somewhat different terms, Dylan's idea of appropriate accompaniment had to seem like a joke, a way of saying, *Get off my back, man—how do you expect me to know what I'm going to do on stage when I haven't the slightest intention of setting foot on one?* When Dylan finally did tour again, in 1974, he used the Band, just as he'd done in 1965 and '66—no girls in sight. Shouting his greatest hits over the crowd, he could hardly have been more insular: the legend walked, but he didn't talk, nor did he crack a smile.

Arriving on waves of bad press for two not-quite-sold-out

shows at the Oakland Coliseum Arena this November, Dylan was plainly out to prove that his new act was no joke. "A lot of writers have called this 'showbizzy' or 'disco,'" he muttered near the end of the two-and-a-half-hour concert I saw, "but you know that isn't true." Some of the music was awful, some of it was dull, but there were moments of real strength, and I found myself caught up in Dylan's performance even when his singing was at its worst.

The show takes some getting used to. There are almost a dozen people on stage, some of them occasionally looking for ways to keep busy; the lighting changes constantly. The music had no body. Dylan remarked with pride that his saxophone man, Steve Douglas, had worked with Phil Spector; it was only after wondering why everything Douglas played was utterly lacking in imagination that I remembered that Spector used sax solos strictly as filler. While Dylan radically revamped his best-known songs, successfully rescuing them from nostalgia—he sang a lot of greatest hits, but they didn't come off that way—the band almost never stretched its arrangements. As hasn't often been the case with Dylan's concerts, there was no edge to the music; the limits were all fixed in advance.

Perhaps for just that reason, Dylan seemed more at home on stage than I've ever seen him. Laconic; hanging on to the mike the way Sinatra used to lean on a lamppost; combative; clumsily but unselfconsciously dancing—always, he communicated hard-won pleasure. When, for his last move of the night, he struck a pose reminiscent of nothing so much as a forties movie queen mugging at a premiere, the release of tension—release from the tension of a cataclysmic big-band version of "It's Alright, Ma (I'm Only Bleeding)," release from the tension of his mysterious career—was overwhelming. I laughed out loud.

As Elvis Presley could only do with parody, Dylan has escaped much of the pressure that weighs on the legendary figure, and unlike Elvis, he's done so without belittling his music. What he may be onto, what may have been brewing all these years, is a lust for the kind of melodrama that is the stock-in-trade of the great soul and country stars: a show that, since Dylan doesn't need a show to orchestrate his status, is paradoxically big enough to bring him down to ordinary size. The most striking number of the concert was a slow, intimate version of "Tangled Up in Blue," a long, biographical (but only archetypically autobiographical) narrative Dylan all but acted out, opening up the song with a physical and conversational freedom he's never before had on stage. The tune, a high point on *Blood on the Tracks,* seemed to expand: it seemed so much richer, so much more *interesting,* that I leaned forward, afraid to miss a word. It may be that this sort of intimacy is possible for Dylan only in a show he can get lost in—a show so unlikely, so unwieldy, that the preconceptions of his mostly white, middle-class audiences (hardly attuned to the trappings of James Brown or Tammy Wynette) bring to his performance cannot survive it. The result, for Dylan, is a new range: a range that takes in playfulness, trash glamour, and entertainment for entertainment's sake, and freezes out life-and-death drama.

There's no image-mongering in such a context, and no mystification. Dylan is not just putting everybody on with his allusions to the style of Neil Diamond (or maybe more to the point, Bette Midler). Nor is he angling for a new career in Las Vegas, though I wouldn't be surprised if he turned up there soon, if only to see if he could pull it off. To see Dylan on stage today is to see the follies of a bohemian in Disneyland. Dylan is delighted to find that he can take pleasure in aspects of American culture that must have seemed alien—but still seeing no reason why, as he works certain of those things into his style, he should do so *exactly.* Like his timing during so much of his singing, Dylan's showbiz gestures are off the mark; they're still his gestures, and not really an imitation of anyone. Bob Dylan has been many things over the years, but he's never been a very good purist.

Bob Dylan, *At Budokan* (Columbia, 1979). Bare on record, an apotheosis of what Tom Kipp calls sludge: musical clichés as their own complete, absolutely self-referential language.

AMAZING CHUTZPAH
New West
24 September 1979

Listening to the new Bob Dylan album is something like being accosted in an airport. "Hello," a voice seems to say, as Dylan twists his voice around the gospel chords of "When He Returns." "Can I talk to you for a moment? Are you new in town? You know, a few months ago I accepted Jesus into my life, and—" "Uh, sorry, got a plane to catch!" "—and if you don't you'll rot in hell!"

Slow Train Coming is the first testament to Bob Dylan's recent embrace of a certain version—southern Californian suburban—of fundamentalist Christianity. Produced by the rhythm and blues legend Jerry Wexler, with Dire Straits' Mark Knopfler and Pick Withers on guitar and drums, it's an initially commanding but ultimately slick piece of music: "a professional record," as Dylan has said. The record offers surprises—Dylan celebrates his belief in Christ with the blues, which is nicely heretical; his singing is often bravely out of control—but they're irrelevant to the burden Dylan is seeking to pass on to whoever will listen. What we're faced with here is really very ugly.

It's not that *Slow Train* is drenched in religious imagery, or that a Jew has decided that the New Testament truly completes the Old. Throughout his career, Dylan has taken biblical allegory as a second language; themes of spiritual exile and homecoming, and personal and national salvation, have been central to his work. In "All Along the Watchtower," Dylan defined a crisis of faith—faith in life. The song remains as profoundly religious as any in pop music. What is new is Dylan's use of religious imagery not to discover and shape a vision of what's at stake in the world but to sell a prepackaged doctrine he's received from someone else. Despite an occasional sign of life ("She can do the Georgia crawl / She can walk in the spirit of the Lord," Dylan sings, and who knows what the Georgia crawl is, or wouldn't like to know?), the songs on *Slow Train* are monolithic. Jesus is the answer, and if you don't believe it, you're fucked.

Religious revival courses through our history as a response to collapsing social structures and the need for values that make sense of struggle. Dylan is preeminently an American artist, and conversion, after one has spent years as a quester and a solitary, is a preeminently American way of continuing one's quest—not within the vast open spaces that once filled the country and still fill the American mind, but within the warmer confines of solidarity, of fellowship, of a church. But conversion is also a way of ending a quest, of falsely settling all questions. With *Slow Train,* we don't touch the liberated piety of the Rev. Thomas A. Dorsey, who abandoned a career as Georgia Tom, master of the dirty blues, to write "(There'll Be) Peace in the Valley (For Me)"; we don't sense the awful tension of Hank Williams and Elvis Presley, who could sing about the light without ever finding a way to live in it. Dylan's new songs have nothing of the sanctified quest in them: they're arrogant, intolerant (listen to the racist, America-first attack on Arabs in "Slow Train," a pretty good tune; listen to what's said about anyone who thinks answers are not the question) and smug. Much of the writing is insultingly shoddy—some of the songs are no more than glorified lists. This is not the music of a man who's thinking something through, but of a man who's plugging in.

"You either got faith or you got unbelief / And there ain't *no* neutral ground," Dylan chants; in case you imagine he's using faith as some kind of spiritual metaphor, he quickly adds: "Sister, let me tell you about a vision I saw . . . You were tellin' him about Buddha / You were tellin' him about Mohammed in one breath / You never mentioned one time the Man who came / And died a criminal's death—" And on and on, screed upon screed.

The best religious music makes me wish I could put aside my emotional and intellectual life and accept what the singer has accepted; though I can't, or won't, I can at least recognize the absence of the singer's joy, clarity, and commitment in my own life. Dylan's received truths never threaten the unbeliever, they only chill the soul, and that is because he is offering a peculiarly eviscerated and degraded version of American fundamentalism. In "Do

Right to Me, Baby," the devastating entreaties of Matthew 5.44 are corrupted. "But I say unto you, Love your enemies, bless them that curse you, do good to them that hate you" turns into you-scratch-my-back-I'll-scratch-yours. Dylan is promoting a very modern kind of gospel: safe, self-satisfied, and utilitarian. There's no sense of his own sin on *Slow Train*, no humility, and it's less God than Dylan's own choice that's celebrated. Thus there are no moments of perfect sight, of deliverance, as there are on Van Morrison's astonishingly rich new album, *Into the Music*. Where Morrison's language is inspired—"Like a full-force gale / I was lifted up again," he sings, "I was lifted up again by the Lord"—Dylan's is ranting, full of promises that are false because they have been made banal. "There's a Man on the Cross / And He be crucified for you," Dylan affirms. "Believe in His power / That's about all that you gotta do."

That's not all you gotta do if you want what Dylan claims to have. What Dylan does not understand—what most New Fundamentalists have neatly sidestepped—are the hard spiritual facts that have always formed the bedrock of traditional American faith. What he does not understand is that by accepting Christ, one does not achieve grace, but accepts a terrible, lifelong struggle to be worthy of grace, a struggle to live in a way that contradicts one's natural impulses, one's innately depraved soul. Sin does not vanish, it remains constant, but now one cannot hide from it, and one must accept the suffering recognition brings. Though one is renewed by moments of unspeakable peace and justification, nothing is finally settled except the fact of one's quest. What sustains that quest is not self-righteousness, but the paradox God has made of life on earth, the tension between what men and women know they could be, and what, in most moments, they know they are. "And I'll be changed," Dorsey wrote in "Peace in the Valley," as so many have sung, from Mahalia Jackson in 1939 to Elvis Presley in 1957 and on from there, "Changed from this creature / That I am."

One never rests. One never claims, as Dylan does throughout *Slow Train*, that redemption is a simple affair. Against Dylan's blithe declaration of allegiance to God, gospel music sets a hymn like "I Would Be True." The distance implied by the conditional, the implication that without God's help one cannot *do* anything, is very great.

American piety is a deep mine, and in the past, without following any maps, Dylan has gone into it and returned with real treasures: *John Wesley Harding* is the best example, but there are many others. *Slow Train Coming* strips the earth, and what it leaves behind is wreckage.

Chuck Berry, who was railroaded into prison seventeen years ago on a Mann Act charge, has a new album out called *Rockit;* it contains strange songs about the passing away of suffering, a chase by the Klan, and one tune, "California" ("Will I ever go to Los Angeles or San Diego / To Redding or Fresno, Needles or Barstow"), that took on new meaning when, last month, Berry entered federal prison here after pleading guilty to tax evasion. Get the record, then write Chuck Berry at the Federal Prison Camp at Lompoc, Box 2000, California 93438, and tell him you're listening.

Bob Dylan, *Slow Train Coming* (Columbia, 1979).

Henry Williams and Eddie Anthony, "Georgia Crawl" (Columbia, 1927). "Hey there, papa, look at sis / Out there in the back yard just shakin' like this / Doin' the Georgia crawl"—and with a keening fiddle, a light guitar beat, and a non-stop leer. Collected on Allen Lowe's heroic *Really the Blues? A Blues History 1893–1959* (West Hill Radio Archives/Music and Arts, 2010).

from LOGICAL CONCLUSIONS
New West
17 December 1979

After canceling a national tour, Bob Dylan opened an unprece-
dented fourteen-show stand at the 2,300-seat Warfield Theater in
San Francisco on November 1—his first concerts since his conversion to fundamentalist Christianity. The material (*Slow Train Coming* and unrecorded new songs) was strictly evangelical; the
performance was lifeless almost beyond credence. Backed by a
pedestrian group of L.A. session men and three lively black vocalists, Dylan sang without expression, without movement, as if the
act of facing a crowd were irredeemably distasteful. The audience
was at times abusive, calling for old favorites, but it was a stupid
response. I was glad Dylan had drawn a line across his career—he's
been a prisoner of the history he made for too long. But for this?

The sold-out hall was almost empty when, after an encore, Dylan returned to the stage, sat down at the piano, and with the three
backing vocalists—Regina Havis, Mona Lisa Young, and Helena
Springs—began a classically styled piece of gospel: "Pressing On,"
which surely had to be straight out of a hymnal. He sang with
every bit of the feeling the concert had denied—he sang with passion, with humility, as a man who knew his worth. I left trying to
figure out what had happened.

I came back November 16, for the last night. The show loosened
up early, when Dylan-as-Adam sang the pig verse of "Man Gave
Names to All the Animals": "He wasn't too small and he wasn't too
big / Ah, think I'll call it a giraffe." A grin spread over Dylan's
face; after a preacher's introduction to "Slow Train" ("This world's
going to be destroyed, we know that, and Christ will set up his
kingdom in Jerusalem for a thousand years, and the lion will lie
down with the lamb—have you heard that before? Just curious,
how many of you here believe that? Well, all right!"), the grin
came back. Later, a shouting match broke out in the crowd—"We

want *Dylan!*" "Do whatever you want, Bob!" "He will!"—and Dylan plainly cracked up.

He hit a lot of high notes on a new tune, "Covenant Woman," and the audience was up for every one of them. "No Man Righteous (No Not One)," a duet with Regina Harris, a bouncy number, kept the mood building; "God Uses Ordinary People," a horrible, Vegas-style solo by Mona Lisa Young, dashed it. The songs from *Slow Train Coming* were still second-rate, the band was little better than functional, and a few of the new tunes were poor, but Dylan was putting himself into the music; he was leaning forward, reaching.

With "Hanging Onto a Solid Rock (Made Before the Foundation of the World)," he took over; his authority was back. This was a huge sound, and Dylan gave it everything. He struck Elvis poses, rocked back on his heels, took his guitar into a crouch; along with the backing singers he shouted out the chorus ("MADE! BEFORE! THE FOUNDATION!") as if the words were being hurled into him.

And then—after more new songs, after an encore, when the show had gone on for almost two hours—it was time for "Pressing On": Dylan's song, as it turned out, and one of his best. Seated at the piano, Dylan traded lines with the other singers, and his voice suddenly grew in range; it was wrenching, scary, and yet completely without strain. It was the high, terrible Appalachian moan of his early ballads: timeless, lean, unforced, inescapable.

Dylan moved to the center of the stage as the band returned to close the song; grabbing the mike stand, he leaned it to one side, just like Rod Stewart, and the performance expanded until it seemed to take in every shade of emotion. As the song hit a surge, Dylan began to jump up and down. The song went on; it might have gone on for ten minutes, and it could have gone on all night.

from THEMES FROM SUMMER PLACES
New West
28 July 1980

This column has been unable to confirm a rumor that Bob Dylan's second born-again album, *Saved,* was held up because of tampering with the cover art, which depicts several hands reaching toward the outstretched, bleeding hand of Jesus Christ. Reportedly, someone broke into the CBS factory one night and very subtly redrew the hand of the supplicant second from the left in such a manner as to make it appear that Jesus was being given the finger. The offender has supposedly been apprehended; a rumor that Elvis Costello's name was found in his address book could not be confirmed.*

Bob Dylan, "Pressing On," from *Saved* (Columbia, 1980). The performance had stiffened up by the time it was recorded; while the opening passage has a light behind it, the rest of the song is overplayed, oversung, hammered with a near-hysteria of orchestration and decoration. The song didn't really find its voice until almost thirty years later, in Todd Haynes's 2007 film *I'm Not There,* with Christian Bale (acting) and John Doe (singing). With half of the combination missing, it wasn't half as convincing on the soundtrack album.

---

*You never know; in 1983 the cover art for *Saved* was replaced by a conventional depiction of Dylan onstage with his band of the time.

from SONGS OF RANDOM TERROR—
REAL LIFE ROCK TOP 10, 1980

New West

January 1981

9) "Like a Rolling Stone" at Longhi's, Lahina, Maui, February 22.
Longhi's is the ultimate laid-back watering hole; as I sat there that
morning, the house radio tuned to KQMQ-FM and playing pop
tunes that functioned strictly as unregistered background, Bob
Dylan's greatest song came on. The languid crowd slowly turned
from its pineapple and Bloody Mary breakfast; feet began moving,
conversations died. Everyone *listened,* and everyone looked a bit
more alive when the last notes faded. It was a stunning moment: irrefutable proof that "Like a Rolling Stone" cannot be used as
Muzak.

As for Dylan himself, his return to the Warfield Theater in San
Francisco far outstripped similar appearances in 1979. The previous shows were one hundred percent holy-writ rock; this time the
ads promised nostalgia: all your favorites! For Dylan, now so fer-
vently committed to Jesus, it seemed like the first real sellout of his
career: a sad concession to his once-doting audience, or a pathetic
admission that he couldn't live without it. That was not how the
music came across. Ending a two-week run, Dylan gave a gruff,
good-humored performance of what, that night, was on his mind:
hard and syncopated gospel, an Appalachian ballad complete with
autoharp, Little Willie John's "Fever," Dave Mason's startlingly
apt "We Just Disagree," a few of his own, older numbers. It was the
seventeenth anniversary of John F. Kennedy's assassination. Dylan
closed with "A Hard Rain's A-Gonna Fall," which has always been
associated with the Cuban missile crisis of 1962—as far as the history books go, Kennedy's finest hour. It was steely, mean, implacable, and forgiving, and it sounded as if Dylan had written it the
night before. Maybe ninety-nine-and-a-half won't do, but it did.

PART THREE

And Eight Years of That, 1985–1993

NUMBER ONE WITH A BULLET
Artforum
May 1985

The late Lester Bangs on the 1976 Second Annual Rock Music
Awards telecast, hosted by Alice Cooper and Diana Ross:

> The highlight of the evening was the Public Service Award. Alice
> Cooper complained that "rock music personalities are foremost
> and basically people—contrary to rumor. People with the same
> dreams, desires and feelings as everyone else. They're ambitious
> but they're not selfish or self-involved—but caring! . . . and I
> can't read this card. Their careers are time-consuming, but they
> still invest whatever time they have in—" Diana: "—what we in
> the industry are most proud of—the Public Service Award." They
> gave Public Service Awards to Harry Chapin for contributing to
> World Hunger Year, and to Dylan for helping get Rubin "Hurri-
> cane" Carter out of jail . . . Then Diana administered the coup de
> grace: "But seriously, folks, there's an incredible movement grow-
> ing in the United States; concerned citizens who believe that
> whales have the right to life. And through words and through mu-
> sic the team of David Crosby and Graham Nash express their own
> concern, by giving a special concert so that the whales are still
> alive. I think that is absolutely incredible and we honor them with
> our fifth Public Service Award. Well, once again I don't think
> they're here, but we'll accept it for them."
>
> Alice made a crack about Flo and Eddie being there, speaking
> of whales, and Diana continued: "No, seriously, I do know that a
> lot of my friends are concerned about this area and it's something
> that I personally would like very much to be interested in."

Things haven't changed much since then. Rock stars still invest whatever time they have in what they are most proud of. The only difference is that the Rock Music Awards have been replaced by the American Music Awards, and whales have been exchanged for Ethiopians.

Following the AMA telecast in January, more than forty performers gathered to make a record to raise funds for Ethiopian famine relief. AMA host and big winner Lionel Richie had already written the song with Michael Jackson; Quincy Jones produced. Diana Ross, Bob Dylan, Bruce Springsteen, Tina Turner, Willie Nelson, Steve Perry, James Ingram, Kenny Rogers, Paul Simon and the rest "checked their egos at the door" and, under the name of USA for Africa, cut "We Are the World." As Oscar Wilde might have said, it takes a strong man to listen without laughing. Or throwing up.

As I was cleaning the floor, I had to admit that as a tune "We Are the World" isn't at all bad—but a more vague composition about specific suffering could not be imagined. Small print on the sleeve claims "United Support of Artists for Africa ('USA for Africa') . . . has pledged to use . . . all profits realized by CBS Records from the sale of 'We Are the World' . . . to address immediate emergency needs in the USA and Africa, including food and medicine," but there isn't a word in the song about how or why this might be necessary. In the first verse one is told that "There are people dying" (STOP PRESS); in the last verse, that "When you're down and out" (Ethiopians are "down and out"?) ". . . if you just believe there's no way we can fall." Literally, that means if Ethiopians believe in USA for Africa the stars will realize their own hopes. That's it for Ethiopia.

While grammar is no help, contextualization comes to the rescue: certainly the superstars of USA for Africa knew their efforts would receive such overwhelming media coverage that their proximate inspiration would be clear to all. Thus once past "There are people dying" the rest of the song can fairly be about not the question but the answer—a celebration of the rock music personalities who are singing.

"There's a choice we're making / We're saving our own lives"—those are the key lines of "We Are the World," repeated again and again. Dylan sings them, Cyndi Lauper sings them, Springsteen sings them, Ray Charles sings them, Stevie Wonder sings them. Within the confines of desperately MOR music, Charles is magnificent, Wonder sounds fine, Springsteen sounds like Joe Cocker, and Dylan—well, if a comedian attempted a Dylan parody this broad he'd be laughed off the stage. But that's irrelevant. Here recognition is all: objective parody is more recognizable, more saleable, than subjective performance. The point is voracious aggrandizement in the face of starvation—a collective aggrandizement, what those in the industry are most proud of. Melanie Klein posited the infant's projection of itself on the world, and its instinctive attempt to devour the world; beneath perfectly decent, thoughtless intentions, that's what's to be heard on "We Are the World." Forget the showbiz heaven of "We are the world, we are the children / We are the ones who make a brighter day"; listen to the way that, projecting themselves on the world, the USA for Africa singers eat it. Ethiopians may not have anything to eat, but at least these people get to eat Ethiopians.

Obviously, I think the subliminal message of "We Are the World" is destructive. The message is, ye have the poor always with you; that there is a We, you and I, who should help Them, who are not like us; that as we help them we gain points for admission to heaven ("We're saving our own lives"); that hunger, whether in the U.S.A. or in Africa, is a natural disaster, in God's hands, His testing—His testing, perhaps, of those Americans who are homeless and starving "by choice," and if they aren't, how in God's name did they reach such a fate? And if they are, aren't the Ethiopians? For that matter, small print and small USA for Africa contributions to American hunger relief (ten percent) aside, doesn't the spectacularization of Ethiopian suffering trivialize American suffering and hide its political causes in a blaze of good will? Bad politics, which can be based in real desires, can produce good art; bad art, which can only be based in faked or compromised desires, can only produce bad politics. Such carping is as vague as "We Are the World"—but there is a message hidden in the song that is more specific than anyone could have intended.

As with Michael Jackson in 1984, the highlight of the 1985 Grammy telecast was the unveiling of the new Pepsi commercial. Lionel Richie, earning $8.5 million as a Pepsi spokesman, strolled through a three-minute spot, advertised as the longest network TV advertisement in the history of the medium. The theme was pressed hard.

"You know, we're all a new generation," Richie said, "and we've made our choice"—most notably, he was saying without saying it, the choice of Pepsi over Coke.

Pepsi first tried this theme in the sixties, when it pushed "The Pepsi Generation" as a slogan. In the time of the generation gap, of seemingly autonomous youth, the line didn't work. As based in abundance as the sixties were, the ideology of the era was antimaterialist; the corporate cooptation rubbed raw. But the new generation of Richie's commercial really was new—the post-sixties generation, which is all-inclusive, which indeed has room for anyone from that passed time; a generation whose members, according to media wisdom, have traded utopianism for self-realization, but nevertheless look hard for quality time to spend on family, friends, and areas they personally would like very much to be interested in, so long as those areas are sufficiently distant, say, eight thousand miles distant.

Actually, the 1985 Pepsi commercial was a lousy commercial: a stiff combination of a Lionel Richie video and an insurance-company ad. Compared to the 1984 Mountain Dew breakdancing commercial it was merely long. But "We Are the World" is a great commercial. It sounds like a Pepsi jingle—and the constant repetition of "There's a choice we're making" conflates with Pepsi's trademarked "The Choice of a New Generation" in a way that, on the part of Pepsi-contracted songwriters Michael Jackson and Lionel Richie, is certainly not intentional, and even more certainly beyond serendipity. As pop music, "We Are the World" says less about Ethiopia than it does about Pepsi—and the true result will likely be less that certain Ethiopian individuals will live, or anyway live a bit longer than they otherwise would have, than that Pepsi will get the catchphrase of its advertising campaign sung for free by Ray Charles, Stevie Wonder, Bruce Springsteen, and all the rest. But that is only the short-term, subliminal way of looking at it. In the long-view, real-life way of looking at it, in terms of pop geopolitical economics, those Ethiopians who survive may end up not merely alive, but drinking Pepsi instead of Coke.

As American singers came together for the USA for Africa sessions, Canadian performers gathered to make their own Ethiopia record. Among the contributors was Neil Young. "You can't always support the weak," he had said in October 1984. "You have to make the weak stand up on one leg, or half a leg, whatever they've got." But the Ethiopia benefit session? Hey, it was something he personally very much wanted to be interested in.

USA for Africa, "We Are the World" (Columbia, 1985, #1) In 2010, Lionel Richie and Quincy Jones, the producer RedOne, and Will.i.am of the Black Eyed Peas staged a twenty-fifth anniversary remake: "We Are the World 25 for Haiti," credited to Artists for Haiti (Columbia, #2). Especially in the video for the song, the performance was simpering beyond belief, with the singers—including Justin Bieber, Tony Bennett, Jennifer Hudson, Jeff Bridges, Barbra Streisand, Usher, Fergie, Janet Jackson, Michael Jackson (in a film clip, not from the beyond), Jamie Foxx (Ray Charles in *Ray*), Enrique Iglesias, Celine Dion, Pink, Lil Wayne, Mary J. Blige, Josh Groban, T-Pain, and dozens of others, including Brian Wilson and Al Jardine of the Beach Boys in the huge chorus—consumed by their own expressions of compassion and pain. It made the original seem like "Ready Teddy."

OVER THE EDGE

on Wilfred Mellers's *A Darker Shade of Pale:*
A Backdrop to Bob Dylan
1985*

This is a confused and confusing book about a confused and confusing figure: Bob Dylan, born 1941 in Duluth, Minnesota, as
Robert Alan Zimmerman. He first made himself known in the early
sixties as self-proclaimed heir to Dust Bowl balladeer Woody
Guthrie, singing songs of social change that got him named conscience of the nation's youth; in the mid-sixties, halcyon times, he
emerged at once as throwback to the dandyist bohemians of Baudelaire's Paris and would-be king of rock 'n' roll, offering metaphors
no one could figure out and everyone could understand, all pow-
ered by a sound so fierce and grand neither he nor anyone else in
popular music has ever matched it; as the decade turned and shattered he stepped back as sly and quiet private investigator of the
ethics of place. In the seventies he performed as walking legend
and stumbling troubadour; in 1979 he became a born-again Christian ("His mother's probably sitting shiva for him right now," his
producer told me as news of the conversion hit), damning the weak
of spirit and the corrupt of soul with all he had, which wasn't
much; as I write he has supposedly come back to the world. On the
surface, a trail so dizzying not even a hired Indian could track it;
beneath the surface, a peculiarly American search, reaching a peculiarly American verge. Bruce Springsteen used to tell a story about
a house he once saw in the Arizona desert: a sculpture, really, built
by a solitary Navajo out of highway junk. The dirt road leading to
the place was headed by a handmade sign: "This is the land of
peace, love, justice—and no mercy." Or perhaps that metaphor is
far too perfect, the search merely personal, its rhythm Dylan's, not
common or shared. "What's it like," a friend asked me about Dy-

---

*Written for the *New York Review of Books;* unpublished.

lan's first Christian album. "It's sneering," I said, "it's sanctimo-
nious, there's not a hint of compassion—" "Oh, well," she cut me
off. "You wouldn't expect him to *change,* would you?"

Wilfred Mellers was an editor of *Scrutiny* when Bob Dylan was
in kneepants. For many years he was a distinguished professor of
music at the University of York; in a nation where the notion of
American culture still brings forth jokes about Australian wine, he
has stood almost alone in taking American music seriously. For that
matter, few if any American musicologists can approach Mellers's
knowledge of American music—the oldest white ballad traditions,
minstrelsy, the 19th century genteel tradition, 20th century art
music, jazz, Broadway, blues, country and western, rock 'n' roll—
and few display his patent love for it. In Mellers's writing knowledge is a form of love: it seeks unities. His unmatched *Music in a
New Found Land* (1964) allowed Charles Ives, thirties Mississippi
bluesman Robert Johnson, Marc Blitzstein, Charlie Parker, John
Cage, and hundreds of others to speak the same deep-structural
language, and without ever compromising their own voices;
Mellers caught meaning in every shading of tone. Taking his cue
from D. H. Lawrence's *Studies in Classic American Literature* (and
perhaps Leslie Fiedler's *Love and Death in the American Novel*),
Mellers let Cooper, Hawthorne, Emerson, Thoreau, Melville, and
Whitman map the territory American musicians would have to inhabit to say anything worth saying about their particular version
of the human condition; then he translated. It is scandalous that
Americans have not followed his lead.

A Darker Shade of Pale frames Bob Dylan in these Americanist
terms, but the presentation is off from the first note. "For more
than twenty years," Mellers writes in his introduction, "Dylan has
been a spokesman for the young . . . he has become the mythic representative of a generation and a culture." The second claim is the
case Mellers means to make, but the cracked cliché of the first begs
all kinds of questions. Is Mellers buying the sixties fantasy of permanent adolescence? The young for whom Dylan has long since
ceased to be a spokesman are superannuated. ("Mr. Masterson has

been known as a distinguished American 'angry young man' for the past twenty years," Frederick Crews wrote in his *Pooh Perplex* parody of Leslie Fiedler—in 1963.) After clumsy curtain-raising, Mellers warms up his New-Found-Land roadster—and drives straight out of his own book. "The Backdrop," which takes up the first half of Mellers's study, traces white folk music traditions from ancient Scottish waulking songs to Elvis Presley, but despite the bizarre pronouncement that "when history comes to be written it may seem that [the] significance" of such towering modern representatives of this tradition as Dock Boggs, Roscoe Holcomb, Jimmie Rodgers, the Carter Family, Hank Williams, and Presley himself "is as precursors of Bob Dylan," Mellers's account of the white vernacular does not lead to Dylan. Mellers doesn't follow it into his section on Dylan proper, he doesn't build on it; a reader forgets the first half of the book a few pages into the second.

A reader forgets because if "The Backdrop" doesn't lead to "Bob Dylan," it doesn't particularly lead anywhere else. While wondering where the black music version of "The Backdrop" is (not in this book, even though Mellers ends the section insisting that a mature American pop music, i.e., Dylan's, must synthesize "white euphoria with black reality"), the reader is continually battered by such Mellersisms as the categorization of all performances as "positive" or "negative," not to mention the categorizations of white euphoria and black reality—and without the fully developed themes of *Music in a New Found Land* the result is a collection of musical facts not endowed with social meaning but stripped of it. The echoes of Mellers's once-lucid sense of wholeness are here—such part titles as "The Monody of Deprivation" and "The Liquidation of Tragedy and Guilt"—but they are only echoes. Mellers's brief but intense tributes to, say, the underappreciated Holcomb, or the far more obscure, wonderfully named Nimrod Workman, are interesting, just as his multiple attacks on Scott Weisman as a country music meliorist are misplaced (though the one-time folk singer Wiseman presumably drove Mellers nuts in the thirties and forties with his duets and comedy routines with his partner Lula Belle, he defines trivial), but neither Workman nor Wiseman are made to speak to each other, let alone to Dylan.* The basic impression one takes away from "The Backdrop" is that as white American musical culture oscillated between positives and negatives lots of stuff happened over a long period and now it's 1962 and time to talk about the first Bob Dylan album. Why not? Got anything else you'd like to talk about?

Mellers's language collapses along with his conceptual apparatus. Throughout, *A Darker Shade of Pale* lacks the clarity and quirky eloquence of Mellers's earlier books; down-to-earth forthrightness is replaced by what seems to be an attempt to sound hip, which only ends up sounding condescending—and I don't think Mellers could intentionally condescend to American music at the point of a gun. Still, the horrible example, one of many, screams out of the book: you can no more call Elvis, who as a boy attended Pentecostal churches, "initially a Jesus freak" than you can communicate anything by calling Jonathan Edwards a cult leader. The links between Edwards, Pentecostalism, and contemporary fundamentalism are real (it's Dylan who is, or was, the Jesus freak), but this sort of thing disposes of them. It's the literary equivalent of eating with your hands.

Tracing Dylan's career, Mellers listens closely, but little connects. There's no drama, no sense of risk or vision—until Mellers reaches the mid- to late seventies, when he takes up Dylan's soundtrack music for Sam Peckinpah's film *Pat Garrett and Billy the Kid* (Dylan had a small and spooky role as one "Alias"), *Desire,* the band-of-hangers-on Rolling Thunder tour and Dylan's resultant film *Renaldo and Clara,* the awful *Street Legal,* and finally crests with an analysis of the Christian albums, from *Slow Train Coming* in 1979 to *Shot of Love* in 1981. Here, examining Dylan's least expressive singing, his most stolid and mute accompaniments, and

---

*Though Dylan did his best to speak to Wiseman, making a home recording of his 1939 "Remember Me (When the Candle Lights Are Gleaming)" in East Orange, New Jersey, in 1961; a fragment of the song even turns up in D. A. Pennebaker's *Don't Look Back,* his 1967 documentary on Dylan's 1965 tour of the U.K.

his most literalistic lyrics—examining work in which Dylan's links to American musical traditions, secular or sanctified, are almost completely absent, where the poverty of the work justifies itself as wealth by the grace of having God on its side—Mellers does not exactly orchestrate his story, but he does press down harder on his material. That done, he reaches his last chapter—and insists on Dylan not merely as representative of a generation, or a culture, but as ur-representative of the American mythos: "Jewish Amerindian and White Negro," Pagan Christian and Insider/Outsider, plus, for good measure, Male Female. Mellers stops short only of claiming Dylan as part buffalo. Nothing has prepared the reader for this; it's all done by fiat. What's going on?

In the mid-sixties, when Bob Dylan made the music on which his legend is still based, when he produced the capital the interest on which he has been living off since, it was common to hear ordinary, everyday conversations invaded by his lyrics: "Let me eat when I'm hungry / Let me drink when I'm dry / A dollar when I'm hard up / Religion when I die," Dylan sang in an early unreleased recording, changing the second person of the old "Moonshiner" folk song to the first person. One can suspect that the Americanisms of *A Darker Shade of Pale,* which make little sense when they are clean-cut and are sometimes tortured into the realm of the weird (Mellers wants at least a poetic acceptance of the 16th–17th century theory that as survivors of the Ten Lost Tribes of Israel, Amerindians *were* Jews), are mainly a pretext for what Mellers really wants to talk about.

Even in *Music in a New Found Land,* Mellers revealed a weakness for the Transcendentalists as against the Nostalgiac (Cooper), the Orgiast (Whitman), and the Blackhearts (Hawthorne and Melville); the essential American experience, he wrote, is that of being "born again," though he wasn't speaking religiously. Even in the sixties, explicitly Christian metaphors were woven into Dylan's songs, and into his persona ("I expect to be hung as a thief," he said at a devastating press conference in 1965; around the same time he posed on his knees clutching a rough wooden cross). Reading *A Darker Shade of Pale,* it's hard not to think that it is less four centuries of American music, or two decades of Dylan music, than Dylan's notorious conversion from nominal Jew to radical Christian that has brought forth Mellers's eighth-decade exegesis.

For more than ten years, this great critic has been obsessed by the problem of transcendence: from *Twilight of the Gods: The Music of the Beatles* (1973) to *Bach and the Dance of God* to *Beethoven and the Vision of God* to the more circumspectly titled Dylan book, which could be called *The Message of Bob Dylan: Believe or Die.* To close the last, Mellers quotes Tocqueville's *Democracy in America,* that fabulous text which, like the culture of American democracy itself, can provide all things to all people, so long as one takes care not to stand in one place too long. "I doubt whether man can support complete religious independence and entire political liberty at the same time," Tocqueville wrote. "I am led to believe that if he has no faith he must obey, and if he is free he must believe." (Why hasn't someone told Solzhenitsyn this?) Dylan's evangelism may appear to go "beyond the bounds of common sense," Mellers says ("not to mention common charity," he adds), but "the evolution of American industrial technocracy" has produced a situation "that may be one with which common sense is incompetent to deal." It's the great deus ex machina of postwar aesthetics: the Bomb. Even Perry Miller dragged it onstage to close *Errand into the Wilderness*—though not, I think, with Mellers's message of believe-or-die attached.

As *A Darker Shade of Pale* ends with its flurry of cross-cultural, cross-racial, cross-gender amputations and grafts, one arm remains outstretched toward the light. Dylan's last word "need not be interpreted in narrowly Christian terms, even by Dylan himself"— still, the "Christian answer may be the most valid in that it is both historical and revelatory" (the Anti-Defamation League and the Muslim Benevolent Society raise their voices: ours aren't?), and anyway, that answer, like all answers, "must be seen as a beginning rather than as an end," which is to say that (by this time the reader is asking, "It does?" even before the reader has been told what the it is) Dylan is correct in affirming that if we are not "born again, our vaunted civilization, whether Christian or pagan, is finished; and will deserve its fate."

Back in 1963, in "Let Me Die in My Footsteps," Dylan sang a protest song against fallout shelters; this is a critic's fallout shelter. Mellers has left himself a lot of outs, but not enough of them. Yes, as the self-invented creature whose mind and soul are as blank as the continent before him (Mellers waves back to John Locke), the American must be born again, and again, and again, if he or she is to be American at all—but what does this tell us about Melville, Lincoln, Faulkner, or Ned Cobb (the real name behind Theodore Rosengarten's *All God's Dangers: The Autobiography of Nate Shaw*), who are the most American Americans we know, and whose works and days were defined by what they imagined they remembered? The white American must be born again in a "creative interfusion" (Mellers) with black and red—so said Melville in *Moby-Dick,* Twain in *Adventures of Huckleberry Finn,* Lawrence, and Fiedler— but weren't they thus saying that the new man or woman is helplessly borne back into the sins and guilts of his or her past? When Dylan kept company with these writers—in the mid-sixties, with the albums *Bringing It All Back Home, Highway 61 Revisited,* and *Blonde on Blonde*—he sought not answers but questions. But what Mellers is talking about is the surrender of the Antinomian will (out of which the new woman or man makes herself or himself)—a surrender to God's order, a subsuming of human diversity into an at least symbolic messiahhood (Dylan as white-black-red-Christian-Jewish-pagan-male-female-leftist-rightist) as the only alternative to nuclear holocaust. A few years ago, I read a profile of Stanley Marsh 3, the Texas millionaire and patron of the Ant Farm's celebrated Cadillac Ranch; he talked about his late nights with the paleoanthropologist Richard Leakey, who would put down his drink, stare hard at the man who could, if he so chose, fund Leakey's next project, and explain to Marsh exactly what lay behind his digs for stray scraps of one-, two-, three-million-year-old bones, which was nothing so tame as the mere mystery of human origins. No, *If I can prove that all humanity derives from a common ancestor, and therefore that as we are all one war is folly, then there would be no more war*—

Remember Bob Dylan? In 1965 he had a hit with "Like a Rolling Stone." In 1984 he told an old friend, a man he had known since they were students and folk-music fans at the University of Minnesota in 1960, that he was stymied. People demanded the old songs, or simply the ones they knew. He had just dutifully put out *Real Live,* a redundant, fourth-time-around set of greatest hits; his label's alternative was a five-record archive fit for a dead man. He felt like a dead man, he said. When he sang people sat still like receptacles; he had turned into a reification and his audience had willfully made itself into another. He wanted, Dylan told his friend, to get out of the big halls where expectations were sealed by the ads announcing the arrival of a legend. He wanted to play small clubs—maybe South America. There he would be only a rumor. He could arrive without encumbrances, traveling, as Melville wrote to Hawthorne in 1851, with "nothing but a carpet-bag—that is to say, the Ego." But Dylan's managers, promoters, his record company, would not hear of it; they had already forced him to stud his evangelical program with old favorites, and then to perform only those evangelical songs that could themselves be presented as old favorites—*Real Live,* had any Bob Dylan album ever carried a title so flat, so stupid, so nihilistic? Compared to that, *Bob Dylan's Greatest Hits, Vol. II,* was poetry.*

---

*The friend was Paul Nelson. Born in Warren, Minnesota, in 1936, he died in New York City in 2006; a great critic, who contributed the essay on Bob Dylan for the original edition of *The Rolling Stone Illustrated History of Rock & Roll* (New York: Rolling Stone–Random House, 1976; edited by Jim Miller), he served as a model for the character Perkus Tooth in Jonathan Lethem's novel *Chronic City* (New York: Doubleday, 2009). What Dylan told Nelson became an undercurrent all through the middle chapters of Dylan's *Chronicles, Volume One*—but while there he pictured himself as a Hurstwood, a bum in the alley outside the back door of a theater in which he himself was performing, he never did make that small-club tour to South America.

We are not talking about the fate of the world. We are talking about an individual struggling to find his way to the next audience, and thus to the next song worth presenting to that audience, or to the next song which might gather that new audience: the pop equation, the pop paradox. We are talking about the next hit, and whether or not Bob Dylan, forty-four-year-old pop singer, can ever produce anything that could make people forget "Like a Rolling Stone." As a pop music artist, Bob Dylan will be born again only when he creates something that will make people forget his greatest hit, and who and what he was when he made it.

Mellers is correct when, glancing over the ugliness of Dylan's 1977 divorce from his wife of twelve years—an event which seems to have led straight to the fundamentalist Christianity which contained the anti-feminist theology necessary to justify the breach—he says that an artist's biography is ultimately irrelevant to an artist's work. Finally, we see what we see, read what we read, hear what we hear, in our own ways, and it's the task of the critic to help us see, read, and hear. Criticism based in personal or social facts only controls work that can't escape such facts; confronted head on by *Moby-Dick* or Lincoln's Second Inaugural Address, nobody really cares about who was who and what was what, then. But if biography is irrelevant, metaphysics may be as meaningless as making connections is fecund.

Mellers's book is set up to make connections, but its goal is elsewhere. When, in 1964, in *Music in a New Found Land,* Mellers wrote about Robert Johnson, dead since 1938, Johnson remained little known. An album collecting his recordings from 1936 and 1937 had been released in 1961; few had heard it. Mellers did not merely register Johnson's existence. In a paragraph, he set out what he heard in the hidden violence of Johnson's rhythms even more than in the explicit violence of Johnson's words: the fulfillment and the superseding of the Mississippi country blues, a form, made by a few men in a small, out-of-the-way place, that would decades later shape pop music all over the world. It's all been blown to pieces, Mellers wrote: they lie here, and those who can pick them up will, and will be remembered, and those who cannot, won't be. Nothing so powerful as this music can ever be killed, Mellers was saying, and indeed it is the explosion itself that has made the once-narrow form accessible to anyone. This was more than prescient for 1964; even in 1973, for Dylan to dedicate his *Writings and Drawings* "To the magnificent Woodie Guthrie and Robert Johnson, who sparked it all off" was only half-obvious. But in *A Darker Shade of Pale* everything is scrambled; what is at stake is not the American musical past ("The Backdrop"), nor even its recent, individualized version ("Bob Dylan"), one person trying to put the pieces together and make a common language new, but a demand for a language which is not particularly American at all, a language which is a good fifteen hundred years older than America black or white. The true weight of Mellers's book is that Bob Dylan—as the ultimate incarnation of what Emerson called the representative man, as "the first white American poet-composer-singer whose genius is both creative" (he writes his own songs) "and interpretive" (based on other people's)—can save the world. No wonder he wants to perform in Tierra del Fuego.

Over the past two decades both Mellers's work and Dylan's have imploded—but perhaps Dylan can take it as a sign of life that *A Darker Shade of Pale* says more about Mellers's career than his own. Maybe his new album will be as good as the advance word says it is; if it's not, *Highway 61 Revisited,* which I have played a dozen times while writing this, still defines what pop music can be. In that record, a string of positive negatives beginning with the unlimited reach of "Like a Rolling Stone" and ending with the long fall of "Desolation Row," containing the shades of Dock Boggs, Robert Johnson, Roscoe Holcomb, Hank Williams, Elvis Presley, and hundreds of others, Dylan created music that today remains utterly unsatisfied by the world that music meant to make— or, as the dandy-thief Lacenaire says in Marcel Carné's *Children of Paradise,* unmake. Dylan merged white euphoria with black realism; Beethoven and Ma Rainey "unwrapped a bedroll"; as in "The Whiteness of the Whale" and the crew's reply to Ahab's speech on the quarterdeck, as in Lincoln's "every drop of blood drawn with the lash, shall be repaid with another drawn by the sword," Dylan shouldered all debts in a spirit of providential ecstasis. On the margins of *A Darker Shade of Pale,* Mellers is right—but it must be to Bob Dylan's comfort that the book that could explain how and why remains as unwritten as the end of his career.

Wilfred Mellers, *A Darker Shade of Pale: A Backdrop to Bob Dylan.* New York: Oxford, 1985. This was Mellers's fourteenth book; he published nine more after it. I've returned to it many times over the years, for stray passages on waulking songs, odd mountain singers who for Mellers represent the poetic heart of their traditions even if those who sell the traditions have never heard of them, even a photo caption:

Dock Boggs the whirligig.

COMEBACK TIME AGAIN
Village Voice
13 August 1985

Big, goopy songs, something like later Elvis ballads with a cranked-up whine instead of that inflated but still grand Presley sweep . . . a few echoes of the basement tapes, "Tears of Rage" on the new "I'll Remember You" . . . "Clean Cut Kid," sort of a "protest song," there's a beat but it's CLUNK NOT FUNK—

Do you care? If it wasn't for prerelease reviews in *Rolling Stone* and *Time* (*This is the one! This is the real comeback! Not like the last one!* raves), it might not be necessary to write off the new Bob Dylan album at all. But here it is, *Empire Burlesque,* one more dead battery, so why not.

Listening to this record quickly dissolves into a search for signs of life; there're just enough to keep you listening, if that's your idea of a good time. Put your ear to the chest: yes, "When the Night Comes Falling from the Sky" is too long (even the title's too long, not to say redundant; didn't he once have a way with words?), but not only does it get going, it keeps going. Hold a mirror up to the mouth—it clouds over, barely. The horns are pointless, the guitar endlessly noodling even more so, but Sly & Robbie, part of any comeback LP's necessary contingent of hired names, find a groove and hold it. There's a shadow of the doomy conviction that drove the 1974 live recording of "All Along the Watchtower," that rescued the 1976 "Hurricane" from its terrible rhymes and made it stick like a knife quivering in a wall—just a shadow, but it's something. In moments Dylan seems to forget he's singing, and so, in those moments, he does sing.

The question is, do you want to listen to this stuff? Do the bits and pieces you might hear on the radio or MTV touch you, do they catch you up short, provoke a response? Does any of it demand as much from you as Foreigner's "I Want to Know What Love Is"? For all the hopeful critical line-toeing about Sly & Robbie 'n' Ron

Wood & Mick Taylor 'n' mixmaster Arthur Baker—*serious record-making* after years of one-take foolishness, etc.—the voice is what does or doesn't reach you; the voice is what counts. And except in moments it's the same voice Dylan has been strangling on since 1978, since *Street Legal.*

Even on *John Wesley Harding,* ten years before that (think about it: in 1968 Dylan's career was seven years on, a fraction of its present entity, and the legend was already in place, already the Gorgon to be faced down, refused, accepted, evaded)—even then, there were instants in which, as a singer, Dylan sounded sick: ill. On "I Pity the Poor Immigrant," say: his voice curled up in his throat, will and desire collapsed under leaden vowels. It was hard to know where the dead weight came from; the lilt of "Down Along the Cove," the nimble turns of "As I Went Out This Morning," made it easy to forget. But since *Street Legal,* that sick sound, that sound of pain, has been close to Dylan's whole voice.

In the domain of cliché, pain suggests blues, but this is anything but a blues voice: a voice that drifts away from its owner, gazes back at its maker, speaks of such things as "my second mind." The pain in Dylan's voice communicates as irritation, at best as bitterness. A whine that most often presents itself as cracker-barrel wise, it's the voice of a crank—a crank who wants you to believe he's seen it all but really just wants to complain that he hasn't liked what he's seen. Or is it that those who've looked at him haven't liked what they've seen, haven't liked it enough, haven't liked it in the precise, proper, mysteriously right way?

Empire Burlesque is no more and no less confused than *Street Legal.* Unlike *Infidels* or the Christianist albums, that record was a career move against confusion, and so is this. It doesn't sound like mud straight off, as *Street Legal* did—the record has a bright, balanced sound—but mud is what it is. Save for the last track, "Dark Eyes," Dylan alone with his acoustic guitar and harmonica, nothing connects to anything else. It's pure entropy: when the night comes falling from the sky it just goes back.

After the 1983 *Infidels,* a decent hit, a five-LP retrospective including much unreleased material was shelved—the balance sheets showed Dylan wasn't ready for the history books. The quickie *Real Live* was shoved onto the market instead. The banality of the title cued the reviews, which were awful when they appeared at all; the album was a stiff. It contained Dylan's most exciting performances since the 1975 *Blood on the Tracks,* the only true comeback album he's ever made. On the *Real Live* version of "Tangled Up in Blue," Dylan went through the verses as if he knew both what they said and what they didn't say, and so he changed words all over the place. He played with the song, laughed with it, brought it to life, no doubt inventing as he sang. He reminded me that in 1965, when he would stand alone on a stage and sing the then-unreleased "Desolation Row," people would laugh out loud, and he would grin. His music wasn't a burden his audience was expected to shoulder; it was an adventure its audience was free to join, and free to reject. It wasn't about Bob Dylan; only fools wondered if this or that song was about Joan Baez.

I hold no special brief for Bob Dylan as folk singer; he was great, but he was a better rocker, one of the four or five most piercing rock 'n' roll singers of all. In the mid-sixties, when he was chasing the Elvis legend, shouting onstage with his hands cupped around his mouth to make a megaphone against the roar of the Hawks behind him, there was more of Dock Boggs, Buell Kazee, and other deep hollow singers in his voice than there ever was before. After closing his shows with "Like a Rolling Stone," he would sneak backstage, sit down at the piano with Johnny Cash, and find his way into an American folk language so old his voice defined culture. He was rooted in history and rooted in the present moment, but there are no roots in his music now. The solo "Dark Eyes" connects not because it calls up some spurious, readymade sense of folkie roots, but because it's the only song on the album where Bob Dylan isn't singing about some undefined, unknown, unknowable, paranoid "they" or "you": "they" who turned the clean-cut kid into a killer, "you" who doesn't love me in just the way I need to be loved. "Dark Eyes" connects because here, as a singer, as a voice, Dylan is talking to somebody. That it's himself is no matter: he's not talking to a fixed object, an enemy, as he is everywhere else. What takes place, as he falls out of his crank-prophet voice and drifts into a reverie, is a conversation. You can imagine yourself part of it.

The theme of *Empire Burlesque,* both in lyrics and in the voice that puts them across, is simply stated: hell is other people. The most characteristic lines are from "Trust Yourself": "If you want somebody you can trust, trust yourself . . . You won't be disappointed when vain people let you down." This dead end is where Dylan has been heading for years now; *Empire Burlesque* is one spirited variation after another on *Street Legal'*s notoriously non-ironic "Can you cook and sew / Make flowers grow / Can you understand my pain?"

I don't think it's worth asking if this signifies anything whatsoever about the state of things in 19 and 85: the collapse of pop community, the fragmentation of the audience, Big Chill—you know the line. I think it's merely personal, and I won't speculate as to the source. What's the way out for someone who once caught fifty states, four hundred years, and four seasons in his voice? I don't know, but perhaps it's something that begins with the voice, something that makes the voice fuller, and less full of itself. Not humility, not regret—maybe cortisone, maybe a lot more Dock Boggs.

Bob Dylan, *Empire Burlesque* (Columbia, 1985).

SPEAKER TO SPEAKER
Artforum
April 1986

In 1984, in his book *Rock Stars,* Timothy White made the heretical statement that the music of Bob Dylan was ultimately less significant than Gene Vincent's "Be-Bop-a-Lula." Dylan's songs were "of the 'time-and-place' stripe," White said, while "Be-Bop-a-Lula" existed "on its own terms . . . It is an emotion preserved in song, unconditional, wholly without boundaries." Dylan's songs were themselves boundaries, and together they simply made a map; they told a certain generation, a certain pop audience, where it was. Once that audience vanished, the songs would go with it. In 1969, Nik Cohn had said much the same thing in *Pop from the Beginning:* "In my own life, the Monotones have meant more in one line of 'Book of Love' than Dylan did in the whole of *Blonde on Blonde.*"

It's time to take up this argument, if only because a quarter-century after Bob Dylan began his professional career in the Greenwich Village folk milieu, and twenty-one years after he seized the center of rock 'n' roll with "Like a Rolling Stone," the market is flooded with the flat insistence that his songs need not exist on their own terms: that the map supersedes the territory it supposedly describes. Wilfred Mellers's critical study *A Darker Shade of Pale,* Robert Shelton's *No Direction Home: The Life and Music of Bob Dylan,* Dylan's own *Lyrics 1962–1985* and the five-LP retrospective *Biograph*—each in its way presents Dylan's music as self-referential, each song meaningful only for its position on the map, which now describes no commonplace territory, but one man's career. The listener plays no part in the affair; one looks on from afar, and feels privileged for being allowed to do so.

The result is that one is led to confront Dylan's work—to think about it, to listen to it, to feel it—either in terms of his mythic status (Mellers), his heroic status (Shelton), or his cultural status (*Lyrics, Biograph*). That is, one is led away from confronting his work. Mellers constructs Dylan's career as a progression from an artist's appropriation of various folk strains to his transformation into the ultimate American, the ultimate New Man: White-Negro European-Amerindian Jewish-Christian Male-Female. Within such a structure, every song functions; none takes place. With Shelton, one follows the chronological odyssey of a man seeking always to "do it his way"; all that matters is whatever his way is, and so songs are simply incidents in an exemplary process of self-realization. On *Biograph,* recordings from 1962 through 1985 are jumbled out of chronological sequence to say that Dylan's music was whatever "Dylan," as a sort of moving concept, was doing whenever he did it. As a flat premise this flattens the music, with "Just Like a Woman" pumping up its next-track neighbor, "On a Night Like This," "On a Night Like This" deflating "Just Like a Woman." Whether the story is told by Mellers, Shelton, or Dylan himself, Dylan's performances, as moments in which he committed an act, in which something was actually happening, are completely trivialized as music, no matter how grand the claims being made for them. Each performance exists only in terms of the larger story being told, which is no longer a large story at all. It becomes impossible to understand the story Dylan's career really tells: to understand that, at certain points (say, *Highway 61 Revisited* in 1965, or the basement tapes in 1967), Dylan actually did something, and that at other points (say, "Blowin' in the Wind" in 1963, or his 1974 comeback tour), he didn't.

"Kinda ersatz," said a friend as we listened to Bob Dylan's version of "Blowin' in the Wind" for the first time, on the radio. He meant contrived, second-hand—received. This great anthem of the Civil Rights movement, no matter how profound its effect on the world (it brought people together, made sense of their hopes and fears, was good for singalongs, made Sam Cooke so envious he wrote "A Change Is Gonna Come"), was from its first appearance a proof of White's time-and-place argument: a song less written about a time and place than by them, an inevitable translation of events into a poeticized reflection. The song itself was blowing in the wind. Dylan picked it out; it was received so readily because, in a way, people had already heard it. With "This Wheel's on Fire," from the basement tapes, something altogether different was going on—in terms of a person creating something that would not have been had that person acted differently, something *was* going on. Real music is universal language because it speaks in many tongues: no matter how effective the apocalyptic images and tones of "This Wheel's on Fire" translated the apocalyptic moods of 1967, the song could not be held to any fixed, time-and-place meaning. It created its own time and place: one would have heard it in 1967, and one hears it today, as an event, not as a comment on an event, or an incident in a career, or an element in a mythos. Such a way of looking at things is not merely absent but expelled from *Biograph* or Mellers's and Shelton's books. Within the settings they establish, there is no way to think about why "This Wheel's on Fire" is real and "Blowin' in the Wind" is false (or, if you prefer, vice versa), or why "A Change Is Gonna Come" is immeasurably richer than "Blowin' in the Wind." One performance validates another, invalidating any other sort of perception while promoting the career as the source of all meaning.

To promote an individual as the source of the meaning of the individual's work is to promote pure solipsism. It is to make it impossible to think about how meaning is made—to experience meaning being made, or to experience the way a given performance continues to make meaning far beyond its presumptive time and place. There is no way to talk about the possibility that Dylan's career describes not aesthetic progress, but the invalidation of the idea of this kind of progress—that it is a story of both triumph and tragedy, that the fact that the 1964 "It Ain't Me Babe" can be placed on an album next to the 1974 "You Angel You" is a denial of everyone's best hopes. But if one ignores the perspective of *Biograph,* and listens for oneself, a real event becomes possible.

"You Angel You" is a bouncy piece of junk, an affirmation of nothing. "It Ain't Me, Babe" was always a fine song, but on *Biograph*—remastered, the voice brought forward, allowed to change its shape with every word—it is overwhelming, and it destroys the smeared setting that has been made for it.

Here Dylan moves from certainty to an ambiguity that frightens him back toward a certainty the falsity of which he has just revealed. His whole career comes into focus—as a continuing attempt to tell the truth as he sees it, supported by economics, mythos, and the lack of anything better to do. His career is an attempt to tell the kind of truth one can discover only in the act of telling what one thinks one already knows, which the act itself exposes as vanity.

It's foolish to expect that anyone could accomplish such an act by the mere fact of being who one is—at any time, in any place. It makes sense that the confluence of who one is with certain times and places would produce such moments, and that other confluences would not. The question of how the performance of a song makes meaning is raised; so is the question of how a song fakes it.

Timothy White, *Rock Stars*. New York: Stewart, Tabori and Chang, 1984, 139.

Nik Cohn, *Pop from the Beginning*. London: Weidenfeld & Nicolson, 1969. Rev. ed. as *Awopbopaloobop Alopbambamboom*. London: Paladin, 1970, 174.

Wilfred Mellers, *A Darker Shade of Pale: A Backdrop to Bob Dylan*. New York: Oxford, 1985.

Robert Shelton, *No Direction Home: The Life and Music of Bob Dylan*. New York: Beech Tree, 1986.

Bob Dylan, *Lyrics, 1962–1985*. New York: Knopf, 1985.

———. *Biograph* (Columbia, 1985).

———. "Blowin' in the Wind," on *The Freewheelin' Bob Dylan* (Columbia, 1963).

———. "This Wheel's on Fire" (1967), on *The Basement Tapes* (Columbia, 1975).

REAL LIFE ROCK TOP 10

Village Voice

21 June 1986

7) Bob Dylan: "Silvio" (Columbia). A tune by Robert Hunter, the Grateful Dead's writer, but the story isn't that the Dead rejected it first. The story is the arrangement, which goes back to Bill Haley for its suppression of elision or surprise. Dylan has always sung in country time, with an idiosyncrasy of rhythm and meter only certain musicians could keep up with: when he sings, he invents or he does nothing, but this is far less than nothing. "Silvio" suggests he has so little left of his style he couldn't make a convincing Budweiser commercial—there's more musical freedom in the average Budweiser commercial than there is here. Dylan's music now has meaning only as neuroticism.

Village Voice

15 July 1986

6) Bob Dylan with Tom Petty and the Heartbreakers: "Lonesome Town" (Greek Theatre, Berkeley, June 13). "Ricky Nelson did a lot of my songs; I'd like to do one of his." A lovely gesture, and it worked. As for the rest of the show, Dylan traded emotional nuance for rote chanting so doggedly that when my seatmate wondered if the next number might not be "99 Bottles of Beer on the Wall" it was impossible to hear what followed as anything else. Two verses later, we deciphered it as a speeded-up "Rainy Day Women #12 & 35."

Village Voice

9 September 1986

9) Robert Shelton: *No Direction Home—The Life and Music of Bob Dylan* (Beech Tree). Shelton published the first Dylan review, and

it turned out to be a hook in his side. In the works for more than twenty years, his book finally arrives at a length of 578 pages, bleeding with incomprehension. Like Myra Friedman in *Buried Alive,* her Janis Joplin biography, Shelton falls helplessly into the role of village explainer. Any sense of play and discovery is banished; the endless search for sources and meanings doesn't open up the story, it narrows it. Still, Dylan's conversations with Shelton, from 1962 through 1985 and all previously unpublished, are unparalleled in their sincerity and frankness: they make the book important. So cut this item out of the paper, take it to the bookstore, pull the book off the shelf, flip to pp. 14–18, 24–25, 38–40, 60, 63, 90–91, 109–10, 124, 129, 131, 188, 195, 279, 280–81, 287, 341–62, 479–81, 485–86, 491–92, and have a good time.

BOB SPITZ, *DYLAN: A BIOGRAPHY*
Washington Post Book World
8 January 1989

This is an obnoxious book, and a very lively one. It's riddled with misspelled names, misquoted songs, and startling errors of fact (rock showman Bill Graham appears as "the guy who employed the Hell's Angels to police his promotions"—a complete falsehood), and as many coups of interviewing and research. Sometimes it's plain that Spitz, author of two other, far less interesting books on pop music, has no idea what he's talking about; sometimes, as he reconstructs a situation twenty or thirty years gone, you can hardly believe he wasn't present himself. Absurd potted histories (American youth may have been "politically active" in 1963, Spitz says, but they "were drifting toward the progressive labor movement and away from civil liberties"—the line defies comprehension) give way to intricate, lucid accounts of the sessions that produced the great albums *Blonde on Blonde* and *John Wesley Harding.* Prose full of sneering hype ("And her Italian temper—*mama mia!*") or clairvoyant blather ("As Suze gazed over the bow of the ship, out across the tranquil sea, how could she predict the chaos that awaited her back in New York?") can turn a reader's stomach, and it can nail a moment—for example, Dylan's first appearances after his 1979 conversion to fundamentalist Christianity, two solid weeks of concerts in San Francisco. "No doubt fans assumed it'd be like one of the city's legendary Grateful Dead marathons," Spitz imagines. "'Fourteen shows, man—outta sight! Let's go to 'em all!' Boy, were they in for a rude surprise."

After nearly three decades of constant press coverage, at least two previous full-length biographies (one, Robert Shelton's *No Direction Home*, published little more than two years ago), and more than a score of critical studies, tour memoirs, anthologies, and coffee-table books, the outline of the Bob Dylan story is almost its own cliché: the middle-class Jewish childhood and rock 'n' roll adolescence in Hibbing, Minnesota, in the 1940s and '50s; the discovery of folk music at the University of Minnesota, then the blazing entry into the Greenwich Village folk scene in the early sixties. The emergence as the conscience-of-a-generation with "Blowin' in the Wind" and *The Times They Are A-Changin'* in 1963 and '64; the shocking abandonment of social realism and protest songs for the corrosive electric drama and paradox of "Like a Rolling Stone," *Highway 61 Revisited*, and *Blonde on Blonde* in 1965 and '66, music so rich, performed in concerts so unflinching, that it did not merely reflect its time but truly changed it. The withdrawal from a self-created maelstrom of fame and excess in 1966 and '67. And the attempt, ever after, through celebrations of family life followed by divorce, through religious fanaticism followed by a surrender to ordinary careerism, to find a voice that could inscribe more than footnotes to what had already been done—an almost quarter-century attempt, by now, to disprove Fitzgerald's maxim that there are no second acts in American lives. Spitz is the first of Dylan's biographers to treat this old story as an opportunity for something other than wonder and reverence; to let loose the ambition, cruelty, confusion, and selfishness ("the hard core of selfishness," as

Raymond Chandler once put it, "necessary to exploit talent to the full") that shaped the story.

Spitz does so through what, by this time, can be called Goldmanisms, after pop biographer Albert Goldman's books on Lenny Bruce, Elvis Presley, and John Lennon: extreme reliance on previously ignored (if often marginal) sources, satirically ironic melodrama ("The concert was *religious,* man! . . . what a mitzvah!"), and the insistence on the author's superiority to his material—his absolute hipness—as means to the authoritative voice. Goldman's books are driven by a puerile distaste for their subjects, a distaste pumped up into an all-consuming contempt. While Spitz is anything but contemptuous of Dylan, his adoption of Goldman's manner spreads contempt on everyone else in the tale, heedlessly, pointlessly, as if empty wisecracks were judgments. "High, wide Finnish cheekbones," Spitz says of Dylan's high-school girlfriend Echo Helstrom, "siamese eyes, pale, chalky skin, and a full steamy mouth that hung limply and begged for masculine sustenance of any kind—Oh Lord, she was a hot little number!" The Dylan who we're to think felt these things turns into a bundle of hormones; Helstrom turns into a whore.

When Spitz attacks the ludicrous scholasticism of the early sixties folk world, where original songs were forbidden and the provenance of a ballad was more important than its interpretation, this approach pays off; fools come forth as fools. Half of the time, contempt fades out in the face of a simple, eager lack of respect for the received pieties of the Dylan story. As Spitz draws out memories of musicians who worked with Dylan, the creation of epochal music is brought down to earth, becomes a fascinating account of boredom, discovery, surprise, satisfaction. Then back to ugly nonsense: when, say, in 1975, Dylan gives a concert at a women's prison—to an audience of "big, black mothers."

What one can get from this book is a sense of the terrific momentum of Dylan's life and work in the early and mid-sixties, the period when Dylan made his mark and made a world; no other book captures it so well, understands so well that this is the period that matters. At the same time, one can get no sense at all of where this transformation came from. It's as if a young man stumbled on the zeitgeist and, for an instant, falling in just the right way, pinned it to the ground, after which the zeitgeist flipped him over and broke his neck. Spitz can recreate the emotions that brought Dylan to a convulsive performance, but he can't write about music, can't tell what happened as the show took place. He can dig up, and make thrilling, untold stories about a black man who introduced a teenage Dylan to the wealth of American music, but give no sense of how Dylan absorbed the lesson. He can render the dangers of the void opened up in "Like a Rolling Stone," carefully dramatizing unreleased film footage of a junked Dylan in the back seat of a limousine, but he can't say what a dive into the void was worth.

Spitz's book is fun; it is repulsive. It's admirable that until page 233 there's no need to record that Dylan ever slept with anyone; the horribly detailed night a lonely man supposedly spent with a woman in 1975 is a violation, an atrocity in a book about someone still living—just because Spitz found some pathetic woman eager to trumpet her story, that doesn't make what happened his business, or ours. So you go back and forth, fascinated, irritated, intrigued, disgusted. Spitz's book proves one thing: the clichés of the Bob Dylan story are still alive, and the story is still waiting for the writer who can tell it.

Bob Spitz, *Dylan: A Biography*. New York: McGraw Hill, 1989.

THE MYTH OF THE OPEN ROAD
Clinton St. Quarterly
Spring 1989*

When I was invited to talk about pop music and the idea of the open road, the first song I thought of was Chuck Berry's "Promised Land," which came out in 1964. With perfect exuberance and un-

---

*A talk given at the Walker Art Center in Minneapolis, 4 October 1988.

paralleled verve, it told the story of "the poor boy," who sets out from Norfolk, Virginia, with "California on his mind." So he takes off—and inside a few minutes Chuck Berry and his hero have mapped the continent. The poor boy has to go by bus, car, train, and finally (he can't believe it) airplane, first class. There are breakdowns and disasters at every turn, but there are always people to help him, and he keeps going.

The best moment comes when he's up in the air, "working on a t-bone steak" ("à la carty," goes the line, and you can see Chuck Berry grinning; *he* knows how to pronounce it, but he knows the poor boy doesn't) and the moment is so complete you wonder why the plane ever has to come down. The arrival in Los Angeles is an anticlimax. Nothing could match the journey the poor boy's just made.

This is a song of freedom: a get-away. It's also a song about money: although the poor boy has none of his own, he has friends and he's never lacking. It's a song about space: the whole lift of the performance, the singing notes on the guitar, the wild life of the melody, each element is dependent on a big country, a country too big to really understand, an expanse so large and varied no geography textbook can truly explain it. And it's a song about confinement. Chuck Berry made trips across the country before he wrote "Promised Land"—bone-rattling bus trips on the barnstorming, one-night-stand rock 'n' roll package tours of the 1950s, with the white performers staying in decent hotels and eating in restaurants, while, in a lot of the country, blacks like Chuck Berry bunked in flops and ate out of paper bags. Berry also made nice, fourteen-hour flights from coast to coast when he went to Hollywood to mime his hits in the movies—but that wasn't what he was talking about in "Promised Land." When he wrote the song in the early '60s, he was in prison, railroaded on a Mann Act charge. He was fantasizing. What would it mean to get away, what would it feel like to see a different place every hour, instead of the same cell every day?

Because as a songwriter Chuck Berry was always a realist, he made the poor boy's journey troublesome. And though to himself he was a cynic, to his audience he was a romantic, so he gave the trip a happy ending. And because as a songwriter he knew that it's detail that makes a song work, that locks a song into a listener's mind, he had to get the details right—and that was a problem. "I remember having extreme difficulty while writing 'Promised Land,'" he said in 1987 in his autobiography, "trying to secure a road atlas of the United States to verify the routing of the Poor Boy from Norfolk, Virginia, to Los Angeles. The penal institutions were not so generous as to offer a map of any kind, for fear of providing the route for an escape."

Listening to this wonderful song, thinking about the images of movement and play the American landscape offers, you have to stop and think about the song Chuck Berry would have written if he hadn't been in prison—about how his version of the open road would have been different if he'd actually been on it. What's missing from "Promised Land" is control: mastery, the singer's hand on his own fate.

In the mid-'50s, when Chuck Berry was just hitting the charts, before he had big money in the bank, he never sang as "the poor boy": just the opposite. He was a *driver*. He had his own machine—first a V-8 Ford, then a Cadillac—and where he went was up to him. "Maybelline," "You Can't Catch Me," "No Money Down"—the road was his. By the end of "You Can't Catch Me," he's airborne: in the '50s, everyone believed that in a few years cars would fly, and Chuck Berry never missed a trick. But the emotion at the end of "Promised Land" isn't triumph, isn't the unlimited sense of release you feel as "You Can't Catch Me" fades out—it's a feeling of relief. He made it; he got there; it's over. There's nothing left to say. The story is finished.

The fact that the freedom behind this great tale of the open road was a fantasy—a prison cell—tells us something about open road songs: in rock 'n' roll, they're fantasies, and mostly cheap fantasies at that. Sooner or later you're going to have to figure out where you want to go, which means you have to acknowledge that you start from somewhere, that you're not absolutely free. You'll carry the baggage of your place and time with you. You'll never get rid of it. You can go anywhere only if you come from nowhere, and no one comes from nowhere.

In that sense, there are no true open road songs in rock 'n' roll at all—no good ones, anyway. By definition, the open road has no fixed destination on it. It's the "Endless Highway," as the Band titled their worst song; "The road goes on forever," as Greg Allman drones in "Midnight Rider," setting the stage for the Allman Brothers' "Ramblin' Man" and everyone else's Sorry-babe-the-road-is-calling-me number. It's Lynyrd Skynyrd's "Free Bird" or a hundred songs like it—none of them with the terrific sense of fate in the Marshall Tucker Band's hard, lovely "Can't You See," where the singer pledges he'll run away from himself "'til the train run outta track." It will? That blues line is the stopper in the song. What will the singer do then? He doesn't know, but he knows he'll have to make up his mind.

You get the same feeling in Bruce Springsteen's "Thunder Road." If you're lucky enough to hear it in your car with some room in front of you, the chords demand more speed; each time Springsteen presses down on a word or a guitar string he presses your foot down on the gas. But even as he sings "These two lanes will take us anywhere," you know, somehow—*he's* saying it, somehow—that the singer and his girlfriend have nowhere to go, that they'll never even make it out of town. The reality of confinement in this affirmation of escape is what gives the song its tension, its power. It's no accident that Springsteen's next road song after "Thunder Road" was "Racing in the Street." It's a couple of years later, and the hero is older, tired. His girlfriend is even more tired than he is. The anywhere those two lanes would take them is reduced to how fast the hero can race a couple of city blocks on a bet, while his girlfriend stays home.

With these songs, we're talking about cars, about money, about ownership, about privacy—but that's not where the American open road song started. It started in 19th century ballads, and it took shape in early 20th century blues and country music. The open road song was the song of a man with no money, nowhere to go, and no home he'd accept. So he left—he took to the road, walking, or hopped a freight car. There was a thin edge of fun in some of the songs, but most were somber, finally doomed. The highway was Hank Williams' "Lost Highway," which can be a terrifying song.

The setting that these old songs called up was always social. The singer was leaving his community, his family, his familiar milieu of friendship, love, obligation, piety, work, and respect. You were born, you did what you were expected to do, and you died; it was, to some, a prison, and so these singers got out, or imagined that they did. Confinement put the element of fantasy into the enormous landscape. When the Mississippi blues singer Robert Johnson sang "Dust My Broom" in 1936, "Chicago" functioned in the lyric as a place as distant as "the Philippine Islands"; "California" was a place as mythical as "Ethiopia." In a manner that is both inspiring and pathetic, it wasn't experience that sparked so many blues and country road songs, it was wish. The road, in other words, was a utopia, and utopia means nowhere.

Before going back in Chuck Berry's and Bruce Springsteen's front seats, we have to stop and remember that when the likes of "Dust My Broom" were being written, the road meant vagrancy, the equivalent of people we see living on city streets today. In Berkeley, where I live, at a coffee bar where I go every morning, I've seen the same five or six homeless men for five or six years. They have no homes—no houses—but they have a place where they live: they don't move. It wasn't so in the twenties and thirties, when vagrancy was a crime; people without money and without hope of getting any lived on the road. It wasn't a romantic adventure. The hobo camps Robert Johnson and Jimmie Rodgers knew were a world of fear, starvation, alcoholism, theft, rape, and murder. Yet sometimes, it was also a world of familiarity, friendship, love, obligation, and respect.

That's the thin edge of affirmation you can hear in the road songs of the time—a very thin edge. In the twenties, as a young man, the future Supreme Court justice William O. Douglas hopped a freight from his home state of Washington (he'd been to college, he had the world in his grasp) and landed in a hobo jungle in Chicago. He squatted with the bums, ate their food, maybe he drank their Sterno, but they could tell he didn't have to be there, and they told him to leave—not because they thought he was slumming, but because they didn't wish their life on anyone.

We're all familiar with road movies: not Audrey Hepburn and Albert Finney in *Two for the Road,* but two men on the lam from this or that, lots of chase scenes. The geography of the country is always a good setup, good visuals, you can fill an hour and a half without trouble. The fact is, I can't remember the title of the last road movie I saw, the one with Robert de Niro and Charles Grodin, the one where all the money runs out but in the end the rich guy pulls a few hundred thousand out of his secret money belt and gives it to the poor guy, but that isn't what road movies were like in the thirties. As the road song was being invented, the road in road movies went nowhere, as in *The Grapes of Wrath,* or *Wild Boys of the Road,* a Warner Brothers film about scared teenagers looking for comradeship when they had no reason to expect anything but death. That's why the road songs of the prewar period always carry a sense of *going down*—not exactly of failure, because success is not even a possibility, but of disaster, or surrender, an acceptance of the fact that you can't do whatever it is you want to do, that you can't be whatever you want to be. You can't even begin to imagine what you'd really like to be, where you'd really like to go. On that road, with no money, no family, no one to meet, every place is just like the last place, and the last place is just like the place you'll be next.

The ruling modern American myths of the road are Jack Kerouac's novel *On the Road* and the movie *Easy Rider*—I confess I never read the book or saw the movie, because both seemed stupid every time anyone told me about what I was missing. I did see the Albert Brooks movie *Lost in America,* where a rich businessman, inspired by *Easy Rider* and with Kerouac sugarplums in the back of his mind, decides to go "on the road" to "discover America," selling his house and buying an $80,000 van—well, things get tough, so what the hell, he takes the job in New York he'd turned down. Just as there is no open road when there's a fixed destination, there's no open road when you can always go home—and these middle-class exercises in Columbus, Part 2, were always fixed. It doesn't matter that in the end of *Easy Rider* Peter Fonda and Dennis Hopper get killed by rednecks: they were slumming. Jack Kerouac went home, moved back in with his mother, and became a right-wing crank. The myth lives, he's still celebrated annually as the apostle of anarchy, the champion of the freedom to do everything and say everything. But freedom is tricky. On the road, slumming, he wrote in *On the Road* that, yes, under this great sky, I wished I was a Negro, full of life and instinct and . . . And, James Baldwin wrote in response, I wish I could have seen you read that stupid passage on the stage of the Apollo Theater in Harlem, and I wish I could have been there to see what happened next. They actually had a hook at the Apollo, but I think Baldwin had something more vehement in mind.

A song about the open road that doesn't contain these contradictions, these confusions, is a lie—and that's why, finally, listening to "Free Bird" is no more satisfying than listening to James Taylor sing "Fire and Rain," listening to him sing about how much he cares about himself, or for that matter listening to Patti Smith sing "People Have the Power," listening to her sing about how much she cares about everyone else. It's safe stuff—no thinking required, no need for a sound that carries doubt or a melody that insists on uncertainty. "Free Bird" is freedom, "Fire and Rain" is sensitivity, "People Have the Power" is noble—if it's that easy, we have nothing to worry about.

There are a lot of rock 'n' roll road songs: songs about a performer being on the road. This road is usually boring, tiresome, but most road songs just shove a little déjà vu or ennui into the fun and games. Bob Seger's "Turn the Page" doesn't, and that's why it's a real road song: there's no end to this road, he doesn't want to be on it, but he has no choice. He's no wild boy on the road, he's no tramp, he's got a job—but he's not his own boss. He doesn't even believe in what he's doing as he sings the song, but he doesn't know how to do anything else. So he writes a song about what he's not doing, and what he's not doing is what he wants to do: to leave his audience changed, make history, leave a mark.

Aside from "Night Moves," "Turn the Page" is Bob Seger's finest song. It's slow, like a bus going down Route 66, which is always slow no matter what the speedometer says—despite its famous, exciting song, Route 66 may be the most boring highway in the U.S.A. The way Seger sings his song, every word seems to question, to undercut, every other. The song is all weariness, a story about the need to get up for the next show, which doesn't turn out well enough to justify the effort. There are details: Seger wrote the song in the early '70s, when to go through many territories between San Francisco and New York with long hair was to get hate stares that hurt, that humiliated, that said, "I'm a law-abiding citizen, and if I weren't you'd already be dead." Seger captures it all in his tone: there's no self-pity in his voice, only shame. This is a road to nowhere—the tour will never end, because he will never be a success—whatever that means. Here's where a song vanquishes its own realism, because it didn't work out that way for Bob Seger. Today he lives in Hollywood, in a penthouse, he's a millionaire many times over, but the tune still rings so true you say "Good! You deserve it! Even if you never write another decent song!"

A few years after "Turn the Page," Seger made "Against the Wind," a lovely song, a huge hit, a sort of follow-up to "Turn the Page." Seger was insisting, explicitly, that no matter how big his bank account, he was still on the road to nowhere, running, escaping, and though in formal terms, in terms of elegance and style, "Against the Wind" was a better song, it was worthless. I love "Against the Wind"—all the romanticism of the middle-class road song is there, which is, at bottom, *Sorry, Mom, the road is calling me*—but I know the song is false, and I know it cost Seger nothing to write it. I know it cost the man who wrote "Turn the Page" everything he had to write that song, and that's why it hurts to listen to it. In "Turn the Page" Seger is William O. Douglas, lacking even someone to take the trouble to tell him to get lost, that he has something better to do with his life.

The open road, as an idea, as a vision of the geographical endlessness of America, makes a promise: it will be a place of surprise, where anything can happen. But as the song of the open road developed over the decades, the open road became the road you already knew, that you knew in your bones, the road you could drive without thinking, without looking. The road song became a cliché that a good songwriter or singer has to consciously *resist*—the writer has to trip you up. The songwriter has to make you say, as you drive the street you've driven all your life, barely conscious, Hey, wait a minute. What's that tree doing growing out of the middle of the road? *That* was never here before!

This is what happens in Bruce Springsteen's music—as the girl on the doorstep in "Thunder Road" turns into Caril Fugate, standing on her front porch in "Nebraska." You remember, or you've heard about it: in 1958, Charley Starkweather drove up to his girlfriend Caril's house in Lincoln; after killing her parents and her baby half-sister, they took off. They were on the road, where they could do anything they wanted to do, and then, as Springsteen has his Starkweather say, tracing the map with his finger, singing in a voice that so plainly comes from beyond the grave,

> Through the badlands
> Of Wyoming
> I killed every
> Thing in my path

Starkweather and Fugate lived out a road song; twenty-four years later, in 1982, Springsteen finally wrote it. But it was already there. They didn't know what they'd find, they didn't know how far they'd get, but they knew two lanes could take them anywhere. They got caught—but, as Starkweather wrote to his father, facing execution, "for the first time me and caril had more fun." Springsteen doesn't shrink from such facts in his song; he goes beyond them. He has Starkweather talking like a man who thinks: "They declared me / Unfit to live / Said into that great void / My soul'd be hurled"—well, *that's* a road song, the promised land, eternity. Promised land—what it really means is that you can do anything you want to do—it means that the feeling of movement you get from the open road makes you want to do things you'd never want to do if you weren't on it. Who hasn't felt this? Who hasn't driven flat out with a good song on the radio, and felt invulnerable? What songs were Charley Starkweather and Caril Fugate listening to, loving, saying yes, that's me, that's us, the car accelerating, the two of them knowing the feeling that nobody could touch them, you can't catch me—what songs did they care about, in 1958? A lot has been written about Starkweather and Fugate: there have been TV documentaries, the film *Badlands,* but no one has ever asked that question. Starkweather is dead; Fugate isn't talking.

The open road in modern American song finally has to come back to Chuck Berry's "Promised Land": absolute freedom containing absolute confinement, or vice versa. If the open road song means a song where there is no fixed destination—if we have to rule out "Route 66"—"It winds from Chicago to L.A.," no detours permitted—then there are two more songs worth mentioning. One is Springsteen's "Stolen Car," which came out in 1980, on *The River,* the same album that produced "Hungry Heart," his first top ten hit.

"Hungry Heart" was a lie like Bob Seger's "Against the Wind," though not a fraction as good a song. A guy with a family on his back walks out and never comes back: that's all you know about him, and all you need to know. "Stolen Car" is the other side of the song: no bouncy chorus, no singalong melody, but spare, quiet, pure death that won't come. The song is short, but its real time is described in lines from the blues: "Minutes seem like hours / Hours seem / Just like days."

The story in "Stolen Car" is the same: a husband leaves. But that's all that's the same. "I'm driving a stolen car / Down on Eldridge Avenue / Each night I wait to get caught / But I never do." The song is too slow for someone who says he's driving—you can feel him moving down the street, ten miles an hour, five miles an hour, passing one cop car after another, as he moves, *waiting*—but the cops don't care, it's as if he'd never been born. He drives in a circle. "She asked if I remembered the letters I wrote / When our love was young and bold / She said last night she read those letters / And they made her feel / One hundred years old." That seems young to him, now.

The detail that "Hungry Heart" slides over is present, the people are real. As the man drives round and round his town in a circle—maybe he's been doing it for weeks, years, maybe he's the guy people point to and say, "You know him, the guy who always passes here at 4 P.M., as if he's expecting someone to notice him"—but like a homeless man on the same corner for five or six years, no one acknowledges his presence. The story he's telling is like a story once told by the guitarist Roy Buchanan, who killed himself last month, a story about the tiny California town he grew up in: "Sometimes it gets so quiet here you feel like you could fire a gun inside yourself"—and, he didn't say, because he didn't think he had to, no one would hear it. The man singing "Hungry Heart" is out on the open road of "Free Bird" and "Ramblin' Man." The man in "Stolen Car" is in his house, his prison cell, fantasizing, like Chuck Berry as he wrote "Promised Land." The open road has become an image of itself—which, perhaps, is what it always was.

There's one more road I want to talk about—Highway 61, which you all know. When I first heard Bob Dylan's song "Highway 61 Revisited" in 1965, I was transfixed. Instantly, it was a mystical road to me, a place of visitations and visions. Two thousand miles away from where I lived, it was plainly a place where anything could happen; where, the song said, if you knew how to look, you could see that everything already had happened. Highway 61 was the center of the universe. Bob Dylan was saying that if you think hard enough, see clearly enough, you can understand that the whole of human history, every possible combination of story and syntax, is right before your eyes, that the open road is the road you know best. The song explodes.

Listening to "Highway 61 Revisited" today, it doesn't matter to me that I know the open road is a narrow, class-based, sexist, race-based theme in American music. Think about it: where are the great road songs from Otis Redding or Wilson Pickett—sorry, "Mustang Sally" isn't it. Aretha Franklin? The only open road song from Al Green is about wandering from bar to bar in search of God. For these singers, you can't leave home until you've settled your affairs at home, and if you leave, what you get is not freedom but exile. Can you imagine Prince singing a song about the open road? Just to ask the question exposes its triviality. What would the idea have to say to him? And "Little Red Corvette" is not about a car—although it might be the ultimate internalization of the image of the open road.

Bob Dylan came out of the tradition of the twenties and thirties blues and country singers. Getting out of here, down the highway, five hundred miles from my home, not knowing where you're going, leaving everything behind. No one, certainly no nice, middle-class, Jewish, ex-college student from Hibbing, Minnesota, ever carried it off so convincingly. When Dylan sang the old blues song "Highway 51" on his first album in 1962, he made it real. The way Bob Dylan sang on his early records, he could have been born in Virginia in the seventeen hundreds, turned up for the Gold Rush in California in 1849, headed up to Alaska in the 1890s, made it down to Mexico in 1910—the road was the story, it told the story, the story told you.

When I came to Minnesota in 1966, all I wanted to do was get behind the wheel and get out onto Highway 61—I was sure transcendence was waiting there at every entrance. I pulled onto the highway, and of course it was just like pulling onto any highway. Nothing happened. Still, the song lost none of its force, and it still hasn't. "OUT ON HIGHWAY 61," Dylan was shouting, and no singer could put more inflection, more wit and irony, into a shout than the Bob Dylan who was singing in the mid-'60s. Abraham gets the command to sacrifice his son—out on Highway 61, God says. A man has to escape, from what we aren't told—Highway 61 is the only route. Garbage has to be dumped (a thousand red, white, and blue shoestrings, you get the idea)—Highway 61 is the place. A drama of miscegenation, incest, and race is played out—where else? And, finally, the last verse. There's a gambler, he's got a great idea—let's put on the next world war. He meets a promoter—well, he's shocked, but he knows where.

That was 1965. In 1974, when Bob Dylan and the Band toured the country for the first time in eight years—and, in those days, adjusting for the inflation that has taken over pop culture, eight years was like a century—Bob Dylan and the Band played "Highway 61 Revisited," which they'd never played in the 1960s. The song was the only one that upset them, that confused them, that forced them to acknowledge, as musicians, that they didn't know where they were going.

Put some bleachers out in the sun, and watch the end of the world. Why not? The open road is full of surprises. Anything can happen. In this song, everything does happen, and so casually. Why not? You're out on the open road, no metaphor, now the thing itself. It's a fact, an experience you're reporting. Just as the open road has no fixed destination, it has no fixed beginning—Sorry-babe-the-road-is-calling-me won't do. What's so shocking about "Highway 61 Revisited" is that its two lanes, which will take you anywhere, describe a place where people actually live, where they have fantasized, where they are stuck.

The song could have been called "No Way Out." There is only one song I know with that title; "I got you, I got you—*and there's no way out*," run the lines that shoot out like the hands of a haunt. All the road movies, all the chase scenes, all the flights of all the free birds come to a halt in "Highway 61 Revisited." You can hear a man at the height of his commercial and mythic success announcing that freedom is confinement—anything can happen, he says, but only at home. He is fantasizing everything within the confines of the familiar; like Chuck Berry in "Promised Land," he is admitting that the journey is not up to him.

The open road song goes back too far—to a time when there were no roads, only wandering. Daniel Boone wanted elbow room, the country had it, he went looking for it. Other people followed in his footsteps; their tracks became roads. Eventually, those roads reached the end of the continent; then doubled back, and criss-crossed the continent with highways.

The strangest open road song is Canned Heat's "On the Road Again"—"We might even / Leave the U.S.A.," Al Wilson sings under the band's fatalistic burr. But this isn't real. "Highway 61 Revisited" is: what's real is the insistence that the open road is your own ground, your own street, where anything can happen.

I believe that it can, and I believe that looking for surprise wherever it is that you live is better than looking for it where you've never been and don't belong: where, in the end, like Kerouac and Peter Fonda, you're slumming. I remember reading "Howl" for the first time in 1970, where Allen Ginsberg says, "The cosmos vibrated at my feet in Kansas"—"In *Kansas?*" I said to a friend with disdain. "What sort of cosmos vibrates in *Kansas?*" But I now know Ginsberg should have named the town where it happened, and the street, as Bob Dylan named "Highway 61." "Look," my friend said, "anyone can get the cosmos to vibrate in Japan, or China, or India. But to get the cosmos to vibrate in Kansas—that means he was really *there.*"

Allen Ginsberg wasn't slumming. Unlike his friend Jack Kerouac, he wasn't looking for what he wasn't, he was trying to become what he wanted to be, what he already was. The cosmos still vibrates for me in "Highway 61 Revisited." Whenever I think of it, when I'm driving—you don't hear it on the radio anymore, but you can call it up out of memory—the number of the highway I'm on doesn't matter.

As a cliché, the open road is a dead end; starting from nowhere, that's where it leads. Yet as an enclosed metaphor—as with "Promised Land," a reach for freedom out of a prison cell, or Springsteen's "Stolen Car," which was never stolen, or "Highway 61 Revisited," just the local road—anything can happen, and you'll recognize it, understand it, weigh its costs.

This, I think, is what the notion of the open road is about today. When we can fly across a continent that once took months to cross in a few hours—and see nothing: it no longer matters how long it takes to drive it, walk it—the fastest time defines the place. But the idea of the open road in your own town, in your own mind, in your own cell is a contradiction in terms, and that is why the idea cannot be closed off. As a fact, the open road is now a fantasy; as a fantasy, we will never get off it.

Chuck Berry, "Promised Land" (Chess, 1964).

———. *The Autobiography.* New York: Harmony, 1987, 216–217.

Bob Seger, "Turn the Page," from *Back in '72* (Capitol, 1973).

———. & the Silver Bullet Band, "Turn the Page," from *Live Bullet* (Capitol, 1976).

Bruce Springsteen, "Thunder Road," from *Born to Run* (Columbia, 1975).

———. "Racing in the Street," from *Darkness on the Edge of Town* (Columbia, 1978).

———. "Nebraska," from *Nebraska* (Columbia, 1982).

———. "Stolen Car," from *The River* (Columbia, 1980).

Bob Dylan, "Highway 61 Revisited," from *Highway 61 Revisited* (Columbia, 1965).

———. "Highway 61 Revisited," on *Before the Flood* (Asylum, 1974).

Joyce Harris, "No Way Out" (Infinity/ Domino, 1961). Included on *The Domino Records Story* (Ace, 1998).

Joyce Harris, 1961.

REAL LIFE ROCK TOP 10
Village Voice
14 November 1989

9) Bob Dylan: *Oh Mercy* (Columbia). Producer's record, shapely and airless. Featuring Daniel Lanois as the director who likes to chalk marks on the floor and Bob Dylan as the actor who has to hit them.

Village Voice
7 April 1990

1) Pete Seeger: "A Hard Rain's A-Gonna Fall," from *We Shall Overcome—The Complete Carnegie Hall Concert, June 8, 1963* (Columbia). I first heard Bob Dylan's song as Seeger sang it, just days before the March on Washington, where Martin Luther King replaced Dylan's Armageddon with a vision of liberation. But both King and Dylan spoke the same apocalyptic language; it was never Seeger's. His version of the song seemed like a final statement twenty-seven years ago, in the flesh or on the original, one-LP Carnegie Hall recording, but today it's plain the moment made the music. Seeger notoriously lacked any blues feeling, and "Hard Rain" is proof he had none for country, not even for Child ballads; as Woody Guthrie or Big Bill Broonzy he was Henry Ward Beecher, Yankee abolitionist to his toenails. This performance documents one of the great musical events of the American postwar period, but the event is no longer musical; to hear how scary the song is, you have to listen to Bryan Ferry sing it.

Artforum
March 1991

1) Various radio stations: format violation (January 15). After so many years devoted to erasing the notion that in the mix of radio

sounds one might expect a subject, it was a shock, on this strange, suspended day, to find the medium talking to you, in a kind of celebration of dread. No matter what button you pushed you were faced with the same conversation, the pressure drop of Edwin Starr's "War," or Bruce Springsteen's cover of it, or Freda Payne's "Bring the Boys Home," Country Joe and the Fish's "I-Feel-Like-I'm-Fixin'-to-Die Rag," Gang of Four's "I Love a Man in a Uniform," Creedence Clearwater's "Bad Moon Rising," Peter Gabriel's "Here Comes the Flood," an unidentified woman's "Will Jesus Wash the Blood from Your Hands," the Beatles' "I Wanna Be Your Man" (relief, violation of the new format within the old format; it felt fabulous). Bob Dylan's "Masters of War" and Plastic Ono Band's "Give Peace a Chance" seemed thin and arch, too far above the mess of confused, violently random emotion, morally insulated (though not so much as Sean Lennon and Lenny Kravitz's Peace Choir smile-button video for their new version of the latter, so removed from fear its basic message might have been that Cyndi Lauper had found a way to get back on MTV). Cutting through the many voices, even those of songs only playing in your head—Elvis Costello's "(What's So Funny 'bout) Peace, Love and Understanding," maybe, or Metallica's "One," or Laurie Anderson's "O Superman" ("Your military arms," so softly, "your petrochemical arms")—was the Pogues' "And the Band Played Waltzing Matilda." It's a long, slow, unbearably bitter first-person account of a mutilated Australian soldier who came back from Gallipoli; Shane McGowan collapses seventy years to make the man explain why he wishes he hadn't come back, shame and wonderment dripping from every line. When the war began the next day HBO had *Top Gun* scheduled and the radio was back to normal.

REAL LIFE ROCK TOP 10
Artforum
Summer 1991

Bob Dylan's *the bootleg series volumes 1–3 [rare & unreleased] 1961–1991* (Columbia) contains a shadow version of his entire career, embedded within fifty-eight performances. They range from a tune taped in a Minnesota hotel room in 1961 to an outtake from the 1989 album *Oh Mercy;* along the way, three CDs collect concert recordings, alternate takes, rehearsals, and publishing demos, programmed roughly year by year. A lot of it is dross, a history of unfinished ideas or untranscended clichés, a book of footnotes. Other parts work as a series of interruptions—of the whole, of whatever you happen to be doing—moments that leap out of the chronology and stop it cold, turn it back on itself. Some seem to need no context, and to make none; some seem to fall together and make a story.

Beginning with the fourth track:

1) "No More Auction Block," from a show at the Gaslight Café in Greenwich Village, late 1962. The song was composed in antebellum times by escaped slaves who had reached the end of the Underground Railroad, in Nova Scotia. As "Many Thousands Gone," it was probably first taken down by Union soldiers in the middle of the Civil War, in 1862, precisely a century before Bob Dylan mixed it into an otherwise undistinguished set comprising mostly New York folk-scene commonplaces: "Barbara Allen," "Motherless Children," "The Cuckoo," and so on.

The number opens here with a few hurried but isolated guitar notes, which instantly promise a weight no other song sung this night will achieve. Throughout, the guitar sound suppresses melody; instead it produces a strange hum, maybe the sound history makes when for a few minutes it dissolves. Not the acting a singer might do, or impersonation, but a transforming empathy breaks down all distance, not of persona, or race, but of time.

When Dylan sings, "No more / Auction block / For me"—and then, much more slowly, "No more / No more"—there's no reference to any symbol. The auction block is a thing, you can touch it, people are standing on it: "Many thousands gone." The hesitations in the singing are so eloquent, so suggestive, that they generate images far beyond those of "the driver's lash" or "pint of salt" in the lyric. I thought of Tommie Smith and John Carlos, black members of the 1968 U.S. Olympic team, standing on the victory blocks in Mexico City after taking gold and bronze medals in the 200-meter dash, each with a bowed head and a raised fist in a black glove. A small protest against racism, a silent no to the assassination of Martin Luther King, and it caused a firestorm: the men were all but arrested, and then sent back. The picture of the two of them that was flashed around the world seemed to terrify the nation; listening now to a twenty-one-year-old Jewish folkie as he sang "No More Auction Block" six years before that event, you can feel the reason why. In the symbolic matrix their gestures made, Smith and Carlos suddenly knew, and everyone else just as suddenly understood, what they were standing on.

Skipping twelve tracks:

2) "Who Killed Davey Moore?" from a concert at Carnegie Hall, 26 October 1963. Fashionable bleeding-heart pieties about a boxer who died after a fight with Sugar Ramos—in 1971 Dylan himself would be present for the first Ali-Frazier match—but also songwriting as intricate and satisfying as Neil Sedaka and Howard Greenfield's "Calendar Girl." With referee, fans, manager, gambler, sportswriter, and opponent each stepping forward in ritual it-wasn't-me denial, the lyric is almost all dialogue; the filler between the lines ("It's hard to say, it's hard to tell") can seem like genius. You can sense a new energy here: the thrill of getting it right.

Skipping one track:

3) "Moonshiner," outtake from *The Times They Are A-Changin'*, 12 August 1963. "I hit all these notes," Dylan said in 1965, in reply to

an interviewer's mention of Caruso, "and I can hold my breath three times as long if I want to." This Appalachian ballad—five minutes of suspension, single notes from the singer's throat and harmonica held in the air as if to come down would be to bring death with them—must have been what he meant.

Skipping one track:

4) "The Times They Are A-Changin'," piano demo, 1963. Dylan presses hard, right through the song's instant clichés. Times are changing; events are physically present; the force of history is driving this performance, and you might feel like getting out of the way.

Skipping one track:

5) "Seven Curses," outtake from *The Times They Are A-Changin'*, 6 August 1963. A horse thief is caught, his daughter tries to buy his life, the judge demands a night with her instead, she pays, her father hangs anyway—seemingly set and written in feudal Britain (that's where the melody comes from), this is a simpler, more elemental version of "The Lonesome Death of Hattie Carroll," perhaps Dylan's greatest protest song, but with the position of the narrator impossible to place. The resentments and hopes of the preceding tunes of oppression and rebellion, "No More Auction Block," "Who Killed Davey Moore?" "Moonshiner," "The Times They Are A-Changin'," or others someone else might choose from *the bootleg series*, all are present in this performance, but with an ending: there is no such thing as change. That old melody turns out not to be the skeleton of the song, but its flesh; it carries its own, unspoken words, which are "there is nothing new under the sun."

Skipping six tracks:

6) "Sitting on a Barbed Wire Fence," outtake from *Highway 61 Revisited*, 15 June 1965. Chicago blues with a Howlin' Wolf laugh. All rhythmic hipness, especially the first time Dylan says, "Al*right*," investing the words with more meaning—more stealth, more mo-

tionless Brando-Dean menace—than any of the number's real lyrics.

Skipping one track:

7) "It Takes a Lot to Laugh, It Takes a Train to Cry," *Highway 61 Revisited* alternate, 15 June 1965. As if he'd waited one year too many to shake it up and put the Beatles in their place, a headlong rush. And after a minute or so, a heedless extremism, as with the last minute of the Velvet Underground's "Heroin"—which, when it was released in 1967, sounded too much like Bob Dylan was singing it.

Skipping one track:

8) "She's Your Lover Now," outtake from *Blonde on Blonde,* 21 January 1965. An unforgiving, barely coherent rant, but less about the unnamed she than the rumble that repeatedly builds up to an explosive convergence of guitar, piano, bass, drums, organ, words, and vocal—a convergence that never arrives in the same place twice. As for the piano, liner notes credit both Paul Griffin (who played on "Like a Rolling Stone" and Don McLean's "American Pie") and Richard Manuel, but it must be Dylan. No other pianist could follow his singing; no singer could follow this piano without playing it.

Skipping twenty-one tracks:

9) "Blind Willie McTell," outtake from *Infidels,* 5 May 1983. Between "No More Auction Block" and "She's Your Lover Now" there are barely three years; between "She's Your Lover Now" and this song, more than seventeen. Seventeen years of good work, bad work, endless comebacks, divorce, musical confusion, a terrible search for a subject producing hopeless songs about Legionnaires' disease and Catfish Hunter, a retreat into simple careerism, and, most shockingly, conversion to a particularly suburban version of fundamentalist Christianity and then reemergence as a Full Gospel preacher. "You came in like the wind," he sang to Jesus in 1981, on

"You Changed My Life," a *bootleg series* number: "Like Errol Flynn." And went out like him, too, maybe; with three explicitly born-again albums behind him, Dylan seemed to come plummeting back to the world with *Infidels,* and critics climbed on for another comeback, a return to form: "License to Kill," "Neighborhood Bully," and "Union Sundown" sounded like . . . protest songs!

Perhaps they were, but "Blind Willie McTell" is much more. It turns all the old, sainted rebels and victims parading across *Infidels* as across Dylan's whole songbook to dust, then blows them away. Led by Dylan on piano, with Mark Knopfler in his steps on guitar, this piece claims the story: the singer finds not evil in the world but that the world is evil. The whole world is an auction block; all are bidders, all are for sale: "Smell that sweet magnolia bloomin' / See the ghost of slavery ships."

The song is detailed, the language is secular, the mood is final. It's the last day before the Last Days, except for one thing, one weird, indelible non sequitur closing every verse, every scene of corruption and failure, like a gong: "Nobody can sing the blues / Like Blind Willie McTell." So the prophet answers his own prophecy with a mystery not even he can explain; the singer sums up and transcends his entire career; and the listener, still in the world, turns off the stereo, walks out of the house, and goes looking for an answer.

10) Blind Willie McTell, *Last Session* (Prestige, 1960). Willie McTell was born in Georgia in 1898 or 1901; he died there in 1959. He first recorded in 1927, and ended his life frequenting a lot behind the Blue Lantern Club in Atlanta, where couples parked to drink and have sex; McTell would walk from car to car, trying to find someone to pay him for a tune. In 1956 a record store owner convinced him to sit down before a tape recorder, and he talked and sang his life and times.

DYLAN AS HISTORIAN
San Francisco Focus
July 1991

Bob Dylan's "Blind Willie McTell" moves in a circle of images—tent meetings of itinerant holiness preachers, antebellum plantations, the slave driver's lash, chain gangs, painted women, drunken rakes—and it calls up many more. You might think of Ingmar Bergman's *The Seventh Seal:* the road traveled early in the film by Max von Sydow's thirteenth-century knight, back from the Crusades to find God on his own ground. Instead he finds plague and the Angel of Death, mad monks and a line of flagellants, torturers and a child witch on a huge pile of sticks and branches, ready to be burned. The witch is convinced of her own guilt, and the knight accepts her punishment, even though he understands that it is his homeland, his realm of knowable good and evil, that's guilty, even if it's a guilt that his world, with curses laid on it six hundred years later by a filmmaker, will never have to pay for. But to say all of this, to say any of it, to dive straight into the world made by "Blind Willie McTell," is to violate the sense of time that governs the tune—to go into it too fast.

The song dates to 1983. It was a discarded track from *Infidels,* Dylan's first commercial step away from the born-again Christianity—the shocking apostasy of one born and raised a Jew—that had ruled his previous three records: *Slow Train Coming, Saved,* and *Shot of Love,* increasingly lifeless works that had all but destroyed a subjective, critical voice with the imposition of a received religious ideology. "How does it feel," the Christian songs seemed to ask, "to be on your own, with no direction home, like a complete unknown," and the songs answered: it feels like perdition. Still, despite its title, *Infidels* seemed secular; it was full of what Dylan had once called finger-pointing songs. War was bad; capitalism was bad; *Infidels* was a hit. Critics approved and the radio played it. Listening now, you can imagine why "Blind Willie

McTell" was put aside. It would have dissolved the certainties and rancor of the rest of the music, upended it, given it the lie.

Still too fast. "Blind Willie McTell" begins slowly, with the hesitations, doubts, but finally irreducible willfulness that defines the blues. It is in fact just a rehearsal. An earlier, full-band recording had been dumped; this sounds like an attempt to find the song Dylan must have heard inside the song. He hits D flat on the piano, in the Dorian mode, which communicates like a minor key, somber and fearful. The mode takes him back to the old ballads and country blues that shaped his first music, and back to the invention of Christian music as it's known, to the beginnings of Gregorian chant and the piety loaded into it. There are following steps from guitarist Mark Knopfler, but this you barely register. What you feel is absence, as if Dylan is for some reason refusing to follow his first note with whatever notes it might imply. Then he hits E flat, then D flat again, and the song gets under way.

No knowledge of musical notation or musical history is needed to catch the drama in the moment. The message is clear because it is coded in more than a millennium of musical culture, high and low, vulgar and sanctified: *this is it*. This is the last word.

Who was, who is, Bob Dylan? In the rush of the mid-1960s, it was obvious that he was, and performed as, someone who was always a step ahead of the times. ("I'm only about twenty minutes ahead," Dylan told John Lennon at that time, "so I won't get far.") In late 1965, as the protest politics of the decade were hardening into slogans, he argued for the substitution of dada over directives on placards (" . . . cards with pictures of the Jack of Diamonds and the Ace of Spades on them. Pictures of mules, maybe words . . . 'camera,' 'microphone,' 'loose,' just words—names of some famous people"). In 1968 he countered the Beatles' super-psychedelic *Sgt. Pepper's Lonely Hearts Club Band* with music that sounded as if it could have been made by a particularly literary and reflective Hank Williams in 1953, just a year before Elvis Presley cut his first singles, assuming Hank Williams wasn't already dead. But today one has no idea who Bob Dylan is. He no longer beats the Jesus drum, but the echoes are there in any interview: his revulsion at wanton women and loose desire, his insistence on someone else's sin. Reading the conversations, the nice career talk suddenly shaken down, you can almost see the eyes that once seemed to freeze an epoch in an image go cult blank. But this is not what happens in "Blind Willie McTell."

It's long been obvious that Bob Dylan can no longer be listened to as any sort of avatar; "Blind Willie McTell" makes it clear that his greatest talent is for bringing home the past, giving it flesh— proving, as the ethnologist H. L. Goodall, Jr., puts it, that "in addition to the lives we lead we also live lives we don't lead." Art is made partly to reveal those lives—to take their lead. And this is what happens in "Blind Willie McTell."

Those slow first notes raise a sign: "Seen the arrow on the door-post / Saying, 'This land is condemned / All the way from New Orleans / To Jerusalem.'" "From New Or-lee-ans to Jer-u-sa-lem," Dylan sings, drawing out words until the line they trace seems to circle the globe. The sign sparks a quest, and the only active incident in the song: "I traveled through East Texas / Where many martyrs fell." Everything else in "Blind Willie McTell" is passive, a witnessing: I saw, I heard. Or an imperative, a demand that the listener witness, too: see, hear, *smell*. As one scene after another opens and fades, the senses are alive, but only to transgression. There's no hope of action or change; all is crime and failure, "power and greed." In Revelation, the last book of the New Testament, the Lamb of God opens the seven seals of a book, and terrible visions burst out with every loosening; it's only the seventh seal that can reveal God's final resolution. In "Blind Willie McTell" the first visions are present, brought down to the ground and into the everyday, but the seventh seal is missing. There is only a plainly irreligious affirmation, which can't be fitted to the forgiveness or even the knowledge of any sin. I've traveled, the singer says, I've seen, I've heard, but I know nothing. Or almost nothing. I know one thing: "I've traveled through East Texas / Where many martyrs fell / And no one can sing the blues like Blind Willie McTell."

As Dylan sang in 1983, Blind Willie McTell was twenty-four years dead. His work is found on archival albums; he sang sacred songs, dirty songs, story songs, rags, blues, whatever people on the street would pay him to play. Most famously he wrote and sang "Statesboro Blues," a 1971 hit for the Allman Brothers. He played twelve-string guitar—which he first heard played, he said, by Blind Lemon Jefferson, who indeed traveled out from his birthplace in East Texas, though he fell in Chicago, according to legend freezing to death on the street. McTell had a light, romancing tone, altogether inappropriate, one might think, for a Bob Dylan song about the resistance of Judgment Day; about the way, as the believer waits for it, Judgment Day recedes.

Perhaps the most entrancing challenge in "Blind Willie McTell" is to hear in its namesake's music what Bob Dylan heard. In Dylan's song, revelation struggles to rise out of every scene the singer witnesses, but only the profane refrain that ends each verse—"No one can sing the blues like . . ." "But nobody can . . ." and once, startlingly, "I KNOW NO ONE . . ."—can take the witness from one place to another. As revival tents are taken down, folded, stowed, and driven off to the next town, the singer hears only an owl, perhaps imagines it himself: "The stars above / The barren trees / Were its only audience." He sees a harlot and a dandy, "bootleg whiskey in his hand," and for that line Dylan's voice reaches a pitch of disgust and pain not matched for lines formally describing things far worse: "See them big plantations burning," he sings with almost laconic nostalgia, "Hear the cracking of the whip / Smell that sweet magnolia blooming / See the ghost of slavery ships."

But those lines need no more disgust. They take you into some immobile past-present that can never be escaped; they make you put your hands into a wound that will never be closed. One hundred and twenty-six years ago, in his Second Inaugural Address, Abraham Lincoln imagined that the Civil War might "continue . . . until every drop of blood drawn by the lash, shall be paid by another drawn by the sword." But the debt hasn't been paid, and "Blind Willie McTell"—most of all in the old and wearied tones of

Dylan's voice—says that it can't be. The singer can't pay it, and neither can Jesus. That the singer has found something Jesus can't pay for is in some way his truest testament of faith, his proof that he took his faith to its limits, and found those limits in the crimes of the world.

One phrase seems to hide silently behind all the lines of the song: "Vanity of vanities, all is vanity"—Ecclesiastes 1:2. It isn't surprising, then, that "Blind Willie McTell" quotes the same source, with "God is in his heaven," or that Dylan changes the words that follow in the Bible from "And thou upon the earth" to "And we all want what's his," turns the words sour, insisting that we have cut ourselves off from God, seeing in his face only our own greed and lust for power. But Ecclesiastes is more than a reference in "Blind Willie McTell"; "Blind Willie McTell" is a version.

Both the song and the lamentations of Ecclesiastes, "son of David, king in Jerusalem," are about the absolute rebuke the world offers every believer—every believer in anything, be it Yahweh, Jesus, earthly justice, money, love, or simply a world better than one finds when one looks, when for an instant one can glimpse not only power and greed but intimations of honor and right. "I have seen the task which God have given to the sons of men to be executed therewith," Ecclesiastes said. "He hath made everything beautiful in its time; also he hath set the world in their heart, yet so that man cannot find out the work that God hath done from the beginning even to the end . . . And he that increaseth knowledge increaseth sorrow." Perfection has been laid in the heart as a rebuke to all, because not even the best are worthy of it. Even the best of humankind sense perfection first and last as suffering, because it is given to them to feel "the evil work that has been done under the sun." "There is nothing new under the sun"; but for the witness every crime is new. Against this, Dylan offers only "Nobody can sing the blues / Like Blind Willie McTell"—but in the constant renewal of the way he sings the phrase, in the infinite reserves of spectral comradeship he seems to find in it, it is for as long as the song lasts, somehow enough.

Always slowly, with Dylan's piano keeping a tricky, unsettled time, sometimes flashing up and rattling as if the Mississippi bluesman Skip James is back from the dead to play the keys, "Blind Willie McTell" rides the bones of the melody of "St. James Infirmary," the standard perhaps done best—certainly most delicately, and most harrowingly—by Bobby Bland. It's a source Dylan acknowledges in his last verse, as the singer finds himself in "the St. James Hotel"—though perhaps there is a second source. Closer in spirit is an early blues recording by the obscure singer Richard "Rabbit" Brown, a man whose most notable brush with common knowledge came in 1962, when he was cited as a favorite in the notes to Bob Dylan's debut album. Set down in 1927, the year McTell too first recorded, though Brown never recorded again, Brown's song is called "James Alley Blues," after the New Orleans street where he grew up.

Dylan's recasting, or rereading, of "James Alley Blues," if that is what "Blind Willie McTell" is, breaks down any useful genealogy of what comes from what in American music. The melody is not similar; no analogue of either Brown's weird percussive guitar figures, or of his comedy ("'Cause I was born in the country, she thinks I'm easy to rule / She try to hitch me to her wagon, she want to drive me like a mule"), is present. But the spirit is: Brown's preternatural, bottomless strangeness, seemingly the voice of another world, right here, where you live, the prosaic dissolved by a faraway ominousness, a sense of the uncanny, an insistence on paradox and curse.

Dylan was singing "James Alley Blues" in 1961, when he taped a poor rendition in a friend's apartment; he may not have listened to it since, but no one who has heard "James Alley Blues" forgets it. As Brown must have with that song, the power of which has very little to do with words, Dylan saw all around his life with "Blind Willie McTell," and as one listens one is given entry to all the lives moving in the song; one is drawn in. The song is rich enough to pull a skeptic close even to Dylan's acceptance of Jesus Christ, for the song is undeniably the fruit of that event, and rich enough to lead one to the sort of sights the singer witnesses, with little more than the song itself as a companion—as, finally, the singer, a solitary, cut off or cut loose from God, has no more than his memories of an old blues singer.

Bob Dylan, "Blind Willie McTell," recorded 5 May 1983 with Mark Knopfler, guitar, included on *the bootleg series volumes 1–3 [rare & unreleased] 1961–1991* (Columbia, 1991).

————. "Blind Willie McTell," recorded April or May 1983, included on *The Genuine Bootleg Series* (bootleg). A pressing vocal, searching for effects, with doggedly conventional backing by a full band: a producer's record. Nice harmonica, though.

————. "Blind Willie McTell," recorded August 1997, included on augmented editions of *Time Out of Mind* (Columbia, 1997/1998). A live "field recording"—as if from the crowd. Stirring, harsh, and passionate, but never on an even keel. Half of a line—"Well, I've traveled"—might come out deep and confident, with the next half—"Through East Texas"—pleading, beaten down. With "Jerusalem," as it is on the Knopfler studio version, changing, as it almost always would on stage, into "New Jerusalem," which can be anywhere; see the 15 March 2009 post on rightwingbob.com.

————. "James Alley Blues," recorded by Tony Glover in Bonnie Beecher's apartment in Minneapolis, May 1961; see *The Minnesota Tapes, disc 1* (bootleg). Recorded 12 April 1963 in Eve and Mac MacKenzie's apartment in New York; see *I Was So Much Younger Then* (Dandelion bootleg).

Richard "Rabbit" Brown, "James Alley Blues" (Victor, 1927). Included on *Anthology of American Folk Music* (Folkways, 1952; Smithsonian Folkways, 1997), and, with Brown's four other recordings, on *The Greatest Songsters (1927–1929)* (Document, 1990). Other notable recordings of "James Alley Blues" include Jeff Tweedy, Roger McGuinn, and Jay Bennett on the anthology *The Harry Smith Connection* (Smithsonian Folkways, 1998), and David Johansen and the Harry Smiths, on *David Johansen and the Harry Smiths* (Chesky, 2000).

REAL LIFE ROCK TOP 10
Artforum
December 1991

6) Brian Morton: *The Dylanist* (HarperCollins). In this novel about a young woman growing up through the lives lived and surrendered by her parents, ex-Communists who still believe, what begins in mildness turns graceful and then quietly hard. Bob Dylan is Sally Burke's talisman—she's a Dylanist, a young union organizer tells her ("You're too hip to believe in anything but your own feelings") as she revels in a bootleg copy of the incomprehensible, never-released basement tapes tune "I'm Not There." "This," she says, "may be the greatest song ever written," and she's right, but she grows past Dylan, too, in her late twenties: "When she looked at his records, she could never find anything she wanted to hear." In the end who she is is more fated, a life made of a contradiction Dylan might have escaped, and even her parents, but she can't: "She would never find a home, as they had, in the effort to transfigure the world. But in her belief that she lived in a world that needed to be transfigured, she'd probably always be homeless."

Artforum
January 1993

1) Lou Reed: "Foot of Pride," at Columbia Celebrates the Music of Bob Dylan, Madison Square Garden, New York, October 6 (radio and pay-per-view TV broadcast). In Bob Dylan's original from 1983, this long and muscular song sounds vaguely influenced by Lou Reed. In Reed's version Judgment Day looms—backed by Booker T., Duck Dunn, and Steve Cropper, the MGs minus the late Al Jackson—and he leads the charge. All debts are paid before the first line closes; from then on the tune is Reed's more than it ever was Dylan's. All those years of clunky talk songs—here Reed grabs

a note, rings it, wrings it: like Jimi Hendrix said, he'll kiss the sky. For the first time in an era Reed *sings,* heading into each chorus like Jan Berry, if Jan Berry were to finally solve Dead Man's Curve—as written the chorus is so strong each one seems as if it has to be the last, because nothing could follow it. Lou, you've got to put this out.

Bob Dylan, "Foot of Pride," from *the bootleg series volumes 1–3 [rare & unreleased] 1961–1991* (Columbia, 1991).

Lou Reed, "Foot of Pride," included on Bob Dylan, *The 30th Anniversary Concert Celebration* (Columbia, 1993).

PART FOUR

New Land Sighted,
1993–1997

REAL LIFE ROCK TOP 10
Artforum
February 1993
with Roots and Branches
Image (San Francisco Examiner)
17 January 1993

2) Bob Dylan: *Good As I Been to You* (Columbia). Solo versions of very old ballads and prewar blues standards, released last November 3, which just happened to be Election Day: "other people's songs," but these songs are as much Dylan's as anyone else's, and he sings them with an authority equal to that he brought to Blind Lemon Jefferson's "See That My Grave Is Kept Clean" in 1962. The authority is not the same, though; there's more freedom in it now. "Little Maggie" is always played for its melody, but Dylan goes for its drama, the drama of a weak, scared man in love with an unfaithful drunk. The music is cut up, stretched, snapped back: each line opens with a stop, and at its end just fades out. The more historical numbers—the likes of "Canadee-I-O" and "Arthur McBride," 18th and 19th century tales of, to be blunt, imperialist class war and primitive capitalist exploitation—are personalized, Dylan inhabiting the first-person narratives as if he lived them twice. As the rough, tested character of the voice and the darkness of the melodies hidden in the guitar link the undatable past of "Blackjack Davey" to the early twentieth century of "Sittin' on Top of the World," you hear the old songs resolve themselves into a single story: variations on the tale of innocents setting out on long journeys into the unknown and the terrible betrayals they find when they reach their destinations. It's only after a time, when the melancholy and bitterness seem too great for one voice, that you hear them as history, as more than one man's plight. Finally all of the story is shared, the singer only its mouthpiece, medium for

private miseries within the great sweep of disaster; these songs are as much yours as anyone else's. As for the guile, the slyness, the pleasing cynicism of the singer's voice, he gets to keep that—leaving you to wonder why, at just this moment in time, one person who has in stray moments seen as clearly as Natty Bumppo is offering *this* story as a version of American legacy.

Artforum
March 1993

3) Michael Jackson, Aretha Franklin, Kenny Rogers, Bill Clinton, James Ingram, Stevie Wonder, Tony Bennett, Dionne Warwick, Michael Bolton, children's choruses, adult choruses, and more: "We Are the World," at An American Reunion, preinaugural celebration on the Mall of America (HBO, January 17). It may be that behind the great good feeling of this performance lies only propaganda, a fabulous sheen of communitarian self-recognition disguising a new administration that means to leave the country as it found it. But as John F. Kennedy proved against his own will, or for that matter his thoughtlessness, false promises can be taken up by those who only hear the tune and don't care about the copyright. If, as Robert Ray of the Vulgar Boatmen puts it, "The *sound* of Dylan's voice changed more people's ideas about the world than his political message did," then the same can be said of the sound of Kennedy's voice and his political acts. The same may prove true of Bill Clinton's demeanor and his political instinct—as opposed to his personal instinct—to pull back at the first sign of trouble. The double-hearted rule but do not govern; desires have been loosed in the air and there's no telling where they'll light.

8) Bob Dylan: "Chimes of Freedom," An American Reunion (HBO). Yeah, he sounded terrible, but did you see that jacket? Purple, with black appliqué? On a night when Michael Jackson looked less human than the Mickey Mouse men in Disneyland commercials, Dylan looked like he'd just bought a Nashville haberdashery.

WHAT'S NEW IN THE CEMETERY

Interview

December 1993

For the second time in less than a year Bob Dylan has released an unproduced, acoustic-guitar-and-harmonica collection of traditional blues and folk songs. A small voice from the sidelines—even the wilderness—in its own way *World Gone Wrong* traces the renunciations of fame, responsibility, and authority Nirvana tries and fails to enact on *In Utero,* their response to the stardom that followed *Nevermind,* which they now see as a failure because too many people liked it. Dylan won't have that problem.

Good As I Been to You, his 1992 Election Day special, was his most striking music since . . . since the last time he cut the ground out from under your feet, whenever that was. It stopped at number fifty-one on the *Billboard* charts and didn't make the *Village Voice* national critics poll chart at all. Their loss: Dylan came to life in the old clothes of "Canadee-I-O," "Hard Times," "Frankie & Albert." As he does on *World Gone Wrong,* he came to life as a singer; then as now, as a singer, in the hesitations and elisions of his phrasing, he came to life as a philosopher.

On both records, the music is all about values: what counts and what doesn't, what lasts, what shouldn't. The performance is modest, but anything but casual. Finding the fatalism—the foreboding—in the old, twisting melodies of "Love Henry" and "Jack-a-Roe" on *World Gone Wrong,* as he did with "Jim Jones" and "Blackjack Davey" on *Good As I Been to You,* as a philosopher Dylan comes to life as a gatekeeper, a guardian. "I have to think of all this as traditional music," he said in 1966. "Traditional music is based on hexagrams. It comes about from legends, Bibles, plagues, and it revolves around vegetables and death. All these songs about roses growing out of people's brains and lovers who are really geese and swans that turn into angels—they're not going to die. It's all those paranoid people who think that someone's going to come and take away their toilet paper—*they're* going to die. Songs like 'Which Side Are You On?' and 'I Loves You Porgy'—they're not folk-music songs; they're political songs. They're *already* dead."

This is precisely the talk Dylan talks in the liner notes to *World Gone Wrong,* where he says where the songs come from and explains what they're about. "What attracts me to the song," he writes of "Lone Pilgrim" (the only composition on *World Gone Wrong* credited to a named author, as opposed to a blues or folk progenitor), "is how the lunacy of trying to fool the self is set aside at some given point, salvation & the needs of mankind are prominent & hegemony takes a breathing spell." Regarding "Stack A Lee," archetypal tale of the black outlaw and perhaps the best-known number on *World Gone Wrong,* "what does the song say exactly? it says no man gains immortality thru public acclaim. truth is shadowy . . . the songs says that a man's hat is his crown. futurologists would insist it's a matter of taste." On Blind Willie McTell's "Broke Down Engine": "it's about variations of human longing—the low hum in meters & syllables. It's about dupes of commerce & politics colliding on tracks . . . it's about Ambiguity, the fortunes of the privileged elite, flood control—watching the red dawn and not bothering to dress."

Dylan is claiming absolute and infinite meaning for the songs he's now singing. The trick is to hear in these songs even a fraction of what he hears: whether it's McTell's 1931 "Broke Down Engine" or Dylan's, Dylan's "Blood in My Eyes" or the Mississippi Sheiks' 1931 original, William Brown's 1942 "Ragged & Dirty" or the same story half a century later. Dylan hears a whole world, a complete millenarian opera, in every tune; the person who buys the record, takes it home, puts it on, is going to hear a small-time drama into which intimations of the uncanny ("roses growing out of people's brains and lovers who are really geese") occasionally, inexplicably intrude. "Ragged & Dirty," a coy blues, is first of all carnal; the way Dylan slides into the piece, barely speeding the pace, is a one-verse seduction. "Stack a Lee" is quickstep true crime, graveyard humor: "Taken him to the cemetery, they failed to bring him back." But Dylan hears as much mysticism in these prosaic American jokes a he does politics in the almost Arthurian "Love Henry," where a parrot bears witness against its murdering mistress.

In "Blood in My Eyes," a man is trying to get something going with a prostitute. You can feel the age in his voice; you can also feel he's probably impotent. The weariness, the fear of humiliation, the despair in the man's voice as he describes the situation, the way he hopes he'll get what he wants, is almost too painful. Only that moment when he drifts out of the dollars and cents of the day's concern and into the chorus, "Got blood in my eyes / For you," is sweet. It's so sweet, summoning desire so plainly outside the realm of fulfillment, that the man's loneliness overwhelms anything else he might bring into his life. And yet, when you're as lonely as Dylan has now made this man—as he's made you, if he has—you'll bring anything into your life in an attempt to turn that isolation into something else: an adventure in a foreign land, a lover' murder, God's kiss.

As *World Gone Wrong* plays, with Dylan's scratchy, seemingly disdainful voice quickly growing full, earnest, urgent, then delicate, all these things do turn into one another. The music traces a circle from which there need be no exit. And if you pick up Dylan's cues and hunt down the originals of the songs as he names them—the Mississippi Sheiks' "I've Got Blood in My Eyes for You," on their *Complete Recordings, Vol. 3,* or Doc Watson's "Lone Pilgrim," on *The Watson Family*—you might find a certain discontinuity between the old versions and the new. The older singers often sound eager to please; Dylan doesn't. He sounds as if his goal has been to get all the way into these old songs, and then get lost.

Bob Dylan, on traditional music, to Nat Hentoff, "The Playboy Interview" (*Playboy,* March 1966), collected in *Bob Dylan: The Essential Interviews,* edited by Jonathan Cott. New York: Wenner Books, 2006, 98.

———. *Good As I Been to You* (Columbia, 1992).

———. *World Gone Wrong* (Columbia, 1993).

Mississippi Sheiks, "I've Got Blood in My Eyes for You" (1931), on *Complete Recorded Works in Chronological Order (1931–1934)* (Document, 1991).

————. "The World Is Going Wrong" (1931), on *Complete Recorded Works in Chronological Order, Volume 3 (15 December 1930 to 24 October 1931)* (Document, 1994).

Doc Watson, with Gaither Carlton, fiddle, "The Lone Pilgrim," from *The Watson Family* (Folkways, 1963; Smithsonian Folkways, 1993); field recordings by Ralph Rinzler, Eugene W. Earle, Archie Green, and Peter Siegel, 1961–1963.

THE 30TH ANNIVERSARY CONCERT CELEBRATION
Spin
November 1993

Aren't tribute albums terrible? You don't look to mass extravaganza concerts—one performer after another trooping across the stage in fealty, in memoriam, or bowing to some good cause—for real music. The artifacts such shows leave behind are just souvenirs. Even legendary Woodstock produced only a single number that's still talked about: Jimi Hendrix's version of "The Star-Spangled Banner."

When more than a score of stars gathered at Madison Square Garden on October 16, 1992, to play Bob Dylan's songs and thank him for supposedly putting a head on the body of popular music, it would have made sense to expect what a lot of people in fact came up with: respectful or wrong-headed or decently satisfying turns by the likes of Eric Clapton, John Mellencamp, or the Clancy Brothers. There was no reason to expect that time and again people would step forward and, reaching for something in a Bob Dylan song that had never quite been heard before, leave their own careers in the dust. It was a shock then and it's a shock now.

Sound recordings are just a map here; the video is the territory. You can hear what Johnny Winter—backed, as were most others this night, by the in-your-dreams combination of Booker T. and the MG's plus drummers Jim Keltner and Anton Fig—does with "Highway 61 Revisited," but you can't exactly hear his performance. The sound is sardonic, hip, fast, uproarious, just as it was on *Second Winter,* the great lost album of 1970. But it's Winter's appearance that takes the song to other worlds. On he comes, impossibly thin, his arms covered with tattoos of hex signs and hoodoo symbols, tattoos that look more like Kaposi's sarcoma than anything else, tattoos that seem to have eaten away most of the flesh he's apparently intending to play his guitar with.

This is a pagan apparition. The song is going to begin with "God said to Abraham, kill me a son," but Winter looks as if he's already been sacrificed. Then out of nowhere, as Winter stands still, his mouth closed, you hear weird hollers and moans. It's as if the song knows what's coming, and it's flinching, as if the song doesn't want to play itself. But Winter is only tuning up. He does play the song, rams through it, leaves.

Lou Reed doesn't look as if he's going to do anything odd. Dressed in black—big surprise—wearing glasses, he comes out to sing "Foot of Pride," a tune Dylan left off his 1983 album *Infidels.* It's a very long song: two or three hundred verses, about half a million words. Reed reads them off a music stand. This is quite distracting, until Reed hits the first chorus; then the biblical curse of the number hits home. The huge roar that emanates from the stage doesn't seem tied to any individual; the vertigo the sound creates is a vertigo of rising, not falling. Reed could be standing on his head for all you'd care. He's created a monster and now he's riding it.

Heard today on *John Wesley Harding,* "All Along the Watchtower" is cool, sinister, a tale about Limbo told in Purgatory: "Two riders were approaching / The wind began to howl," it ends, leaving the listener in a wasteland. Jimi Hendrix's version of the windstorm has been riding the airwaves for twenty-five years; it's probably the strongest cover of a Dylan song anyone has ever produced.

Neil Young steps out to prove the song has just begun to speak. As Jon Landau once said about Wilson Pickett's "In the Midnight Hour" (perhaps Booker T. and the MG's finest hour), this is not a classic, it's an epic. "All along the watchtower," Young says to himself over and over after he's all but ended the performance, as if the power of the image has only just now hit him. It's all modern war, what he's done with the song; go back and listen to Dylan's version after Young's and it's like hearing Robert Johnson for the first time, a man who died before you were born in a place you'll never get to, exiled by the fact that you'll never catch up with him.

All of this, though, is merely art. What happens with Roger McGuinn and "Mr. Tambourine Man" is something else: real life, the transformation of a man before your very eyes. Looking fine and just a bit uncertain, at once proud and shy, he strides out to join Tom Petty and the Heartbreakers. He launches into the song with the same ringing Rickenbacker twelve-string notes and the same fey, Beach Boys voice that made "Mr. Tambourine Man" a number one hit in 1965. But then he passes the single verse the Byrds used all those years ago, and lunges for the next one.

He is a different person. The voice is thicker; the body rocks back and forth. There's a vehemence here that no one has ever heard from this man before. On the "and" in "And if you hear vague traces," his voice lifts into the air and the word fragments, then floats down as pieces of some Scots ballad, but McGuinn is already making the hard consonants of the next words into weapons, a blacksmith with "skkkkkipping reels of rhyme"—the performance is cruel, heedless, vengeance for a crime that isn't named.

That act—that vengeance—is something one can hear all through Dylan's own work, even if he once said that all of his songs end with "Good luck." You can hear that, too: there are a lot of good smiles in the show, but the best of them comes almost at the end, when Dylan and everyone else have finished "Knockin' on Heaven's Door." The taciturn mask Dylan has worn for the last numbers of the concert breaks; just barely, he seems to acknowledge that he might have heard something he hadn't heard before, even in his head.

Bob Dylan, *The 30th Anniversary Concert Celebration* (Columbia, 1993).

———. *The 30th Anniversary Concert Celebration* (Columbia Music Video, 1993). The only currently available DVD release is the botched *Tribute to Dylan* (101 Distribution, 2009), which omits the Winter, Reed, and Young performances in favor of John Mellencamp's hideous "Like a Rolling Stone," Nanci Griffith and Carolyn Hester's simpering "Boots of Spanish Leather," and the oleaginous Richie Havens on "Just Like a Woman."

REAL LIFE ROCK TOP 10
Artforum
Summer 1993

7) Bob Dylan: on Guns N' Roses' cover of his "Knockin' on Heaven's Door," in *The Telegraph* 42 (Summer 1992). "Guns N' Roses is OK, Slash is OK, but there's something about their version of the song that reminds me of the movie *Invasion of the Body Snatchers*. I always wonder who's been transformed into some sort of clone, and who's stayed true to himself. And I never seem to have an answer."

"LIKE A ROLLING STONE" AFTER TWENTY-NINE YEARS

Interview

April 1994

Reading *Sweet Nothings,* an anthology of poems about rock 'n' roll, I kept thinking about two scenes in Jim Sheridan's film *In the Name of the Father.*

In the first, the Daniel Day-Lewis character, Belfast petty thief Gerry Conlon, is running from cops and soldiers. As he hurls himself down tiny back alleys, the huge, devouring chords of Jimi Hendrix's "Voodoo Chile (Slight Return)" pursue him like a dinosaur in *King Kong.* Hendrix's guitar might be a mouth with fire coming out of it: his noise, his presence, is all over Conlon, breathing down his back, laughing in his face, tangling his feet. The chase is thrilling, scary, and the music is just right—it adds so much. Still, that's all it does. The use of the Hendrix tune is a simple, conventional orchestration, the sort of thing you can find anywhere. You've seen it before—for that matter, you've seen it in a sequence in *The Harder They Come* that uses the Maytals' "Pressure Drop" on Jimmy Cliff in exactly the same way.

The second scene comes shortly after. Gerry Conlon's stolid, responsible father has decided to get his good-for-nothing son out of Belfast and send him to London. Conlon's all for it: London 1974, still full of hippies and squats, drugs and free love. He can't wait. He boards a ferry out of Belfast, meets a friend. They get beers, drop a coin in the jukebox, and as the first notes of Bob Dylan's "Like a Rolling Stone" come on, they hoist their glasses in a toast to their new adventures, to life in a new land.

Here the music does not orchestrate what the actors are doing; they are orchestrating the music. The chase could exist without Hendrix; this scene could not exist without the sound on the screen. All Sheridan uses is the fanfare that opens the song—that thick, swirling, implacable rising tide of hope and fate, promise and threat. It's just Dylan's band taking its first steps into the song, as Conlon and his friend are taking their first steps; the music is faded off the soundtrack as Dylan begins to sing. The event is so strong, so emotionally lucid, it can take you right out of the story, freezing this perfect moment, this tiny utopia that, over the next hour or so, will be torn to pieces.

There are orchestrations like Sheridan's use of Hendrix among the poems in *Sweet Nothings: An Anthology of Rock and Roll in American Poetry,* as with Yusef Komunyakaa's "Hanoi Hannah," where a North Vietnamese DJ harangues GIs waiting for the next attack: "Her knife-edge song cuts / deep as a sniper's bullet." When the music is simply used, you get the equivalent of bad rock criticism. It's the instances when poets make room for a song to make its own claim in a new way that make the book sing, that let it remind you of your own experiences as a listener trying to hold on to one of those instantaneous musical utopias as it vanished. The example I keep coming back to is David Rivard's "Cures."

A man and a woman are sitting in their living room, after a fight that's left them disgusted, ashamed, and bored. They've turned the stereo up to drown their own thoughts; for some reason they're playing "Mystery Train," "where Elvis relates some dark to himself." The scene doesn't develop; it just sits there, like the two people, "each doubt a little larger / than desire."

The poem goes on, but Rivard has closed it with those lines; as the couple listen to this song of movement, of danger, fear, lust, chase, and triumph, it freezes them, shows the depth of their paralysis. Each doubt a little larger than desire, and the longer each doubt lasts, the larger it grows.

This wasn't why Elvis Presley and Sam Phillips made "Mystery Train" in Memphis in 1955, presumably: to expose people to their own weakness. But people don't use songs according to anyone's intent. In their truest moments, songs, like microbes—without intent, without brains—use people. The real mystery Rivard's poem opens up has nothing to do with a train; it's about the way songs enter people's lives, the way people can't get them out. Their beauty, at its most intense, might be more a rebuke than a promise. In "Cures," it's the passion and the heedlessness of the music that define how much the two people listening have given up, how much they've given up on each other, on themselves—just as the jukebox notes in *In the Name of the Father,* lifting like a curtain in a theater, define the preciousness of everything that's about to be taken away.

Sweet Nothings—An Anthology of Rock and Roll in American Poetry, ed. Jim Elledge. Bloomington, IN: Indiana University Press, 1994.

DOCK BOGGS
Interview
August 1994

We were driving in the coal country around Norton, an Appalachian mountain town in the southwestern tip of Virginia. The radio was all country music, and it was a bland-out. Travis Tritt, Tanya Tucker, Randy Travis, a crew of smaller names, all of them milking the current formulas of rural references, I'm-your-pal vocals, bright old-timey fiddles, and happy endings—to the point where a snatch of Billy Ray Cyrus's "Words by Heart" on a convenience-store cassette player stood out as an explosion of passion and pain, of reality.

Maybe it was a bad-luck day: There was no Garth Brooks beyond "American Honky-Tonk Bar Association," a pastiche of everyone else's songs. No George Jones, just Alan Jackson's smarmy "Don't Rock the Jukebox." "I wanna hear some *Jones,*" Jackson sang, his phrasing bleeding phoniness, just like everything else he does. The fiddles were the worst. After a bit they were semiotics, not music; nothing was communicated but the sign of traditionalism. It wasn't simply that one fiddle part sounded like another, doing the same job in every tune. It was as if there were no people actually playing, as if each part came from the vault in Nashville where they keep the all-purpose fiddle sample.

Iris DeMent would have made a difference. Her prim, neat, and fearful warbles, catching the fear of one's own desires along with the fear of the world at large, would have told a different story. But DeMent's music, in which traditionalism is only the doorway to a house you have to build yourself, wasn't just not on the radio, it was nowhere near it. I gave up and stuck a Dock Boggs tape into the car's cassette player.

Dock Boggs was born in Norton in 1898. For most of his life he worked the coal mines in the area, save for time as a moonshiner in the twenties and as a professional musician between 1927 and 1929, when he recorded twelve sides for the Brunswick and Lonesome Ace labels. In 1963, at the height of the folk-music revival, he was rediscovered, right where he'd always been, and went on to record three albums and play festivals and concerts around the country. He died in Norton in 1971. He was—as Thomas Hart Benton had recognized from the first, pressing Boggs's version of the old ballad "Pretty Polly" on anyone who would listen to it— possessed of one of the most distinctive and uncanny voices the American language has ever produced.

On Bogg's 1927 "Country Blues" a wastrel faces ordinary, everyday doom. The banjo, which as a white man Boggs plays like a blues guitar, presses a queer sort of fatalism: fate in a hurry. At the close ("When I am dead and buried / My pale face turned to the sun"—Boggs worms you into the old, common lines until you sense the strange racial transformation they hint at), the singing rises and falls, jumps and plummets in a rush, as if to say, Get it over with. In 1963 Boggs recorded "Oh Death"—"Won't you spare me over for another year?"—and you can imagine Death's reply, which would have been as fitting thirty-six years before, when Boggs was first singing the song. Sure thing, man, what the hell. It's no skin off my back. You sound like you're already dead.

In Norton, I bought a copy of *The Coalfield Progress* ("A progressive newspaper serving our mountain area since 1911," the year after Boggs went to work at the mines). It announced a talk at the nearby Clinch Valley College by Sharyn McCrumb, who started out writing comic mysteries set in England and now writes serious, complex, spooky mysteries set in the Appalachian highlands, each taking its title from one of the murder ballads that cling to the mountains like the haze that turns them blue. In the first of these books, *If Ever I Return, Pretty Peggy-O,* a folk singer is talking to a sheriff about one of the mountain songs, which turns out to be a clue to a present-day murder: "'It dates from around 1700, but people have always changed the words to fit whatever local crime is current . . . There's always a new dead girl to sing about . . . Isn't it funny how in the American versions they never say why he kills her,' she mused. 'She's pregnant, of course . . . So many songs about that. "Omie Wise." "Poor Ellen Smith" . . . So many murdered girls. All pregnant, all trusting.'"

"Pretty Polly" might be McCrumb's basic text; in its English versions Polly's pregnancy is part of the story. In Boggs's version there is, true to McCrumb's thesis, no mention of it—but there is something more, or anyway something else. The evil in his singing, a psychotic momentum that goes beyond any plain need to do-this-to-achieve-that, overwhelms the song's musicological history. As Boggs sings, the event is happening now.

Driving around Norton, you can see remnants of a cultural war, between the likes of Boggs's "Country Blues" or "Pretty Polly" and the churches and signs that dot the landscape: JESUS IS THE ANSWER, JESUS IS WAITING, or, in a hollow, a modest, somehow implacable white frame house, with three stark crosses underneath the words HOUSE OF PRAYER. Against the lust for escape, for a private exile, that you can hear in Boggs's songs, the church stood as the nihilist singer's final temptation, beckoning him to surrender his anger, his refusal, his freedom.

And the war goes on today. Around Norton there wasn't a song on the radio that would have dreamed of writing a check God couldn't cash. Except one: high up in the mountains, pressing the radio scanner, Genesis's "Jesus He Knows Me" turned up. On a pop station and in its video, it's a cheap British traveler's satire of televangelists. Surrounded by the piety, reassurance, and easy answers of this year's country music heroes, though, it was a shock, and as mean as anything in "Country Blues." "My God," said the person in the car with me. "What's that doing here?"

Dock Boggs, *Country Blues* (Revenant, 1997). Recordings 1927–1929. Notes by Jon Pankake and GM.

————. *His Folkways Years 1963–1968* (Smithsonian Folkways, 1998). Notes by Mike Seeger and Barry O'Connell.

Sharyn McCrumb, *If Ever I Return, Pretty Peggy-O* (1990). New York: Ballantine, 1991, 161.

REAL LIFE ROCK TOP 10
Artforum
February 1995

5) James Marsh, director: *Highway 61 Revisited* (Arena Television/BBC, 1993). Part of a "Tales of Rock 'n' Roll" series unseen in the U.S., this one-hour documentary—"a biography of a song"—focuses on one of Bob Dylan's most inspired recordings and the spine-of-the-nation highway it's named for. There are surprises everywhere: "Blind Willie McTell" orchestrates footage of Civil Rights demonstrations, a specter dissolving the words of heroes; a rough, clanking piano demo of "Like a Rolling Stone" turns into the anthem everyone knows as New York City looms up; Dylan's old buddy John Bucklen shares high-school tapes. Bucklen and then Bobby Zimmerman talk into the tape recorder self-consciously, as if they know someday we'll be listening, judging whether Dylan's claim that Johnny Cash is more boring than dirt, or that Elvis was a thief, sounds convincing (not completely).

Dylan hammers out Little Richard's "Jenny, Jenny" on the piano. He sings "Little Richard"—the song. His song. Good, too.

"Little Richard," "Jenny, Jenny," and twelve other segments from tapes made by John Bucklen in Hibbing, Minnesota, in 1958, can be found on *I Was So Much Younger Then* (Dandelion bootleg).

BOB DYLAN AFTER THE 1994 CONGRESSIONAL ELECTIONS
Interview
March 1995

I admit I was thrown by the Bob Dylan segment of the NBC News end-of-the-year wrap-up on December 30. After the requisite Bobbits-Simpson-Tonya-Michael Jackson montage, and a similar smear of Rwanda-Bosnia-Haiti-Chechnya, there was bright footage of Newt Gingrich and other Republican stalwarts celebrating their November triumph—with Dylan's 1964 recording of "The Times They Are A-Changin'" ("Come senators, congressmen / Please heed the call / Don't stand in the doorway / Don't block up the hall") churning in the background. Despite Gingrich's immediate post-election identification of the seemingly long-gone counterculture as the enemy within, the song sounded so weirdly apt it was as if the Republicans had now seized all rights to it, along with the rest of the country. The NBC orchestration conflated all too perfectly with the new TV commercial Taco Bell began running about the same time, announcing a burrito-plus-CD promotion (you can pick up a sampler with General Public, Cracker, the Spin Doctors: "Some call it 'alternative' or 'new rock'—we just call it 'dinner music'") with footage of happy young people turning Taco Bells into dance clubs. "Don't let it pass you by," said the announcer in a friendly voice, which suddenly, unexpectedly, turned hard: "Because there is . . . no alternative."

On the other hand, it didn't bother me at all that Dylan recently licensed "The Times They Are A-Changin'"—certainly his most famous, catchphrase-ready protest song, in the mid-'60s an inescapable affirmation of the power of the Civil Rights movement to redeem the nation's soul—to be used in a TV commercial for the Coopers & Lybrand accounting firm. I think all songs should go up on this block. As with the NBC collage (perhaps inspired by Tim Robbins's *Bob Roberts,* in which a right-wing folk singer–politician storms the heights with "The Times They Are A-Changin' Back"), it's a way of finding out if songs that carry people with them, songs that seem tied to a particular time and place, can survive a radical recontextualization, or if that recontextualization dissolves them.

The Beatles'' "Revolution" may never recover from its Nike commercial, but Coopers & Lybrand didn't lay a glove on "The Times They Are A-Changin." When Bob Dylan sang it on his MTV *Unplugged* show—taped November 17 and 18, little more than a week after the election, it aired December 14—the song was full of new life. With a lively band around him, Dylan took the lead on acoustic guitar, making more of the song's inner melodies, its hidden rhythms, than ever before. He slowed the song down, as if to give it a chance, as it played, to catch up with the history that should have superseded it. Or was the feeling that the song was still lying in wait, readying its ambush? As he did throughout the performance, Dylan focused certain lines, words, syllables, looking around behind impenetrable, blacker-than-black dark glasses, as if to ask, "Are you listening, are you hearing, who are you, why are you here?" By design, the people in the front rows of the audience were young enough to go from this show to the taping of the Taco Bell commercial without skipping a beat, but breaking such a rhythm seemed to be what Dylan was doing this night with "The Times They Are A-Changin."

Emphasis was the motor of the performance, with quietly stinging notes highlighting especially "If your time to you is worth savin'," a phrase that in 1964 felt certain and today can feel desperate and bereft—a deeper challenge. Or perhaps those words, sung and played as they were, were now a challenge for the first time. If Dylan was celebrating anything as he retrieved the number, it was menace. The song took on a new face, and you could hear it as if it were putting a new face on a new time. Instead of Great Day Coming, the feeling was, Look Out. What opened out of the song was not the future, but a void. It was all done lightly, with a delight in music for its own sake: Dylan's gestures and expressions, like his black-and-white polka-dot shirt, radiated pleasure. You didn't have to hear anything I heard, but what you couldn't hear, I think, was an old warhorse of a greatest hit trotted out to meet the expectations of the crowd.

"The Times They Are A-Changin'" was not in any way the highlight of the show; that was probably "With God on Our Side." With its circa 1952 grade-school-textbook summary of American wars, it brought the same displacement the Cranberries play with in "Zombie." There the word 1916 leaps out, because today the mention of an event that took place before the song's intended audience was born is a bizarre use of pop language. It's a strange violation of an art form that sells narcissism more effectively than anything else.

Seven years ago, describing Bob Dylan at the Live Aid concert in 1985, Jim Miller, in perhaps the best short overview of Dylan's career, spoke of a "waxen effigy," a "lifeless pop icon," "a mummy." The guy onstage in 1994 was more like a detective, investigating his own songs—and then treating them as clues, following them wherever they led, to the real mystery, the real crime. For the last year or so, the most ubiquitous appearance of this pop icon in pop media has been that moment in Counting Crows' "Mr. Jones" when Adam Duritz shouts, "I want to be Bob Dylan!"—and it's a wonderful non sequitur. What in the world does it mean? As it seemingly was not a few years ago, what it means to be Bob Dylan is now an open question; as Taco Bell insists, there may be fewer open questions around these days than one might have thought.

Bob Dylan, *MTV Unplugged* (Columbia, 1995).

NEW LAND SIGHTED, 1993–1997   185

Cranberries, "Zombie," on *No Need to Argue* (Island, 1994).

Jim Miller, "Bob Dylan," *Witness* 2-3 (Summer/Fall 1988). Collected in an abridged version in *The Dylan Companion*, ed. Elizabeth Thomson and David Gutman. New York: Delta, 1990.

Counting Crows, "Mr. Jones," from *August and Everything After* (DGC, 1993).

————. "Mr. Jones," album and acoustic versions (DGC, 1994).

FREE SPEECH AND FALSE SPEECH
Threepenny Review
Summer 1995*

I was very struck by something Ruth said in the last sentence or the second-to-last sentence of her talk, where she said, "I ask you to consider." That little transitional phrase went off like a small bomb in my head. That very same phrase, "I ask you to consider," was used near the climax of Mario Savio's famous speech on the steps of Sproul Plaza, thirty years ago yesterday, just before the big sit-in that led to the culmination of the Free Speech Movement. It has always seemed to me to epitomize the kind of talk that went on during the Free Speech Movement, the respect for the audience or the listeners or the crowd or whatever you want to call it, the complete lack of any assumption of any sort of superiority of special knowledge, the complete absence of any sense that the speaker was

---

*A few weeks after the elections of 1994, when the Republican Party turned out the Democratic majorities in both houses of Congress, a thirtieth anniversary celebration of the Free Speech Movement was held on the campus of the University of California at Berkeley. This extemporaneous talk, transcribed from a recording, was given at a December 3 panel called "The Current Political Situation"; the other speakers were Ringo Hallinan, Jack Weinberg, Ruth Rosen, and Mario Savio, who spoke last. *Threepenny Review* published Savio's talk, also unwritten, and mine, both without any rewriting into essay form.

there to convey to you, the listener, something he or she knew and you didn't—it was a kind of civility, but it was also the antithesis of rant, the antithesis of a speaker coming forward with certainty, knowing exactly what the truth was and expecting you only to accept it. So I just wanted to point that out. It was a moment I liked.

Now, I'm a critic. I write about music, mostly, I write about novels, movies. And I was asked here to provide a kind of cultural perspective on the current political situation. And maybe I do have a perspective, but I don't know how current it is. I know that I can't begin to imagine the kind of crunch that the country is going to be experiencing in the next few years. I've done a very good job in the last few weeks of not imagining it. A friend of mine sent me a top ten of songs to play following the election, and I amended it, and my number one was an old Rod Stewart song called "I've Been Drinking." I've been playing that song over and over in my head.

One thing that I thought of before coming here—obviously, the notion of free speech comes to mind first of all. A novelist named Steve Erickson has a comment on free speech that I like. He says, "The Constitution grants no one free speech. It assumes you already have it. It simply says the government can't take it away." I think this is something that is misunderstood by some of our more famous performance artists, who seem to equate free speech with receiving a government grant, and seem to equate losing a government grant or being denied one with being deprived of free speech. I don't think that's how it works. I think free speech comes in some ways when you least expect it. And what's most important in the domain of free speech is being able to recognize it.

Now, I simply want to present today two examples of speech, one free and one unfree. Simply as things that you might keep in mind, because over the next few years we're all going to be faced with many, many examples of false speech, of speech that pretends to be speech of resistance, speech of refusal, speech of an alternative to what we read about in the papers and see on the news every night, but won't be. And we're going to come across, less frequently, explosions, some of them stillborn, some of them silent, where real free speech takes place.

In order to present these two examples, I'm going to go back to exactly this weekend, not thirty years ago, but twenty-nine years ago. Twenty-nine years ago in Berkeley, two events took place that I've thought about over and over and over again. The first was a celebration of the Free Speech Movement, and of course the date that was chosen, then as now, was the date of the big sit-in. And the strangest tableau was presented on the steps of Sproul Hall. There were figures dressed in enormous papier-mâché masks. I mean, not just masks of head size, but at least if my memory isn't playing tricks on me, masks that seemed to go up three or four feet high. They looked like Mr. Peanut figures, almost as if they could barely walk with these enormous things on their shoulders. Well, I seem to remember that there were several figures, but one of these figures was Mario Savio, who was not in Berkeley that year, and the other was Clark Kerr, the president of the university. And so there was a kind of jousting match between the Savio figure and the hapless Kerr figure. It was a Punch and Judy show, really; the Savio figure vanquished the Kerr figure, who slunk off in shame and despair. This was funny, it was enjoyable, and it was a nice substitute, since the man that people really wanted to hear was not there.

But then something happened that turned the entire event into something ugly. The person inside the Savio contraption had a speech that he wanted to give against something the university had done that was an attempt to roll back free speech gains that had been made the previous year. And so he delivered his speech from inside the Savio construction. It was possibly the most alienated, the most self-canceling, the least human, the most robotic attempt at political speech I've ever seen. I think we're going to see a lot of people dressing up in other people's clothes, so to speak, denouncing, criticizing, claiming to offer alternatives, but doing so in a way that really only takes away an individual sense of self, of confidence, of power, of imagination.

That very same weekend, maybe it was the night of that day, I don't remember, but it was December 3rd of 1965, Bob Dylan came to town. He played at the Berkeley Community Theatre with a band that in later years became known as the Band, in those days was called the Hawks—it was a blues bar-band that he'd picked up. That was a time when there was a tremendous dispute raging around the country, a dispute that now seems utterly quaint, over whether Bob Dylan had sold out by abandoning folk music and acoustic guitar to play commercial, corrupt rock 'n' roll and make a loud noise. It was very refreshing, it was very interesting, that at Berkeley Community Theatre that night, nobody cared. People sat fidgeting while Bob Dylan went through the acoustic/folk music part of his show, like "Get on with it, get on with it, we want to see the band."

Well, Bob Dylan was performing at that time—as a friend of mine named Howard Hampton has said—as if he had a knack for turning a casual aside into a condemnation of an entire social order. There was a way in which he could turn a phrase, and suddenly you'd turn your head, as if someone had just slapped you in the back of the neck. There was a way in which he would move an arm out, and you'd feel as if you'd been grabbed, as if someone was questioning all the basic assumptions by which you lived your life. Well, that night, he put on a show that without any question was the most powerful performance I've ever seen by anyone.

My friend Howard Hampton said something else about Bob Dylan's music of that time. This is a young person—he's in his early thirties, he wasn't around, he's not thinking nostalgically. He's simply basing a critique of the present on what he hears in the past. And he made this argument: to say that what a person like Bob Dylan is doing today, when he attempts to continue his career for its own sake, is the equivalent of what he did years ago when he gave his career a meaning for being in the first place—to say that the two things are equivalent is obscene. And, he said, it's also to continue the politics of the last twenty years, which have taken shape in order to suppress the kind of demands that Bob Dylan's speech once made.

A cultural war is inaugurated and a counterattack is made. Part of that counterattack is to simply destroy the notion that a performance can be more than a performance, that entertainment can be more than entertainment. What were the demands that Bob Dylan, that night in Berkeley in 1965, was making on society?

They were, in the simplest and most complex terms, a demand to be free. He performed a drama of freedom. And it was scary, it was confusing. It was a drama where first you clear away the debris—everything that gets in the way. You're sighting what it might mean to be your true self in a mirror that doesn't exist. Once that is cleared away, there is the joy of discovering that, "My God, I can say out loud what I think." Then there is the fear, once having made that discovery, of actually having the burden of putting it to use, and actually standing up, as someone did a few minutes ago, in the middle of a crowd, and saying something that maybe people don't want to hear. Whether or not you agree with what's being said, it's always worth remembering what kind of nerve it takes to do that. It takes a lot of nerve.

What happened that night, and what I've always remembered, is the complete antithesis of the kind of reduction, the kind of shrinking of speech, that I saw in Sproul Plaza on the first anniversary of the Free Speech Movement. It was a kind of expansion that I learned about during the Free Speech Movement here, and that I've seen happen in politics since, occasionally. It's a shout. It's a gesture. It turns into a conversation. It begins, perhaps, when a refusal meets a rule. And right off the bat, you're questioning whether you should take one step forward or one step back. Very quickly, you're questioning, "Well, whether or not I want to do this, do I have the right to do it?" Very quickly, you're questioning whether the institution that presumes to give you that right or to withhold it has any legitimacy whatsoever. Very quickly after that, you're questioning the nature of institutions themselves. And by the end—and this could be five minutes later, five days, five months—you're questioning the meaning of life. That's what happened in that performance. That's what happened in some speeches I've heard over the years, speeches that in one way or another, if not in these words, contain that "I ask you to consider"—

think now, don't take what I'm saying on trust, see if it makes sense.

I think the great cultural challenge of the next few years is going to be to distinguish between speech that's true and speech that's false. And there's going to be a lot more of the latter than the former, coming from all of us here in this room. Thank you.

Mario Savio's speech in Sproul Plaza on 2 December 1964 was collected on *Is Freedom Academic? A documentary of the Free Speech Movement at the University of California at Berkeley* (KPFA-Pacifica Radio LP, 1965). Film of his speech can be found on YouTube.

Bob Dylan, *Long Distance Operator* (Wanted Man bootleg, recorded at Berkeley Community Theatre, 4 December 1965).

REAL LIFE ROCK TOP 10
Artforum
January 1997

5) Bob Dylan: "All Along the Watchtower," from *The Concert for the Rock & Roll Hall of Fame* (Columbia). For the moment, the only licensed, recorded proof that what Dylan and his shocker of a combo (Winston Watson, Tony Garnier, Bucky Baxter, John Jackson) were doing on stage in 1995 was more than an illusion—and, until *Having a Rave Up with Bob Dylan* appears, the only proof that reinventing yourself in your fifties as a lead guitarist embracing syncopation as the source of all values is a brilliant idea.

Concert for the Rock & Roll Hall of Fame (Columbia, 1996). With one song each from Aretha Franklin, James Brown, Johnny Cash, Booker T. and the MGs, Sam Moore, and Bob Dylan, and three by Melissa Etheridge.

ALL THIS USELESS BEAUTY

at the conference Stars Don't Stand Still in the Sky,
Dia Center for the Arts, New York
14 February 1997

When Elvis Costello released "All This Useless Beauty," the title song of a 1996 album, the song went right past me; I didn't really hear it. It wasn't until Costello put the song out again, in a live version recorded in May 1996 in San Francisco, when he was doing dates around the country accompanied only by his pianist, and then in a version he'd asked the band Lush to record, that I began to hear the song. I was hearing it—particularly the Lush version—as the theme song for this conference, or the anti-theme song, because in this song, stars do stand still. Time stops.

According to "All This Useless Beauty," time stopped a long time ago. The song begins in a museum. "This is song about a woman who's walking in a beautiful gallery," Costello said when he introduced the tune in San Francisco. "It's full of pictures of classical antiquity and idealized beauty. And she looks across to her less than fabulous, late-twentieth-century lover—and she goes, *'awwwwwwww* . . .'" Costello sings the song full-throated, the words all rounded. I ran into him a few years ago in the Accademia in Florence, both of us staring at Michelangelo's *David*—I can't hear Costello sing this song, this song about all this useless beauty piled up in a museum, without picturing a setting that perfect, that marbled. In the San Francisco performance, Costello even sang a chorus in Italian. You can imagine for yourself what paintings the woman in Costello's gallery might be looking at—I see Pre-Raphaelite scenes, like Edward Burne-Jones's *The Golden Stairs,* with a score of Hellenic maidens descending toward some unseen ceremony, or his *Tree of Forgiveness,* with Eve clutching Adam and Adam desperately trying to escape from her embrace. Whatever she's looking at, in the sing-songy, up-and-down-the-stairs cadence of "All This Useless Beauty," the woman in the gallery,

Costello says, "imagines how she might have lived / Back when legends and history collide."

It's a striking line, thrown away in the song—Costello just lets it drift out of the story he's barely telling—and the sense of wonder in the words, their air of loss and surrender, matches Bob Dylan's comment on Peter Guralnick's biography of Elvis Presley. "Elvis as he walks the path between heaven and nature," Dylan said, and those words are as good as any he's written in two decades. Those words are so balanced and explosive, they turn the next phrases of his comment, which aren't bad, into clichés: "in an America that was wide open, when anything was possible."

This is what stopped time for me. "When legends and history collide"—when what we believe to be hard facts and what we know to be dimly remembered and barely describable ideals go to war against each other, or turn into each other. I think that's what both Costello and Dylan were talking about: history turning into legend, heaven turning into nature, and vice versa, in a painting of an ancient forest or in a new kind of rhythm and blues record. But the promise is there only to be taken away. In this song, the time "when legends and history collide," that time of all-things-are-possible, is gone, if it ever was. "Those days are recalled on the gallery wall," the song goes on, but the woman in the gallery was born too late; she missed those days. She missed it—that's exactly the word Costello uses, like some sixties person telling someone about Woodstock: "I was there, man, and you *missed* it." Now all the woman has is a fact, a hard fact in the form of a soft fact, her lump of a boyfriend slumped at her side with all the ideals of the past, recalled on the gallery wall, mocking her. She waits, the singer says, "for passion or humor to strike," and nothing happens. It's the collision of history and legend that produced all the useless beauty on the walls—useless because now its only function is to remind whoever looks at it of what's no longer possible, if you're stupid enough to believe that anything, or rather everything, ever was.

Costello sings the song as a tragedy; a beautiful tragedy. The irony burns off as he goes on. The words—taken slowly, carefully, as if something in them, or him, might break—seem to shake in his throat on the choruses. It's painful. But as Lush do the song, it's altogether different. Over twenty years, a whole constellation of singer's singers has taken up residence in Elvis Costello's voice: Billie Holiday, Frank Sinatra, Tony Bennett, George Jones, Patsy Cline, Sarah Vaughan, Dusty Springfield, Lotte Lenya. When he goes all the way into a piece of music, it lifts off the ground; in a way, it goes onto that gallery wall, keeping good company with whatever useless beauty is up there at any given time. As a punk he was always a classicist; he was always too much of a record fan to let the world get in the way of his sound for too long. Lush is a much younger band, guitarists and singers Emma Anderson and Miki Berenyi leading a two-man rhythm section. As a pop group they've always looked for the punk in their sound, and on "All This Useless Beauty" they find it. There's no pose, no preening; what they do with the song makes Costello seem like an actor. Like that moment in the Human League's "Don't You Want Me" when the female singer comes in, earnestly telling her story in a manner so naturalistic it's an effort to remind yourself that she's singing, what Lush create with "All This Useless Beauty" is the shock of realism.

The tragic cast Costello gives his tales of the worlds that are now behind us is what lifts, what beautifies, his own tale of useless beauty. But Anderson and Berenyi take their places in the gallery like schoolgirls who've been brought in on a class trip—for the tenth time. They're too smart for their own good; that's what's always getting them into trouble on trips like this. They're suspicious, they think too much, they're always asking questions—and so what was tragic in Costello's original is now just bitter. These girls, acting out the most ordinary, everyday events in this gallery, in this song, know what the idealized images of classical antiquity are for. Where Costello feels loss, Anderson and Berenyi see a trick—and their thin, reedy, determined voices, pressing through the tune word by word, nothing at all taken for granted, say one thing. This stuff on the wall—do you think you can fool us with that?

A whole world of mystification opens up out of this performance, a whole social con, or a quick, frozen glimpse of an entire
society organized around a con: the con of beauty, of idealism, the
con that takes reality away from the life you actually live, every
day, and delivers that reality up onto a wall, or into the past, for
safekeeping. There are moments of coyness in Costello's performance; there are none in Lush's. Listen to it more than a few times,
and in its restraint, in the way it makes ordinary talk out of
Costello's elegant chorus, Lush's "All This Useless Beauty" is as
hard, as resistant, as betrayed, as anything in "Anarchy in the
U.K." And yet—when you're sitting around in the limbo of the
present age, dreaming of times when history and legend collided,
waiting for passion or humor to strike, one of the things you're
waiting for is a song like this, a song that can change shape and
color according to who's singing it, a song that is like a magic
lamp. Here Costello's version and Lush's collide; so do the past and
the present, the tragic and the commonplace, beauty as a useless
rebuke and beauty as an inevitable by-product of pressing down
on some stray incident or emotion until it seems it can contain the
whole of life. Pressing down—that's all the woman in the gallery
does with her disappointment over her boyfriend. With Emma Anderson's disembodied contralto floating behind Miki Berenyi's
gritty, plain-speech lead on the choruses—with idealism, a legend
of how things should or could be, floating behind hard facts, behind anyone's history of everyday defeats, insults, humiliations—
the song is beautiful, and only as useless as your life. It reveals
itself as a song about what's missing when a mythic dimension is
missing from life—and what's missing is a sense of being part of a
story that's bigger than yourself, a story that can take you out of
yourself, outside of the pettiness and repetition of your life, cir-
cumscribed as it might be by whatever city or town you live in.
The fact is, though, that history and legends collide every day, and
we are always part of the collision.

    Take what is perhaps the greatest and most pervasive of pop
myths: the myth of rock 'n' roll as an agent of social or even revo-

lutionary transformation. As a myth, it isn't necessarily a false story; whether it is or not, it's a big story, a story with room in it—room for whoever might want to join the story, for whatever beginning or ending one might want to try to put on it. This story has been told many times; depending upon intellectual or political fashion, it's told with aggression or apology, hubris or embarrassment, presented as a testament of ambition or naïveté. Recently I came across the most extreme version of the story I've ever seen, in *Twigs of Folly,* an unpublished memoir by the historian Robert Cantwell, the author of *When We Were Good,* by a long ways the finest book on the folk revival of the fifties and sixties.

One of Cantwell's themes is that of a type he names "the remorseless spitting American." He takes the phrase from Fanny Trollope, an Englishwoman who, visiting the new United States in 1830, found herself amazed by the new democratic race she encountered: rounders and roughnecks and women who lived in dugout houses—people who, in Cantwell's description, had made the leap from "all men are created equal" to "all men are equal."

For Cantwell, these are the true carriers of the myth of equality, down through the decades: not all of them lawbreakers, exactly, but surely a line of moral outlaws, all of them in some final manner uncivilizable. They scorn all differences and all claims to superiority. They are the romantic, the resentful, the heroic or petty outsider Americans who are nevertheless the only real Americans: the likes of Abraham Lincoln and Lyndon Johnson, John Henry and Calamity Jane, Mike Fink and Jack Johnson, Railroad Bill and Georgia O'Keeffe, Louise Brooks and Marlon Brando, James Dean and Charles Starkweather. To give the story over to Cantwell:

> If the remorseless spitting American was a flatboatman, or a trapper, or a trader in the 1830s, a blackface minstrel in the 1850s, a Confederate soldier in the 1860s, a western cowboy in the 1880s, a dustbowl refugee in the 1930s, by the 1950s he was singing from every jukebox, radio and record player. Who were Buddy Holly, Jerry Lee Lewis, the Everly Brothers, Carl Perkins, Eddie Cochran,

Gene Vincent, Sanford Clark, George Hamilton IV, Roy Orbison, if not remorseless spitting Americans all—and, ahead of the rest, Elvis Presley.

The remorseless spitting American had become a rockabilly star.

The opening strains of "Heartbreak Hotel," which catapulted Presley's regional popularity into a national hysteria, opened a fissure in the massive mile-thick wall of postwar regimentation, standardization, bureaucratization, and commercialization in American society and let come rushing through the rift a cataract from the immense waters of sheer human pain and frustration that had been building up for ten decades behind it. Elvis was desirable and desiring, the son of a Mississippi sharecropper with no advantages but the God-given erotic force that put the gleam on his 300-horsepower hair, the Hellenic beauty in his face, the genital nerve-endings in his voice, and on his lips a sneer with more naked repudiating ideological power than the writings of Thomas Paine, Karl Marx, and V. I. Lenin put together.

Put aside any thoughts as to whether this myth, this story Cantwell is telling, or retelling, is true or false, a vision of wholeness or self-congratulatory generational nonsense. Whatever it is, as Cantwell sets it out it is a story you can become part of, that can situate you precisely where history and legends collide, can help you perhaps to define your own place in your society, or outside of it. It's a complex story—a tale of debts coming due, of the return of the repressed, and much more—but first and last it is a myth of liberation, of legacy and starting over all mixed up together.

You could join this myth by listening to or arguing about or buying records, or writing about them, or making them yourself, by aligning yourself for or against this or that pop figure—or by publicly professing allegiance to one such figure while, secretly, maybe in a secret you half kept from yourself, you identified most completely with a figure mocked and scorned by everyone you knew. This was a myth you could join by allowing it to judge the choices you made: between friends, between going to college or not going, studying one thing and not another, between clothes you put on and those you set aside—the choice you made, finally, over just what country, as you defined it, you would be part of, if you were to be part of any country at all.

That is the myth—as it was acted out in the sixties, as it was received, transmitted, invented, codified, and then taken as a natural fact, as a legend of history. In the fifties—Cantwell's epoch of the flood, of the moment when everything changed—this legend wasn't present. There were only events. The myth had to wait—and by the time it arrived, history had faded, faded enough for legend to replace it. At bottom, that's how you join a myth: you join in constructing it, in making it up. Making up this particular myth was to one degree or another the sense or nonsense left to the world by the first generation of pop critics. Does that make the myth untrue? Of course not. It makes it a strange and shadowing standard, a standard all pop music that followed upon the first emergence of rock 'n' roll has to be seen to match, or overtake, or overthrow, or render irrelevant. It's a standard every record, every performance, has to somehow affirm or dismiss.

But as Robert Cantwell writes out the myth of pop transformation—which he is writing plainly, if dramatically, as history—it isn't hard to see another, poisonous myth inside of it, as if biding its time: a germ in the idea of equality, the idea carried forth so ferociously by Cantwell's "remorseless spitting Americans," a germ that will emerge not to prove that all might exist on the same plane of legitimacy, but to prove that some people are true and some are false. This is the myth of authenticity, or purity—the idea that true art, or true culture, exists outside of base motives, outside even of individual desires, particular egos, any form of selfishness, let alone mendacity, let alone greed.

This myth rewrites the past no less than the myth of pop transformation does, and more violently. The earliest version of this myth wasn't written out; it wasn't a story. It was acted out. It was the payola investigations of the late fifties and early sixties, all based in the certainty, on the part of certain guardians of public morals, and politicians who knew a good horse to ride when they saw one, that the only reason the airwaves were filled with garbage, and that decent children, white children, had turned away from decent culture, was that someone was paying disc jockeys and radio programmers to play what otherwise would have never been heard. Rock 'n' roll, in other words, was itself payola: a conspiracy. It was a trick, not unlike that other fifties media panic, subliminal advertising. Both the fear of payola and of subliminal advertising were versions of the ruling postwar myth: that, like the seedpods in *Invasion of the Body Snatchers,* communism could creep up on America as it slept. At the time, in the late fifties, this argument—which was itself vaguely subliminal—didn't even feel like a metaphor. Communist messages secreted in Hollywood movies, like fluoride in public water systems, would weaken the will or the brain tissue itself, until Americans were powerless to resist. And on the radio, among teenagers everywhere, it had already happened.

A different version of this argument came out of the folk revival that took shape concurrently with the payola scandals. Pop music, rock 'n' roll, was looked on as trash, the adolescent indulgence society at large said it was, something to grow out of. It was corrupt; it was all about money; it was all about imitation, every emotion a counterfeit, every gesture second hand. But with folk music—old mountain music, blues, reels, and story songs, ballads that sounded as if they'd been written by the wind—the soul of the singer came forth. Stripped of artifice in its performance, the music produced a naked person, who could not lie. The speech that issued from his or her mouth was pure; the motive, simply to tell the truth, was pure; and the performance made both singer and listener into authentic beings, who could not lie because they could not want to.

A present-day version of this version of the anti-pop myth comes in Fred Goodman's book *The Mansion on the Hill,* which is about the presumed clash between art and commerce in contemporary pop music. Here, because pop music takes shape in a capitalist milieu, it is inevitably deformed and corrupted, until nether performer nor listener can tell truth from lie. Never mind that pop music might as usefully be seen as a form of capitalism as any kind of art—Goodman's version of this myth is bizarre.

Before Bob Dylan stepped from folk music into rock 'n' roll in 1965, Goodman argues, rock 'n' roll was a "pop-trivial medium." There was no such thing as expressiveness, no authenticity of any kind, just—stuff. Money and sounds. But rather than a resurgent, Beatle-driven rock 'n' roll wiping folk music off the cultural map— as the story is usually told—Goldman argues that, through Dylan's agency, folk music completely rewrote the rules of pop music. Now, according to Goldman, suddenly the rock 'n' roll sound could carry truth: true messages and true beings. You could be true to yourself; to thine own self you had to be true. But because there was still money to be made off of rock 'n' roll—in fact, more than ever before—a fatal contradiction loomed.

Despite suggestions in *The Mansion on the Hill* that the man who once wrote "Money doesn't talk it swears" kind of likes to, you know, swear, Bob Dylan, Goodman said on the radio in an interview about his book, had stayed pure. "There's Dylan and there's everybody else," he said. "He's never made a record to make money; he's never made a record to make a hit." Any good pop fan should answer that with, "Well, if Bob Dylan never made a record to get a hit, he ought to. It's not too late." But the whole concept, the whole division, is ludicrous—and still this myth of purity, this folk virus, is today as defining a pop myth as any other. In England it defined punk from the beginning, with some fans all but demanding written proof of working-class status before a record might be considered, and it defines much of the punk milieu today. That's the world Adam Duritz of Counting Crows came out of in Berkeley—and it was this myth, far more than anything that can be reduced to an attitude, that drove him out of town. He wrote his songs, formed this band and then that one, made his music, followed where it led, and his music hit—and then, in a drama that Kurt Cobain acted out within himself, arguing with himself, raining abuse on himself, Duritz found himself a pariah on the streets of his own city, cursed by those onetime friends and fellow scenesters who did not cross the street or turn their backs and walk the other way when they saw him coming. Not only had he betrayed the purity of the Berkeley punk community, he was like a disease: get too close, and you could catch it. It all goes back, so seamlessly, to the folkies who decided that the Kingston Trio, never mind that they'd somehow gotten the word out first, were phonies.

Given the weight of pop myths—and there are scores of them, intertwined and overlapping stories about what it means to be a performer or part of an audience, about love and death, identity and facelessness, and on and on—it can be a shock to encounter performances that seem utterly free of myth, that seem to come forth completely on their own terms, as if they came out of themselves. That this might be possible is perhaps the most alluring pop myth of all. Myth or not, it's what I heard on *Golden Vanity,* a Bob Dylan bootleg a friend in Germany sent me.

Bob Dylan acted out an odd, to many incomprehensible or irrelevant little cultural drama in the early and mid-nineties. Onstage, he offered often shockingly powerful versions of his old songs, performed with a tight, relentless band, with himself as lead guitarist, to the point that long, snaking instrumental passages, doubling back and descending into near silence, and then, like the Isley Brothers' "Twist and Shout," erupting into a greater noise, would overwhelm the parts of the song that were actually sung. Sine 1990 he has issued no new songs of his own, instead substituting records of old blues and folk standards. It's these sorts of songs that are collected on *Golden Vanity*—the oldest of the old songs, ballads, and airs that are hundreds and hundreds of years old, collected in the form of audience recordings made at Dylan shows from 1988 through 1992. Some of the songs are common coin, numbers everyone sang in the days of the folk revival, "Barbara Allen" or "Wild Mountain Thyme." Some are obscure, at least to me: "Eileen Aroon." These are the sort of songs Bob Dylan recorded in St. Paul and Minneapolis in 1960 and 1961, on cheap tape recorders in cheaper student or dropout apartments, because in those days these songs seemed like a key: a key to another country or another self, a strange music carrying, like all strange music, the call of another life.

In the early sixties, Dylan, then twenty, twenty-one, could invest these songs with flesh and blood. As he sang, men and women, lords and ladies, ghosts and demons, all the figures of the old ballads appeared before you. But now, as Dylan sang these same songs in his late forties, in his early fifties, all that these songs once meant, as talismans of the folk revival, charm pieces of purity and authenticity, as keys to a kingdom, has been forgotten. As knowledge, as rules, what the songs once meant has been passed down in the form of punk, not in the form of "Little Moses" or "Two Soldiers" or "The Wagoner's Lad"—and so these songs appear, on a bootleg CD, not as culture at all, but as some sort of contradiction, anomaly, or disruption, coming out of nowhere: speech without context, a foreign language.

In a dark, bitter, chastened voice, Dylan sings these old songs as if he knows they contain the truth of being, from birth to death, and as if that truth would be plain to all if only the songs could be sung as they were meant to be sung, or heard as they were meant to be heard—if only the world were, for an instant, in perfect balance. Passion lifts the songs, a yearning so fierce it's hard to credit, hard to listen to. A retreat, a withdrawal in the face of a world that was always the way it is and that will never be any different, backs the singer away from himself, and he seems barely to sing at all. But inside the audience, where these recordings were made with handheld microphones and hidden tape recorders, there is an utterly different world, and people live in it.

People are shouting, cackling, growling like dogs, yelping Deadhead yelps and whooping hippie whoops, imitating each other, vocally high-fiving, barking and drunk. It's the weirdest thing. This is no collision of history and legend—the collision from which myths arise, the myth emerging as a new language no one has to learn, as with teenagers and rock 'n' roll in the fifties, or whether the collision was arranged, the myth set forth as a new language everyone has to learn. Here, in these recordings, as what the singer is doing and what the crowd is doing cancel each other out, there is no history and there is no legend. The centuries of persistence in the ancient songs Dylan is singing, and the ancient singer he appears to be, make the noise of the crowd seem like vandalism; the refusal of the crowd to listen makes the wisdom of the songs, and the passionate body of the singer, seem like vanity. The result is the most compelling music, or the most compelling event, I've heard, or become part of, in a long time: irritating, confusing, impossible to hear and in moments impossible to pull away from. You hear someone struggling to turn what he believes to be timeless, outside of historical time, back into ordinary time, and the instinctive effort of others to stop him.

There's no myth I can pull out of that or drape around it. It's a new incident, without a story, so far—like the two shouts that open Sleater-Kinney's "Little Mouth," the film-noir theme in DJ Shadow's "Stem/Long Stem," or a thousand other things anyone could name.

Elvis Costello, "All This Useless Beauty," on *All This Useless Beauty* (Warner Bros., 1996). Costello writes in his notes to a 2001 reissue that the song was written for the British folk singer June Tabor, who recorded it for her 1992 album *Angel Tiger* (Green Linnet), where it was "actually delivered with more anger than on my version"—though to my ears it's a concert recital in a long dress. "None of these lyrics," Costello wrote of "All This Useless Beauty," "Little Atoms," "You Bowed Down," and other songs, "contained any anger toward the characters, only disappointment that they had settled for so little."

———. "All This Useless Beauty," from Costello & Nieve, on "San Francisco Live at the Fillmore (15 May 1996)," from *Los Angeles San Francisco Chicago Boston New York* (Warner Bros., 1996). A unique document of a unique tour: a box of five short CDs (five or six songs per city) drawn from live radio broadcasts of shows by Costello and Attractions pianist

Steve Nieve from May 1996. The highlight might be a more than seven-minute version of "My Dark Life," also from San Francisco. Throughout the performances are at once pristine and explosive, reserved and inviting, private and common, with crowd noise that is by turns fawning and obnoxious, responsive and hushed, the real ambiance of real rooms. "It's not a record of well-produced, high-tech concerts," Costello said at the time. "It's a record of overheard concerts."

Lush, "All This Useless Beauty," included on Elvis Costello & the Attractions, *You Bowed Down* (Warner Bros., 1996).

Robert Cantwell, "Twigs of Folly" (unpublished, 1997).

Fred Goodman, *The Mansion on the Hill*. New York: Times Books, 1996.

Bob Dylan, *Golden Vanity* (Wanted Man bootleg). Songs include "The Girl on the Green Briar Shore," "When First Unto This Country," "Trail of the Buffalo," "Man of Constant Sorrow," and "Lakes of Pontchartrain." Courtesy Fritz Schneider.

PART FIVE

New Land Found,
1997–1999

PREEMPTIVE OBITUARIES

Interview
August 1997

I was in England in late May, trying to get people to read a book about Bob Dylan's 1967 basement tapes recordings, when the story that Dylan might be near death from a rare heart ailment hit the papers. The queer thing about the news was the seeming eagerness with which it was reported. You could almost hear a sigh of relief: "My liege, I bring great news—the '60s are over! Finally, we can close the book!"

You might figure that if the era wasn't over by 1997, it never would be. That didn't explain why what should have been straight news—diagnostic reports, information on the cancellation of Dylan's then-imminent U.K. and European tours—was freighted with preemptive obituaries. In paper after paper, lengthy career summaries were appended to the medical updates. Some dailies ran full-page essays probing the likely longevity of the influence of the Voice of a Generation, if not the man, or the Generation itself. But it wasn't just in the U.K. American papers, too, put out the call for obit writers. The network news shows wanted critics—not doctors—to draw deep breaths and wrap it all up. Showing its usual flair for matching the slick with the glib, *Newsweek* caught the mood with surpassing vulgarity, burning off the veil of solemnity adopted elsewhere: "The scary news blowin' in the wind last week was that Bob Dylan might be dying . . . Bob Dylan's heart in danger? It sounded like a death knell for the counterculture." You can almost hear them salivating, can't you? But why this breathless anticipation of a death that in truth took place long ago?

Part of it, I think, is a fear that a singer who once seemed able to translate the vague and shifting threats and warnings of his time into a language that was instantly and overwhelmingly understood might be able to do it again. Part of it has to do with what Gerri Hirshey, in a recent *Rolling Stone* story on Dylan's son Jakob (in the top ten with his band, the Wallflowers, for all of the spring of this year) called the "foolish cultural myopia that has long plagued this country: We don't know what to make of artists who have the audacity to outlive their own revolutions." There's something more, though. As Dylan hinted in the basement tune "This Wheel's on Fire"—theme song, rather frighteningly, for the BBC/Comedy Central series *Absolutely Fabulous,* where it's repeatedly keyed to Julie Driscoll's sly, certain reading of the line "If your mem'ry serves you well"—artists who stick around after their putative moment has passed are troublesome reminders of promises their audiences, perhaps more than the artists themselves, have failed to keep. So you can almost imagine the elegiac, funereal editorial cartoon, picturing a scattering of ashes and a caption: "Now Bob Dylan, too, is blowin' in the wind . . ."

Empowered media arrogance and arrant media stupidity bucked up against the perhaps little-known but immovable fact that, as this near-celebration was taking place, Bob Dylan, no matter how ill—he did say, on leaving the hospital, "I really thought I'd be seeing Elvis soon"—remained not merely a real person, but an artist doing work that ranks with his very best. Throughout the 1990s he has been reshaping his music, honing a tight, cool little band, clearing his long-blocked throat with two dank, vitriolic, surreptitiously ambitious albums of traditional songs, and reinventing himself onstage, not as a prophet or a careerist or a ruined reminder of better times, but as a guitar player. His shows began to jump: when I last saw him, two years ago, the long shout that kicked off his first number was like a flag unfurling.

The man so hopefully buried, dead or alive, as a creature of the past, as a prisoner of a counterculture he left behind long before it disappeared on its own, has spent the better part of seven years biding his time. Earlier this year he recorded a new album, his first collection of original songs since 1990—unlikely to be released, I'd imagine, until Jakob Dylan makes room for it on the charts. If it does come out, it should be the first Dylan album in well over twenty years likely to get whoever might hear it wondering what in the world it is.

The record is not like any other Dylan has released, though the music isn't unlike some he's made: it has a dirt-floor feeling, with loose ends and fraying edges in the songs, songs that sound both unfinished and final. The music seems more found than made, the prosaic driving out the artful. It all comes to a head with "Highlands," a flat, unorchestrated, undramatized monologue, wistful and broken, bitter and amused, that describes both a day and a life. The song, as I heard it one afternoon this spring in a Sony Records office in Los Angeles, is about an older man who lives in one of Ed Kienholz's awful furnished rooms in the rotting downtown of some fading city—Cincinnati, Hollywood, the timeless, all-American Nowheresville you see in David Lynch's *Blue Velvet*—getting up and going for a walk, maybe for the first time in weeks. In the course of the song he recounts his adventures, recalls the people he met and those he avoided. In a certain sense nothing happens; from another perspective, a life is resolved. The song is someone else's dream, but as Dylan sings, you are dreaming it. And you can't wake up.

"How long was that?" I asked the man who'd left me with the tape. "Seven minutes? Eight?" "Seventeen," he said. This is from the man so many were ready to bury: a singer who, at the age of fifty-six, no longer a factor in the pop equation, can still beat the clock.

REAL LIFE ROCK TOP 10
Artforum
September 1997

9) Midway Stadium/Ticketmaster: advertisement for upcoming concert (*City Pages*, Minneapolis, June 18) You know how in the ads for once-mighty rock heroes now reduced to playing local bars you've

never heard of, the promoter always sticks the title of the one big hit under the marquee name, since you might remember the song even if you've forgotten who did it: EVERY MOTHER'S SON ("COME ON DOWN TO MY BOAT")—GINO'S NO COVER ONE NITE ONLY? But this was a shock, and for a show at the Minnesota State Fair, no less:

Featuring . . . IN PERSON
"Sensational!!"
BOB
DYLAN
"Blowing in the Wind"

Not to mention that it's "Blowin'," not "Blowing."

Artforum
October 1997

10) Bob Dylan: *Time Out of Mind* (Columbia). A western. It starts with Clint Eastwood's face at the end of *Unforgiven,* then turns around and heads back east like bad weather.

A MAP YOU CAN THROW AWAY
San Francisco Examiner Magazine
2 November 1997

The challenge of Bob Dylan's *Time Out of Mind*—his first collection of self-written songs since 1990—is to take it at face value. There is no point searching for autobiographical confessions ("It's a breakup album, right?" said a friend, referring to all the tunes about lost love and a broken heart) or messages of hope. This is as bleak and blasted as any work a major artist in any field—and by major artist I mean an artist with something, a reputation, an audience, to lose—has offered in ages. *Time Out of Mind* is hedged only by craft, by the performer's commitment to his material. The world may be meaningless; he has no choice but to try to shape that void.

At first the music is shocking in its bitterness, in its refusal of comfort or kindness. Then it settles in as something like a conventional set of songs, and then a curve in one of them—the finality of a life left behind in the way Dylan gets rid of the seemingly traditional lines "I been to Sugartown I shook the sugar down" in "Tryin' to Get to You," perhaps, or the quiet drift of "Highlands," a nearly seventeen-minute number so unassuming and mysterious you feel it could have unwound its ball of string over the entire length of the record without exhausting itself—upends any casual listening and throws every bit of word-play or muffled testimony into harsh relief, revealing a tale seemingly complete and whole.

The story opens with the singer, the tale-teller, walking dead streets and ends with him walking the streets of an almost deserted city: "Must be a holiday," he mutters to himself, as if he could care less if it is or not. Images of homelessness and endless wandering drive song after song. Sometimes that motif suggests a man who doesn't want a home ("I know plenty of people," he tells you at one point, "put me up for a day or two"); sometimes it calls up the tramp armies of the Great Depression, or the film director in Preston Sturges's *Sullivan's Travels,* disguised as a hobo, riding the boxcar like a railroad bum in order to meet the masses, the dispossessed and the defeated—and finding that the rags of poverty and anonymity are easier to put on than to take off, that they don't merely hide the signs of wealth and celebrity, but dissolve them.

As in that old movie, made as the Depression was about to disappear into the maw of the Second World War, when *Time Out of Mind* plays, another country comes into view. It's less the island of one man's broken heart than a sort of half-world, a devastated, abandoned landscape where anyone might end up at any time, so long as that time is now.

This is a land as still as the plains, its flatness broken only by a violence of tone or the violence of syncopation, of hard truths or a band's rhythms rushing up on each other like people running out of a burning house. "I thought some of 'em were friends of mine, I was wrong about 'em all," Dylan sings in "Cold Irons Bound," letting the whiplashed rhythm carry his words around their corner. On that rhythm, the word "all" isn't simply emphasized; the drama of *Time Out of Mind* is in its moments of queerly shared vehemence, when a solitary seems to speak for anyone who might hear him, maybe especially for those who won't, but that vehemence is never obvious. Here the whole line is not stressed but swung—"*Wrrrrong* about 'em *alllll*"—with the first word tipped up, the last tipped down, an organ sweeping up the song like wind. For a moment, the landscape—which from song to song takes names, "Missouri," "New Orleans," "Baltimore," "Bostontown"—is erased by the movement taking place upon it, and the singer moves out of earshot; when he returns nothing has changed.

The country that emerges is very old, and yet fresh and in sharp focus, apparently capable of endless renewal. At the same time the place is very new, and all but worn out: "I got new eyes," Dylan sings coolly, in one of the deadliest lines of his writing life: "Everything seems far away." Verbal, melodic, and rhythmic signatures from traditional blues and folk songs fit into the songs on *Time Out of Mind* as naturally, seemingly as inevitably as breaths—say in the way Dock Boggs, standing on the railroad platform in his "Danville Girl" in 1927, passes the song's cheap cigar to the singer on the platform in "Tryin' to Get to Heaven." That the reappearance of the forgotten past in an empty present is a talisman of *Time Out of Mind* is sealed by the art Dylan has chosen to be imprinted directly onto his disc: the "Viva-tonal/Electrical Process" Columbia label from the late 1920s, a label that ran one series for "Race" or Negro recordings, another for "Old Time" or country.

Dylan's record spins on that label in the way certain of its choruses and verses seem to write themselves, tossed off with a throwaway gruffness that suggests Dylan knows that on hearing half of a line the listener will automatically complete it even before Dylan himself has sung it: "That's all right, mama, you / Do what you gotta do," as he drawls in "Million Miles." But the label also spins backwards, until nothing on it can be read. As many incidents in the music seem to come out of nowhere, the nowhere that is both the present and the future of the country where the story Dylan is telling takes place: "Maybe in the next life," Dylan says elsewhere in "Million Miles," "I'll be able to hear myself think." Over and over, with resignation and sly, twisting humor, with the flair of a Georgia string band or the dead eyes of a gravedigger, the tale-teller poses the same question, sometimes almost smiling when he asks if "everything is as hollow as it seems."

So often, listening to the songs on *Time Out of Mind* is like watching people pass through revolving doors: the ambiance is that abstract and vague and untouchable. You have as much right to expect someone to reappear as quickly as she vanished as to expect never to see her again. That's how it is in the central incident in "Highlands," where a man walks into a restaurant, empty except for a waitress. They banter, almost flirt, and in an instant—an instant of fatigue, of boredom, of his or her memory of too many instants just like it, any of that or just a single word uttered with an edge it shouldn't carry—the mood dies. The room, the city outside, the nation around it, its entire history and all of the pieces of music and dramatic scenes that so quietly enter and depart from this one—Josh White's "One Meat Ball," Skip James's 1931 "Hard Time Killin' Floor Blues," Jack Nicholson's diner dialogue in *Five Easy Pieces,* Dylan's own "Desolation Row" cut down by Robert Burns's half-original folk song "Farewell to the Highlands"—all of that, from song to nation, turns hostile and cold. For a moment the waitress turns her back, and the air in the restaurant is now so mean you're as relieved as the singer when he quietly slips out of his chair. You can feel yourself tensing your muscles as he tenses his. Yet the singer barely has to go out the door, or the song down its Boston street, for you to imagine that this might have been the last conversation the tale-teller ever had—or, in Boston, on the ground where his nation began, the last conversation to even begin to suggest the possibility of a story that hasn't been told before.

That is what is new in *Time Out of Mind,* and in the country it traces as if it were a map you can read once and then throw away, because you won't be able to forget it whether you want to or not. Though crafted out of fragments and phrases and riffs far older than anyone living, bits of folk languages that joke and snarl as if for the first time, this is a picture of a country that has used itself up, and the peculiar thrill of *Time Out of Mind* is in its completeness, its complete refusal to doubt itself.

This new story does not come out of nowhere, or at the least it is not a solitary voice in the wilderness. The same cynical, damaged, sardonic, absolutely certain acceptance of one's own nihilism has been all over Bill Pullman's face in the last few years, in *The Last Seduction, Malice, Lost Highway,* in Wim Wenders's recent *The End of Violence*—for just as *Time Out of Mind* is an end-of-the-American-century record, closing with a fantasy of a retreat to the Scottish highlands, to the border country where the oldest ballads first came to light, Bill Pullman, in these films, is the ultimate end-of-the-American-century man. His face may have the cast of knowledge as a movie begins, or it may take most of a movie for the sheen of unsurprise to settle over his features. He may walk with the looseness of the already dead, as in *The Last Seduction,* or shatter before your eyes, as in *Lost Highway*—regardless, as in *The End of Violence* and as with the narrator in *Time Out of Mind,* the fact that in some essential way the story he has to tell ended before he even took the stage only increases his wariness.

In *The End of Violence,* Pullman is a movie producer whose life, not unlike that of Preston Sturges's John L. Sullivan (played by all-American boy Joel McCrea), is turned upside down. We first see him in his aerie looking down over all of Los Angeles, surrounded by computers and cell phones; soon he is dressed in rotting clothes, part of a crew of Spanish-speaking gardeners, hefting his leaf-blower, moving invisibly through perfectly groomed estates where, only days before, he looked past his own gardeners as a lord. With an old baseball cap on his head, his eyes squint against the sun; weirdly, they also squint inward, as if it's only with a squint that he can bear to look at himself. Unseen by everyone else, a drifter, unshaven and penniless, he misses nothing, but the more he understands, the less need he has to say anything to anyone. Who would listen?

Blowing his harmonica through passages of "Tryin' to Get to Heaven" until the song builds on itself like a folk version of the Ronettes' "Be My Baby," it's not a question Bob Dylan has to ask himself. Though most often spoken of today as a figure from the past, as someone now marginalized along the dimmer borders of the pop world, Dylan might well answer that when the music is as uncompromised as it is on *Time Out of Mind,* it's the old songs and the people in them that listen; the dead streets of his new songs, as depopulated, somehow, as the streets in his 1963 "Talkin' World War III Blues," will have to take care of themselves. And Dylan may be far less marginalized than he seems; he may be less of a crank, or a pop outsider, than an embodiment of the sort of cultural memory he plays with in *Time Out of Mind.*

Last May, in the college town of Iowa City, on the Dubuque Mall, a soul band set up its amplifiers, and soon a woman was belting out Chaka Kahn imitations, driving the afternoon street singers into corners, where their acoustic-guitar-and-harmonica renditions of Prince's "Purple Rain" and the Replacements' "I Will Dare" could barely be heard. As night came on the crowds got younger, the basement bars noisier, the street singers more numerous—by ten, there was one every twenty feet or so, each looking equally bereft and ignored, each with a girlfriend in idolizing attendance—and the repertoire more ambitious: "These Foolish Things," "You Belong to Me," the old folk song "Railroad Bill," something that must have been by Phil Ochs, the Rolling Stones' "The Singer Not the Song." Every singer seemed to want nothing more than to sound like Bob Dylan, and in his own way, every one did.

Bob Dylan, *Time Out of Mind* (Columbia, 1997). 1998 edition includes a second CD with live "field recordings" of "Love Sick," "Cold Irons Bound," "Can't Wait," and a time-stopping "Blind Willie McTell."

————. Not Standing in the Doorway with the Dirt Road Blues (Just Yet) (Rhythm Rhizome/Wild Wolf bootleg of 1997–1999 live recordings of Time Out of Mind Songs).

————. Life on the Square (Boss bootleg of 1999–2004 live recordings of all the songs from Time Out of Mind).

ONE STEP BACK
New York Times
19 January 1998

In 1997, Jakob Dylan's band, the Wallflowers, sold four million copies of its second album, *Bringing Down the Horse*. Led by the hit single "One Headlight," it stayed in the Top 10 for most of the year and, sustained by the single "Three Marlenas," the album is still on the radio.

Thirty-five years after the release of his first album, Bob Dylan, Jakob Dylan's father, was all over the news. Death-scare headlines circled the globe in May when he was hospitalized for a heart infection. In September, he performed for the Pope in Bologna, Italy. In October, he released *Time Out of Mind,* his first album of original songs in seven years, to universal critical acclaim. In December, he was honored at the Kennedy Center in Washington.

This confluence of circumstances prompted a major metropolitan daily to send out calls to various they-should-knows asking if in thirty-five years Jakob Dylan would loom as large as his father does today.

Why should he? It's a dumb question; it's also irrelevant. Because so much money is at stake, pop music seems to be about careers. But beneath the surface, perhaps on the level where the money is actually made, pop music is really about a social fact. At any moment, anyone might have something to say that the whole country, even the whole world, might want to hear, and maybe only one such thing. The ruling values of pop music might seem to be situated in the accumulation of fame and riches. They might be found in the way a song can turn your day around and then disappear.

A singer reaches you with a song. He or she has no responsibility to reach you with another one, and you have no responsibility to respond if he or she tries. Heard or overheard, a song—on the radio, in a bar, hummed by someone standing next to you in line—diverts you from the path your day has taken. For an instant, it changes you. But you can forget about it as surely as you may feel shadowed until you hear it again.

Or, rather, you may try to forget about it. You may not be allowed to. A hit song you don't like is an oppressive mystery. Granted that almost every female person of my acquaintance considers Jakob Dylan the cutest thing currently walking on two legs, what was he doing dully offering "One Headlight" until spring turned into fall? It was like watching someone do a jigsaw puzzle with four pieces, over and over again.

As omnipresent hit singles go, "One Headlight" was too flat to be more than a mild headache, and of course you could always change the station. It takes a great single, like Hanson's "MMM-Bop," the most ubiquitous record of last year, to produce a migraine. You need a piece of music so deliriously catchy, so insidiously marvelous, that you can't change the station, a song you can't stop hearing even if you turn the radio off.

That was the story in a skit built around Hanson's recent appearance on *Saturday Night Live*. The three teenage Hanson brothers enter an elevator. Suddenly two terrorists (the guest host Helen Hunt and the cast member Will Ferrell) rush in, shut the door and hold the boys at gunpoint. "MMMBop" has driven them insane, and they want nothing less for Hanson. Earplugs in place, the terrorists stop the elevator between floors, put "MMMBop" on a boombox set to REPEAT, and wait.

It takes only an hour or so for the first Hanson to crack; his mouth jerks up in a horrible grin. A few hours later a second Hanson succumbs. The third just keeps on happily tapping his feet. Mr. Ferrell takes out his earplugs; a smile spreads over his face, and he too begins to move. Realizing he's gone over to the other side, Ms. Hunt has no choice but to execute him on the spot.

That's one way to settle the mystery of a hit single. But some singles, like the Wallflowers' current "Three Marlenas," are mysteries that intensify until they finally float off the airwaves and disappear into the air.

The song walks in and out of the struggles of people who have no money and expect none. Jakob Dylan plays the simplest cadence on his guitar, never varying it. A piping organ makes the people you're hearing about seem bigger than their small lives, even heroic. Then all the orchestration falls away, and only the guitar is left, counting off the time. The whole piece pauses, and the singer says the hell with it. He's going to get a car and drive it, with the top down and the radio on. The eavesdropping tone of his descriptions of other people is replaced by a bitterly casual James Dean snarl. "I'm going right out of state," he says. "Now, I ain't looking back until I'm going / Right through heaven's gate."

He stretches the word "heaven" as far as it will reach. He bets all he has on that word and the next, but without tipping his hand. Though his face remains impassive, the phrase "heaven's gate" works as a magnet, pulling in metaphors from every direction, filling up the hole that has opened in the music.

The hole is filled with thirty-nine members of Heaven's Gate, the seekers who killed themselves last March, well after "Three Marlenas" was recorded but before it reached the radio and stuck there. It is filled with Genesis 28:17, where Jacob, in terror, dreams his way up his ladder to "the gate of heaven," and with "Hark! hark! the lark at heaven's gate sings," from the seduction song in Shakespeare's *Cymbeline*.

Jakob Dylan's song is filled with the slowly building disaster of the 1980 Michael Cimino movie about the Johnson County War, where "Heaven's Gate" were words painted on a tented roller rink in Sweetwater, Wyoming, in 1892. In that roller rink, for what it's worth, the musician T-Bone Burnett, the onetime Bob Dylan accompanist who produced the Wallflowers' *Bringing Down the Horse,* was the leader of the film's "Heaven's Gate Band."

Merely working in culture, with all questions of intent moot, Jakob Dylan has called up these metaphors. With his song weighted by events he could never have foreseen and analogues he may never have known, he creates the sense that wherever the singer in his song is going, he isn't coming back. It's as if he expects to find heaven's gate closed and even hopes it will be, so he can drive right through it and break it down.

Listening, you can almost see it happen, but the picture won't come into focus. So you listen harder every time you come across "Three Marlenas," wanting nothing more than to go all the way into the mystery it has presented, until finally you just get tired of trying. The day comes when you find the song playing and you hear nothing at all. Like so many singles, the record has gone back where it came from, wherever that is.

Wallflowers, "One Headlight" and "Three Marlenas," on *Bringing Down the Horse* (Interscope, 1996).

Hanson, "MMMBop" (Island, 1997).

Michael Cimino's "Heaven's Gate"—Original Soundtrack, music composed by David Mansfield (United Artists, 1980; reissued Rykodisc, 1999).

THIRTY RECORDS ABOUT AMERICA
Rolling Stone
28 May 1998

1) Chuck Berry: "Promised Land" (Chess, 1964). This is the map, as "The Poor Boy" sets off from Norfolk, Virginia, to discover the country: a journey that moves from poverty to wealth, from a bus to a plane setting down at LAX. All pop music that takes America

as a subject—whether winding toward tragedy or toward the sweetest harmony—runs off this mountain.

2) Carl Perkins: "Blue Suede Shoes" (Sun, 1956). "Don't tread on me," with a smile and an open hand.

3 & 4) Chuck Berry: *More Chuck Berry* (Chess, 1955–1960) and the Beach Boys: *The Best of the Beach Boys, Vol. 2* (Capitol, 1962–1966). The map begins to fill up, with blacks and whites, cars and girls, grand adventures into the night. "Let it rock," Berry commanded; "I get around," the Beach Boys respond coolly, a car full of guys on top of the world. There's no threat in this land a good song can't answer.

5) Dion: "Abraham, Martin and John" (Laurie, 1968). It breaks my heart; sometimes I can't bear to listen to it, to hear the country that isn't there.

6) Bob Dylan: *Highway 61 Revisited* (Columbia, 1965). Out here it's one endless game of chicken. A squinting eye sees a land that's all threat, and a voice that could have come from any state or all of them describes a nation defined by hysteria and redescribes it as an awful, somehow thrilling joke—without a punch line.

7 & 8) ZZ Top: *Eliminator* (Warner Bros., 1983) and Tarnation: *Gentle Creatures* (4AD, 1995). Same road, but no problem: you want all-night convenience stores, hot-sheet motels, we got 'em on the Interstate, and cheap, too.

9) Bobby "Blue" Bland: *Two Steps from the Blues* (Duke, 1961). You also have the St. James Infirmary—and a nation of strangers.

10) Pere Ubu: *Pennsylvania* (Tim/Kerr, 1998). So you turn off the Interstate, into forgotten small towns, and pretend that you, too, could belong in that diner—that you, too, could be one of the ghosts.

11) Bruce Springsteen: *Nebraska* (Columbia, 1982). The map shrinks to a single state where, once, as Chuck Berry was singing, a teenager and his girl friend got in their car and drove: "And ten innocent people died," Springsteen as Charlie Starkweather sings without glee or apology. It's the early Reagan years; wealth has become the measure of all things, and Starkweather has returned as the prophet of that nihilism.

12) "5" Royales: "The Slummer the Slum" (King, 1958). But the map can open up at any moment. "Don't try," says the singer in deadly stop-time, "to figure out / Where I come from," and you can't. Though there are two Americas in the number—one black and poor, one rich and white—there is also a single, shared church. It's what the late Robert Palmer called the Church of the Sonic Guitar, which Lowman Pauling burns down and rebuilds from the ground up.

13) Barrett Strong: "Money (That's What I Want)" (Anna, 1960). Money as the measure of freedom, the sound of a riot, the pursuit of happiness grabbed like a handoff and taken straight through the line.

14) Allen Ginsberg: *Holy Soul Jelly Roll—Poems and Songs, 1949–1993* (Rhino Word Beat, 1994). Citizenship: how to get it, how to use it.

15) Prince: *Dirty Mind* (Warner Bros., 1980). An orgy, staged in Minnesota, by blacks and whites, Christians and Jews; the First and Fourteenth Amendments acted out and put to the test.

16) Randy Newman: *Sail Away* (Reprise, 1972). A slave ship as the *Titanic:* nothing can go wrong. The ship sails gloriously into Charleston Bay, and sinks the country.

17) Jimi Hendrix: *Woodstock* (MCA, 1994). As he told it, "The Star-Spangled Banner" was the story of a nation ripping itself to pieces, then stitching up the flag as a crazy quilt. His face is still in it.

18 & 19) Fastbacks: *In America—Live in Seattle 1988* (Lost and Found, 1991) and Martina McBride: "Independence Day" (RCA, 1993). Patriotism from Seattle and Nashville: "Who says the government's on your side?" a woman asks flatly as another fills her lungs with the realization that the government doesn't matter at all—not on home ground, where "The Declaration of Independence makes a difference" (Herman Melville).

20) Bill Parsons: "The All American Boy" (Fraternity, 1958). Elvis meets Uncle Sam: "Ah, I'm gonna cut yo' hair off . . ."

21) Geto Boys: *We Can't Be Stopped* (Rap-A-Lot, 1991). Inside the never-ending pageant of self-congratulation that is white America, there's a black hole—a few blocks of Houston's Fifth Ward—where life is so unfixed, it's not that bodies can't find their souls, it's that souls can't find their bodies.

22) Bob Dylan: *John Wesley Harding* (Columbia, 1968). A 1950s black-and-white western as staged by an 1870s minstrel troupe made up of 17th-century Puritans and veterans of the Revolution.

23) Alexander "Skip" Spence: *Oar* (Columbia, 1969). Another western: cowboys sit around a campfire and sing old cowboy songs. The only thing bigger than the land, they think, is the sky. The vastness of the nation overwhelms them. Then it swallows them up.

24) Sly and the Family Stone: *There's a Riot Goin' On* (Epic, 1971). There was, anyway. This is the sound left when it's over and nobody wants to talk about what happened, and what didn't.

25) X: *Los Angeles* (Slash, 1980). They shot Philip Marlowe up with heroin. He stayed on the case. He stayed on the needle.

26) James Brown: "Night Train" (King, 1962). Still on the rails.

27) The Stax/Volt Revue: *Vol. 1, Live in London* (Stax, 1967). "Hold On, I'm Comin'" is a reenactment—not of the record, but of V-E Day.

28) Firesign Theatre: *How Can You Be in Two Places at Once When You're Not Anywhere at All* (Columbia, 1969). Oh, you didn't hear? The U.S. *lost* World War II. But hey, if you lived here, you'd be home by now.

29) Laurie Anderson: "O Superman" (One Ten, 1981). If there were a home, that is. There's not, a woman says, so softly, so carefully, each word clipped to its note. Maybe long ago, on the plains, on the river . . . now there is only power, and we're mere figments of its aura, a dream that doesn't need us, a dream so complete we'd dream it ourselves if we could.

30) Sam Cooke: "A Change Is Gonna Come" (RCA, 1965). Cooke was dead when his answer record to Dylan's "Blowin' in the Wind" appeared on the radio. The new country he demanded—an old country, really, that promised land, without the catch, without separation, without exclusion—flared up with the passion in his voice, in his whole body; then it faded away. The song remains a rebuke to the decades that followed it, passing by the tune the way you pass a bum on the street.

TABLE SCRAPS
East Bay Express Books
August 1998

Reading to a small group of listeners at Black Oak Books in Berkeley, Scott Spencer began his seventh novel at the beginning. It's 1973, and Billy Rothschild, the first-person narrator of *The Rich Man's Table,* is nine. He and his best friend, neither of whom has

ever met his father, are on 6th Avenue in Greenwich Village, playing their favorite game: "Is That Your Dad?" One boy points out a
man on the street—could be a rotting junkie, could be a handsome
painter—asks the other, "Is that your Dad?" and the kid who's it
has to go up to the man and *ask* him.

When I read the book—putatively about a young man's quest
to force his world-famous, beyond-legendary father to acknowledge him as his son—this struck me as a terrifying premise. Just as
Spike Lee knows how to make you watch, Spencer knows how to
make words move. The boys get the game going, Spencer carries
you into it, and it seems a lot scarier than ringolevio. What's the
kid going to say? How's the man going to react? And what if—
what if it's him, whoever he is? It couldn't be, of course, but what
if it is? What do you do then?

At Black Oak, Spencer didn't push the story, he unrolled it.
Nervous on the page, the story as Spencer told it was all about the
weightlessness of boyhood. A lot of writers on book tours go either
flat or florid as they back away from what they've written, until
you lose all connection between the person before you and the
words coming out of his or her mouth, or they pump up the significance of every comma and period, unashamedly in love with the
magic they've made. Spencer seemed at home with his story; he
read as if he trusted it, which is to say he read as if he trusted his
readers.

This day, as Billy and his friend play their game, the mark
comes across: whoever he is, he somehow knows Billy, calls him by
name. So Billy rushes home to his ur-bohemian mother, Esther
Rothschild, and she realizes it's time: she's going to have to give up
all the vague, phony stories she's doled out over the years about
why there's never been a father around and tell her son the truth.
So she does. "It's Luke," she says. "Luke Fairchild . . . He was my
boyfriend for a couple of years. More like three, I guess." Billy gets
down on his knees and pulls out one of his mother's old LPs, and
there it is, there they are on the cover: "Luke and Esther were hur-
rying along Bleecker Street, with the wind at their back, lifting the

collars of their matching buckskin jackets, whipping their hair around. They seemed entirely happy and in love. They wore boots, jeans, their bodies exuded confidence and satisfaction. Luke had a guitar case slung over his left shoulder; Esther carried a string bag filled with oranges and a skinny loaf of bread from Zito's . . ."

The Rich Man's Table remains compulsively readable after this—waiting in line at another bookstore, I saw a stack, picked up a copy, found my place, and read half a page before my turn at the counter—as a comic book. Any reader likely to be drawn to *The Rich Man's Table,* pulled in by its jacket photo of a mid-sixties Bob Dylan lookalike coyly holding a cape over the lower half of his face, will recognize the figures on the album cover described above—the jacket, we're told, of a Luke Fairchild record called *Village Idiot.* It's Bob Dylan and Suze Rotolo on the cover of *The Freewheelin' Bob Dylan,* his breakthrough second album, the two of them arm in arm. It was one of the most romantic and indelible images of its time. As an LP cover, it summed up so much of its moment, and the future that moment seemed to promise, that it remains a sort of black hole, complete in itself, pure gravity, still sucking in all the failures and betrayals of its moment, and all those to come. Spencer can't imagine himself away from this tableau—or he doesn't try.

It becomes impossible to read anything about "Luke Fairchild" without thinking *Dylan, Dylan, Dylan*—without thinking that as Spencer takes you through all the histories of masturbation, heroin, disloyalty, dishonesty, schizophrenia, and plain selfish pettiness in Luke Fairchild's career, you're getting the inside dope and secret dirt no straight Bob Dylan biography could get away with. At Black Oak, Spencer denied any such intent, or commercial tease. He knew little more about Bob Dylan than what he got from liner notes, he said; he started to read one of the standard biographies, then put it down, realizing he'd find his story imprisoned by facts. But while his book may not be imprisoned by facts, it is entirely imprisoned by Bob Dylan's place in the popular imagination. For close to forty years, people have seen themselves in Bob

Dylan, and read the books they wished they could write into his songs. That Bob Dylan is a tar baby. As if wanting to smear just a touch onto his forehead, Spencer got his hand caught.

I think that what propels a reader through the book—as an older Billy, who is himself writing a book about Luke Fairchild, goes off to interview various lovers and rivals, so all the gaps are filled in as he anguishes over his sort of purposeless meaning-of-life quest to, as a grown man, ask Fairchild "Are you my dad?" and have him say yes—is the suspense of wondering if Spencer will somehow get his hand unstuck. You keep hoping he will—because then a real life might open up into a new story, or anyway give a new dimension to an old one.

It never happens. It less than happens: the whole book is punctuated by lyric quotes from Fairchild's songs, and the problem isn't that they read like the most convoluted slipknot bad poetry in the Dylan songbook, from "Sad-Eyed Lady of the Lowlands," say, or "Chimes of Freedom"—

> Now the tents are all folded
> The circus shrinks in the rain
> The kid's disappeared on a southbound train

—the problem is that Spencer, or rather Billy, just like the sort of Dylan fan who explains every Dylan song in terms of what drugs or what woman Dylan was using when he wrote it, explains every Fairchild song in the same reductionist, idiot-autobiographical manner. In these pages, to imagine that any of these songs ever existed in the world, on their own, loosed from the clef of their roman, is to doubt the existence of the world. Really, why have the millions and millions of desperate fans in *The Rich Man's Table* been hanging on Fairchild's every word as the sixties turned into the seventies, right up to the present day, if all the man has ever done is talk about himself?

That taking on Bob Dylan as the subject, or springboard, for a novel does not have to lead straight to novelist's prison was nailed a clean quarter-century ago, in Don DeLillo's 1973 *Great Jones Street*. DeLillo's Dylan, here called Bucky Wunderlick, the first-person narrator of *Great Jones Street*, has, as Dylan did in 1966, disappeared from the pop world. As Dylan did in 1967, he has made a set of strange, instantly mythologized recordings that everyone wants to hear, that Wunderlick is almost certain he wants no one to hear: stuff close enough to Dylan's basement tapes that DeLillo just calls them "the Mountain Tapes." So DeLillo sets himself up—and within pages he has circled his Bob Dylan (who in 1973, the year *The Rich Man's Table* begins, remained a specter, a singer who in the previous six years had not appeared in public more than a handful of times) with a set of characters so odd, threatening, and insistent that their own paranoid versions of reality altogether subsume those of everyone else.

Bucky Wunderlick is tired; his skepticism has grown so hard he has begun to doubt whether he actually exists, or, if he does, if he ought to. As far as Bob Dylan goes, he disappears into the same doubts, which soon enough belong to the reader. By the time the novel nears its end, Wunderlick is ready to believe anything, and so are you. "You're soft, not hard," one of the many people trying to get their hands on the Mountain Tapes tells Wunderlick over the phone. "You're above ground, not under it." He explains everything, as others in DeLillo's pages have already done.

"The true underground is the place where power flows. That's the best kept secret of our time. You're not underground. Your people aren't underground people. The presidents and prime ministers are the ones who make the underground deals and speak the true underground idiom . . . This is where it happens . . . This is where the laws are broken, way down under, far beneath the speed freaks and cutters of smack."

The whole hipster world is just a scene, the man tells Wunderlick, and the scene is just an illusion, a costume for the streets: "Illusions forced me to change my life." He did it, he says: "Shall I tell you how I tried to cope? Where I went and how I got there?" "Sure," Wunderlick says. He sounds vaguely interested: at this point in the book, for him the secret of being is about as compelling as the third question of the night on *Jeopardy*. But you can't wait to find out.

"Shall I tell you then? Shall I tell you what I did?"

"Sure."

"I took a walk down lonely street to Heartbreak Hotel."

You've forgotten all about Bob Dylan by now; so has DeLillo. Like him, you're loose in the air of a story that, wherever it began, has found its own power principle, that has created its own reason for being. That's why I read novels, to breathe that air; I have no idea why Scott Spencer wrote *The Rich Man's Table*.

Scott Spencer, *The Rich Man's Table*. New York: Knopf, 1998.

Don DeLillo, *Great Jones Street*. Boston: Houghton Mifflin, 1973.

FOLK MUSIC TODAY— THE HORROR
Interview
October 1998

When people talk about folk music today, I don't think they're talking about the big night around the campfire Bob Dylan spent with the ghosts of old American music on *Time Out of Mind* last year, or the ruined country music of Palace and Wilco, which in moments comes from as deep a mine. ("You sound like a hillbilly," sang Dylan in 1962, offering a booker's response to his first attempts to get work in New York coffee houses. "We want folk singers here.") The folk music you can trip over just about anywhere now is not trying to get you lost, as that other stuff is. It's trying to convince you of something—to get you to agree with it. It may want your money, but most of all it wants your vote.

This music comes in a rattling basket of styles. There are Patti Smith's sermons and elegies, and Ani DiFranco's hectoring confessionals and secret handshakes, all orchestrated as a high-concept celebration of authenticity and autonomy—look, she's put out eleven albums in nine years on her own Righteous Babe label and won't sign with a major! There are the burgeoning revivals and tributes organized around Pete Seeger and Woody Guthrie, from a pile of reissues on Smithsonian Folkways to *Mermaid Avenue*—a hard-nosed Billy Bragg–Wilco workup of unfinished Guthrie songs—to Steve Earle's putrid where-have-all-the-lefties-gone lament "Christmas in Washington" to Bruce Springsteen's often heart-stopping *The Ghost of Tom Joad*.

There are Dan Bern's dogged attempts to embody both Bob Dylan and Mother Teresa, the Indigo Girls actually mixing sex, humor, rhythm, and politics in a convincing manner with their hit "Shame on You," and the James Taylor–soundalike radio commercials for Lucky Supermarkets. There's something for everybody. But before one takes the possibly risky step of, say, listening to Nanci Griffith sing "If I Had a Hammer" on *Where Have All the Flowers Gone: The Songs of Pete Seeger,* or Bern suffer over Monica Lewinsky and the Oklahoma City bombing, it's worth casting back to a scene from *Animal House.*

It's toga night at the lowest fraternity on campus, somewhere on the East Coast sometime during the Kennedy administration, and John Belushi, dressed as a Roman senator and already drunk, descends from his room to join the festivities. On the staircase he encounters a neatly dressed preppie (Stephen Bishop, who might as well be playing himself) charming several steps' worth of sorority sisters with his rendition of "I Gave My Love a Cherry." Belushi pauses. A quizzical expression falls over his face, as if he's contemplating a fundamental question of ontology, or about to deliver an address on the destruction of Carthage. His face darkens. You begin to hear this innocent little folk ditty as he does: as a contradiction of all that is vital and true in the history of mankind. Thus Belushi calls upon the spirit of "Louie Louie": he grabs Bishop's guitar from his hands and smashes it with a single blow. "Sorry," he says, handing back the wreckage. Sometimes, he seems to be telling us as he stumbles down the stairs, you just have to do what's right.

There are thirty-nine performances in the opera of sententiousness, sentimentality, condescension, and children's choruses that is *Where Have All the Flowers Gone,* and not all of them are bad, any more than all protest songs are bad. Roger McGuinn couldn't do a bad version of "The Bells of Rhymney," which is a great protest song, and John Stewart couldn't harm "Old Riley," which is about playing the banjo. But the purity of heart, the certainty of righteousness, the inexplicability of doubt, and the smooth, genteel, utterly harmless surfaces of the music, whatever the style, is like a disease. As one wades across this double CD—which has a lot less to say about the indomitability of the human soul than the recently released four-CD set *Bird Call! The Twin City Stomp of the Trashmen,* a band known only for its single hit, the 1963 "Surfin' Bird"—one realizes that Pete Seeger's songs, whether sung by him or by Judy Collins, Richie Havens, Bragg, Tim Robbins, Odetta, DiFranco, Bruce Cockburn, or any number of others, really are about one world: his. "So I ask the killers, do you sleep at night?" Kim and Reggie Harris sing with deep concern and insufferable piety on "Those Three Are on My Mind," Seeger's tribute to civil rights workers murdered by police and Klansmen in Mississippi in 1964, and in the real world there is a simple answer: "Yes."

Dan Bern isn't obvious about the fact that he belongs in this company; for that matter, he comes on as a sort of folkie John Belushi. A Midwesterner who knows he's going to be pegged as a New Dylan and figures he'll live through it, he wears his sense of humor on his sleeve. He has an exuberant grasp of broken rhythms that translates as an affirmation of radical individualism: a song is what he says it is, even if it sounds like a collection of mistakes. He wants desperately to be annoying: class clown, practical joker, fart champion, arsonist. Whatever it takes, he's game. He kicks off his second full-length album, *Fifty Eggs,* with a half-crazed rant about how big his balls are; it's stupid and it's funny. But halfway through, even if you're laughing, the insistence that this is a satire of male bragging takes over. Bern doesn't want you to think he thinks his balls are as big as Jupiter. Call him an asshole, no problem; on the wrong side, never. It's the same with "Cure for AIDS," "Chick Singers," "Different Worlds," about sexual freedom, sexism, and racism; they aren't bad songs, they're fun to listen to, for a while, but they want so badly to please while pretending they want to get under your skin that before long you may not trust a sound out of Bern's mouth. He acts like the last guy on earth you'd want cornering you at a party.

Legend has it that John Belushi could be pretty horrible at a party himself, but it's too bad he's not here to take up the good fight once again. The whole way of being in the world that he smashed on that staircase long ago is with us still.

Billy Bragg and Wilco, *Mermaid Avenue* (Elektra, 1998).

Where Have All the Flowers Gone—The Songs of Pete Seeger (Appleseed, 1998).

Trashmen, *Bird Call! The Twin City Stomp of the Trashmen* (Sundazed, 1998).

Dan Bern, *Fifty Eggs* (Work, 1998).

OLD SONGS IN NEW SKINS
Interview
April 1999

The pop moment I've found most affecting in the last few months comes at the end of *Little Voice*, when Michael Caine's wiped-out sleazeball promoter gets up drunk on a nightclub stage and sings a horrible, self-flagellating version of Roy Orbison's "It's Over." The classic song has been rubbed smooth by decades of overplay, but now it's ripped into someone else's story so violently you may never again be able to hear it as an innocent object, as a kind of toy. Now it has been brought into a play about real life—or the play of life as such.

I couldn't get Caine's scene out of my head. I began to think about how songs survive—and one of the ways songs survive is that they mutate. Once you start thinking this way, it's like listening to a new radio station: a vampiric, surrealist station where nobody knows what time it is and everything happens at once.

Sometimes this happens subtly, around the margins, in soundtracks or commercials. The song is moved just slightly off the map we normally use to orient ourselves—but in a way that, in a year or ten, may completely change how we hear it, what associations we bring to it. Pop songs are always talked about as the soundtrack to our lives, when all that means is that pop songs are no more than containers for nostalgia. But lives change, and so do soundtracks. Even if they're made up of the same songs.

Etta James's "At Last" was a number two R&B hit in 1961, and a bare pop hit. After that it lived a quiet life in a small, neat house on a poor street—until last year, when the musical director for *Pleasantville* came knocking. In James's hands the record was a soft exhalation after years of silent suffering, a sweep of passion so full of doubt it all but turns in on itself, and it was used to orchestrate the most romantic scene in the movie: a boy and a girl, connecting for the first time, driving into the sylvan glade of Lover's Lane as the novelty of their emotions brings new color streaming into their black-and-white 1950s sitcom world. The bucolic set-up was too good to leave to the movie, though—and now, just months after the film's release, you can see the scene replayed, tree for tree and leaf for leaf, in a Jaguar commercial. But while in the movie the song is a forgotten voice brought back to speak as if for the first time, blessing the young lives it's dramatizing, in the commercial the song completely escapes. It's too unrushed, too patient, to be used as the commercial wants to use it: to make you want something, right now. So it turns and walks away—not back to the history books, but back to Pleasantville.

Where Bob Dylan's "The Lonesome Death of Hattie Carroll" has gone is a trickier question. Dylan supposedly wrote it after attending the 1963 March on Washington, where he and others sang for equal justice. There was a story in the paper about a white rich man's son in Baltimore, William Zantzinger, who, drunk at a society party, had beaten a black woman to death.* The song Dylan wrote was solemn, elegant, and almost unbearably painful. In the last verse his song turned bitter and ugly, and he sprang the fact on which, for him, the story turned: "For penalty and repentance . . . A six-month sentence." When you listen, it's as if Dylan can barely expel the last word. It breaks and stumbles, as if the singer will never not be shocked.

Thirty-four years later, in 1997, the Baltimore cop show *Homicide* ran three episodes about the murder of a Haitian maid employed by a rich Baltimore family; the father, played by James Earl Jones, had shielded his guilty son. Why? Because of William Zantzinger, the Jones character says, and he tells the old story in Bob Dylan's words, as if they are now part of a bible, as if a white man's crime should pay for a black man's, an eye for an eye, a tooth for a tooth—even if in both cases the eyes that close are those of a poor black woman. "In the courtroom of honor, the judge pounded his gavel, to show that all's equal and that the courts are on the level," Jones explained to Andre Braugher's detective, too young to remember, and so long after the fact, or before the new fact, that it was impossible to read his tone: "The ladder of law has

---

*Zantzinger, twenty-four, screamed racial epithets at Hattie Carroll, fifty-one, who was working at the hotel where the party Zantzinger was attending was held, and struck her with a toy cane. She later suffered a stroke and died. After a sordid life, during which he was convicted of crimes including extorting rents from poor black families on property he did not own, Zantzinger died at sixty-nine in 2009. To the end he cursed Bob Dylan for making his name a byword for evil: "He's a no-account son of a bitch," he says in Howard Sounes's 2001 *Down the Highway: The Life of Bob Dylan*. "He's like the scum of a bag of the earth."

no top and no bottom." But the law had a top and a bottom for Zantzinger, Jones was saying: Doesn't my boy deserve the same? A song that was once so clear, that sounded as if its words might be chiseled over some courthouse door, now seemed to make no sense at all.

Then last December 8, testifying before the House Judiciary Committee, the Princeton history professor Sean Wilentz stirred the broth one more time. Among a group of scholars arguing against Bill Clinton's impeachment on various Constitutional grounds, Wilentz seemed to come out of nowhere, pugnacious, angry, granting Republican representatives no more respect than he would a well-dressed lynch mob. He denounced the argument "that if we impeach the president, the rule of law will be vindicated if only in a symbolic way, proving forcefully that no American is above the law and that the ladder of law has no top and no bottom." Nonsense, he said: the offenses of which Clinton is accused put no Constitutional principle in jeopardy—and if you vote for impeachment for any reason found outside the Constitution, out of vengeance or for gain, "History will track you down."

With those last words, Wilentz recovered the voice of the song that, through blind quotation, he had made part of the official historical record of the nation—a voice of suppressed and bitter fury. ("I got tired of Henry Hyde describing Clinton as if he were William Zantzinger," Wilentz says.) In his way, Wilentz was singing a Bob Dylan song as badly as Michael Caine sings "It's Over" in *Little Voice*—and as fully. I can't listen to Roy Orbison's original anymore: compared to Caine's version it sounds bloated and strained, where Caine's is all sweat and self-loathing. The song itself may be over—or, rather, definitively appropriated, never to be given back. As for Dylan's song, like Etta James's, you can think it has just begun to travel, a mutant now, limbs fallen off, strange sores appearing, the sores growing into whole new bodies.

Little Voice, directed by Mark Herman (Miramax, 1998).

Pleasantville, directed by Gary Ross (New Line, 1998).

Bob Dylan, "The Lonesome Death of Hattie Carroll," from *The Times They Are A-Changin'* (Columbia, 1964). On 9 February 2010, Dylan sang a slow, spare, musing version of the title song from the album at the White House for A Celebration of Music from the Civil Rights Movement; it's hard to imagine that "The Lonesome Death of Hattie Carroll" could ever lose its flesh, or that had Dylan offered it instead that night, it wouldn't have stopped the night dead in its tracks. For an unparalleled reading of the song, see Christopher Ricks, "Bob Dylan," in *Hiding in Plain Sight*, edited by Wendy Lesser, San Francisco: Mercury House, 1993.

Homicide: Life on the Street (NBC), "Blood Ties" episodes 79–80, Oct. 17, 24, 31, 1997. *Homicide: The Complete Season 6* (A&E Home Video, 2005).

PART SIX

Hopscotch,
2000–2001

THE MAN ON THE LEFT
Rolling Stone
20 January 2000

The best words on Rick Danko, who died in his sleep on 10 December 1999, at fifty-six, were written thirty-four years ago, almost to the day he died, by the late Ralph J. Gleason. Bob Dylan had come to San Francisco with his new backing band, the Hawks. The noise they made was stupendous, and most eyes were focused on the center of the stage, where the action seemed to be, with Dylan and lead guitarist Robbie Robertson facing each other for the choruses, playing head to head, hand to hand. Gleason, though, was drawn to the left, where the young bass player moved with an uncannily graceful yet somehow violent rhythm, as if he were cracking the rest of the band like a whip—as if, secretly, he were the scientist behind the alchemy. Writing in the *San Francisco Chronicle* on Dylan's Bay Area shows, Gleason, thinking of the concrete cylinder that shoots up over the city from Telegraph Hill, summed up Danko more directly: "He looked," wrote a man who had covered Hank Williams, Louis Armstrong, Dizzy Gillespie and Elvis Presley, "like he could swing Coit Tower."

You can hear that happen on a song that emerged on the Dylan-Hawks tour, "Tell Me, Momma," as it was played in Manchester, England, on 17 May 1966. By then the combo was using the tune as the kickoff for its shows; this performance, this night, cracks it open. Now, there was always a lot of gospel in Rick Danko's bass, a lot of Motown, with Funk Brother James Jamerson's fingers reaching the short distance from Detroit to Danko's home ground in Ontario, just across the border. The muscular, syncopated thumps that open the Band's "Up on Cripple Creek," the stiffening attack in its demo cover of Marvin Gaye's "Don't Do It," the pulse in "Chest Fever"—it's all power, all control. But on "Tell Me, Momma," you're hearing a hipster, someone who can't be surprised, who knows there's a twist he can put in every story, someone who'll be looking the other way when it hits you. With a heedlessness that would rarely be present when the Hawks turned into the Band, everybody on the Manchester stage is hurling himself into this performance: Dylan is soaring like an eagle diving in and out of a stampede just to egg the cattle on, but off to the side, a funny grin on his face, Danko is both keeping the charge going and waiting for the moment when he will ease right out of it, step back and seal it. It's just a three-note pattern, coming up again and again when for a second the song needs to be suspended, when the boys have shot over a cliff, looked down, decided they don't care and kept going. *Rrrrum-bum-bum,* Danko says with his bass, flipping the whole enormous piece of music to the drummer. The move is so casual, so striking, that there's a split second before the drummer accepts the song, slashing down on his cymbal, kicking the music back to the group as a whole. It's the coolest thing I've ever heard.

But what allowed the Band to redefine rock 'n' roll in 1968 and 1969, with *Music from Big Pink* and *The Band,* was that it played and sang with such musical sympathy, it was meaningless to untangle one man's contributions from another's. Was that bass or guitar, drums or strings, Danko's voice behind Levon Helm's, Richard Manuel's calling out to Danko? On the invaluable video documentary *Classic Albums: The Band,* Helm, Garth Hudson, Robertson, Danko and producer John Simon let you see and hear how the songs were built. They sit at a control board, separate the tracks, isolate the sounds. It's a magical exercise, but even separated, you can, at this moment in the group's career, hear that each sound was far more about connecting to another than about calling attention to itself. There, along with that of the rest, is Danko's deepest legacy in those brief years, in a few songs—"The Weight," "King Harvest (Has Surely Come)," "To Kingdom Come" "Chest Fever," "Up on Cripple Creek"—when great artists could lose themselves in the anonymity of their art, in music that seemed to predate them and was sure to outlast them.

When, in the 1970s, the camaraderie went out of the Band's music, Danko's singing—with "Stage Fright," or his version of the Four Tops' "Loving You Is Sweeter Than Ever"—exchanged the style he had as part of something bigger than himself for the mannerisms of a singer who would not expose himself. The catch in his voice became a kind of trick; the abandonment of his fiddle playing in "Rag Mama Rag" collapsed into the stiffness of a singer imitating his own records. And yet, in what at the time seemed like anything but his last years, the soul singer that had been trapped inside Danko all his life finally made it out. On *High on the Hog* and *Jubilation,* little-noticed albums that Danko, Helm and Hudson put out in the 1990s as the Band—with Robertson gone after 1976 and Manuel dead by his own hand in 1986—Danko spoke a new language. "Book Faded Brown" and the gorgeous, painful "Where I Should Always Be" were made of forgiveness and regret, of a self-knowledge one might rather not have, of loss and the kind of smile only a missed chance can bring. As it turned out, they were last chances, and not missed at all.

Bob Dylan, "Tell Me, Momma," from *The Bootleg Series Volume 4—Bob Dylan Live 1966—The "Royal Albert Hall" Concert* (Columbia, 1998).

The Band, "Don't Do It," included as "Baby, Don't You Do It" on *Crossing the Great Divide* (Genuine Bootleg Series bootleg).

———. "Where I Should Always Be," from *High on the Hog* (Pyramid, 1996).

———. "Book Painted Brown," from *Jubilation* (River North, 1998).

Classic Albums: The Band, directed by Bob Smeaton (1996; Eagle Rock, 2005).

REAL LIFE ROCK TOP 10

Salon

7 February 2000

10) Bill Clinton, State of the Union Address (January 27). "We remain a new nation," Clinton said. "As long as our dreams outweigh our memories, America will remain forever young." "Could Reagan have said it better?" asked a friend, and the answer is, no, he couldn't have said it better, or half as well. Reagan couldn't have brought off the Dylan reference as if it had come to him out of the air. And I doubt if Reagan would have done what Clinton did just a paragraph earlier—when, caught in the coded metaphors of American speech, he had a Founding Father ("When the framers finished crafting our Constitution, Benjamin Franklin stood in Independence Hall and reflected on a painting of the sun, low on the horizon. He said, 'I have often wondered whether that sun was rising or setting. Today,' Franklin said, 'I have the happiness to know it is a rising sun') name a house in New Orleans. Or, as another friend said, "Cue the Animals."

WHERE IS DESOLATION ROW?

Threepenny Review

Spring 2000

James Ensor's 1888 panorama *Christ's Entry into Brussels in 1889* is a picture of what you see when you look out from Bob Dylan's "Desolation Row." It's worth remembering that both works are screamingly funny—or at least Ensor's picture today looks funny before it looks like anything else, and when people first heard Dylan performing "Desolation Row," they couldn't stop laughing.

   Nobody laughed at *Christ's Entry into Brussels* when Ensor first presented it. Almost nobody saw it. The Twenty, the supposedly avant-garde Brussels artists' group which had first shown his work in 1884, rejected it. They'd rejected his paintings before; he was sure his enemies in the group were keeping his work from the public so they could steal his ideas. He was only twenty-eight, but for the previous three years the themes of his best work had been rejection, humiliation, mockery, torture, crucifixion, with Christ at the center of the pictures, until Ensor replaced Christ with himself. But the Twenty wouldn't give Ensor the satisfaction of recognizing him for who he was, nailing him up in the center of town; then everyone might have had to look him in the eye.

They simply froze him out. The year before, Ensor's father, an outcast in a family of female shopkeepers, a useless man who lived for music and alcohol, had died drunk on the street; on a greater stage, his life was now Ensor's to live. Ensor had fantasized himself crucified, but now his great painting was his own cross, bending him under its weight as he and his picture were banished from the city. Thus was he confirmed, the art historian Libby Tannenbaum wrote in 1951, just two years after Ensor's death, as an artist of "resentment and hatred of mankind," not to put too fine a point on it—or, as the Belgian-American critic Luc Sante put it just last year, as "the most deadly cynic in the entire history of art."

Just by its enormous size, its overwhelming visual noise, its thousands and thousands of citizens crowding into Brussels to celebrate Mardi Gras and the incredible coup the city fathers have pulled off with this year's parade master—LADIES AND GENTLEMEN, YES, STRAIGHT OUTTA JERUSALEM, HERE HE IS, JESUS CHRIST!—the picture was meant as an unanswerable last word. In its way it was: nobody answered. If nobody hears you, did you even speak? The whole city, the whole world was present in the painting: businessmen, soldiers, the government, art critics, the bishop, the devil, people in masks, people whose faces looked made out of dough, all caught up in a frenzy of joy over the chance to get close to a really big celebrity—a forlorn, confused-looking Jesus, riding on an ass in the middle of it all—and, at the end of the parade, to crucify him. What a fantastic allegory of the utter bankruptcy of modern society, of the entire history of mankind! And none of it mattered.

Ensor took the huge thing back to his rooms over his mother's souvenir shop in the seaside tourist town of Ostend, hung it up on his own wall, and for the next sixty years sat gazing at the vortex he'd made, that he'd seen, that had been made for him: all the hypocrites and liars and frauds and fools in Brussels, in Belgium, in Europe, for that matter everyone on earth, everyone who didn't understand his genius, who didn't even try—everyone, everyone, everyone in the picture, everyone who would ever look at it.

Everyone: those who saw it when it was finally shown in public for the first time, in Brussels in 1929, at an Ensor retrospective where the king made him a baron—when, in Libby Tannenbaum's cutting words, he was celebrated for his post-Impressionist, pre-Expressionist, early 1880s experiments with definition and color, and his blasphemous, threatening work of the late 1880s and 1890s was written of "as the unfortunate result of some extraordinary disease which had enfeebled the artist in his early twenties." Everyone: those who in later years came to his rooms to pay him compliments, to gaze at his pictures while the old man himself sat in a corner, playing his own songs on a harmonium, just like Allen Ginsberg. Everyone: those who come to see it at the Getty Museum in Los Angeles now. The picture was a giant, final insult, and nobody at the Twenty had trouble figuring that out. One look would do it. The face with cheeks like sausages, that rotting white monstrosity that looks more like a maggot than a man, those people with noses as long as arms—is that supposed to be me? Nobody thought that was funny.

Bob Dylan has made a career out of dropping hints no one picks up. As he frankly admitted as "Desolation Row" spun to its close, you can recognize everyone in the tune without recognizing yourself: everyone knows Einstein, Ophelia, Romeo, T. S. Eliot, Ezra Pound, Casanova, the Good Samaritan, Cinderella, Cain and Abel, the Hunchback of Notre Dame, the Phantom of the Opera, and everybody knows they're somebody else. So the lines just slip by: "I had to rearrange their faces, and give them all"—the word "all" expanding, "aaaaaaaallllllllll," until it swallows the words that precede it—"and give them all another name." Well, you could reply from the audience, that still couldn't be me: Bob Dylan doesn't even know my name. Which is like the late Robert Shelton, in the 1960s a Dylan chronicler and confidant, insisting that the clueless reporter in "Ballad of a Thin Man" couldn't possibly be based on him: "I'm fat," he said.

As in Ensor's picture, in "Desolation Row" the listener's eye is directed toward a circus of grotesques: a beauty parlor filled with sailors, a commissioner masturbating as he caresses a tightrope walker, a whole city in disguise. But whoever they are, nearly all of the characters in the song share one attribute: they're not free. They are prisoners of judges, doctors, torturers, an entire secret police, and the worst part is they may have recruited its troops from their own hearts. If they are not free it is because they are prisoners of their own ignorance, their own vanity, their own compromises, their own cowardice. By the way they are sung, the saddest lines in the song echo with all that one man used to be, could have been, will never be again: "You would not think, to look at him, but he was famous, long ago," the "long" stretched out just as long as it will go, *lonnnnnng,* all the way back to the time when the Einstein the man was then wouldn't even recognize the Einstein he is now.

Dylan recorded first "Desolation Row" in New York, on 2 August 1965—which was also probably the first time he ever sang it. He recorded it again, for the version that would end his album *Highway 61 Revisited,* on August 4. Little more than a week had gone by since his performance at the Newport Folk Festival had brought boos, catcalls, rage, confusion, and silence. It was the first time the troubadour known for his folk guitar and proletarian harmonica had performed with a rock 'n' roll band since high school. If one of his first original songs, written in Hibbing, Minnesota, in

1958, was called "Little Richard," Little Richard wasn't Woody Guthrie, voice of the dispossessed, poet of the Great Depression, a man blown by the wind and made out of dust. Little Richard was not Of The People; Little Richard was a freak, a foot of pomade, a pound of makeup, and purple clothes. Rock 'n' roll was pandering to the crowd, cheapening everything that was good in yourself by selling yourself to the highest bidder, putting advertising slogans on your back if that's what it took, just as one of the banners in earlier and later versions of Ensor's *Christ's Entry into Brussels,* a banner right up there with the painting's "Hail Jesus King of Brussels" reads "Colman's Mustard."

"What about the charge that you vulgarized your natural gifts?" the critic Nat Hentoff asked Dylan in his famous *Playboy* interview; it was early 1966, when the fury over Dylan's heresies had yet to reach its climax. "I'm only twenty-four," Dylan answered. "These people that said this—were they Americans?" They were; to many in the world of folk music—people who had heard their own voices in Bob Dylan's, who had found their own righteousness confirmed when they responded to his songs against racism and war, his calls to replace a society of lies with a community of truth—to many who felt these songs as their own, an electric guitar and a loud band were nothing more than a version of the Colman's Mustard ad. At Newport, a prophet they had trusted with their own best selves had turned his back on them, and on his back was not the blue denim of the worker, the costume he had always worn, but a black leather jacket.

Four days after his performance at Newport, Dylan recorded "Positively Fourth Street," his bitter, sardonic reply to the Greenwich Village folkies who had fawned and gossiped over him for years, who were at that very moment trying to decide which side to take. It was probably the most complete putdown ever committed to tape—though in Minnesota, where Robert Zimmerman of Hibbing first became Bob Dylan, people have always been sure the song was about Fourth Street in Minneapolis. Filled with heroes and villains from all across Western culture, "Desolation Row" was less specific, less local, because it was a whole world—and for that matter the song was not always easy for even the singer to find.

At first Dylan tried to record it with bass, played by Harvey Brooks, his own acoustic guitar, and electric guitar played by Charlie McCoy, up from Nashville and the most versatile musician in Music City U.S.A. But there is no groove; again and again McCoy tries to focus the hodgepodge of people Dylan is singing about with a jangling, needling guitar sound, tries to wrap up the verses with a scratching, treble-heavy rhythm, but Dylan seems to fall back from the story, and you never see more than a bunch of people dressed up in costumes. A month later, at the Hollywood Bowl, singing the song in front of an audience for only the second time, Dylan retreats to a strident, humorless voice, and makes this then-shockingly long song, eleven minutes long, into something much smaller: a protest song, though as Dylan finishes it you can hear an ecstatic young girl shouting, "It's so groovy!" It was the second time through the tune in New York, with Charlie McCoy now playing lead acoustic guitar, that the song took its shape.

The guitars are not electric, there are no drums, but the song is rock 'n' roll in what it asks for, in the way that it asks. McCoy's playing is florid as the performance opens, very decorative, and it relaxes the listener, and maybe the singer too. Catching the south-of-the-border feeling that would hover over so much of *Highway 61 Revisited,* McCoy relies most strongly on Marty Robbins's 1959 bordertown hit "El Paso," just as Dylan had drawn on a 1958 Ritchie Valens hit for "Like a Rolling Stone," the number that would begin the album—as Phil Spector put it a few years later, "It's always very satisfying to rewrite the chord changes to 'La Bamba.'" But McCoy presses harder as the tune goes on. He looks more for rhythm than for melody. In the instrumental passage after the verse in which, as in so many American folk songs of the century, the *Titanic* sails, McCoy hammers back at Dylan's steaming harmonica playing until they seem to be driving the ship down as one man. There is nothing discreet about Dylan's performance. He sings—sometimes he shouts—as if he's fronting an entire band, as if he has to fight to make himself heard. He's hoarse but holding nothing back, rushing some verses, slowing others, dramatizing the song's right to take its characters from any land and any era, dressing himself as Scheherazade for the Einstein verse, and he sweeps you up. The song doesn't come off as funny, but as a sad, broken allegory, not as if the song's tale is a mystery, but as if it's obvious, as obvious as the last war, or the next one.

Dylan sang the song in public a little more than three weeks after recording it—two days before the song and the album it sealed were to be released—on August 28, at Forest Hills in New York. It was his first show since the Newport Folk Festival. For the opening half of the concert he would appear solo, with his acoustic guitar; then he would come back with a band and, as he knew, the trouble would start. People were primed, for and against; in fact, it would be the meanest, most outraged crowd Dylan would ever face in the United States. But for the time being, listening to familiar songs played in a familiar way, those in the crowd who have come to protest the former protest singer are reassured—at the least, they have dropped their guard of suspicion.

Dylan's tone for the new song is cool, and his style of emphasis, the way he comes down on this word or that, is hilarious. The whole performance is entrancing, as if full of confidence that everyone will get the joke. No one present has heard the song before, but the crowd is with it instantly, laughing with wonderful good humor at every other line, cracking up completely at the words "Everyone is either making love, or else expecting rain," as if "expecting rain" is the funniest thing they've ever heard. The feeling is that of liberation, of people absolutely at home in their own skins; there's also a sense of privilege. It's a sense of people being in the right place—here, where the tribune of a new culture is speaking a secret language that, for the moment, needs no translators—at the right time—now, when the world seems to be changing and you can feel yourself one step ahead, already looking back.

"Did you ever have the standard boyhood dream of growing up to be president?" Nat Hentoff asked Dylan for *Playboy*. "No," he said. "When I was a boy, Harry Truman was president; who'd want to be Harry Truman?" "Well," Hentoff said, "let's suppose you were president. What would you accomplish during your first thousand days"—a weird slip, referring not to Franklin Roosevelt's first hundred days, the traditional standard for presidential accomplishment, but to the thousand days of John F. Kennedy, assassinated barely two years before—as if President Dylan might have more time. "Well," Dylan said, "just for laughs, since you insist, the first thing I'd do is probably move the White House. Instead of being in Texas"—not a slip at all, but Dylan's way of saying what he thought of Kennedy's replacement, President Lyndon B. Johnson—"it'd be on the East Side in New York. McGeorge Bundy would definitely have to change his name, and General McNamara would be forced to wear a coonskin cap and shades. I would immediately rewrite 'The Star-Spangled Banner,' and little schoolchildren, instead of memorizing 'America the Beautiful,' would have to memorize 'Desolation Row.'"

As Dylan made his way back and forth across the country, all through the fall of 1965 "Desolation Row" remained a comedy, or people continued to hear it that way, to hear it as something to see from a distance, as if they were not in it. But in the spring of 1966, when the tour reached England and the furor over Dylan's entry into the pop arena reached a pitch of hatred beyond anything Dylan had seen in his own country, the number changed.

On May 10, in Bristol, Dylan seems to be seeking the smile in the melody, the song a boat to sail. "Puts her hands in her back pockets / Bette Davis style"—when he sings those lines it's as if the whole story is a regret, a tale of sorrow, its only subject all that has been lost. On May 27, at the Royal Albert Hall—"Desolation Row" would not be sung again for eight years, until Dylan's barnstorming comeback tour of 1974, and then only once—the performance is a house of mirrors, now sardonic, now funny, now not so funny.

The characters in the song are dramatized; they seem physically present, because for the first time, perhaps, they are: the people in the audience are in the song, and there is no obvious way out. The song is presented as a vision, as gnosis, as secret knowledge—as something that might be accessible to those who are listening, and might not be.

In Manchester, ten days before, the song perhaps found its true body; the performance is emotionally complete in a way that others are not. At first Dylan clips his words, cutting himself off from them, putting himself at a distance from the action, making himself as much an observer as anyone in the crowd. But as the song goes on, even as the actual cadence holds, the song seems to go into slow motion. There is a flatness, a lack of dramatic effect, which, given the stories being told—Cinderella making her own Desolation Row, Casanova punished for visiting it, Ophelia not being allowed in—is itself dramatic. This is the feeling: someone is telling a very old story, or, more closely, acting out a ritual, a mystery everyone knows and no one has ever solved. The song ceases to be Bob Dylan's at all; in tone, manner, diction, in his lack of fear, he could be singing "Barbara Allen."

Listening to "Desolation Row" when it appeared—drawn toward its scrap heap of Western civilization—you could almost hear an answer-record to Richard Huelsenbeck's 1920 memoir *En Avant Dada,* where he raised the serious question, "What is German culture?" and replied peremptorily, with a colon in a parenthesis, as if the answer was too plain to really bother with: "(Answer: Shit)." Huelsenbeck and the rest of the dadaists were trying to get the world to look in the same mirror James Ensor had raised almost thirty years before they set up their Cabaret Voltaire in Zurich. The dadaists' wordless poems and crazy dances, their denunciations of whoever paid to hear them, were their answer-record to *Christ's Entry into Brussels*. Like them, Dylan is saying in "Desolation Row" that culture is decay at best, betrayal at worst. As his characters move through the song he follows them, only to learn that almost no one keeps what they have, their essential humanity, their "special gift"—to learn that almost everyone sells a birthright for a mess of pottage. So that scrap heap gives off a sickening but intoxicating smell of missed chances, of folly, error, narcissism, sin. In this atmosphere—and the song truly does make its own atmosphere, its own weather—everything seems worthless. "Desolation Row": the words seem merely to give the scrap heap a name. But as a friend said with shock after listening to the song twenty times in a row, that wasn't it at all: "He likes it on Desolation Row!"

Al Kooper played organ and piano with Dylan on *Highway 61 Revisited,* at Forest Hills and at the Hollywood Bowl; Desolation Row, he says in a tossed-off aside in *Backstage Passes and Backstabbing Bastards,* his autobiography, is Eighth Avenue in New York City. At the time it was the kind of place where they tell you to walk down the middle of the street if you want to be safe at night; you're better off with the drivers who don't see you than with the people on the sidewalk who do. You get a picture of life from the inside of Desolation Row, a map of it, in "Visions of Johanna," released in May 1966 on Dylan's *Blonde on Blonde,* though he had been performing the song, as "Seems Like a Freeze-Out," since the previous fall. You could very well be in an apartment on Eighth Avenue, looking out the window.

The song makes a dank room where a draft blows balls of dust across the floor. In the corners some people are having sex; others are shooting up or nodding out. It's the perfect bohemian utopia, a place of withdrawal, isolation, and gloom. It's fourth-hand Poe, third-hand Baudelaire, handed down by the countless people who've bought into the myth of the artist who cannot be understood, the visionary whom society must exile for its own protection—must exile within itself, so that his or her humiliation is complete, is final, but that's the danger. That's the one card left to the artist, and with that card the artist can change the game. The artist will return society's vitriol with mockery and scorn of his or her own. The difference is that while society speaks only in shibboleths and clichés—as a banner hoisted up in *Christ's Entry into Brussels* reads, "The Standard Fanfares Are Always Appropriate"—the artist invents a new language, to speak as strangely, with such power. That's the idea.

The dank room where this magic is made is its own cliché, of course, but is there anywhere else you'd rather be? Nowhere else the singer in "Desolation Row" would rather be—or Cinderella, Casanova, Einstein back when he still played the electric violin, or the Good Samaritan, who in *Christ's Entry into Brussels* is just part of the crowd. They stick their heads out the window to call to those few they might judge worthy of joining them, laughing at the crowds rushing through the street, at all those who don't even know enough to beg to be let in. This voice in "Desolation Row" and "Visions of Johanna" is Jack Kerouac's voice, his narration for Robert Frank and Albert Leslie's 1960 life-among-the-beatniks movie *Pull My Daisy*. "Look at all those cars out there," he says. "Nothing out there but a million screaming ninety-year-old men being run over by gasoline trucks. So throw a match on it." From inside the room in "Visions of Johanna," that's the feeling, except that there's also a kind of lassitude that suggests you could throw matches all day and nothing would catch fire.

From the mid-1880s through the rest of the nineteenth century, James Ensor went much farther than Bob Dylan did in 1965, or in the years since; he also lived much less of a life. As a prophet, he issued his prophesies and let the world suffer them. Ensor's 1891 *Skeletons Fighting Over a Herring* contains not only the meanness of the new petit bourgeois but the Battle of the Somme; as Luc Sante has written, this horrible picture, of "two skeletons in hussars' uniforms each tugging with its teeth at the end of a kippered herring, is an eloquently encapsulated summary of his century and prediction of the one to come." Ensor's 1880s Christ etchings— where, for *Cavalry,* the letters INRI over the middle cross are replaced by E N S O R—culminate with *Christ in Agony,* on the cross, his flesh being eaten by devils, apes, people. The tangles of the picture, the unnatural postures its protagonists assume as they twist in the air, call up fifteenth-century Central European woodcuts of the Antichrist, held in the air by demons, to prove that he can fly, that he is God. The 1888 etching *Combat of Demons* is an explosion of scatology, sadism, and terror, as crowded and as unstable as one of Sue Williams's contemporary orgy pictures: no matter what detail you focus on—the sword plunged into the anus, the crab with the human face, the vomiting bat—there is something worse happening right next to it. George Grosz's most powerful painting, the 1918 *Funeral Procession,* with Berlin a cauldron of corruption lit by reds that look black and blacks that look red, is only a confirmation of Ensor's 1896 prophecy *Death Pursuing the People,* where a giant skeleton wields his scythe from the rooftops as the fleeing crowds seem to wave in the streets like wheat.

There is no piety in these pictures, as there is none in *Christ's Entry into Brussels,* and there is something beyond blasphemy. Ensor was anticlerical, his biographers will tell you, but like many who hated the church he loved the idea of Jesus: pure, innocent, truthful, the first martyr and the last. Some even say that *Christ's Entry into Brussels* was made not to condemn, but to call the wicked to the path of righteousness. But Ensor's Christ pictures, where before he puts his name on the cross he substitutes his face for the Savior's, do not open the path of righteousness; they make their own kind of black mass, just like Ensor's quiet, unassuming 1885 painting *Scandalized Masks.* A man sits in a room at a desk, a bottle before him, hat on his head and a pig-snout mask on his face. A woman stands in the doorway, holding a staff, a pointed hat on her head, black glasses over her eyes. Her nose is huge and bulbous, her chin sticks out like a growth; you can't tell if she's wearing a mask or if you're looking at her real features. Yes, they're going to Mardi Gras—but at the same time, in this sadistically prosaic scene, you know something unspeakable is going to happen as soon as the two leave the room. You know that the carnival they're going to is not in the public streets but on Desolation Row, that place where the old heretics, the witches, the ancestors of the bohemians of the modern world perform their ceremonies.

Ensor may have seen his own rejection in Christ's, or wished for one to sanctify the other, but his work gives its own testimony, which is not all that different than testimony cited by Wilhelm Fränger in his study *The Millennium of Hieronymus Bosch:* testimony given by one Konrad Kannler, who in 1351, in a court of heresies, declared himself to be not only "the Brother of Christ," and "The New Adam," but also the "Anti-Christ in a good sense," and, into the bargain, felt himself called, in his capacity as "the image of the innocent Lamb," to be the supreme judge at the Last Judgment.

Luckily for Bob Dylan, he had one foot in the heretic's chamber, the bohemian's garret, the privileged space of Desolation Row, but as a pop musician, which, in 1965 he had so glamorously become, his other foot was in the street, where he could not pretend he was all that different from anyone else. As time moved on, then, "Desolation Row" became more and more a picture, fixed in time, a story that could be heard as if for the first time in its original voice. It also became a place that could not really be revisited, unlike the highway for which the album that carries "Desolation Row" is named. When Dylan performed the song on MTV in 1995, for his *Unplugged* show, with his inspired 1990s band, the song was not a thing in itself, but a reference to something else.

By then, as Bob Dylan would make clear in 1997, when he closed his album *Time Out of Mind* with the long, meandering "Highlands," the borders between Desolation Row and the outside world had long since collapsed. Dylan's highlands, like the fields of his fellow Minnesotan F. Scott Fitzgerald's old American republic, recede as they are pursued, so they stay in the air as an image of the good: an image, the singer says as he walks through a world where he can hardly bring himself to speak, where no one hears him if he does, that he can bring down into his mind if he must. If he does that, though, it will no longer hang in the air, as a picture of the world as it ought to be, so he leaves it there.

That old dank room is still there too, but no one else has been there for years; the singer would like company, but he can live without it. As Dylan told Richard Avedon's collaborator Doon Arbus around the time "Highlands" was first being heard, "One of the feelings" of the old folk milieu "was that you were a part of a very elite, special group of people that was outside and downtrodden. You felt like you were part of a different community, a more secretive one . . . That's been destroyed. I don't know what destroyed it. Some people say that it's still there. I hope it is . . . I hope it is. I know, in my mind, I'm still a member of a secret community. I might be the only one, you know?"

Bob Dylan, "Desolation Row," recorded 30 July 1965, with Harvey Brooks, bass, and Charlie McCoy, electric guitar. Included on *The Genuine Bootleg Series* (bootleg).

————. "Desolation Row," with Charlie McCoy, acoustic guitar. From *Highway 61 Revisited* (Columbia, 1965).

————. "Desolation Row," Los Angeles, 3 September 1965. Included on *We Had Seen a Lion* (VigOTone bootleg). With a fabulous concert review by Shirley Poston.

————. "Desolation Row," Bristol, UK, 10 May 1966. Included on *Away from the Past* (Wild Wolf bootleg).

————. "Desolation Row," recorded at the Royal Albert Hall, London, 27 May 1966. Included on *Genuine Live 1966* (Wild Wolf bootleg).

————. "Desolation Row," recorded at Manchester Free Trade Hall, 17 May 1966. From *The Bootleg Series, Vol. 4—Bob Dylan Live 1966—The "Royal Albert Hall Concert"* (Columbia, 1998).

————. "Desolation Row." *MTV Unplugged* (Columbia, 1995).

Al Kooper, *Backstage Passes & Backstabbing Bastards* (1998). New York: Hal Leonard, updated edition, 2008.

Wilhelm Fränger, *The Millennium of Hieronymus Bosch: Outlines of a New Interpretation*. Chicago: University of Chicago, 1951. On the triptych better known as *The Garden of Earthly Delights* (c. 1500), 30.

Doon Arbus, in Richard Avedon and Arbus, *The Sixties*. New York: Random House, 1999, 210.

The Superhuman Crew: Painting by James Ensor, Lyric by Bob Dylan, edited by John Harris. Los Angeles: J. Paul Getty Museum, 1999. Ensor's

Christ's Entry into Brussels in 1889 orchestrated by the words to "Desolation Row." The piece here was originally given as a talk at the Getty Museum on 14 October 1999 to mark the publication of Harris's book.

HOPSCOTCH

REAL LIFE ROCK TOP 10
Salon
12 June 2000

7) Bob Dylan: "Blowin' in the Wind" (live) on *The Best of Bob Dylan, Volume 2* (Sony UK). In this seven-minute, undated 1990s "field recording" the song is less a message than an occasion for music, with a lot of guitar. The song itself is now blowing in the wind, and has long blown away from its author; on this night people have momentarily attached themselves to it, the author with little more claim to the composition than the audience. The confidence and condescension of a younger man—*Don't you get it?*—have turned into the regret of an older one. The song is no oldie, though. Singing alongside Dylan, Charlie Sexton and Larry Campbell take the tune to a new, higher register, and suddenly "Blowin' in the Wind" is not only an occasion for music, not when it's daring the future to shut it up.

Salon
26 June 2000

7) Favorite Albums of Senatorial Candidates in Minnesota, from "So You Want to Be a Senator" questionnaire (*City Pages*, Minneapolis, May 31). Mike Ciresi (Democratic-Farmer-Labor, 54): "Ann's Favorites" (wife's compilation of his favorites); David

Daniels (Grassroots—party, not group—45): Bob Marley & the Wailers, *Natty Dread;* Leslie Davis (Independence, born 1937): *Janis Joplin's Greatest Hits;* Mark Dayton (DFL, 53): Jefferson Airplane, *Volunteers;* Dick Franson (DFL, 71): "All of Frank Sinatra's albums"; James Gibson (Independence, 47): "my wedding album"; Jerry Janezich (DFL, 50): Meat Loaf, *Bat Out of Hell;* Steve Kelly (DFL, 47): Mary Black, *Collected;* David Lillehaug (DFL, 46): Kansas, *Greatest Hits;* Steven Miles (DFL, 50): Bob Dylan, *Time Out of Mind;* Erik D. Pakieser (Libertarian, born 1969): Beastie Boys, *Paul's Boutique,* Ice Cube, *Death Certificate,* Beatles' "white album"; Ole Savior (DFL, 50): Rolling Stones, no album named; Rebecca Yanisch (DFL, 47): Van Morrison, *Moondance;* Rod Grams (Republican, incumbent): did not respond.*

Salon
10 July 2000

5/6) Colson Whitehead: *The Intuitionist* (Anchor) and Bob Dylan: "I'll Keep It with Mine," from *the bootleg series volumes 1–3 [rare & unreleased] 1961–1991* (Columbia). Dylan's weary 1966 piano demo is about whether or not to get on a train; Whitehead's 1999 novel is a metaphysical mystery about elevator inspection; and these lines, from Whitehead's gnostic textbook "'Theoretical Elevators, Volume Two,' by James Fulton," could have been written to translate the song: "You are standing on a train platform. A fear of missing the train, a slavery to time, has provided ten minutes before the train leaves. There is so much you have never said to your companion and so little time to articulate it. The years have accreted around the simple words and there would have been ample time to speak them had not the years intervened and secreted them. The conductor paces up and down the platform and wonders why you do not speak. You are a blight on his platform and timetable. Speak, find the words, the train is warming towards departure."

---

*Mark Dayton won.

Salon

7 August 2000

10) *Bob Dylan: The American Troubadour,* directed by Stephen Crisman, written by Ben Robbins (A&E, Aug. 13). This two-hour documentary is a thrilling exercise in the legal doctrine of fair use. With no permissions forthcoming for any material controlled by its subject, let alone a contemporary interview, the drama proceeds according to occasional fragments of old recorded Q&A's, enough panning of still photos to make you think the career in question predated the invention of motion pictures, never more than a single chorus of any given song, and a great deal of time devoted to the pronouncements of not very many talking heads, one of whom, Todd Gitlin, in the sixties a head of Students for a Democratic Society and currently a sociology professor at NYU, emerges as his generation's David Halberstam. Around the edges are traces of an untold story: a circa-1958 audio tape of Dylan's high-school combo the Golden Chords harmonizing on a piece of original doo-wop ("I'll be true, I love you, yes I do"—after a moment it sounds just like Fargo's Bobby Vee on his earliest Buddy Holly imitations) is really not that far from the 1967 basement tapes Dylan tune "Dontcha Tell Henry" as performed here by Levon Helm of the Band. At sixty he's been through cancer and looks it. He sounds it: his barely audible rasp, mandolin clutched to his chest, calls up a simple music that will outlive its singers, not that people like Helm or Dylan seem likely to grant that death's mortgage on their bodies ought to take priority over the music's lien on their souls.

Salon

13 November 2000

1) Ethan and Joel Coen: *O Brother, Where Art Thou?* (Touchstone Films). Three white prisoners escape from a Mississippi chain gang and run straight into a series of blackouts about old-time music—starting when they stop their jalopy to pick up a young black man

in suit and tie, bluesman Tommy Johnson, fresh from selling his soul to the devil for guitar prowess and ready to rock. Unlike the younger Robert Johnson, Tommy Johnson ("Cool Drink of Water Blues," 1928, though here he's given Skip James songs to play) actually bragged of the transaction. (What could be cooler?) When in the Coen Brothers' version he's seized by the Ku Klux Klan for ritual lynching, he figures it's just payback coming sooner than he bargained for.

It's a scene that recalls *The Birth of a Nation,* but so culturally blasphemous there are really no precedents for it. In a clearing in the dead of night, hundreds of Klansmen in pure white robes whirl about like a college marching band at halftime, executing lightning moves as if they were born to them. They come to rest in formation, facing a red-robed Grand Master. Johnson is brought before them—and then, from a high platform, from inside the Master's mask, issues the most horrifying, the most full-bodied, the most perfect rendition of the ancient plea "Oh Death" imaginable. As the long, tangled song goes on, with no accompaniment but the audience, the victim, and the night, a lynching becomes a philosophy lesson—and the slapstick escape that follows takes off none of the chill.

2) *O Brother, Where Art Thou?—Music from the Original Soundtrack* (Mercury). Typically, the dynamism of the film doesn't carry over into disembodied recordings—even if, with the torrential "Man of Constant Sorrow" that the cons plus Johnson cut in a radio station, it's the same recording. Pick to click, among the modern recreations by the likes of Ralph Stanley, Alison Krauss, Gillian Welch, Emmylou Harris, the Cox Family, and the Whites: running under the titles, Harry McClintock's 1928 version of the hobo jungle anthem "The Big Rock Candy Mountain."

3) November 3, from the ether: A friend writes: "I went to sleep when the networks called Florida for Bush, woke up ninety minutes or so later to see they were recalling it again, down to 500 votes at that point—and, shortly, someone cut to a shot of an Elvis

impersonator (in black street clothes, but with the sideburns/hair/ aviator glasses), presumably in Nashville, clasping his hands in silent prayer. It was that kind of night."

4) Al Gore: Huntington, West Virginia (November 4). Lest we forget, as we will, at the close of the campaign, with Gore taking up George W. Bush's truthful but (simply because of, in Bush's mouth, the accidental nature of its truthfulness) bizarre claim that "The people in Washington want to treat Social Security like it's some federal program," Gore finally hit the note that had eluded him for so long: "It wasn't a slip of the tongue. It was an expression of ingrained hostility, a preference on the other side for a dog-eat-dog, every-person-for-himself mentality that—" And here the words vanish into the next four years.

5) Bono: "Foreword" in *Q Dylan* (*Q*, October 2000). "The best way to serve the age is to betray it," Bono says of Bob Dylan, quoting Brendan Kennelly from *The Book of Judas*. He goes on: "The anachronism, really, is the '60s. For the rest of his life he's been howling from some sort of past that we seem to have forgotten but must not. That's it for me. He keeps undermining our urge to look into the future."

6) Richard Carlin and Bob Carlin: *Southern Exposure: The Story of Southern Music in Words and Pictures* (Billboard Books). Mostly pictures, from the 1880s to the 1950s—pictures of musicians who made the music that in the 1920s was already the last word of another world. It's the real world of *O Brother, Where Art Thou?* especially in one mottled, degenerating photo: it shows a dashingly handsome, dark-haired man with dark, hooded eyes looking you in the face under a broad-brimmed hat. Foulard tie, jacket, vest, watch chain: holding his five-string banjo, he is the dandy, the woman stealer. You wake up next to him and he's already gone. In Warren Smith's irresistibly slow, beckoning 1957 rockabilly tune he's the man with a "Red Cadillac and a Black Moustache," but all

through Lee Smith's 1992 novel *The Devil's Dream,* back from her to the Carter Family in 1940, making a circle with Bob Dylan's 1992 *Good As I Been to You,* he's Black Jack Davey. Given what stories, regrets, laments, fond memories, or erotic dreams he might have left behind in Hope, Arkansas, where he stands as his picture is taken, sometime in the 1890s, he's also Bill Clinton.

7/8) Kasimir Malevich: *Dynamic Suprematism,* 1915/16, and Bill Woodrow: *Twin-Tub with Guitar,* 1981, at the Tate Modern (London, through 2000). In a huge, insistently conceptual long walk through twentieth-century art, these pieces jumped out. In the

Manifesto Room of the History/Memory/Society sector, the old broadsides covering the walls shout and stamp their feet, announcing Futurism, the Bauhaus, Kandinsky's New Theater, Suprematism itself, while off in a corner Wyndam Lewis is Blasting England to bits. Among a few other paintings is the Malevich, a tilted but upright triangle: it's quiet, modest. From somewhere in Russia it pulls all the noisy declarations of the future into its own abstraction and silences them. In its abstraction, the piece at least seems to speak clearly—about the *ease* of remaking and rearranging the world, its constituent elements of life. If

you keep looking, though, the triangle begins to seem like a figure, an idea, a person, someone with a name. With the bars and squares that score the triangle now arms, eyes, and hats, the figure gestures. It is now obese, absurd, threatening, its identity so obvious: Alfred Jarry's loathed and loved Pere Ubu, in Jarry's own woodcuts the same shape, the same fascist trod across whatever might be in his way—and now, with Ubu on the march into the New Day, somehow morally cleansed.

Ivan Chtcheglov, 1953, "Formulary for a New Urbanism": "Given the choice of love or a garbage disposal unit, young people all over the world have chosen the garbage disposal." Not so fast, says Bill Woodrow, born 1948 in the U.K., in his own room in the Still Life/Object/Real Life sector. For his piece he's cut the outline of an electric guitar out of the grimy metal casing of a post-war Hotpoint washing machine but not removed it, so the two remain attached like a parasitic twin still part of its host. The curators comment: "The sculpture wittily combines two potent symbols of Western consumerism." Not so fast: why not art out of functionalism, or the art hiding in object of utility, desire hiding in need? Woodrow: "The guitar was a pop icon and the washing machine was an everyday, domestic item. So it was bringing the two things together like a slice of life." Not so fast: why not the urge to create sneaking out of the wish for comfort, and superseding it? There's no trouble imagining this as Pete Townshend's diddley bow, his first guitar.

9) Middle-aged man shaking a cardboard coffee cup full of change like maracas (6th Avenue and 13th Street, New York, November 5). He was hammering out a tremendously effective R&B number that sounded halfway between anyone's "C. C. Rider" and almost anything by Bo Diddley, and it wasn't until I'd added my change to his and was halfway down the block that the song revealed itself out of its own beat: Elvis Presley's first record, "That's All Right."

10) Pere Ubu 25th Anniversary Tour (Knitting Factory, New York, October 14). "The long slide into weirdness and decay," leader David Thomas announced. When synth player Robert Wheeler moved his hands over two homemade theremins—to play the theremin you can't look like anything but someone casting spells—the small pieces of metal seemed less like musical instruments than UFOs, and the high-pitched sounds coming from them, drifting through the rest of the music like swamp gas, nothing but the cries of creatures trapped inside. Like any number of people other than myself must feel as I write, the day after the election.

Salon
28 November 2000

Special bizarre all-quotation edition!

1/3) Alan Berg and Howard Hampton on Election night and after: Berg, November 6. "I am trying to cope with my jitters by listening to the five CDs of Dylan's Basement Tapes bootlegs and nothing else till it's over." November 9: "I didn't think I'd have time to listen to all *five* CDs. When things got rough, right before Pennsylvania came in, 'Clothesline Saga' came on and that took care of

Pennsylvania. Right now it just went to 'We carried you / In our arms / On Independence Day.' No question about what this will be resolved on: 'I'm Not There.'" Hampton, November 18: "Today I played the only appropriate song I could find: 'I Was in the House When the House Burned Down.'"

4) Fran Farrell: "I Want to Be Teenybopped: Teen Star Sex Fantasies" (*Nassau Weekly,* Princeton, N.J., October 19). "Jordan Knight, of the New Kids on the Block, was the first person I ever masturbated about . . . While my friends were playing with Barbie, I was imagining having sex with Jordan, and sometimes a threesome with Joey, on their big tour bus. See, I met Jordan when I was 10; it was downhill from there. Fast forward 10 years, to London, England. I'm walking down the street when I see a sign, the most beautiful sign I've ever seen—Jordan Knight, performing at 4 o'clock today. I couldn't believe my luck. Then I thought, this isn't luck, it's fate. We met 10 years ago, but now it's legal for him to have sex with me!!!! So I wait in line for FOUR HOURS. Yes, four hours for that has-been. The line was full of 15-year-old girls with thick British accents, acne and very bad teeth. I was squished in the middle of a crowd of sweaty, ugly girls screaming for a washed-up '80s pop star. But when he came onstage . . ."

5) Sen. Joseph Lieberman: Fiftieth birthday greeting for Bob Dylan (U.S. Senate, 24 May 1991). "Twenty-five or thirty years ago, I would have had a very difficult time imagining Bob Dylan, whose music was so much a part of my life at the time, being fifty years old, an age he attains today, his birthday. I would have had even greater difficulty imagining me taking note of his achievements in remarks in the Senate of the United States.

"Back in 1963, it is hardly likely any member of Congress would have been talking about Bob Dylan, at least not on the floor or either chamber; at least not in favorable terms. After all, it was he who said of them, 'Come senators, Congressmen, please heed the call / Don't stand in the doorway, don't block up the hall.' So times have changed, though Dylan's sentiment still holds true when we consider how many problems we still have to heed. I am sure he sings those words with the same spirit and intensity today as he did twenty-eight years ago.*

"There is a mystery to Bob Dylan, which is surprising, in a way, given how freely he has expressed himself through his music. But the mystery results, I think, from Dylan's refusal to play roles society might seek to assign him—roles like superstar, rock idol, prophet. 'I tried my best to be just like I am / But everybody wants you to be just like them.'"

6) David Thomson: *The Big Sleep* (BFI Publishing). On Lauren Bacall, director Howard Hawks, and *To Have and Have Not* (1944): "Betty was born in 1924, and grew up looking like nothing else on earth. I mean, how does one describe that young woman who could look like a Jewish teenager, a Eurasian doll, a Slav earth mother and the smoke that gets in your eyes—and all that before Hawks got hold of her? Add to that the allegation that she was only seventeen, and you can see what a wide-open country America was then."

7) Ishmael Reed: on the dance mania "Jes Grew" sweeping the nation after the election of Warren G. Harding, "the first race president," in 1920, and the conspiracy of the "Antonist Wallflower Order" to stop it, from *Mumbo Jumbo* (Scribner, 1972). "It has been a busy day for reporters following Jes Grew. The morning began with Dr. Lee De Forest, inventor of the three-element vacuum tube, which helped make big-time radio possible, collapsing before a crowded press room after he pleaded concerning his invention, now

---

*As noted above, but with more detail: "WASHINGTON—Half a dozen legislators sat a few feet away, under the crystal chandeliers of the East Room of the White House, as Bob Dylan sang 'The Times They Are A-Changin',' poker-faced. 'Come senators, congressman, please heed the call,' he rasped. 'Don't stand in the doorway, don't block up the hall.' His tone was rough but almost wistful; he had turned his old exhortation into an autumnal waltz. Afterward, he stepped offstage and shook President Obama's hand. It was part of 'In Performance at the White House: A Celebration of Music from the Civil Rights Movement.'" Jon Pareles, "Music That Changed History and Still Resonates," *New York Times,* 10 February 2010.

in the grips of Jes Grew: 'What have you done to my child? You have sent him out on the street in rags of ragtime to collect money from all and sundry. You have made him a laughingstock of intelligence, surely a stench in the nostrils of the gods of the ionosphere.'"

Tycoon Walter Mellon: "Jes Grew tied up the tubes causing Dr. Lee De Forest to cop a plea at the press conference . . . At the rate of radio sales, 600,000,000 dollars' worth will be sold by 1929, correct?"

Hierophant I of the Wallflower Order: "That is true, Mr. Walter Mellon."

"Suppose people don't have the money to buy radios. It will be an interesting precaution against this Jes Grew thing, isn't that so?"

"I don't get what you're driving at, Mr. Mellon."

"The liquidity of Jes Grew has resulted in a hyperinflated situation, all you hear is more, more, increase growth . . . Suppose we shut down a few temples . . . I mean banks, take money out of circulation, how would people be able to support the appendances of Jes Grew, the cabarets the juke joints and the speaks. Suppose we put a tax on the dance floors and get out of circulation J.G.C.s like musicians, dancers, its doers, its irrepressible fancy. Suppose we take musicians out of circulation, arrest them on trumped-up drug charges and give them unusually long and severe prison sentences. Suppose we subsidize 100s of symphony orchestras across the country, have government-sponsored Waltz-boosting campaigns . . ."

"But wouldn't these steps result in a depression?"

"Maybe, but it will put an end to Jes Grew's resiliency and if a panic occurs it will be a controlled panic. It will be our Panic."

8) Hal Foster: Election "Diary," on a word soon to disappear from our lexicon (*London Review of Books,* November 30). "Chad . . . For some reason I think of Troy Donahue, and imagine him dimpled, pregnant, hanging or punched."

9) Colin B Morton: on Metallica and Napster in "Welsh Psycho: Extracts from the Teenage Diary of Colin B. Morton" (*Clicks and Klaangs* #3, October/November). "William Hague, leader of the UK

Tory Party, has recently come out in defense of a man who shot dead a youth who was trespassing on his private property. Even more recently, the Tory Party has used, without permission, the music of Massive Attack to help promote the idea that we shouldn't have to pay tax or care about the sick. Hague's own logic dictates, therefore, that Massive Attack's Daddy G and 3D should have the right to shoot all members of the Tory Party for trespassing on their Intellectual Property. Either Intellectual Property doesn't exist, or they can have that right. Hague can't have it both ways. (Well, he can, but that's another story entirely.)"

10) Special "Forward into the Past" Election Update—Francis Russell, *The Shadow of Blooming Grove: The Centennial of Warren G. Harding* (McGraw-Hill, 1968), quoting Progressive newspaper editor Brand Whitlock on the Republican Party's nomination of Warren G. Harding as its candidate to replace Woodrow Wilson: "I am more and more under the opinion that for President we need not so much a brilliant man as solid, mediocre men, providing they have good sense, good and careful judgment, and good manners."

Salon
19 March 2001

4/5) Low: *Things We Lost in the Fire* (Kranky) and Peter S. Scholtes, "Hey, We're in Duluth" (*City Pages*, February 7). "When they found your body / Giant Xs on your eyes / And your half of the ransom," Alan Sparhawk sings in "Sunflower," "The weather hadn't changed"—I made the last line up, but it wouldn't be out of place. From Duluth, where forty-two years ago Bob Dylan sat in the audience at the National Guard Armory as Buddy Holly played his third-to-last show, this notoriously unhurried trio captures the insignificance of human desire as opposed to the fact of a Minnesota winter even as they suggest they might prefer that the weather never change at all. Or, as Scholtes puts it in his Twin Cities visitor's piece on "the emerging sense among Duluthians of an emerging sensibility among Duluthians"—that is, signs of a termite culture going public—"if there is one certainty at the heart of Duluth's mystique it is Lake Superior. The lake is always there and it is always cold. It will always be there and it will always be cold. Nothing about the physical landscape of the lake's corner should make a visit this spring more pressing than one the next."

7) *When Brendan Met Trudy*, directed by Kieron J. Walsh, written by Roddy Doyle (Collins Avenue/Deadly Films 2). As culture—the picture it draws of what it means to live happily, almost fully, in a funhouse of representations—the writing in this movie is as sexy as the smile in Flora Montgomery's eyes. "He makes movies," Montgomery's young thief says to her warden, describing her schoolteacher boyfriend, and he does: home movies, as scripted by Godard, Iggy Pop, Kevin Spacey, Jean-Claude Van Damme starring in *Remedial Action*. As when he runs into one of his teenage students, whose name he can never remember. "Dylan," the boy reminds him, as his parents beam at the one remaining sign of a hipness long since erased by the class system. "Mr.—Tambourine Man," the teacher says, having already forgotten the student's name again but translating the reference into a bigger story. The kid has no idea what he's talking about.

Salon
2 April 2001

5) *The Early Blues Roots of Bob Dylan* (Catfish). The tribute album backward—assembling the originals, the set makes the present-day man pay homage to his forebears, whether he wants to or not. But Bob Dylan is not at issue—right off, with the Mississippi Sheiks' 1931 "I've Got Blood in My Eyes for You," you hear how completely sixty-two years later he entered the song and changed it from the inside out. The structure remains the same; only the soul is different. Rather, it's the wide range of the compiler's ear—picking up Booker T. Sapps' obscure 1935 "Po' Laz'rus," Will Bennett follow-

ing the melody of "Railroad Bill" in 1929 like a man going downstream in a canoe, the Rev. J. C. Burnett chanting "Will the Circle Be Unbroken" in a black church in 1928—that makes you realize what an undiscovered country remains to be found. When, just before the end, in the Parchman Farm Penitentiary in Mississippi in 1939, Bukka White begins to hammer the high, ringing chords of "Po' Boy," his voice an eternal whine, as if he knows this is the only way to get God's ear, you reach that country, and you can't believe you have to leave. You can; he couldn't.

Salon
1 May 2001

2) No Depression in Heaven—An Exploration of Harry Smith's *Anthology of American Folk Music,* produced by Hal Willner (Getty Center, Los Angeles). The sixties Cambridge folkie Geoff Muldaur led the assemblage. He looked like the kindly town pharmacist; when he opened his mouth Noah Lewis' 1928 "Minglewood Blues" came out like a tiger. "You're going to be killing a lot of people tonight, aren't you?" fiddler Richard Greene asked Rennie Sparks of the Handsome Family, who was one of only four or five people under forty, or maybe fifty, on the stage. "That's what I do best," she said sweetly. Sparks writes lyrics about murder and clinical depression for her husband, Brett, to sing; she introduced the Blue Sky Boys' 1936 "Down on the Banks of the Ohio" as a song in which "a woman is slaughtered to ensure the river remains full." "This record sounds like it came from Mars," Greene said, kicking off Floyd Ming and His Pep Steppers' 1928 "Indian War Whoop" (a new version orchestrates Baby Face Nelson's arrest in *O Brother, Where Art Thou?).* It sounded just like Slim Whitman's "Indian Love Call," which in *Mars Attacks!* makes all the Martians' heads explode.

The fourteen-person band was heading toward cuteness when Garth Hudson began to play. He was everywhere at once. As soon as you thought you caught a tune—"Home Sweet Home," "Shenandoah"—it vanished. He was an avant-garde pianist in a 1915 grind

house, forgotten girlie flicks and In-a-castle-dark epics turning profound under his fingers. And then, like a sermon, came a low, thick,
unbending voice from the back of the stage, insisting on the Great
Depression as God's will, punishment for sins unknown, even un-
committed, and insisting on the only solution, which was suicide.
"I'm going where there's no Depression," as the Carter Family sang
in 1936, on their way to heaven. "There'll be no hunger, no orphan
children crying for bread / No weeping widows, toil or struggle."
The singer was Maud Hudson, and when, with absolute dignity,
she reached the lines "No shrouds, no coffins / And no death," you
realized the song was calling for nothing so small as the end of a
life, but for the end of the natural order: the end of the world.

Salon
14 May 2001

Special Absurdity of Worldwide Commemoration of Bob Dylan's
May 24 60th Birthday Edition!

1) This column has been unable to confirm a report that at his May
1 concert in Asheville, N.C., Bob Dylan performed his Oscar®-
winning song, "Things Have Changed," with the Thing Itself
prominently displayed on a speaker cabinet. True or false, the
story doesn't touch the night Michael Richards showed up on *The
Tonight Show* wearing his new *Seinfeld* Emmy as a necklace.

2/3) Bob Dylan: "You Belong to Me" on *Natural Born Killers—A
Soundtrack to an Oliver Stone Film,* produced by Trent Reznor
(nothing/Interscope, 1994) and "Return to Me" on *The Sopranos:
Peppers & Eggs—Music from the HBO Original Series* (Sony). Listening to his startlingly gentle version of "You Belong to Me" on
the *Natural Born Killers* soundtrack, you could figure that Jo
Stafford would have smiled at Dylan's cover of her 1952 smash, her
biggest record. And you can imagine what Dean Martin would
have to say about this cover of his 1958 smash—and his best

record. Probably he wouldn't say anything, just give Dylan the same sneer Robert Mitchum gives Johnny Depp in Jim Jarmusch's *Dead Man*. A look that says, "Are you still here?"

4) *A Nod to Bob: An Artists' Tribute to Bob Dylan on His Sixtieth Birthday* (Red House). Suzzy and Maggie Roche can't help letting you know how clever they were to choose "Clothesline Saga," one of Dylan's coolest songs—and their bohemian posing stands out as rock 'n' roll raunch on this collection of bored and pious folkie tributes, most of which somehow project condescension through the veil of homage. But if you're ever yearned to hear "I Want You" done as a prayer, this is for you.

5) New Dylan Alert! Robbie Fulks: *Couples in Trouble* (Boondoggle). Fulks has an uncanny ability to write songs as if they were remembered from a previous life—a life lived in England in the 17th century. This album leads off with "In Bristol Town One Bright Day"—"A stranger he came calling," that other person says through Fulks. It's a new—or unfound—version of "The Daemon Lover," dripping blood: "And on his lips the strangest words seemed so meek and common." You want a warning? That's a fire alarm. This is the sort of song Dylan would be sneaking into his shows next week, if he hadn't already recorded it as "House Carpenter" (1962, on *the bootleg series, volumes 1-3*) and "Blackjack Davey" (in 1992, on *Good As I Been to You*). As for Fulks, the rest of the record is Don McLean in loud clothes.

6) *Duluth Does Dylan* (Spinout). Bands who still live where Bob Dylan was born dive in with no respect and come out sounding as young as they are. Not all of it is good, and some of it's horrible, but little is predictable—not Chris Monroe's deep winter cover drawing, the First Ladies' wasted "Father of Night," or the way the chorus of "Like a Rolling Stone" keeps surfacing in the Black Labels' *Where did you say we are? And who are you, anyway?* reading of "Rainy Day Women #12 & 35." Everybody must get stoned, like a rolling stone—why didn't anyone think of that before?

7) Old New Dylan Alert! Bob Marley & the Wailers: *Catch a Fire: Deluxe Edition* (Tuff Gong/Island). Before releasing the Jamaican sessions that made up this 1972 album—songs included "Stir It Up," "Kinky Reggae," "400 Years," "Slave Driver," and "Stop That Train"—producer and label owner Chris Blackwell had some overdubbing done in London. This set presents the originals—including two numbers left unrevised and unissued—on one disc, plus, on a second, *Catch a Fire* as it almost, but not quite, caught fire around the world.

"Concrete Jungle"—here in its first form as a Jamaican single—was always the test between the real thing and its adulteration. This profound protest against the specific political and economic realities of Jamaica in the moment, and against the weight of history, of slavery, pressing down like an elephant's foot every time the singer tried to think, speak or act, is smaller as the Wailers made it on their own—spare, the sound open, the backing vocals word-by-word clear. Despite the backing singers, and the careful, impeccable rhythm of the band, this is one man's testament, a work of dignity.

In London, John "Rabbit" Bundrick of Texas added organ, and Wayne Perkins of Alabama added guitar; the backing vocals were muffled, and somehow given even greater presence. There is a long, slow introduction, Perkins edging his way into the theme like a stranger trying to walk into a bar without anybody noticing, though after one turn into the music he's got his money out. Aston Barrett's bass, a counter in Jamaica, is huge here; as much as Bundrick's Garth Hudson–like tentacles, it's this that makes a mood in which you can't tell curse from judgment, the future from too late. Straight off, the sound puts everything in doubt, and everyone on the record in jeopardy.

As the song goes on, the backing singers seem to circle Marley's lead, pointing at him, smiling, frowning, offering approval, withholding it, and soon the prosaic has vanished from the performance: the crying chorus is made up of the "many thousands gone" of "No More Auction Block." "Where Dead Voices Gather," Nick Tosches calls his forthcoming book on 1920s blackface minstrel Emmett Miller; this remixed "Concrete Jungle" is one place they gather.

All through the progression of the song, Perkins has been waiting, offering up a sign or a riff, a comment or a counterpoint, like the man in the bar looking a split-second too long at the guy who seems to own the place, holding his glass in a way not quite the same as anyone else, calling another drink with words that are English but sound like Spanish. As Marley steps back, then, Perkins steps in. The solo he plays is so restrained in form, and so passionate in tone, it translates the pain of Marley's story into a dream beyond words or even images. It is a dream of flight, of the running man trapped, escaping only to be trapped again, until, in a shocking moment, the solo turns over, and turns back on itself, as if to say, this record will end, but the story can't end. Not well; not even badly. And you can't wait it out. "400 Years"? You thought that meant from then to now, but it means from now to then.

8) Bob Dylan: *Live: 1961–2000: Thirty-Nine Years of Great Concert Performances* (Sony Japan). Sixteen tracks, from "Wade in the Water," taped in 1961 in Minneapolis, to "Things Have Changed," from Portsmouth, England, last year. Killer: "Dead Man, Dead Man," studio version on *Shot of Love,* 1981. Taped in New Orleans that same year, "Dead Man" is a textbook warning against the devil, if you listen as if you're reading; if you hear it, it's a poker game, and the singer's winning.

9) Pre-Dylan Alert! Robert Cantwell: "Darkling I Listen: Making Sense of the *Folkways Anthology,*" talk at Harry Smith: The Avant-Garde in the American Vernacular (Getty Center, Los Angeles, 20 April 2001).* About old American music, as first recorded in the 1920s and assembled by Smith in 1952 as his anthology *American*

---

*Collected in Cantwell's *If Beale Street Could Talk: Music, Community, Culture.* Urbana and Chicago: University of Illinois, 2009; and in *Harry Smith: The Avant-Garde in the American Vernacular,* edited by Andrew Perchuck and Rani Singh. Los Angeles: Getty Publications, 2010.

Folk Music—which, given the degree to which he absorbed it, in the late fifties and early sixties might have been Bob Dylan's pillow. The records were not quite the songs, and the performances of the songs were not quite the songs either, Cantwell argued: when seven decades ago those who Dylan once called "the traditional people" faced new machines, what resulted were "thought experiments, science fictions—newer than new, as it were, and older than old. They lead us, finally, to the *Anthology*'s central mystery: How can *these* performances have found their way to *those* records? Or better, these records to those performances?—questions that would not arise at all were it not for the still deeper question with which Harry has confronted us: *What is a record?*"

With the strange old sounds ("It is the sound of the old records we have, not the records themselves"), Cantwell said, Smith "placed us roughly where the listeners to Edison's phonograph were, phenomenologically speaking, in the early weeks of its public unveiling, when, according to the editor of the *Scientific American*, 'the machine inquired as to our health, asked how we liked the phonograph, informed us that [it] was very well, and bid a cordial goodnight.' At succeeding demonstrations young women fainted; eminent scientific heads were convinced it was a trick of ventriloquism; a Yale professor pronounced it a flat-out hoax. What was this machine that could steal the human voice? That could make absent people present—or was it that it rendered present people absent? That immortalized the human voice, but at the same time abolished it? What can one say of a machine that brings the dead back to life, but in the same instant buries them again?" No one has ever come closer to rendering Smith's selections—the likes of the Alabama Sacred Heart Singers' "Rocky Road" or Blind Lemon Jefferson's "See That My Grave Is Kept Clean"—in mere words, as opposed to, as with Dylan's versions of the latter, on his first album in 1962, and in the basement tapes sessions five years later, more recordings.

10) Anonymous Dylan fan (e-mail, May 7). "Bob birthday blast of coverage reminds me of fifties country song—*I forgot to remember to forget*—except updated—*I forgot, then remembered then forgot*

then remembered then remembered why I never should have forgotten in the first place."

TOMBSTONE BLUES
Los Angeles Times Book Review
20 May 2001

Richard Fariña died in a motorcycle accident near Carmel on 20 April 1966, just following a party celebrating the publication of his first novel, *Been Down So Long It Looks Like Up to Me;* he was just twenty-nine. A musician, songwriter, singer, and fabulist as well as a novelist, he seduced many people in life, and many in death. David Hajdu, author of the well-received biography of Billy Strayhorn, the Duke Ellington collaborator, is one of the latter.

"Who reveled in the act of living more than this man who tried to make every meal a banquet, every task a mission, every conversation a play, every gathering a party?" Hajdu asks in *Positively 4th Street: The Lives and Times of Joan Baez, Bob Dylan, Mimi Baez Fariña and Richard Fariña.* "Being with Dick was a feeling," a Carmel friend said. "It wasn't something outside of you that you looked at or saw. It was something that went through you." Thomas Pynchon, friend from college and ever after, worshiped him. Women could not resist. Did Fariña truly carry out secret missions for the IRA, as he claimed? We will never know.

A little of this goes a long way. Hajdu bets that a life unlived— cut short—a life unsullied by failure, decline, or betrayal, can overshadow lives that were lived, that went on past the golden moment when all things seemed possible, i.e., the world of American folk music from the late 1950s to the mid-1960s.

In this story, the Cambridge folk singer Joan Baez, who from the time of the release of her first album in 1960 was for many the embodiment of a moral purity that could not be found in American society as it advertised itself, and her younger sister, guitarist

Mimi Baez, Fariña's second wife, function as confused, manipulated, lovesick women caught between two powerful men.

On the side of life there is Fariña, from Brooklyn, handsome, exotic (his father Cuban, his mother Irish), a deep male friend, a capricious lover, dedicated to laughter and to his art. On the side of death there is singer and songwriter Bob Dylan, "a Jewish kid from the suburbs."

He is profoundly talented, but principally as a thief; he is able to ride the times as if they were a horse, even to become the voice of a generation, without ever truly engaging with the times, his eye always on the way out. As a person he is distant, less a comrade in the folk milieu than a spy; he is sour, "pallid and soft . . . childlike, almost feminine," "a little spastic gnome"—"that little toad," as Baez describes him to Hajdu. And without Fariña—who, a friend recalls, conceived the idea of merging folk with rock ("Dick said, 'We should start a whole new genre. Poetry set to music, but not chamber music or beatnik jazz, man—music with a beat. Poetry you can dance to. Boogie poetry!'")—Dylan would have had no career: not even the remarkable idea of carrying around a notebook in which to write down ideas, "as Richard Fariña had been doing since college." "Fariña gave Bob this lecture," the folk singer Fred Neil tells Hajdu, as Fariña told others: "'If you want to be a songwriter, man, you'd better find yourself a singer.' You see," Neil says, "Bob and me, we were both writing, but I knew how to sing. Fariña told him straight, 'Man, what you need to do, man, is hook up with Joan Baez. She is so square, she isn't in this century. She needs you to bring her into the twentieth century, and you need somebody like her to do your songs. She's your ticket, man. All you need to do, man, is start screwing Joan Baez.'" It was 1961, in New York; by 1963, it would be true. They sang together; they slept together. And of course it was a freak show: "As soloists, each of them had always had a public image that was elementally desexualized and androgynous—Joan the virgin enchantress, Bob the boy poet," Hajdu writes. "The idea of either of them sexually engaged was not so much titillating as it was startling and puzzling: How will *this* work?"

But perhaps one can draw a deep breath, wipe the sweat from one's brow, and leave Hajdu's career-and-relationships reconstructions; his utter credulousness when it comes to anyone who, having been left behind, might resent the fact that Bob Dylan, having entered history, still writes and sings songs people want to hear; his feats of research (the unpublished or unexpurgated 1960s interviews by the late Dylan biographer Robert Shelton with Dylan and others, now archived at the Experience Music Project in Seattle); his ability to get people to speak in ways that hardly cast themselves in a favorable light ("When I started, I used a lot from Debbie's act," Baez says of the Cambridge singer and guitarist Debbie Green. "She was modestly talented, but not ambitious. I was going someplace, she wasn't. I didn't hurt her. I only helped myself"); and his inability to dramatize, which is ultimately his inability to convey any sense of why his story is of any import at all, and listen again to how, for the country at large, the story took shape.

"Fair young maid, all in the garden," begins the probably 17th century English ballad "John Riley" as it appears on the 1960 album *Joan Baez*. It's the quieting of the tale as Baez moves it on, a little melodic pattern on her guitar flitting by like a small bird as a hushed bass progression follows it like a cat, even more than the voice—the voice of someone departed, but walking the earth to warn the living—that told the listener then, and can tell a listener now, that he or she has stumbled into a different country. It was like waking up as an adult, or nearly so, to discover that all the fairy tales of one's childhood were true—and that, if you wished, you could, instead of the career or the war awaiting you, live them out. In a few old songs, making a drama of hiding and escape, material defeat and spiritual conquest, investing that drama with the passion of her voice and the physical presence of the body that held it, she beckoned you toward a crack in the invisible wall around your city. What would it mean, people all across the country asked the music they were hearing, as the music asked them, to feel anything so deeply?

Bob Dylan, whose fellows in the northern Minnesota town of Hibbing would have been unable to say just what it was a suburb of, appeared on *Bob Dylan,* in 1962, as a tramp. That is: as someone who had slept in hobo jungles, seen men go mad from drinking Sterno, and forgotten the names of people who, one night, seemed like the best friends anyone could ever have. Though in Hajdu's book there is not a hint that Dylan ever evinced humor beyond a private joke, many of the songs are funny ("Been around this whole country," he says of the place name that in 1962 was a folk talisman, "but I never yet found Fennario"), but shadowed. All in all, the album is a collection of old songs about death. They dare the singer—can you sing me?—and he dares them—can you deny me what is mine? It was a time when almost everyone assumed that nuclear war would take place, somewhere, sometime, if not every-where for all time; it was a time when black Americans risked their lives, and sometimes had them taken, whenever they raised their voices, or took a step outside of the country into which they had been born and into a new one, the country they and everyone else had been promised. Death is real, the twenty-year-old singing on *Bob Dylan* said; knocking on a door perhaps built especially for that purpose, the sound Dylan made was not ridiculous because he was right.

This is the public drama that, in Hajdu's book, is only a figment of private life, and, as its players followed that drama over the next years, Fariña added nothing to it. Fulsome accounts of the 1965 Fariñas albums *Celebrations for a Gray Day* and *Reflections in a Crystal Wind* cannot hide the fact that Mimi Fariña could not sing, or that with the exception of "Reno Nevada," Fariña's most notice-able compositions were stiff, shallow imitations of "A Hard Rain's A-Gonna Fall" and other Dylan songs. Because the case for Fariña as a cultural innovator cannot be made—his novel, despite its blaz-ing encomium from Pynchon, is a sixties curio—Hajdu spends far more time on Fariña as a movable feast, as a boundless spirit, as the man who already was what, in the better world Baez and Dylan seemed to be singing about, everyone would be. Hajdu quotes a letter from married Fariña to teenage Mimi: "Things is, Mishka mine, I'm weary of hopping around the cities of this tired world & not knowing what was happening 'fore I got there. For me alone I guess it's all right but I'm not me alone anymore . . . Take my hand a little, baby, and squeeze it some."

Why are we reading this? Because Mimi Fariña gave the letter to David Hajdu? It's creepy, and not just because the posing style of 1963 doesn't travel well, but because you are violating someone's privacy by reading other people's embarrassing letters, and when you do that, you are made to violate your own privacy. But because Fariña did not live long enough to prove the truth or lie of his life, that is what Hajdu is left with.

"Richard never started the next book he planned to write," Hajdu says. "It was to be a memoir of his experiences with Mimi, Joan Baez, and Bob Dylan." Those are the last words of Hajdu's book. Fariña's torch has been passed, one is to understand, but the music and the writing that remain, Baez's, Dylan's and Fariña's, give the lie to the notion that it was ever really lit.

David Hajdu, *Positively 4th Street: The Lives and Times of Joan Baez, Bob Dylan, Mimi Baez Fariña and Richard Fariña*. New York: Farrar, Straus & Giroux, 2001.

WHEN FIRST UNTO THIS COUNTRY
Granta
Winter 2001

I live in Berkeley, California. Almost every day for nearly twenty years I've walked up the same steep, winding hill, up a stretch of pavement named Panoramic Way, which begins right behind the University of California football stadium. A few years back, when my fascination with Harry Smith's *Anthology of American Folk Music*—a fascination that began around 1970—was turning into obsession, I began to imagine that Smith had lived on this street.

I knew that Smith was born in 1923 in Portland, Oregon, and grew up in and around Seattle; that as a teenager he had recorded the ceremonies and chants of local Indian tribes, and in 1940 had begun to collect commercially released blues and country 78s from the 1920s and 1930s. In 1952, in New York City, when his collection ran into the tens of thousands, he assembled eighty-four discs by mostly forgotten performers as an anthology he at first called simply, or arrogantly, *American Folk Music:* a dubiously legal bootleg of recordings originally issued by such still-active labels as Columbia, Brunswick and Victor. Released that year by Folkways Records as three double LPs—two each for "Ballads," traditional or topical story-telling numbers, "Social Music," from dance music to the church, and "Songs," where the singer presents whatever commonplace tale he or she is telling as if it's his or her story alone—what was soon retitled the *Anthology of American Folk Music* became the foundation stone for the American folk music revival of the late 1950s and the 1960s.

Slowly at first, Smith's set found its way into beatnik enclaves, collegiate bohemias and the nascent folk scenes in Greenwich Village, Cambridge, Chicago, Philadelphia, Berkeley, Detroit, Wichita—wherever there might be an odd record store or an imaginative public library. By the early 1960s the *Anthology* had become a kind of lingua franca, or a password: for the likes of Roger McGuinn, later of the Byrds, or Jerry Garcia, founder of the Grateful Dead, for folk musicians such as Dave Van Ronk, Rick von Schmidt and John Fahey, for poet Allen Ginsberg, it was the secret text of a secret country. In 1960, Jon Pankake and others who were part of the folk milieu at the University of Minnesota in Minneapolis initiated a nineteen-year-old Bob Dylan into what Pankake would later call "the brotherhood of the *Anthology*"; the presence of Smith's music in Dylan's has been a template for the presence of that music in the country, and the world, at large. From then to now verses, melodies, images and choruses from the *Anthology,* and most deeply the *Anthology's* insistence on an occult, Gothic America of terror and deliverance inside the official America of anxiety and success—as Smith placed murder ballads, eruptions of religious ecstasy, moral warnings and hedonistic revels on the same plane of value and meaning—have been one step behind Dylan's own music, and one step ahead.

As Smith said in 1991, with fifty years of experimental film-making, jazz painting, shamanistic teaching, and most of all dereliction behind him, accepting a Lifetime Achievement Award at the ceremonies of the American Academy of Recording Arts & Sciences, he had lived to "see America changed by music." He died in 1994.

Three years later, when his anthology was reissued as a six-CD boxed set by Smithsonian Folkways Records, its uncanny portrayal of the American ethos would unsettle the country all over again. But that event had yet to take place when I started musing about Harry Smith and Panoramic Way. I knew that Smith had lived in Berkeley in the mid- to late 1940s, and that he'd done most of his record collecting there. Well, he had to live somewhere, and Panoramic, I decided, looked like where he would have lived.

It's a crumbling old street, with unpredictable, William Morris–inspired Arts and Crafts touches on the brown-shingle and stucco houses—a weird collection of chimneys on one, on another a fountain in the shape of a gorgon's face, sculpted out of a concrete wall, so that water comes out of the mouth, drips down, and, over the decades, has left the gorgon with a long, green beard of moss.

Most of the houses on the downside of the hill are hidden from view. You almost never see anyone out of doors. No sidewalks. Deer and wild turkey in the daytime; raccoon, possums, even coyotes at night. Berries, plums, loquats, wild rosemary and fennel everywhere. Woods and warrens, stone stairways cutting the hill from the bottom to the top. An always-dark pathway shrouded by huge redwoods. The giant curve of the foundation of a house designed by Frank Lloyd Wright. A street where, you could imagine, something odd, seductive, forbidden, or unspeakable was taking place behind every door. Absolute Bohemian, absolute pack rat—where else would Harry Smith live if he lived in Berkeley?

I'd read that Harry Smith had lived for a time in the basement apartment of Bertrand Bronson, professor of anthropology at the University of California, ballad scholar and record collector, so I looked for basement apartments that seemed right. I settled on one, in a dramatic house that looked as if it had grown out of the ground, surrounded by a wild garden dotted with ceramic monsters and a replica of the Kremlin, just off of one of the stone stairways. Then I forgot the whole thing.

A couple of years later I was in a San Francisco bookstore, doing a reading from a book I'd written that had a chapter on Smith's *Anthology* at its center. Afterwards a man with a long white beard came up to me and started talking about Harry Smith, record collecting, a warehouse in Richmond that closed just days before they got the money to buy it out, the Bop City nightclub in the Fillmore district, one of its walls covered by Smith's giant bebop mural, a painting of notes, not performers—I couldn't keep up.

I barely caught the man's name, and only because I'd heard it before: Lu Kemnitzer. "That little apartment," he said, "that's where we were, on Panoramic Way in Berkeley—" "Wait a minute," I said. "Harry Smith lived on Panoramic?" It didn't seem real; Kemnitzer began to look like the Panoramic gorgon. I got up my nerve. "Do you *remember*," I said to Kemnitzer, who now seemed much older than he had appeared a minute or two before, "what the *number* of Harry Smith's apartment was?" Kemnitzer looked at me as if I'd asked him if he remembered where he was living now—if he could, you know, find his way home. "Five and a half," he said.

By then it was late—on Panoramic, much too dark to look for a number. I could hardly wait for the next morning. And of course there it was: a dull, white door in grey stucco; tiny windows; a cell. Maybe ten steps across from the place I'd picked out.

Every day since, as I've walked up the Panoramic hill past Harry Smith's place and then down past it, I've wanted to knock on the door and tell whoever is living there—in four years, I've seen no one, typical for Panoramic—who once lived there. Who once lived there, and who surely left behind a ghost, if not a whole crew of them. "Wanted," ran a tiny ad in the September 1946 issue of *Record Changer* magazine:

PRE-WAR RACE AND HILLBILLY VOCALS.
Bascom Lamar Lunsford, Jilson Setters, Uncle Eck Dunford, Clarence Ashley, Dock Boggs, Grayson and Whittier, Bukka White, Robert Johnson, Roosevelt Graves, Julius Daniels, Rev. D. C. Rice, Lonnie McIntorsh, Tommy McClennan, and many others. HARRY E. SMITH, 5 1/2 Panoramic, Berkeley 4, California.

They were still in that little room—they had to be. They sounded like ghosts on their own records, long years before Harry Smith began looking for them; deprived of their black 78 rpm bodies, they were certain to sound more like ghosts now.

I began to fantasize how I might explain. There's a plaque a few steps from the door of 5 1/2, dedicated to Henry Atkins, the designer who created the neighborhood in 1909. So I would say, "Hello. I wonder if you know who used to live in your apartment. See that plaque over there—well, there ought to be a plaque for this man. You see, he did—remarkable things." No, that wasn't going to work. It already sounded as if I was recruiting for a new cult. A better idea: take a copy of the thing. Hold it up. "This is a collection of old American music. Just this year," I could say (referring to the London art curator Mark Francis), "a man speaking in Paris said that only James Joyce could remotely touch this collection as a key to modern memory. And it all came together right here, in your apartment. I just wanted to let whoever was living here now know that."

After a few weeks this fantasy took a turn and tripped me up. I'd offer the *Anthology,* then walk away, good deed accomplished— but then the person would ask a question. "Sounds really interesting," she'd say. "What's it about?"

Well, what is it about? How do you explain—not only to someone who's never heard the *Anthology,* never heard of it, but to yourself, especially if you've been listening to Smith's book of spells for years or decades? An answer came right out of the air: "Dead presidents," I'd say. "Dead dogs, dead children, dead lovers, dead murderers, dead heroes, and how good it is to be alive."

That sounded right the first time it ran through my head; it sounded ridiculously slick after that. I realized I had no idea what Harry Smith's collection was about. When, in the fall of 2000, I taught a faculty seminar on the *Anthology,* including what for decades had seemed the apocryphal Volume 4, Smith's assemblage of mostly Depression-era records, finally released that same year on the late John Fahey's Revenant label, I realized I had no idea what it was. A group of professors—from the English, German, Philosophy, Music, History, American Studies and Art History departments—sat around a table. Their assignment had been to listen to the CDs; I asked each to pick the song he or she most liked. "The song about the dog," one woman said, referring to Jim Jackson's 1928 "Old Dog Blue." "Why?" I asked. "I don't know," she said, just like any listener. "I played the records when I was doing the dishes, and that one just stuck." There were several votes for "the Cajun songs"—for Delmar Lachney and Blind Uncle Gaspard's "La Danseuse," Columbus Fruge's "Saut Crapaud," both from 1929, and Breaux Freres's 1933 "Home Sweet Home"—names and titles that in thirty years of listening to the original anthology—but, obviously, not altogether hearing it—I'd never registered.

To these new listeners, these performances—all from "Social Music," the part that in the 1960s people usually found least appealing—leaped right out. I was disappointed no one mentioned Bascom Lamar Lunsford's 1928 "I Wish I Was a Mole in the Ground," the most seductively unsolvable song I've ever heard, or Richard "Rabbit" Brown's 1927 "James Alley Blues," which I think is the greatest record ever made. Well, I thought, there's no accounting for taste. And they don't really *know* this stuff—it's not like I got it the first time through. I did mention "James Alley Blues," though. "You mean the one that sounds like Cat Stevens?" someone said. I was horrified. I dropped the subject.

The discussion picked up when I asked each person around the table to name the performance he or she most hated. There was a philosophy professor who, when in later meetings we took up Smith's *Volume 4,* insisted on the instantly unarguable lineage between the Bradley Kincaid of the 1933 "Dog and Gun" and anything by Pat Boone. His first contribution to the seminar was to note "the startling echoes of the Stonemans"—in their 1926 "The Mountaineer's Courtship" and 1930 "The Spanish Merchant's Daughter"—"in the early work of the Captain and Tennille." "Hattie Stoneman," responded an art history professor, "ought to be drowned."

An English professor confessed she really couldn't stand the "flatness of the voices"—she meant the Appalachian voices, Clarence Ashley, Dock Boggs, the Carter Family, G. B. Grayson, Charlie Poole, Lunsford. "What's that about?'" she said. "What's it for?" "Maybe it's a kind of disinterest," a young musicology professor said. "Everybody knows these songs, they've heard them all their lives. So they're bored with them." "It's like they don't care if anyone's listening or not," said the first professor. "Maybe that's what I don't like. As if we're not needed." "I don't think that's it," said a German professor, who, it turned out, had grown up in the Kentucky mountains. "It's fatalism. It's powerlessness. It's the belief that nothing you can do will ever change anything, including singing a song. So you're right, in a way—it doesn't matter if you're listening or not. The world won't be different when the song is over no matter how the song is sung, or how many people hear it."

"Uncle Dave Macon isn't like that," someone said of the Grand Ole Opry's favorite uncle. "No," the let's-drown-Hattie-Stoneman professor said, "he's *satanic.*"

I realized I was completely out of my depth—or that Harry Smith's *Anthology of American Folk Music* had opened up into a country altogether different from any I'd ever found in it. "It's that 'Kill yourself!'" another person said, picking up on the notion, and quickly it seemed as if everyone in the room saw horns coming out of the head of the kindly old banjo player, saw his buck-dancer's clogs replaced by cloven hoofs. They were talking about his 1926

"Way Down the Old Plank Road," one of the most celebratory, ecstatic, unburdened shouts America has ever thrown up. Where's
the devil?

"Kill yourself!" Uncle Dave Macon yells in the middle of the
song, after a verse, taken from "The Coo Coo," about building a
scaffold on a mountain just to see the girls pass by, after a commonplace verse about how his wife died on Friday and he got married again on Monday. "Kill yourself!'" He meant, it had always
seemed obvious to me—well, actually, it was never obvious. He
meant when life is this good it can't get any better so you might as
well—kill yourself? Does that follow? Maybe he's saying nothing
more than "Scream and shout, knock yourself out," "Shake it
don't break it," or for that matter "Love conquers all."

That's not how he sounds, though. He sounds huge, like some
pagan god rising over whatever scene he's describing, not master
of the revels but a judge. "Uncle Dave seems much too *satisfied*
about the prospect of apocalypse," the agent-of-satan advocate
said. Everyone was nodding, and for a moment I heard it too: Uncle
Dave Macon wants you dead. I heard what was really satanic about
the moment: when Macon says "Kill yourself!" it sounds like a
good idea—really *fun*. And you can hear the same thing in "The
Wreck of the Tennessee Gravy Train," which Harry Smith slotted
into his *Volume 4*. It was 1930, and Macon compressed as much
journalistic information as there is in Bob Dylan's "Hurricane" into
just over a third of the time, dancing through the financial ruins of
his state—the phony bond issue, the collapsed banks, the stolen
funds—while crying "Follow me, good people, we're bound for
the Promised Land" over and over. "Kill yourself!" This is what the
devil would sound like singing "Sympathy for the Devil": correct.

Hearing Macon this way was like hearing Bob Dylan's one-time
sidekick Bob Neuwirth's version of "I Wish I Was a Mole in the
Ground." Thanks to Harry Smith, the song was a commonplace in
Greenwich Village: in 1966 Bascom Lamar Lunsford's lines "A railroad man, he'll kill you when he can / And drink up your blood
like wine" turned up in Bob Dylan's "Memphis Blues Again."
Neuwirth sang the song's most mysterious lyric, "I wish I was a

lizard in the spring," as "I wish I was a lizard in your spring." Oh. Right, Sure. Obvious.

In most of the vast amount of commentary that greeted the reissue of the *Anthology of American Folk Music* in 1997, the music was taken as a canon, and the performers as exemplars of the folk. Neither of these notions had reached the room we were in. There people were arguing with Uncle Dave Macon, not with whatever tradition he might represent. It was Hattie Stoneman who had to be drowned, not white Virginia country women in general. There was no need to be respectful of a song if you didn't like it.

In 1940, folklorists Frank and Anne Warner taped the North Carolina singer Frank Proffitt's offering of a local Wilkes Country ballad called "Tom Dooley," about the nineteenth-century murder of one Laura Foster by her former lover, Tom Dula, and his new lover, Annie Melton. The song travelled, and in 1958 the Kingston Trio, a collegiate group from Menlo Park, California—my home town, as it happened, and in 1958 the most comfortable, cruising-the-strip postwar suburb town imaginable—made the song number one in the country.* The whole story is in Robert Cantwell's book on the folk revival, *When We Were Good*—or at least the story up to 1996, when the book was published.

In 2000, Appleseed Records released *Nothing Seems Better to Me,* a volume of field recordings made by the Warners, featuring Frank Proffitt. The liner notes included a letter from Proffitt, written in 1959. "I got a television set for the kids," he wrote.

> One night I was a-setting looking at some foolishness when three fellers stepped out with guitar and banjer and went to singing Tom Dooly and they clowned and hipswinged. I began to feel sorty sick, like I'd lost a loved one. Tears came to my eyes, yes, I went out and balled on the Ridge, looking toward old Wilkes, land of Tom Dooly . . . I looked up across the mountains and said Lord,

---

*"I believed Dave Guard in The Kingston Trio," Bob Dylan would write in 2004 in his book *Chronicles*. "I believed that he would kill or already did kill poor Laura Foster. I believed he'd kill someone else, too. I didn't think he was playing around."

couldn't they leave me the good memories . . . Then Frank Warner wrote, he tells me that some way our song got picked up. The shock was over. I went back to my work. I began to see the world was bigger than our mountains of Wilkes and Watauga. Folks was brothers, they all liked the plain ways. I begin to pity them that hadn't dozed on the hearthstone . . . Life was sharing different thinking, different ways. I looked in the mirror of my heart—You hain't a boy no longer. Give folks like Frank Warner all you got. Quit thinking Ridge to Ridge, think of oceans to oceans.

This is the classic sixties account of what folk music is, how it works, how it is seized by the dominant discourse of the time and turned into a soulless commodity—the classic account of who the folk are, of how, even when everything they have is taken from them, their essential goodness remains. As Faulkner put it at the end of *The Sound and the Fury*, summing up the fate of his characters, naming the black servant Dilsey but at the same time dissolving her into her people, her kind of folk: "They endured."

There wasn't any *they* in the seminar room as the Smith records were passed around the table. The all-encompassing piety of Frank Proffitt's letter—a letter which, I have to say, I don't believe for a moment, which reads as if it could have been cooked up by a Popular Front folklorist in 1937, which is just too ideologically perfect to be true—would never have survived the discussion that took place there. It wouldn't have gotten a word in.

I went home and put the *Anthology* on. I had read somewhere that, in the fifties, the photographer and filmmaker Robert Frank used to listen to the twentieth song on the "Social Music" discs, the Memphis Sanctified Singers' 1929 "He Got Better Things for You," over and over, as if there didn't need to be any other music in the world. I'd tried to hear something of what he must have heard; I never could. But this day it was all there—as if, again, it had all been obvious.

Smith hadn't credited the singers individually, no doubt because he couldn't find their names. In the supplemental notes to the 1997 reissue by the folklorist Jeff Place, you find them: Bessie Johnson, leading, followed by Melinda Taylor and Sally Sumner, with Will Shade, of the Memphis Jug Band, on guitar. Johnson starts out deliberately, with small, measured steps. "Kind friends, I want to tell you," she says in a friendly way. Then her almost mannish vibrato deepens; it's getting rougher, harder, with every pace. When she says "Jesus Christ, my savior," he's hers, not yours. Her throat seems to shred. With that roughness, and the roughness of the words that follow—"He got the Holy Ghost and the fire"—right away it's an angry God that's staring you in the face. Uncle Dave Macon, agent of Satan? This is much scarier. But then, as the first verse is ending, the whole performance, the whole world, seems to drop back, to drop down, to almost take it all back, the threat, the rebuke, the condemnation. Every word is made to stand out starkly, right up to the point of the title phrase. "He got better things for you"—the phrase seems to slide off Bessie Johnson's tongue, to disappear in the air, leaving only the suggestion that if you listened all the way into this song your life would be completely transformed.

The *Anthology of American Folk Music* had been turned upside down and inside out, that was for sure. I was still certain that Rabbit Brown's "James Alley Blues" was the greatest record ever made, but now another performance I'd never really noticed before, the Alabama Sacred Heart Singers' 1928 "Rocky Road," suddenly stood out. It wasn't a record, it was a children's crusade. On the *Anthology*, the spiritual "Present Days," the same group's recording from the same year, has a deep, mature bass, a reedy lead by a man you can see as the town barber, then a farmer or a preacher taking the most expansive moments of the tune, their wives filling out the music. The piece goes on too long—you hear how well they know the number, how complete it is, how finished. It's a professional piece of work. But in "Rocky Road"—"Ohhhhhh-La la / La la/La la la," ten or twenty or a hundred kids seem to be chanting while circle-dancing in a field on the edge of a cliff. As if it were something by Little Richard and I was eleven, I didn't hear an English word, or want to. You didn't need to know a language to hear this music; it taught you. Not that it had ever taught me a thing before. You have to be ready to accept God, songs like this say; you have to be ready to hear songs.

When you're listening to old records, or looking at old photographs, the more beautiful, the more lifelike the sensations they give off, the more difficult it is not to realize that the people you are hearing or seeing are dead. They appeared upon the earth and left it, and it can seem as if their survival in representations is altogether an accident—as if, as the Apocrypha quoted by James Agee at the end of *Let Us Now Praise Famous Men* reads, in truth "they perished, as though they had never been; and are become as though they had never been born." But that's not what the Alabama Sacred Heart Singers sound like on "Rocky Road." Here the persons singing are getting younger and younger with every line. By the end they are just emerging from the womb. Play the song over and over, and you hear them grow up—but only so far. You hear them born again, again and again.

It's impossible to imagine that these people can ever die. That's what they're saying, of course—that's their text. Thousands and thousands of people, over thousands of years, have said exactly the same thing. But they haven't *done* it.

Harry Smith once said that his primary interest in American folk music was the "patterning" that occurred within it. It isn't likely he meant what other record collectors would have meant: the stereotypically male, adolescent interest in classification, adding it up: trainspotting. Sorting it all out by region, style, genre, instrumentation, song-family, and, most of all, race.

Smith's placement of recordings and performers make patterns all through his anthologies. Some of these patterns are easy enough to follow, such as the string of murders, assassinations, train wrecks, sinking ships, and pestilence that ends his original "Ballads" section. Some patterns are utterly spectral—you simply sense that two songs which in any formal sense could not be more dissimilar have been commissioned by the same god. But in no case is the performer imprisoned by his or her performance—by the expectations the audience might have brought to it, or that the performer himself or herself might have brought to it. One singer is sly, a con man; another singer has already gone over to the other side, past death, past any possibility of surprise; a third laughs in the second singer's face.

It's interesting that most of the songs collected on Smith's first *Anthology*, and many of those found on his *Volume 4*—the testimony of killers and saints, tales of escape and imprisonment, calls for justice and revenge, visitations of weather and the supernatural, songs that, overall, leave the listener with a sense of jeopardy, uncertainty, a morbid sense of past and future—had been sung for generations before Smith's recordings were made. But the recordings he chose testify to the ability of certain artists to present themselves as bodies, as will, as desire, as saved, as damned, as love, as hate—as if their singularity has removed them from the musical historiographies and economic sociologies where scholars have always labored to maintain them.

In folk music, as it was conventionally understood when Smith did his work, the song sung the singer. But Smith's work is modernist: the singer sings the song. His anthologies are a dramatization of subjectivity—a dramatization of what it might be like to live in a town, or a country, where everyone you meet has a point of view, and nobody ever shuts up.

Such a society does not merely decline to ask for a canon, it repels it. Look at the supposed canon-maker. Smith spoke of "the universal hatred" he brought upon himself. He dressed as a tramp and often lived as one. He claimed to be a serial killer. He denied he had ever had sexual intercourse with another person, and many people who knew him have agreed they could never imagine that he had. Enemies and even friends described him as a cripple, a dope fiend, a freak, a bum. "When I was younger," Smith said in a lonely moment in 1976, speaking to a college student who had called him on the phone for help with a paper, "I thought that the feelings that went through me were—that I would outgrow them, that the anxiety or panic or whatever it is called would disappear, but you sort of suspect it at thirty-five, [and] when you get to be fifty you definitely know you're stuck with your neuroses, or whatever you want to classify them as—demons, completed ceremonies, any old damn thing."

A canon? What you have behind the anthologies is a man who himself never shut up—a young man in his late twenties in 1952, from the West Coast, now in New York City, who was imposing his own oddness, his own status as one who didn't belong and who may not have wanted to, his own identity as someone unlike anyone else and as someone no one else would want to be, on the country itself.

It was his version of the folk process. He would presuppose a nation, a common predicament, a promise and a curse no citizen could escape; he would presuppose a national identity, and then rewrite it. He would rewrite it by whim, by taste—in terms of what he, the editor (as he credited himself), responded to.

No pieties about folk music, about authenticity, about who the folk really are and who they are not, about whose work is respectful of the past and whose exploitive, can survive such a stance—and that may be why Smith's project has proved so fecund, so generative. He suggests to Americans that their culture is in fact theirs—which means they can do whatever they like with it.

In the seminar I taught on Harry Smith's anthologies of American folk music, I brought up the notion of the characters in all the performances—the characters named and shaped in the ballads about historical events as well as those only implicit and anonymous in the fiddle pieces and calls for deliverance, those representative fictional men and women in the tales told as if they really happened—as peopling a town, a community. If the songs did indeed make up such a town, what townspeople-like roles would those around the table assign the various performers on the anthologies?

This did not go over very well. "Well," someone said finally, "I can see Uncle Dave as the town dentist." "If this is a community," another person said, "it's not one I'd want to be part of." "Of course no one wants to be part of this community," a librarian said after class, frustrated and angry. "All of these people are poor!"

But no one is just like anybody else. No one, in fact, is even who he or she was ever supposed to be. No one was supposed to step out from their fellows and stand alone to say their piece, to thrill those who stand and listen with the notion that they, too, might have a voice, to shame those who stand and listen because they lack the courage to do more than that.

I think it's a great victory, a victory over decades of losing those who had the courage to speak out in the sociologies of their poverty, that anyone can now hear these men and women, and those they sing about, as singular, as people whose voices no particular set of circumstances could ever ensure would be heard. But once that perspective is gained, it has to be reversed. If we now see the artists Harry Smith found gazing on a common predicament, each from their own perspective, it may be time to return them, not to the sociologies that once ignored them, but to their republic, where each is a moral actor: a citizen.

This republic is not a town, but a train—a train that, at least as a song, left the station only a short time ago. "You know you won't be back," Bruce Springsteen says at the beginning of his song "Land of Hope and Dreams," which he began performing in 1999—take what you can carry. "This train," he says—reversing the gospel train that "don't carry no gamblers"—"Carries saints and sinners / This train / Carries losers and winners / This train / Carries whores and gamblers." "This train," he sings, as the voices of the members of his band circle him like shades, "Carries lost soul ramblers / This train carries broken hearted / Thieves and souls departed / This train / Carries fools and jails."

Anthology of American Folk Music, edited by Harry Smith (Folkways, 1952; Smithsonian Folkways, 1997).

Harry Smith's Anthology of American Folk Music, Volume 4 (Revenant, 2000).

Bob Dylan, *Chronicles, Volume One.* New York: Simon and Schuster, 2004, 256.

Robert Cantwell, *When We Were Good: The Folk Revival.* Cambridge: Harvard, 1996.

Nothing Seems Better to Me: The Music of Frank Proffitt and North Carolina—The Warner Collection, Volume II (Appleseed, 2000). Includes seventeen performances by Proffitt, including "Tom Dooley" from 1940 and 1959.

Bruce Springsteen and the E Street Band, "Land of Hope and Dreams," from *Live in New York City* (Columbia, 2001).

LIVE 1961–2000—
THIRTY-NINE YEARS OF GREAT
CONCERT PERFORMANCES

Rolling Stone
5 July 2001

Covering not thirty-nine but forty years—that's what recordings from 1961 to 2000 add up to—the sixteen tracks on this official but bootleg-like Japanese collection seem to come out of nowhere. "Dead Man, Dead Man," from New Orleans in 1981, rushes by like a gang of thieves. The posturing gospel of "Wade in the Water," recorded in a Minneapolis apartment in 1961, is somehow not as fake as it sounds. "Things Have Changed" was recorded last year in Portsmouth, England; heard now, it seems as unimpressed by its Oscar as it is by the price of gas or the meaning of life.

This album is a Bob Dylan show. When he takes the stage today, no song is older than any other. "Handsome Molly," from the nineteenth century, recorded in New York in 1962, seems in this performance hundreds of years older than its provenance, like a dream of the past—but wherever he is tonight, Bob Dylan could make it seem older still, which is to say even more present.

But the same is true of Dylan's own "Knockin' on Heaven's Door," recorded with the Band in 1974. This too takes you back to the nineteenth century, where it holds—but what doesn't hold is the face on the song. The old man in the music is no longer Slim Pickens, sitting on the ground in Sam Peckinpah's 1973 *Pat Garrett and Billy the Kid,* ready to die as the song plays in the background; the old man is the singer, or whoever is listening. "Slow Train," from Dylan's 1987 tour with the Grateful Dead, is no longer the flag of the singer's late-1970s conversion to fundamentalist Christianity but a sign of hope little different from the bluegrass spiritual "Somebody Touched Me," from Portsmouth in 2000, which opens the album—a song no less scary than the version of "Things Have Changed" recorded the next night.

As with any show, there are the numbers you take away and those that might never have been played, and which those are depend on who you are. I keep coming back to "Grand Coulee Dam," recorded with the Band at a 1968 Woody Guthrie tribute—and done as a drunken rockabilly rave-up at the party thrown by the men who built the thing, on the night they opened the spillway for the first time. That, and "Dead Man, Dead Man." The singer and the people around him look the devil in the eye, daring him to take their lives. Suddenly you can feel the devil tremble, like a vampire with a cross shoved in his face. Then comes "Born in Time," and you figure it's time to hit the restroom.

There's a long line, though, and you lose out on "It Ain't Me, Babe." It will never be sung and played quite like it is this night in 1975. You missed it. Or would have, if this record didn't exist.

HANDSOME MOLLY
Mojo
June 2001

Listening to *Live 1961–2000,* it strikes me that the most outrageous act Bob Dylan has ever performed was to sing "Handsome Molly" the way he does here—which is to say the way he sang it in the Gaslight Café in the fall of 1962.

Imagine walking into the Greenwich Village joint in late October, maybe early November. "Folk music" is it, really all that matters now, if you can get your mind off John F. Kennedy and Nikita Khrushchev playing chicken with the world, Freedom Riders being beaten and left for dead in Alabama, and whether you're going home alone tonight. You've probably seen Bob Dylan before; of course you've heard of him. You're too cool to admit to admiration, let alone envy. Maybe you're a little scared. Isn't it about time for this guy to expose himself for the fraud he has to be?

You came in late, to show you could be here or not be here, just checking the scene on your way to somewhere else. "'No More Auction Block,' man," someone says, indicating what you've missed. Sure, like he's a slave, you've seen people try that act before. You feel comforted when he goes into "Ain't No More Cane on the Brazos." He seems a little bored with the song, or the place, or maybe people like you. (*Stop thinking that way! He's got nothing on you!*) "Cocaine"—everybody does that, big deal. The guitar is pretty but—anybody can fingerpick, and he's out of tune. Then "Coo Coo." For a moment, you're not quite in the club anymore; the walls are suddenly transparent, and it's as if you can see the bird flying by outside right through them. Then he says he's going back to West Texas and you know he isn't.

And then he's a hundred years old and you are too. "Oh, I wish I was in London, or some other seaport town—I'd put my foot on a steamboat, sail the ocean 'round." "Londonnnnnnn-ummmmmm," he says, as if it isn't a real place, just a notion, too far away to credit. Now it isn't the walls that are about to fall away, it's the ground beneath your feet. He seems to have all the time in the world; the dead are like that. They're not in a hurry. Anything you can show them, they've seen it all before.

He's just strumming, with a chord to point towards a melody he doesn't quite bother with, not on the guitar—the voice drifts over the melody, letting you imagine it for yourself. You were about to say it again—anybody can do that strum—but your mind isn't quite your own anymore. Your memories are not your own. Your memories are now replaced by those of a lovesick man who died before your parents were born. He's traveling the world, to get away from his memories of Handsome Molly, knowing that the further he goes, the more indelible her face will be. You see it; right now, in this moment, it beckons you towards everything you've ever lost.

You leave. This isn't folk music, not as Mark Spoelstra or Tommy Makem or Joan Baez or Pete Seeger or Martin Carthy make folk music. This is not a gesture. This is not respect. This is not for good or evil. You realize you have the rest of your life to catch up. After all, somewhere, some time, he'll stumble.

Bob Dylan, *Live 1961–2000—Thirty-nine Years of Great Concert Performances* (SME, 2001).

———. *Live at the Gaslight 1962* (Columbia Legacy, 2005). Includes "The Cuckoo," "Cocaine," "West Texas," and "Handsome Molly." Notes by Sean Wilentz.

———. "No More Auction Block," on *the bootleg series volumes 1–3 [rare & unreleased] 1961–1991* (Columbia, 1991).

———. *Second Gaslight Tape* (Wild Wolf bootleg). Includes "Ain't No More Cane on the Brazos."

REAL LIFE ROCK TOP 10
Salon
16 July 2001

2) Clarence Ashley: *Greenback Dollar—The Music of Clarence Ashley, 1928–1933* (County). Ashley (1895–1967) was one of the greatest of the old-timey singers—those who, in the first third of the twentieth century, sang as if the new century was a trick that would disappear soon enough, as if only songs made long before you were born could hold your interest for more than a season. He was born Clarence and recorded under that name, but everyone knew him as Tom; when the bottom fell out of the old-timey market in the '30s, the recording artist Clarence Ashley disappeared and the performer Tom Ashley kept on. In 1960, at a fiddler's convention in North Carolina, he and guitarist Clint Howard and fiddler Fred Price were approached by folklorist Ralph Rinzler, who asked if they had knowledge of a Clarence Ashley, whose bottomless recordings of "The Coo Coo Bird" (1929) and "House Carpenter" (1930) had been collected on Harry Smith's *Anthology of American Folk Music*. "Clint Howard recalls the moment," one can read in the *Greenback Dollar* notes: "Fred and me had known Tom all our lives, but we just knew him as Tom. So I said, 'No, I don't. Do you know a Clarence Ashley, Tom?' Tom started to say, 'No,' but then he had a second thought: 'Hell, I'm Clarence Ashley!'" As a public artist, he began a second life, but musically there was really no change from his first.

Even as a young man, Ashley had a squeaky, baffled old-codger's tone. He reveled in the deadpan mysteries of "Haunted Road Blues" and "Dark Holler Blues." But those songs, like "The Coo Coo Bird" and "House Carpenter," are the high culture of old-timey. On *Greenback Dollar,* drawn from Ashley's various string bands as well as his solo recordings, low culture pulls harder; hokum rules. Ashley performed in blackface on the minstrel show–medicine show circuit; you can hear the blackface snigger in his remarkably obscene "My Sweet Farm Girl," which gets cunnilingus and analingus into a single verse. You can hear the common, secret culture of the south in Ashley's detailed versions of the true-crime ballads "Frankie Silvers," "Old John Hardy," and "Naomi Wise." And in an extremely vicious reading of "Little Sadie" you can hear a man who might have had reason to forget his own name.

Legends of Old Time Music (Vestapol/Rounder). A video anthology notable for Ashley's performance of "The Cuckoo"—recorded on the street in the early sixties. Accompanied by Fred Price, Clint Howard, and guitarist Tex Isley, Ashley explains to folklorist D. K. Wilgus what it meant to travel to New York in the twenties to record for Columbia: "How much did the people who making the records know about his music?" "Not anything," he says, and then he cuts the cards.

The Other Side of the Mirror—Bob Dylan Live at the Newport Folk Festival, 1963–1965, dir. Murray Lerner (Columbia Legacy). Includes Bob Dylan singing the likes of "Only a Pawn in Their Game" and "Blowin' in the Wind" (with Joan Baez on "With God on Our Side") as Ashley, seated directly behind him, adjusts his hat, repositions an unlit cigar, moves his banjo from his knee to the floor and back to his knee, and altogether does everything he can to remain as polite as possible.

SOMETIMES HE TALKS CRAZY, CRAZY LIKE A SONG
New York Times
2 September 2001

Bob Dylan: *"Love and Theft"*
(Columbia 85975) to be released on September 11

There's an old man who lives in your neighborhood, drinking away his days as if they were bottles. He lives by himself in a small house, though others are known to disappear into it: "Samantha

Brown, lived in my house for about four or five . . . months," he announces one day on the street, his voice tearing like cloth. "I never slept with her eeeeeven once." As if anyone cares.

An odd character, in his funny way of nodding as you walk by, in the cadence of his speech when he stops to pass the time—one moment he might be whispering a confidence, the next giving a speech—but also ordinary. He does nod, he does pass the time. On occasion he asks you in, you and your spouse or another neighbor, asks you into his parlor—which really is a parlor. A few old, comfortable chairs, shelves of books. There's a spinet piano with a collection of sheet music in the compartment in the piano bench, some of it handwritten: his own songs.

Not everything is old-fashioned. The '65 Mustang in the garage and the '59 Cadillac at the curb seem to promise a future that merely hasn't arrived yet. Along with the floral lampshades and throw rugs there's a CD player and hundreds of CDs, though most are of blues and country tunes recorded in the 1920s and 1930s. "See if there's anything you want to hear," he always says, without taking his eyes off you as you choose.

He's an explainer. One of the songs he sings at the piano, one of his own, is called "Po' Boy," though the tune sounds like the folk song "Cocaine." With a wry couplet ("Call down to room service, say send up the room") and a knock-knock joke, it tells a story about the Prodigal Son. Seeing you pick a Bukka White CD with his version of the song, or anyway the title—recorded at Parchman State Penitentiary in Mississippi in 1939, the man points out—he leans back and lets the burst of guitar notes that seem to send this "poor boy long way from home" straight to heaven wash over him like rain, then shows you Ramblin' Thomas's 1929 "Poor Boy Blues" ("A Dallas street singer," he says), then Chuck Berry's 1964 "Promised Land," about the odyssey of "the Po' Boy" from his hometown, Norfolk, Virginia, to Los Angeles.

The song was written when Berry was in federal prison in Springfield, Missouri, the man tells you ("When he wanted an atlas to get the route right, they thought he was planning an escape!''), but he's just warming up. "See, what the song is really about is the civil rights movement, the Freedom Riders, the way he plans the Po' Boy's bus route to avoid Rock Hill, that's in South Carolina, a Klan town, then the bus breaks down in Birmingham, where the Klan blew up a church and killed four little girls, that was in 1963, 'turned into a struggle,' see? It's all in this book by a professor named W. T. Lhamon, *Deliberate Speed.*" Nobody has any idea what he's talking about, but the story is romantic, somehow.

The man's own songs have pleasant names like "Bye and Bye" or "Moonlight." The way he sings and plays them, with a phony-looking toothpaste smile, suggests how he once tried to sell them. In moments they sound ridiculously corny—less like Hoagy Carmichael's "Stardust" than Jeanette MacDonald and Nelson Eddy's "Indian Love Call"—or it's a parlor from the 19th century that comes into view, and you almost hear the old sentimental songs of home and courtship, family, death, and renewal, even though the songs are off. They're not as slick as the published tunes that keep them company in the piano bench—though you can tell they were meant to be. Often they end with a sourness, a sting, even a violence, that parlors were made to banish from their doors.

The man takes midnight walks, tramping the streets even to the edge of town, muttering about all he hates, about everything he wants to destroy, preaching or telling dirty stories, gesturing wildly, his hair flying. One night you heard him going on about a woman, it seemed, but then he turned into a general on his horse as quickly as the horse then turned into a pulpit and the general into a prophet. "I'm going to spare the defeated, I'm going to speak to the crowd," he said, whoever he really was. "I'm going to teach peace to the conquered, I'm going to *tame* the proud."

Sometimes he sounds crazy, but the same sound can be seductive, especially in his seeming disdain for all those he wants dead, banished, out of his world. You catch something strange and glamorous in his voice: how you might feel if you had the nerve to talk like this. And it can happen right in his house. Suddenly he is speaking with such intensity that you hear his rants as songs and imagine a band behind them. He begins to speak loudly, angrily, hitting random blues riffs on his piano, then slamming down hard and turning to you to speak of the fun he's had and that he might—and here he is weirdly threatening—have again. "You say my eyes are pretty and my smile is nice," he says, though you haven't said a word. "I sell it to you at a reduced price."

Once he told a story about a flood, then began to sing it, without the piano: "You have to hear a banjo now," he'd said. What followed felt more mystical than real. It was the great 1927 Mississippi flood, it was Noah's flood, it was Iowa just last spring, it was the entire last century as a giant mistake, crying out for its own cleansing, asking to be washed away before it was too late. "Made it to Kansas City," he says of someone called Big Joe Turner: in his mouth the words seem to name as well Davy Crockett, Jesse James, John Henry, Stagger Lee, Railroad Bill, each bestriding the continent. He plays with old songs inside the story—the mountain ballad "The Coo Coo," say, turning the benign lyrics inside out, or revealing their true menace.

"The coo coo, she's a pretty bird, she warbles as she flies," he says with easy pleasure, then changing into Robert Mitchum's preacher in *The Night of the Hunter,* still smiling: "I'm preaching the word of God, I'm putting out your eyes." Then he goes back to the piano and sings about how he hopes she'll meet him in the moonlight. Then he passes out, and everyone leaves.

The stories people tell of the nights they've spent with the man have long since become local legend. But the legend that sticks hardest comes from what people will call "Sugar Baby": the message the man leaves on his answering machine when he leaves town. Given what people have heard before, as they listen they can almost spin the slow, deliberate words of the message into singing, and the singing into an elegant orchestration of slow, deliberate chords—something that years from now they won't be able to get out of their heads. "Sugar Baby," they'll still say to each other, probably long after the man himself is dead; it's become a saying, meaning "That's life" or "There's nothing we can do about it."

Some people will remember how the man used to take out an album by a stone-faced character named Dock Boggs, a singer from the Virginia mountains, who first recorded in 1927, the man would carefully explain; he'd play a song called "Sugar Baby." That was real killer-inside-me stuff; "Sugar Baby" was what Boggs called his lover, who you weren't sure would survive the song. On the message the man leaves, "Sugar Baby"—the words leading off every refrain—seems to be the name of a horse. The feeling, though—the sense of a life used up, wasted as every life is finally wasted, leaving the earth as if one's life had never been—is the same. The feeling is that there is all the time in the world to take stock, if only in the ledger you keep in your heart to settle accounts, to tell jokes you half hope no one will get. "I'm staying with Aunt Sally," the man says on the machine, "but you know she not really my aunt." You laugh, and then something in his tone pulls you down into the emptiness he's speaking from. As in the parlor, he has led you to relax into his exile.

That is just a story. But *"Love and Theft,"* Bob Dylan's first collection of new songs in four years, is an album of stories, some told to the end, some of the most remarkable only hinted at. "High Water (For Charley Patton)" is both.

Born likely in 1891, Patton, a founder of the Mississippi Delta blues, recorded from 1929 until his death in 1934. "His vowels were stretched out, inflated from within; they expanded until they were all but unrecognizable," Tom Piazza wrote recently about how hard it can be to hear him—but in the teasing murk of his sound, Piazza said, "he opened a window in time for himself." It's that window Dylan walks through as if it were a door. While you can find a transcriptions of the lyrics of Patton's 1929 "High Water Everywhere," Patton's singing could hardly be more underwater: "I firmly believe, and have believed for years," a man for whom old blues is a second language says, "that Charley Patton is not singing in English on 'High Water.'" Compared with the dirt in

Patton's voice, the rubble in Dylan's may sound as smooth as glass, but the impenetrability of Patton's song is there in Dylan's: in riddles and parables.

Verse by verse in Dylan's "High Water Everywhere," the flood spreads, takes in and upends more lives, making everyone understand that your freedoms under the Constitution are nothing compared to what God wants from you this night. "You dancing with whom they tell you to," Dylan has one Bertha Mason say, "or you don't dance at all."

"It's bad out there," a verse ends. "It's tough out there." "Things are breaking up out there." But then in the midst of the disaster, a fable stands out as if clearing its own space in the maelstrom. "Well," Dylan says, "George Lewes told the Englishman, the Italian and the Jew" (who just walked into a bar):

You can't open up your minds, boys, to every conceivable point of view
They got Charles Darwin trapped out there on Highway 5
Judge says to the High Sheriff, I want him dead or alive
Either one, I don't . . . care

Dissolving into mystery as soon as it seems clear, the story will be there as long as any in Dylan's signature *Highway 61 Revisited,* from 1965; this could be a verse from it. But the heart of *"Love and Theft"*—the window Dylan's new music itself opens up in time—is in that final "care," dropping off its line like a body falling out of a window, with the same thud. A whole world of rejection, of nothingness, of the humor shared by dead men walking because the graveyard is full—a whole way of being in the world, and a whole way of talking about it, opens up out of that single word, out of the way it's thrown away, and what it throws away with it. As Raymond Chandler had his detective Philip Marlowe say in 1953 in *The Long Goodbye,* in the same voice: "It all depends on where you sit and what your private score is. I didn't have one. I didn't care." Then Marlowe went out and solved the case.

REAL LIFE ROCK TOP 10
Salon
4 September 2001

1) Great Pop Moments (That Should Have Happened Even if They Didn't Division): Valerie Mass, People column (Denver *Post,* Aug. 6). "Elton John spilled the beans about his former liquor-soaked, drugged-out life in an interview with *The London Mirror* . . . John said he met Bob Dylan and George Harrison at a party he was hosting in Los Angeles but was unable to talk any sense to them. 'I'd had quite a few martinis and [God] knows how much cocaine. So I started babbling on about how [Dylan] had to come up to my room and try on my clothes . . .'"

2) Bob Dylan: "Summer Days," from *"Love and Theft"* (Columbia). Speaking of trying on new clothes—four years ago, Dylan's celebrated *Time Out of Mind* mapped a country of abandoned roads and emptied cities, and nothing like what's happening here could have happened there. *"Waaaal"*—in this song, "Well" is always "Waaaal," "Yes" is always "Yaaaaaaassss," pure minstrel diction, as befits an album seemingly named for Eric Lott's 1993 study *Love and Theft: Blackface Minstrelsy and the American Working Class*— "Waaaaal, I'm standing on a table, I'm proposing a toast to the King," the singer shouts from inside a roadhouse where a western swing band is running a jitterbug beat as if it's twirling a rope. On the dance floor women are flipping in the air and couples snap back at each other like towels in a locker room. The singer high-steps his way across the room, Stetson topping his Nudie suit. How much proof do you want that the night can't go wrong? "Why don't you break my heart one more time," he says happily to the woman at his side, "just for good luck?" He stretches out the last word as if he can't bear to give it up.

HIGH WATER EVERYWHERE
Rolling Stone
25 October 2001

"Where is the building? Did it fall down? Where is it?"
—**Joe Disordo,** on the collapse of Two World Trade Center,
New York Times, 16 September 2001

* * *

Looking down they could see the last convulsions: The lights of the cars were darting through the streets, like animals trapped in a maze, frantically seeking an exit, the bridges were jammed with cars, the approaches to the bridges were veins of massed headlights, glittering bottlenecks stopping all motion and the desperate screaming of sirens reached faintly to the height of the plane . . .

The plane was above the peaks of the skyscrapers when suddenly, with the abruptness of a shudder, as if the ground had parted to engulf it, the city disappeared from the face of the earth. It took them a moment to realize that the panic had reached the power stations—and that the lights of New York had gone out.
—**Ayn Rand,** *Atlas Shrugged,* 1957

Everything was absolutely ideal on the day I bombed the Pentagon. The sky was blue. The birds were singing. And the bastards were finally going to get what was coming to them.

I say "I" even though I didn't actually bomb the Pentagon—*we* bombed it, in the sense that Weatherman organized and claimed it . . . Some details cannot be told. Some friends and comrades have been in prison for decades; others, including Bernadine, spent months and months locked up for refusing to talk or give handwriting samples to federal grand juries. Consequences are real for people, and that's part of this story, too. But the government was dead wrong, and we were right. In our conflict we don't talk; we don't tell. We never confess.

When activists were paraded before grand juries, asked to name names, to humiliate themselves and to participate in destroying the movement, most refused and went to jail without saying a word. Outside they told the press, I didn't do it, but I dug it. I recall John Brown's strategy over a century ago—he shot all the members of the grand jury investigating his activities in Kansas.

—**Bill Ayers,** *Fugitive Days,* September 2001

"You don't know where she is?" I asked again. He shrugged again, and I said, "OK." I let the automatic dangle from my hand as I waited for the sound of a jet making its final approach over the motel. "Last chance," I said before the noise was too loud for him to hear. He shrugged again. "You know I'm not going to kill you, don't you?" I said. He shook his head, but his eyes smiled. He might be a piece of shit but Jackson had some balls on him. Either that or he was more frightened of his business associates than he was of me. That was a real mistake on his part. When the landing jet swept over the motel, I leaned down and pumped two rounds into his right foot.

"You didn't have to shoot him twice," Trahearne said.

"Once to get his attention," I said, "and once to let him know I was serious."

—**James Crumley,** *The Last Good Kiss,* 1978

*   *   *

The terrorist attacks were major atrocities. In scale, they may not reach the level of many others—for example, Clinton's 1998 bombing of the Sudan with no credible pretext, destroying half its pharmaceutical supplies and killing unknown numbers of people.

—**Noam Chomsky,** 13 September 2001

Over the years since the seizure of the American embassy in Tehran in 1979, the [American] public has become tolerably familiar with the idea that there are Middle Easterners of various shades and stripes who do not like them . . . With cell phones still beeping piteously from under the rubble, it probably seems indecent to most people to ask if the United States has ever done anything to invite such awful hatred.

—**Christopher Hitchens**, *The Guardian* (London),
13 September 2001

"What we saw on Tuesday, terrible as it is, could be miniscule if, in fact, God continues to lift the curtain and allow the enemies of America to give us what we probably deserve . . . The abortionists have got to bear some burden for this because God will not be mocked. And when we destroy forty million little innocent babies, we make God mad. I really believe that the pagans, the abortionists, the feminists, and the gays and the lesbians who are actively trying to make an alternative lifestyle, to secularize America, I point the finger in their face and say, 'You helped this happen.'"

—**Rev. Jerry Falwell**, 700 Club, 13 September 2001

Responsibility for violence lies with those who perpetrate it.

—**Salman Rushdie**, "In Good Faith," 1990

*   *   *

The water was rising, got up in my bed
Lord, the water was rolling, got up to my bed
I thought I would take a trip, Lord, out on the days I slept.

—**Charley Patton**, "High Water Everywhere Part II," 1929

I was stranded in Chicago until late last night. On the runway in Newark on Monday at 8 A.M.—that was OK by one day; on the runway at O'Hare on Tuesday at 8.30—that wasn't so great. The airport shut down, and we were left to make our way into a chaotic Chicago of semi-evacuation. After three days and five plane reservations cancelled, I finally found a car and drove home. Eight hundred miles of flags, licenses from everywhere and bumper stickers like MY PRESIDENT IS CHARLTON HESTON and HOW'S MY DRIVING /

DIAL 1-800-EAT-SHIT. With my finger on the pulse of the nation, I pulled in about 10 P.M.

—Hal Foster, Princeton, New Jersey, e-mail, 15 September 2001

For the first time in America, except during the Civil War and the World War, people were afraid to say whatever came to their tongues. On the streets, on trains, at theatres, men looked about to see who might be listening before they dared so much as say there was a drought in the West, for someone might suppose they were blaming the drought on the Chief! . . . Every moment one felt fear, nameless and omnipresent. They were jumpy as men in a plague district. Any sudden sound, any unexplained footstep, any unfamiliar script on an envelope made them startle; and for months they never felt secure enough to let themselves go, in complete sleep.

—Sinclair Lewis, *It Can't Happen Here,* 1935

Gloom and sadness and bereavement just hang in the air. My local firemen were killed, and the whole area is plastered with missing-people flyers: someone's little daughter who had accompanied her mother to work, endless husbands and wives and daughters and sons and best friends; destroyed people.

—Emily Marcus, Charles Street and Greenwich Avenue,
Manhattan, e-mail, 15 September 2001

High water rising, rising night and day
All the gold and silver being stolen away
Big Joe Turner looked east and west from the dark rooms of his mind
He made it to Kansas City, Twelfth Street and Vine
Nothing standing there

—Bob Dylan, "High Water (For Charley Patton)," September 2001

*   *   *

"The ship? Great God, where is the ship?"

—Herman Melville, *Moby-Dick,* 1851

PART SEVEN

Find a Grave,
2001–2004

REAL LIFE ROCK TOP 10

Salon
26 November 2001

3) findagrave.com. It was Connie Nisinger, a high school librarian in the Midwest, who decided that this interesting site needed a picture of the final resting place of Billy Lyons, shot dead in St. Louis on Christmas Day, 1895, his corpse kicked through time ever after in the countless versions of "Stag-o-lee," "Stacker Lee" and "Stagger Lee." Click "Search by name," type in "William Lyons," and there is Lyons's plot in St. Peter's Cemetery in St. Louis, sec. 5, lot 289. The site allows you to "Leave flowers and a note for this person": keep clicking and you can leave a cigar or a beer instead. Advertising bars include "Contact Your High School Classmates"— to find their graves?

Salon
10 December 2001

10) Cameron Crowe: director, *Vanilla Sky* (DreamWorks/Paramount). Charles Taylor writes: "In *Vanilla Sky*, the Cruizesuzs, Tom and Penelope, recreate the cover of *The Freewheelin' Bob Dylan*. May God have mercy on us all."

NOT SINGING TOO FAST

Interview
February 2002

"I don't think she could bear not to be in the headlines," said a professor two weeks after Susan Sontag's instantly notorious *New*

Yorker comment on the September 11 mass murders as "a consequence of specific American alliances and actions"—there apparently being no need to name what they were. The woman speaking had lived through Auschwitz and, as a dissident intellectual, through three decades of a postwar Stalinist regime; at seventy-two she suffered no fools. But Sontag was no different from so many others, from novelists to reporters, from columnists to philosophers, who after that day stepped forward to deny that anything had been done that required any rethinking of anything at all. None had changed his or her mind in the slightest about anything. Nearly every argument was intended to congratulate the speaker for having seen all the way around the event even before it happened. The speakers could have said what President Dwight Eisenhower once said: "Things are more like they are now than they ever were before."

Perhaps more than those called to other callings, artists work in the dark—and without artists, society would enter the future blind. "I accept chaos. I am not sure whether it accepts me," as Bob Dylan once put it; the best artists trust that instinct. Especially in a time of chaos—when so many are insisting that what one might feel as chaos is still order—artists can explore, track and map the wilderness of uncertainty and doubt that ordinary political speech means to deny. Rather than calculating what will do the most good or please the most people, artists can trust their own blind bets, without calculating any effects whatsoever. That doesn't mean art has no effects; it means the best artists accept that they have no control over what those effects might be. But the speech of artists—the language their work speaks—can be as impoverished as that of anybody else.

I think one reason so many people think of the firefighters and police officers who were called to the World Trade Center on September 11 as heroes—those who lived and those who didn't—is that as they acted to save their city and their fellow citizens, they kept their mouths shut. They had neither the time or the need to justify, apologize, or explain. Perhaps singers and musicians, who like political actors engage in public speech, have something to learn from firemen and police officers, from people whose extraordinary but also everyday heroism now keeps the word hero from being too easily applied.

What singers and musicians might have to learn is this: when you have nothing to say, it is not incumbent upon you, as a public person, to say anything. "[He] made it very clear he'd written the song about the state of things post 9/11," *San Francisco Chronicle* critic James Sullivan said to me about Rufus Wainwright's debut of his song "Eleven Eleven" during a performance last November. "The first lines were 'Woke up this morning, it was 11:11,' or '. . . the clock said 11:11'—I distinctly remember thinking, 'Uh-oh. The dreaded journal entry.' I like Rufus plenty, but the song struck me like it was his dutiful songwriter's homework project." At the austere September benefit concert "America: A Tribute to Heroes," Bruce Springsteen offered his song "My City of Ruins"—and, really, you could answer its chorus of "Come on, rise up! Come on, rise up!" with, "Shut up, God damn it! Give me time to despair! Give me time to hate!" Did the song, written two years ago for the residents of Asbury Park, New Jersey, need to be sung in this utterly different context? Wouldn't it have been more powerful, more shocking—more of an affirmation of the terrorist attacks not as a "dose of reality," as Susan Sontag described them, but as a rent in reality—for an artist as eloquent and honest as Springsteen to step forward and attest that for the moment he had nothing to say?

"Let us not talk falsely now," Bob Dylan sang in "All Along the Watchtower," three years after his comment on chaos, by then in the middle of the Vietnam War, just before the assassinations of Martin Luther King, Jr., and Robert Kennedy. How do you do that? In a time of public crisis, when, more than oneself, one's community is in jeopardy, from within or from without, it may be that a citizen, and especially a citizen who is also an artist, avoids speaking falsely by offering nothing less than the very best of what he or she has to say—which sometimes might mean nothing at all.

REAL LIFE ROCK TOP 10
Salon
25 February 2002

4/5) Dave Van Ronk: *The Folkways Years, 1959–1961* (Smithsonian Folkways) and *No Dirty Names* (Verve Folkways, 1966). When he died February 10th at sixty-five, Van Ronk left behind a well of generosity and affection. Many of those who passed through the Greenwich Village folk milieu in the 1960s, perhaps most, learned the classics from him—"In the Pines," "Careless Love," "Spike Driver's Moan," "Betty and Dupree"—but as *The Folkways Years* makes plain, what set Van Ronk apart from those with whom he shared his place and time was not his ability to bring the old music to life. Only rarely, as on the shattering "Zen Koans Gonna Rise Again" from *No Dirty Names,* one of his few original compositions—the sardonic title instantly dissolving into a chant of self-loathing as the "Mayor of MacDougal Street" looks down from his railroad flat at the junkies hustling their women in the doorways—did he sing anything you couldn't have heard someone else sing better. Van Ronk was different because he was what so many people think they want to be, if only they could find the time: a man whose life was a gesture of welcoming, a storyteller whose stories allowed those who were listening to imagine that they themselves were in the story, at the same time sitting back in the warmth of Van Ronk's presence, listening to their own adventures.

HOW GOOD CAN IT GET
Interview
November 2002

"How Good It Can Get" is a typically expert Wallflowers tune—and a key to why their new *Red Letter Days* is a break through the wall of craft and moderation the group has always played behind.

Since the band's debut ten years ago with *The Wallflowers,* when leader Jakob Dylan was twenty-two, their music has rolled through the radio with an ease Dylan's own father never mastered. "One Headlight," from the huge 1996 album *Bringing Down the Horse,* so dominated the radio in 1997 that some people figured Bob Dylan wouldn't release his rocks-and-gravel comeback *Time Out of Mind* until his son made room for it.

On "How Good It Can Get" the singer is introducing a woman to sex. "We'll make a lover / Out of you yet," he promises with infinite condescension—with an *and who is this "we"?* hanging in the background as the song moves on. *Red Letter Days* has already kicked off with the life-is-great testament "When You're on Top"—which on the radio sounds more like a commercial than a single (music this vapidly enthusiastic can sell anything) and will end with "Here in Pleasantville" (few will be surprised by the revelation that all is not pleasant in a place called Pleasantville). But a certain momentum is building in "How Good It Can Get," and you might wonder why the musician in Jakob Dylan seems never to have asked himself the same question not even hiding in the phrase.

He answers the question of how good it can get on *Red Letter Days*—and it's something to hear. The violence of "Everybody Out of the Water," the hammering choruses of "Too Late to Quit," the rising groove in "See You When I Get There," the fists-shaking-in-your-face noise of "Everything I Need," the grinding of brags against doubts in "Feels Like Summer Again"—something as apparently small as the willingness to throw a phrase like "makes me sick" into a melody that seems to promise no trouble for anyone—all of it testifies to a willingness to break through to the other side, and to what you can send back when you make it.

"Everybody Out of the Water" (originally called "New Frontier") is part watching television last September, looking at the ruins in downtown New York, trying to believe what you were seeing. It's part "London Calling"—as it appears on the Clash's 1979 album of the same name, not in this year's creepy Jaguar commercial (pronounced "Zshag-u-ahr" by the pitchwoman). It's part answer record to Bob Dylan's 1967 "Crash on the Levee (Down in the Flood)," or his 2001 "High Water (For Charley Patton)"—itself an answer record to Patton's 1929 "High Water Everywhere," which was an answer to the 1927 Mississippi flood. The promise of John F. Kennedy's presidency—the New Frontier, named, some cynics have suggested, after the hotel where Elvis Presley made his Las Vegas debut in 1956—hangs over the music as the summation of all broken promises, or what's left when the floodwaters finally recede. The song gives no quarter, quiets down only to let the clouds gather again, to make the climb of the rhythm back to the top of the song's mountain more exciting than it was the last time around. "On your mark / Get set, let's go" is the first line: Can the music keep up with its subject, or even outrun it?

"Everybody out of the water!" Jakob Dylan shouts again and again. When he says, "The city's been leveled," right at the start, you don't quite believe him—not yet. But the guitar figure snaking closely around a spot the whole song is circling from a shrinking distance convinces you the story is for real. "This is the New Frontier / Everybody out of the water" is suddenly frightening.

And then Dylan is doing things he's never even hinted at before. The word "shit" hurts. The word "sucks" is a void—the way Dylan mouths the word is pure American speech, a complete rejection of all authority, particularly the authority of people saying everything is going to be all right.

That is the message Dylan's own music has communicated in the past. Now he has opened up a hole deep enough to bury his previous hits—and so when on *Red Letter Days* the suggestion comes that things might indeed be all right, you can believe it's not an idle notion. But it won't feel as good as the argument that everything has gone to hell.

Wallflowers, *Red Letter Days* (Interscope, 2001).

REAL LIFE ROCK TOP 10

Salon

4 November 2002

10) Bob Dylan: "Train of Love," from *Kindred Spirits: A Tribute to the Songs of Johnny Cash* (Lucky Dog). Aren't tribute albums terrible? Dylan almost never does good work on them, but here, surrounded by Dwight Yoakam, Steve Earle (it's against the law to make a tribute album without him), Travis Tritt, Keb' Mo', the unspeakable Hank Williams, Jr., Bruce Springsteen, Mary Chapin Carpenter, Sheryl Crow, Emmylou Harris, and Rosanne Cash, he gets real, real gone, though not before pausing to wave goodbye: "I used to sing this song before I ever wrote a song," Dylan says before "Train of Love." "I also want to thank you for standing up for me, way back when." Way back in 1965, onstage at the Newport Folk Festival, where, as the current revisionist line has it, nothing actually happened.

Salon

9 December 2002

Special Bob Dylan at Madison Square Garden Number!

1) Announcement (MSG, Nov. 11). For years, the same voice has opened every show with the same words: "Ladies and gentlemen, please welcome, Columbia recording artist, BOBDYLAN!"—the name always squashed into a single word. Last August 9, though, in anticipation of a date in Hamburg, N.Y., a looking-back piece appeared in the *Buffalo News*. As print it was boilerplate; hearing it appropriated word for word as Dylan's new fanfare was pure media shock, the displacement that takes place when the conventions of one form are shoved into those of another. This is what the audience hears today: "Ladies and gentlemen, please welcome the poet laureate of rock 'n' roll. The voice of the promise of the '60s

counterculture. The guy who forced folk into bed with rock, who donned makeup in the '70s and disappeared into a haze of substance abuse, who emerged to find *Jay-sus,* who was written off as a has-been by the end of the '80s, and who suddenly shifted gears, releasing some of the strongest music of his career beginning in the late '90s. Ladies and gentlemen, Bob Dylan!"

2) "Masters of War" (MSG, Nov. 11) In 1991, with the Gulf War under way, Dylan stepped onto the stage at the Grammys telecast with his band and played "Masters of War," from 1963—but you couldn't necessarily tell. The song was buried in its performance, as if history were its true audience.

With a second Gulf War looming, there was no disguise when, seven songs into the first of two New York shows, Dylan gathered his small band into a half-circle for an acoustic, almost chamber-music version. Played very slowly, very deliberately, the performance made you understand just how good the song is. It wasn't a matter of relevance. You could imagine that if the last war on earth had occurred thirty-nine years ago—if the song had, by its very appearance, ended war—the song would still speak, just as a 7000-year-old god excavated in Jordan and recently installed in the Louvre is still speaking, reminding you of what you came from, of who you once were.

3) Cover: "(The Angels Wanna Wear My) Red Shoes," from Elvis Costello, 1977 (MSG, Nov. 11) He didn't sing about the shoes; having apparently invested more wisely than the angels, he wore them.

4) *The Bootleg Series, Volume 5: Live 1975—The Rolling Thunder Revue* (Columbia) Confusion in almost every vocal, a pound of sugar in almost every arrangement. Right, the famous "donned makeup in the '70s" period.

5) Paul Muldoon, "Bob Dylan at Princeton, November 2000," from *'Do You, Mr. Jones?'—Bob Dylan with the Poets and Professors,* ed-

ited by Neil Corcoran (Chatto & Windus, U.K.) Muldoon is a poet (author most recently of *Moy Sand and Gravel*), co-writer on Warren Zevon's "My Ride's Here," and a professor at Princeton. Leading off this new essay collection with a new poem, Muldoon goes back to a show Dylan played at Princeton in 2000—which took place in Princeton's Dillon Gym. "You know what, honey? We call that a homonym," the narrator of the poem says to the woman he's at the concert with. Muldoon lets the suggestiveness in "homonym"—homage, homunculus, Homoousian—take over; the prosaic moves over an odd surface. Then Dylan's only previous appearance at Princeton enters the poem—in 1970, when Dylan was present not to play but to accept an honorary degree. "He wouldn't wear a hood," the narrator remembers. "You know what, honey? We call that disquietude."

6) Cover: "Something," from George Harrison, 1969 (MSG, Nov. 13) A final encore, done very straight. Musicians love this song; musicians admire the ability to craft anything that's at once generic, anonymous and likely to generate income for a hundred years.

7) "Summer Days" (MSG, Nov. 11) The turnaround cut from the seven-years-overdue unreleased live album "Having a Rave-up with Bob Dylan!"

8) "Yea! Heavy and a Bottle of Bread" (MSG, Nov. 11) Dylan's first performance of the song since he recorded it with the Hawks in a basement of a big pink house in upstate New York thirty-five years ago. Two of the five who were there then are dead. The house was recently on the market as a prime Dylan collectable. The tune still blew the air of pure American fedupness: "Pack up the meat, sweet, we're headin' out."

9) "It's Alright, Ma (I'm Only Bleeding)" (MSG, Nov. 11) From 1964. The audience always waits to cheer for "Sometimes even the president of the United States must have to stand naked." By now the number has outlasted almost as many presidents as Fidel

Castro: Lyndon Johnson (no problem, for a man who liked to re-ceive guests while sitting on the toilet), Richard Nixon, Gerald Ford, Jimmy Carter, Ronald Reagan, George Bush, Bill Clinton (who as president was stripped naked, and who you can imagine singing the line to himself) and now George W. Bush. The line took nothing away from him. He lives in the armor of his own entitlement, and he may outlast the song.

10) "All Along the Watchtower" (MSG, Nov. 11) The second of two encores, it began very strangely, with guitarist Charlie Sexton rolling a few spare notes that seemed to call up a distant Western—Jim Jarmusch's *Dead Man,* maybe, with Neil Young's improvised and timeless guitar soundtrack. It was in fact the opening of Fer-rante & Tiecher's 1961 twin-piano hit "Theme from *Exodus,*" from the movie based on Leon Uris's 1958 novel about the creation of the state of Israel. Whether you caught the reference or not, it took the song about to emerge from its own history—one of Dylan's most world-ending, from 1968, a year that over and over again felt like the end of the world—out of itself. Now the song was going to speak with a new voice: that was the promise that little introduc-tion made.

It was impossible to imagine that Dylan ever played the song with more vehemence, or that, this night, six days after the mid-term congressional elections, the performance was not utterly po-litical, as much a protest song as "Masters of War." Not when, after Dylan, Sexton and guitarist Larry Campbell led an overwhelming instrumental climb through the tune's themes following the clos-ing verse, Dylan came back to the mike to sing the opening verse again in a wild voice, throwing the last lines across the seats and out of the hall like a curse: "Businessmen they drink my wine, plowmen dig my earth / None of them, along the line, know what—any—any of it—any of it is—worth."

Salon
3 February 2003

6) *The Portable Sixties Reader,* edited by Ann Charters (Penguin). At more than 600 pages, a definitively clueless anthology ending with bad poems about the deaths of the decade's top ten dead people. Count down! Ten! Hemingway! Nine! Marilyn Monroe! Eight! John F. Kennedy! "When I woke up they'd stole a man away," says Eric von Schmidt—hey, who's "they"? As Donovan used to say, "I really want to know," but never mind, Seven! Sylvia Plath! Six! Malcolm X! Five! Martin Luther King, Jr.! Four! *Robert* F. Kennedy! Three! Neal Cassady! Two! Janis Joplin! And topping the chart: Jack Kerouac! With a straight obit from the *Harvard Crimson!* Solid! But Janis died in 1970. If she can get in, why not Jimi Hendrix? Captain Beefheart played a soprano sax solo for him the day his death was announced that said more than anything here.

City Pages
9 April 2003

3) Bob Dylan for Victoria's Secret (Fox, March 4) "Only two things in this world worth botherin' your head about and them's sex and death," says a "debauched Midwestern businessman" in Michael O'Donoghue and Frank Springer's 1968 comic serial *The Adventures of Phoebe Zeitgeist.* That's the only explanation for the commercial that uses Dylan's suicidal 1997 "Love Sick" to orchestrate a montage of underwear models looking dour under their hooded eyes. But it's a better Dylan setting than the nearly four-hours-long God-blessed-the-Confederacy film *Gods and Generals,* which features his "'Cross the Green Mountain." I haven't seen the picture, but I have seen the TV trailer featuring Robert Duvall sitting in a chair as Robert E. Lee and opining, through a mouthful of molasses, "'s in Gawd's han's naw," as if to say, "Hey, don't blame me." On the other hand, "Love Sick" is an actual song. At more than eight dying minutes, "'Cross the Green Mountain" might as well be the movie.

City Pages
16 July 2003

2) Bob Dylan in *Charlie's Angels: Full Throttle* (Sony Pictures) Ken Tucker writes in: "Not on the KICK-ASS soundtrack album to this KICK-ASS movie—who needs him there, when you've got Nickelback and Kid Rock collaborating on a KICK-ASS version of Elton's "Saturday Night's Alright for Fighting"? No, Dylan sneaks in during the scene in which a KICK-ASS Drew Barrymore gathers her belongings to leave Angel headquarters, and we clearly see that one of her few cherished possessions is a vinyl copy of *Bringing It All Back Home*. So the real mystery of the movie is, who wanted that product placement in a film filled with shots plugging Cingular Wireless and Body By Demi? My guess? Crispin Glover had been using the album on the set to get himself in the mood to play a bitter, religion-warped mute, and director McG did what he does best, which is stealing cultural totems and reducing them to throwaway junk-jokes that make the viewer feel as though the ASS of anything in life that matters has been KICKED."

THE LOST WALTZ
Threepenny Review
Fall 2004*

There's a great sweep to the Band's story, beginning in Arkansas and Ontario in the 1950s, tracing an arc through to the last year of the twentieth century. It's a far-reaching bow that carried Levon Helm (born in 1940 in Marvell, Arkansas), Robbie Robertson (1943, Toronto), Rick Danko (1942, Green's Corners), Richard Manuel (1943, Stratford), and Garth Hudson (1937, London) through their barnstorming years as Ronnie Hawkins's and then

---

*Drawn from liner notes written for *The Band—A Musical History* (Capitol, 2005), and understandably rejected.

Levon's Hawks in the early sixties, into the noise they made as the unnamed musicians backing Bob Dylan's furious shows in 1965 and 1966, and to their fraternal refounding as the Band in the Big Pink house in Woodstock, New York, in 1967. The curve brought their offer of a new music and a new point of view—a point of view that was also a sense of weight, a sense of weight that in the fractured, whirling America of the late 1960s and early '70s was as much as anything a kind of gravity. The arc circled over the finale of the Last Waltz in San Francisco in 1976, after which Robbie Robertson left the group and the rest played on as the Band, but with barely any new music of their own, without, in some cursed way, a voice, playing back through their own past in small clubs like the Cheek to Cheek Lounge in Winter Park, Florida, where, following a show in 1986, Richard Manuel hanged himself. It was an arc that bent toward an end but even through another decade did not reach it—an arc that touched down only in the last month of 1999, when Rick Danko died in Woodstock, and Levon Helm and Garth Hudson let the working name of the Band die with him.

That is one way to tell the story—but there are moments all through the Band's music where the Band's story seems to tell itself. In "King Harvest (Has Surely Come)," these are moments which are also incidents, or events, where something happens and then is over, or lost, left behind by the story which is also the song, a story that returns to what was lost as the song rounds its next turn, and so the cruelest moment of the song is when it ends.

It was 1969 when the song appeared as the last track on *The Band,* the group's second album, but there is no fixed time in the music. The music sounds old, but in the way a landscape can feel old; in the same way that a landscape promises it will renew itself, the music points to the future. It seems to assume its own permanence, that it is a language that will always be understood, and it's a shock when you realize the singer seems most of all convinced that no one will understand what he's talking about, or care if they do.

"Corn in the fields . . . Listen to the rice as the wind blows cross the water": as if speaking for the landscape, not as someone with a name and a fate, Levon Helm leads the first chorus. As he taps his cymbals, drawing a circle around himself, Garth Hudson's clavinette drops rain into the image of a farm alive with movement and sound, weather and work, so alive you can believe you can hear the crops grow. "I remember from my youth, people out there in the country somewhere, in a place we all know, it may have been there, it may have not," Robbie Robertson said nearly thirty years after he wrote the song, fixing it in "the idea of 'Come autumn, come fall'—*that's* when life begins. It's not the springtime, where we kind of think it begins, it is the fall—the harvests come in."

Richard Manuel, the tale-teller, is less a singer than an actor inside the verses of the song. In an instant, drawing words out of his throat as if the act takes all the strength he has, as much strength as the Band itself uses as it pulls the rhythms of the song against its melody, he makes it plain that the pastoral vision of the opening chorus is inhuman. It has no room for failure, defeat, fear, shame— everything this man's voice is made of. The warm assurance of each prayerful "Corn . . . in the fields" is his memory mocking him, the ruined farm he left behind now leaving him walking city streets filled with bums and drunks. As he describes the disasters of his life, never mentioning the family that must have worked the farm with him, that he has left behind as well, the desperation in his voice grows stronger, more pathetic, more absolute. Each time the promise of the trees, the meadow, the moon, of people celebrating the harvest, circles him in a chorus, the promise seems at once irredeemable and undeniable, a truth that is also a lie, a lie that is also the truth.

Nothing in the man's voice is so flesh-crawlingly pitiful as the faith he puts in the union that he insists will save him and all those like him, a union for farmers at the mercy of speculators, a union for factory workers treated like machinery, to be discarded when they break—it isn't clear and it doesn't matter. The desperation is greatest in the man's awful cry of belief, so great its language breaks into pieces, the classic pledge "I'm a union man, now and always" falling apart as it's spoken: "I'm a union and now always . . ." But that terror may even be worse in the utter lack of irony with which the man describes the promise of the union, even as the broken promise of the land he has abandoned, that has cast him out, shadows his words: "Here come a man with a paper and pen, telling us our hard times are about to end—" In American folk language, the man with a paper and pen means only one thing: the con man who will shake your hand, look you in the eye, and charm you into signing away everything you have, even if it is only your name. "I'm bound to come out on top," the singer says, and Richard Manuel makes you believe that the man in the song believes what he says, and then you do turn away, ashamed to listen any longer.

Or rather you would, if the song did not, when the singer finishes his story, turn into a different story: more complex and impossible to fix. In a few stanzas, the song has caught a repeating story—a farmer and his farm in Wisconsin in the horrifying depression of the 1890s, in Oklahoma and Arkansas in the Great Depression of the 1930s, in the depression that doesn't make the news, the depression that for a family farm in any state or province can arrive at any time. But the man has only told you what he can put into words, and there is a way in which it is only when the words end that the song begins.

You don't want to separate one element of the music from another; you want the music to sweep you up and take you away, and it does that. But over the years, as you return to the song, or find it returning to you, on the radio, on a CD player in a store—or in the instant of first playing it, then finding yourself unable to play anything else, playing the song again and again, as if to prove the music is as inexhaustible as it seems to be—the parts of the music stand up in turn.

The man Richard Manuel portrays has told you what he can; now the other members of the Band take a single step forward to tell you what he can't. Out of the man's fright, his hopeless embrace of any way out, comes a different story altogether. Robbie Robertson begins a guitar solo, made of the thinnest notes, notes so edged and brittle you can almost feel them break as they bend. The story these notes tell is about holding on, not letting go; about determination and courage, about a quest and an escape. You no longer see a ruin, or a fool; you see a man with his eyes level and clear, with a life ahead of him, a life he has begun to lead.

Far beneath the quick and wary steps in Robertson's solo is something like an underground stream—or whatever image Garth Hudson's organ calls up. The stream breaks the surface, and makes an image of freedom, of a man racing the banks of what is now a river, then lying in the grass and looking up at the sky, an image of harmony. Hudson had pushed the drama when the singer poured out his heart, poured out his fears and the hopes he was almost scared to voice; now there is no drama, only a horizon that recedes as the man gazes on it, promising there will never be an end to it. We believe in linear time, in an accumulation of events that leave both us and the world changed; that story is in the solo Robertson is playing on top. Ancient peoples believed in circular time, where there was change within a circle, as one season gave way to another, but the circle did not change, and farmers feel that rhythm no matter what their calendars: "A dry summer, then comes fall / Which I depend on most of all," the farmer has told you, and the perfection of that circle is what you can hear in the music Hudson is making far below. The sound grows quieter and quieter, making you strain to hear it, right up until the point where the sound, fading out, stops cold.

The truest story, or the hardest, the most fragmentary and at the same time the most complete, is beneath even the one Hudson tells.

Throughout the song, there has been a submerged but constant sense of struggle, of resistance, against—what? Fate? The ultimate triviality of one man's failure in the face of the world that doesn't notice and doesn't care? The beauty of the world, of grass and sky, flowers and the rising of the moon, all of it a trick to fool men and women into thinking that, the gospel song they sing to the contrary, the world really is their home? From the start, this feeling of resistance has come from Levon Helm's bass drum and Rick Danko's bass, locked in a dance that is one step forward, one step back. But at the close of "King Harvest," as the rhythm the two are making emerges from the music, you realize it is primary, the foundation of everything in the song, but also its last word, the song's judgment on itself.

Listen: the slow, steady tapping of Helm's stick is the sound of a man rapping his knuckles on a porch railing, a hundred times, a thousand times, never a change, never a sign that anything will change, or can, or even should. And the sound Danko makes—thick, twisting, strong—is the sound of a man listening to his own heart, or to something he cannot see and cannot name, moving below the ground beneath his feet. Robertson's guitar solo opens a road out and takes it, Hudson's enveloping melodies are an embrace that never breaks, and Helm and Danko's two-step, as uncanny as it is plain, is a door swinging open in the wind in a house abandoned years ago.

The Band's strongest music would always seem unfinished, as if there was always more to be said—as Ronnie Hawkins's 1963 cover of Bo Diddley's "Who Do You Love" will always seem unfinished. The band locks into place with the first beat, Robertson shooting out flashes, giving Hawkins's weak vocal the support it needs. And then the first verse ends and the song goes right over a cliff. An otherworldly growl comes up as if out of the ground, turning into a scream that all but reaches out of the speakers, then falls back, as if whoever is making this sound has turned his back and run away, as scared of the sound he's making as you are. Robertson takes over, his lead lines scattered, fractured, what ought to be a straightforward blues progression matching Hawkins's nightcalls with an abstraction no less impossible to track. Another verse, another roll of madness, then a flurry of "Rollin' and Tumblin'" licks on the guitar, wrapping everything up—except that it's at this moment that the monster returns, charging through the back door when you're watching the front, rising with a rhythm Hawkins never had as a mere singer of words and melodies, his final scream his hands around your neck, and Robertson sealing the moment as if he's been in cahoots all along.

The abstraction would remain, growing into a sensibility, shared by all the musicians in the Band: a bet that the pieces did not have to fit, that nothing had to be explained, that you could communicate more deeply through hints and warnings than through statements and clichés. But "Who Do You Love" also left a question: as Helm, Robertson, Danko, Manuel, and Hudson went on, as they took their name and found their sound, as audiences turned to their music as if was not only a set of songs to be listened to but a country that could be lived in, would they ever match those screams? Could any country be complete without them?

Two years later, playing in a half-circle around Bob Dylan, the Hawks—with Mickey Jones in the place of Levon Helm, who had left in despair over audiences enraged by the turn of a folk singer whose words you could understand toward a sound so big it demanded you surrender one kind of meaning for another—are not tight. They are loose. You can hear the Band they will turn into a year later, when Helm rejoined the fold in Woodstock. "We had played together for years," Danko would say long after. "We could almost predict what we would do next." Here, in "Tell Me, Momma," the thrill is in hearing just that, but also hearing that you cannot hear what the musicians must be hearing. It doesn't seem real, how a bounce off of Danko's bass falls into a cymbal smash as if nothing like it had ever happened before, the way the sounds from Hudson's organ seem to slither around everyone's feet, forcing them to jump as they reach for the next change, the rhythm section—whatever instruments it's made of at any given moment—seemingly running on its own track, Robertston playing here as if he's one person and there as if he's someone else, each musician trusting that the others know him better than he knows himself, so that when it feels as if the music is a Ferris wheel spinning too fast not to break free and roll straight out of the carnival, the music can always call it back, just like that.

With the Band's own voices lining out the territory of the music, this is what you hear in *Music from Big Pink* and *The Band*. You hear the trust of one musician for another, of each for all, and you hear that musical value turn into a social value: you hear that trust as comradeship. You hear that sense of comradeship expanding to take in another sort of territory, as the names and faces, places and incidents in the songs make their own town, and then their own new nation. That nation may feel as if it is somewhere in the past, but as with "King Harvest," the songs use old motifs to act out a drama in which change is illusory and novelty a form of vanity. "The Band came from nowhere specific and their evocations were indistinct but they were the whole of the American past and all its space," the critic Nik Cohn wrote in 1973. "Small towns in the Civil War, at the turn of the century, during the Depression; saloons with cracked windows, and dance-halls with leaky ceilings, and hotel rooms with naked lightbulbs . . . gold rushes and oil strikes, eternal dreams of wealth; bad debts, hangovers." So they meet and turn away, the characters in "The Weight," "Across the Great Divide," "We Can Talk About It Now," "Chest Fever," "Get Up Jake," "Up on Cripple Creek," and half a dozen more: they find themselves pulled toward one another even as they look for an exit, opening their mouths to say a simple "Yes" or "No" and hearing parables come out instead.

The people in the town the songs make don't trust each other, certainly; why should they? Looked out your front door lately? Read the newspaper? But they are incapable of pretending they don't see or hear. Against his will, the singer in "Lonesome Suzie" finds himself embracing her; the man in "Chest Fever," his face whipped from one direction to another as different singers take his voice, is trying to save the woman in the song, or anyway find out who she is, what she looks like, what her name is—as you give yourself up to the teeming wilderness of the sound, where those old screams from "Who Do You Love" again and again find their match in hilarity and confusion, you can't imagine the people in the song understand the words any better than you do. In "The Weight," a traveler arrives with a task to accomplish, everyone he meets adds to his burden, he asks everyone for help, and everyone who doesn't smile at him laughs at him. It's a modernist minstrel show, every character in a kind of blackface, made up as someone they're not. It's pure comedy—but as the historian Constance Rourke wrote in 1930, in the minstrel show there was always a dark undertone, something no blackface could ever lighten: an undertone of defeat, and of tragedy.

Here the looseness of "Tell Me Mama" is more playful, and the trust between the musicians deeper. "Tell Me Momma" took a fast tempo, which can hide almost anything; "The Weight" seems to slow down with every verse, revealing more in every chorus. The sound is full of air, full of space, but too much is happening—vocally, instrumentally, emotionally, the story telling shaped less by plot than by a shaggy dog, by the abstractions of gaps and non sequiturs—to hear all at once, or, for that matter, ever. There's hardly a funnier moment in the Band's music than the traveler arriving in town and, after asking the first person he meets if he knows "where a man might find a bed," gets his answer: "No." You're as baffled as the singer, you figure what the hell just as he does, but the chill he pretends not to feel is already in your bones. One riddle follows another, the singer can't tell if the townspeople are dead or alive, real or phantoms; shadow voices echo in the verses, and in the chorus they rise up.

The singer, Levon Helm, splits into himself, Rick Danko, and Richard Manuel, or rather they come together, the three of them, as the one man the singer has to be. Not as one, but one following the other, their voices come together, letting you know that what you first heard as echoes were fully present all along. With the chorus ringing, each voice now reaches for the last syllable of the last word that the voice before it has left behind, and when they fall almost together on a single word, the word "free," they make that single voice. It's unstable, dissolving even as it forms, and while every word that led to it—"Take a load off Fanny, take a load for—"—is full of puzzlement, of the-joke's-on-me-but-at-least-I-get-it, with this word, for an instant, that undertone of defeat, more than anything of regret, wipes out everything else. The song opens up like a well, and the word drops into it like a stone; in certain moods, even as the song goes on, you cease to hear the song, listening for the sound of the stone hitting the water, which you never do hear.

The town made by the simpatico of the Band's music was not necessarily a place anyone would want to live in: sometimes, as with "Up on Cripple Creek," it offered magically easy answers, but often it allowed for no answers at all. And the Band didn't live in it long themselves. In anyone's art, if there's luck, hard work pays off, and a moment emerges where one does what one could never do before—in the case of the Band, what none would ever do without the rest. Even as that moment makes itself known, even as you recognize it for what it is, you may recognize that the moment will not last, and so you take everything it will give. It didn't last: as the Band went on you could hear voices and instruments separate where before you could hardly tell them apart. An alternate version of "Daniel and the Sacred Harp," from the sessions for the 1970 *Stage Fright,* is an intimate drama, with Helm humming parts that on the finished recording would be played by Danko on fiddle; you can hear people reaching out to each other, but you can hear their estrangement before and after you hear them reaching out.

In a score of recordings—in Richard Manuel's "Share Your Love," from the 1973 *Moondog Matinee,* Levon Helm's singing on the unreleased take of "A La Glory," Robbie Robertson's cracked and soulful demo for "Twilight," in "Chest Fever," and especially "The Night They Drove Old Dixie Down" from the *Last Waltz,* where what in 1969 had been a story, told face to face as the singer stopped you on the street and made you listen, became an event, history collapsing on the singer as if it were a house that in his guilt and fury he was pulling down upon himself—you hear what slipped out of the grasp of the group. You hear what one person must now give to the full, where once Helm, Hudson, Danko, Robertson, and Manuel could only take a song to the full if no one's contribution could be separated from any other. You hear what was lost, and you hear what few others ever touched.

REAL LIFE ROCK TOP 10
City Pages
3 December 2003

7) Bobdylan.com store. Featured items: "Self-Portrait Throw Blanket," "Masked & Anonymous Tee," "Johnny Rock 'I'll Be Your Baby Tonight' Corset."

City Pages
5 May 2004

5–7) Leslie Bennetts: "Not Across My Daughter's Big Brass Bed You Don't, Bob" (*Los Angeles Times*, April 16); Mel Gibson, producer: *The Passion of the Christ—Songs Inspired by* (Universal South); Mirah with the Black Cat Orchestra: "Dear Landlord," from *To All We Stretch the Open Arm* (YoYo). Bob Dylan Sellout Alert! Bennetts, who made her name attacking Hillary Clinton in the pages of *Vanity Fair,* again raises the flag of moral outrage. This time it's because of the way "an artist who once had a profound effect on American culture" can now be found in a Victoria's Secret commercial. There he is in the city of gondolas and Titian; as his poisoned "Love Sick" plays, he squints at a woman in bra, panties, and angel's wings, thus giving a whole new meaning to "See Venice and die." But what about "Not Dark Yet"—like "Love Sick" from the wasteland of Dylan's 1997 *Time Out of Mind*— appearing on a collection of mostly old recordings that Mel Gibson has put to work celebrating his very own movie to the point of claiming that he himself is somehow responsible for their creation? Bennetts thinks an underwear commercial is pedophilia, Gibson thinks a song following a man down a dead road is about Jesus, and they may be right—but not as right as the one-time riot grrrl chanteuse Mirah Yom Tov Zeitlyn, who, like so many before her, understands that a profound Bob Dylan song can, in other hands, sound like anybody's common sense.

Interview
August 2004

4) Peter Carey: *Theft* (Knopf). "We had been born walled out from art, had never guessed it might exist," says an Australian painter in Carey's new novel, "and then we saw what had been kept from us." The resentment is patent, but still it's a shock when fragments of pop songs—art the man wasn't born walled off from—explode in his mouth as he rails against a 16th century art critic: "You went to the finest schools all right but you are nothing more than a gossip and a suck-up to Cosimo de' Medici. I was a butcher and I came in through the bathroom window."

PART EIGHT

Beat the Clock,
2004–2010

CHRONICLES

Artforum
December 2004

Bob Dylan's *Chronicles* could be subtitled "A Life in the Arts" rather than *Volume One*—art is what it's about. In a humble, modest, very literary way, Dylan sets off sparks all across his career as a performer, which he describes most of all as a career as a student coming face to face with wonders. Early rock 'n' roll singers "sang like they were navigating burning ships." "What the folk songs were lyrically, Red's stuff"—Red Grooms's—"were visually—all bums and cops, the lunatic bustle, the claustrophobic alleys—all the carnie vitality. Red was the Uncle Dave Macon of the art world." The book is about getting it right, and then throwing it away, to see where it lands—whatever *it* is. Every reviewer seems to have quoted a line about Dylan's early-sixties immersion in the archives of the New York Public Library, living out the nation's story by reading newspapers published during the Civil War, discovering "the all-encompassing template behind everything that I would write": "America was put on the cross, died and was resurrected." That line calls attention to itself, in a way that takes you right out of the story—but then come the throwaway lines that slam you into it again. "I crammed my head full of as much of this stuff as I could stand and locked it away in my mind out of sight, left it alone. Figured I could send a truck back for it later." This book is the truck.

CHRONICLES
Rolling Stone
13 January 2005

Last November 2nd, on election night, in Oshkosh, Wisconsin, Bob Dylan played "Masters of War," his 1963 protest song against arms merchants. It sounded ham-handed and self-righteous even when Dylan was first performing it; why, this night, was the song so frightening, the delivery so deliberate?

Why is the song still alive? There's a hint of an answer in Dylan's *Chronicles*. It's not a memoir, where everything revolves around the author; it's a bildungsroman, where a questing young man relates the tales of his education in art, life, and the ways of the world. *Chronicles* is an account of learning and discovery, most deeply in Minneapolis in 1959 and 1960, then in Greenwich Village in the early sixties, and an account of frustration and failure in the decades to come. The old man looks back at his younger self less to find out where he took the wrong road ("The mirror had swung around and I could see the future—" Dylan writes of himself in 1987, "an old actor fumbling in garbage cans outside the theater of past triumphs") than to begin again, from the beginning. It's not a tease that Dylan's sixties glory years and the startling break-throughs from the early nineties on are ignored: the book revolves around those poles where the writer knew nothing and where he could do nothing. So it is keen-eyed, doubting, but with the writer giving phrases that leap to mind free rein ("The mirror had swung around"—my god, what happens when the mirror *swings around?*) but also reining them in to serve the story, to push it forward or pull it backward—and the story is that of someone with a gift to live up to, if he can figure out what it is.

That's what the book is about: figuring that out. The tale-teller is a detective ("I cut the radio off, crisscrossed the room, pausing for a moment to turn on the black-and-white TV," Dylan writes in perfect pitch, as if walking Philip Marlowe around his Los Angeles apartment. "*Wagon Train* was on"), a pathfinder, looking at other people's footprints on the forest floor. He watches the world from a distance; he watches himself only as a reflection of the light the world gives off.

Because he is a musician, the reflections are sometimes echoes, and some of the echoes are words. "My father," Dylan writes of Abraham Zimmerman, "wasn't so sure the truth would set any-body free"—and those words sound down through the book. This isn't just the stiff-necked Jew turning his back on Jesus pronouncing that "the truth shall set you free"; it's the truth as, again and again in *Chronicles,* Dylan applies it to songs. Folk songs. Old songs. Songs that resist the singer, that change shape as soon as he thinks he knows what they are. Songs that may force the singer to exchange facts for mystery and knowledge for ignorance.

"The singer has to make you believe what you are hearing, and Joan did that," Dylan says of Joan Baez and her 1960 rendition of "Silver Dagger," a Shakespearean Appalachian ballad about a mother who carries a knife to keep men from her daughter. "I be-lieved Joan's mother would kill someone that she loved . . . folk music, if nothing else, makes a believer out of you." "I didn't know what age of history we were in nor what the truth of it was," he writes, speaking of Greenwich Village and the mainstream cul-ture that surrounded it. "If you told the truth, that was all well and good and if you told the untruth, well, that's still well and good. Folk songs had taught me that . . . Whatever you were think-ing could be dead wrong." Folk music opened the door to a "paral-lel universe": "a culture with outlaw women, super thugs, demon lovers and gospel truths . . . landowners and oilmen, Stagger Lees and Pretty Pollys and John Henrys—an invisible world."

> Folk music was a reality of a more brilliant dimension. It exceeded all human understanding, and if it called out to you, you could disappear and be sucked into it. I felt right at home in this mythi-cal realm made up not with individuals so much as archetypes, vividly drawn archetypes of humanity, metaphysical in shape,

each rugged soul filled with natural knowing and inner wisdom. Each demanding a degree of respect. I could believe in the full spectrum of it and sing about it. It was so real, so more true to life than life itself.

Songs that say, *I am true, but there is no truth. Figure that out, buddy.* It was, Dylan recounts, the dare behind his whole career—the poker game he's still playing. And that is why, on a certain night, an old protest song like "Masters of War" can change shape, swing the mirror around, and dare the singer to sing it, to make it true— "the truth about life," as Dylan writes of folk songs, "even if life is more or less a lie." No, it probably wasn't going to set anybody free, except, for an instant, maybe the singer. But of course you never know.

Chronicles, Volume One. New York: Simon and Schuster, 2004.

THE WORLD PREMIERE OF
NO DIRECTION HOME
Telluride Film Festival
2 September 2005
Studies in Documentary Film
January 2007

The thirty-fourth Telluride Film Festival opened Friday night, September 2. I saw the slithering man-and-woman-meet-at-a-wedding drama *Conversations with Other Women,* and *Capote,* which is good—but Philip Seymour Hoffman as Capote is so good he almost silences everyone around him. People were talking about William H. Macy in *Edmund* and *Brokeback Mountain.*

The next morning *No Direction Home* went up on the daily TBA boards. As the festival was not permitted to include the film in the program, and could only show it once, as a sneak, there were no notes to explain what exactly it was—or, for that matter, that it would only be shown once. Some people had read about the movie—the three-and-a-half-hour Martin Scorsese documentary on Bob Dylan—but nothing very clear or helpful had been published. People didn't know it stopped at the end of May 1966, when Dylan ended a world tour in the U.K., in a storm of abuse, and then had a motorcycle accident and stayed off the road for eight years. They didn't know if it was a project Scorsese had been working on for a decade—or if it was, as it was, what Scorsese made of hours upon hours of interviews with Dylan and compatriots from Minnesota, New York, and anywhere else conducted over the last years by Jeff Rosen, Dylan's manager, plus a mountain of performance and news footage, archival photographs, and music famous and unheard. So there were plenty of people at the festival who didn't know what the picture was, and a lot of people who did, and who figured—this was the buzz all day Saturday—that the crowd would be so huge they'd never get in and so didn't bother to try. At Telluride everyone stands in line for a movie, usually on the first days lining up an hour or more ahead of a screening, and often people don't get in—though most films play three or four times, with screenings added as the festival goes on, so by the end everyone has a chance to see what they want to. For the one-shot of *No Direction Home,* the result of confusion, ignorance, and self-intimidation was that the theater, the biggest in town, holding 650 people, was at best two-thirds full.

Nevertheless there was great tension and anticipation in the audience. When I introduced the film, I mentioned that while another, unnamed festival was hosting the official world premiere of the picture, this would be the first public screening of the movie anywhere, and that people could put that into their own words as they chose. It set a tone of eagerness: right from the start, the entire crowd responded to what was on the screen with an engagement—a sense that combined recognition and surprise—that had no analogue at any other screening I attended during the festival (the Dardennes Brothers' *L'Enfant,* Michael Haneke's horrifyingly uncompromised *Caché, Walk the Line,* the Johnny Cash story). People were laughing out loud at anything remotely funny or ironic. They were with Dylan—his flinty, thoughtful, mystical, straightforward narration—all the way. There were murmurs and gasps of assent or approval. There was the displacement the film insists on: starting off with an unspeakably intense, suffused-with-danger "Like a Rolling Stone," onstage in Newcastle in May 1966, with Dylan a dervish possessed by a god you don't want to meet, and then the weird title, "Many Years Earlier," as if to suggest that this would be a film about a quest, the tale of what sort of journey it would be that could take anyone, never mind Bob Dylan, to a place as strange and self-immolating as the one that opens the picture.

At the end of the first section of the film, about two hours in, the crowd erupted into long and hard applause, with shouts and cheers, even though it had been made clear that no one associated with the film was present (very unusual at Telluride, where the director of a film is almost always there to introduce and discuss his or her movie, and often the producer or writer or leading actors— for *Capote,* both Hoffman and the director, Bennett Miller, were there for the entire weekend). During the twenty-minute intermission, there were constant "Did you believe that"s and "Did you see"s, people pinpointing this moment or that (at the beginning, Dylan describing himself as a child, discovering another world when he accidentally encountered Bill Monroe's "Drifting Too Far from the Shore"—the metaphor strikes like a clock as the movie goes on—or Allen Ginsberg speaking of Dylan becoming "at one with his own voice, turning into a column of air"—I couldn't help thinking, "a pillar of salt": "Don't look back"—*or else*). The screenwriter Larry Gross came up and said, "Do you know what this film reminds me of?" "What?" "Peter O'Toole in *Lawrence of Arabia!*" He went on to talk about how, in that movie (and in John E. Mack's biography, *A Prince of Our Disorder*), Lawrence, without ever losing his uniqueness, or, in contrast, ever truly revealing himself, becomes the emblematic figure of his age. In *Lawrence of Arabia,* Gross said, the social and political history of the time takes shape, but it is Lawrence who gives it shape, not because he is a figurehead or a spokesperson, but because in some essential and ultimately indefinable way he enacts the age—acting out or performing the essence of its drama, what the age both needs and wants—but in a way that no one else ever would or could. Other people came up to ask what happened next, in Part 2, as if they didn't know—as if the way Part 1 had unfolded, moving chronologically but continually circling around the cauldron of fury in England in 1966, had cast real, already familiar events into doubt. Or as if they were watching what was on the screen not as the-story-of-their-own-lives but as a movie, where anything can happen.

When the second part began, there was an evident sense of jeopardy. You could feel the stakes being raised minute by minute. The absurdity of so much of the footage from the U.K.—a photographer at a press conference ordering Dylan to "Suck your glasses," a death threat phoned into a hall and Dylan in his dressing room, saying, "I don't mind being shot, I just don't want to be told about it"—was simultaneously ugly and hilarious. A lot of people were tremendously impressed by Joan Baez's interviews (I was one: her humor, her bluntness, her lack of gentility). Scorsese showed enormous flair, and an invisible hand, not only for picking out appropriate moments from Rosen's interviews (the Greenwich Village veteran Liam Clancy or Baez saying one thing, Dylan then contradicting or denying) but for finding *the* moment, such as the musician Bruce Langhorne on the perfect tip of the band into "Bob Dylan's 115th Dream." People were completely caught up, loving the details, but also, slowly, enveloped by the growing dread. By the time the narrative has doubled back on itself, at the end, day after day in May 1966, fans attacking, Dylan's performances becoming more assaultive, there seems to be no exit, no way out, no way this can go on, no way this can end.

In *Walk the Line,* there's a fascinating scene, early in the straight this-then-that biopic story, where Joaquin Phoenix as Cash, in Memphis in about 1954, takes his little amateur group to audition for Sam Phillips's Sun label. They do a gospel number,

and Phillips says, "I don't believe you." Phoenix as Cash is outraged: "What, you don't believe I believe in God?" Phillips explains that it doesn't matter what Cash thinks he believes; he has
to convince other people: "Make me believe something." So Cash
begins to fumble out "Folsom Prison Blues." It isn't until the end
of the picture, when Cash goes into Folsom Prison itself to play,
that you believe Phoenix believes he is Cash, or could have been.

That lack of reality isn't present in *No Direction Home,* and not
because it's a documentary. Either through Rosen's interviewing,
or Scorsese's sense of picture, the people who speak—Dylan's
Freewheelin' girlfriend Suze Rotolo, beautiful and exuberant, the
poker-faced harmonica player Tony Glover, Dylan's one-time
fellow-traveler Bob Neuwirth, people who passed through Dylan's
life and whose lives he passed through—don't seem to be trying to
impress anyone, to come off well, to flatter themselves. And there
is a kind of reality that people may have difficulty integrating with
aesthetic representations. That is, you can be overwhelmed by
Walk the Line, and at Telluride a lot of people were—but if you are
seeing *No Direction Home* at more or less the same time, or connect
the two, *Walk the Line* can't explain itself when set against the
scene in *No Direction Home* of Dylan and Cash, backstage in Leeds
in May 1966, singing "I'm So Lonesome I Could Cry." (The footage
has never been seen before—D. A. Pennebaker shot it, but he
didn't use it in his own, unreleased film of the 1966 tour, and Dylan didn't use it in his barely released *Eat the Document.*) Here's
Johnny Cash, he's thirty-three, he looks sixty, he looks dead, his
face deformed by abuse and guilt, and the question of how he got
to this little room, of how he's going to get out of it, becomes, in an
instant, the question that opens *No Direction Home* itself, with that
Newcastle "Like a Rolling Stone."

At the end, people broke out into two or three minutes of sustained applause and cheering—again, even though they knew
there was no one there to receive it. The audience stayed for the
entire, long credit roll, perhaps thinking there'd be something
they'd regret missing. At the end of the credits, people burst into
applause again. And then a lot of people simply did not leave their

seats, as if they thought there might be an extra reel of outtakes for those who truly demonstrated their commitment.

No Direction Home, directed by Martin Scorsese (PBS, Spitfire Pictures DVD, 2005).

BOOKSHELVES—
PAUL NELSON, 1936–2006
City Pages
12 July 2006

Sometime in the early 1970s, I visited Paul Nelson's apartment in New York, on Lexington Avenue. I'd seen Paul often in the years before, but this was the first time I'd seen him without a cap: the day I found out that underneath that cap, he was completely bald. In his own house, he could be himself.

Paul was a serious book collector: a maven, a fetishist. His shelves were filled with endless editions of 1940s and 1950s hard-boiled detective fiction. First editions in perfect condition; battered paperbacks with lurid covers. Placed here and there were books on stands, as artworks. They were there to be stared at, to fall into, to reflect back, like mirrors. He handed me *Five Sinister Characters,* a 1945 paperback collection of Raymond Chandler stories: "Trouble Is My Business," "Red Wind," "I'll Be Wait-

ing." On the cover were pictures of a rich woman in a heavy necklace, a mean-looking cad in a pencil moustache, a World War I offi-cer, a Chinese thug, and a woman in a veiled hat—a woman who was clearly a man. The crude portraits were like a scrim over the writing inside, teasing you that, as you read, you'd be able to tell who was who, when the whole point was that you wouldn't.

Paul was a humble, generous man with the driest sense of humor imaginable, all in the way he dropped an eyebrow; you knew you weren't seeing a fraction of what was there. The apartment was an airy, pleasant place, but it was also a cave. "P.N. has a Phone-Mate automatic answering machine, which he leaves on twenty-four hours a day, to screen out all calls he does not want," Paul's close friend and collaborator Lester Bangs wrote about that time in a set of notes for a book he planned, "All My Friends Are Hermits"—in those days, you still had to explain what an answering machine was. "Sometimes, after I hear the beep and say who it is, he immediately picks up. Often he does not. Sometimes the latter option obtains for weeks." Paul hid from his own writing. In 1974, when Jim Miller and I were trying to get the chapters Paul had promised for *The Rolling Stone Illustrated History of Rock & Roll* out of him—on Bob Dylan and Rod Stewart, people Paul loved, and who loved him—we left what we thought were funny, then what we hoped were threatening messages on his machine, pushed his buzzer, shouted up from the street, mailed ransom notes (I can't remember who the hostage was supposed to be). We had no idea if he was in the apartment or not. We fantasized—it's a commonplace, banal fantasy, everyone's had it—that he was in there dead, not to be found until the neighbors couldn't ignore the smell. We gave up, and began looking for other writers.

Finally the pieces came. The one on Dylan was a detective story. Paul was the Op; culture was his beat. His clients (from "the Manhattan Institute of Critical Enterprise" and "the Majorities Enter the War League") were looking for a hero to promote, and thought Dylan might still do the job.

"In the mid-sixties Dylan's talent evoked such an intense degree of personal participation from both his admirers and detractors that he could not be permitted so much as a random action," the detective explained. "Hungry for a sign, the world used to follow him around, just waiting for him to drop a cigarette butt. When he did they'd sift through the remains, looking for significance. The scary part is they'd find it—and it really would be significant."

"Mystical mumbo jumbo," one of the clients said; it was a whole career in seventy-five words. Those words took Paul weeks to write, and over the last thirty years they've bounced back to me again and again and again. A lot of writers live their lives without ever getting anything quite so right, in words that would come to no one else.

Paul Nelson, "Bob Dylan," in *The Rolling Stone Illustrated History of Rock & Roll*, edited by Jim Miller. New York: Random House, 1976.

———— with Lester Bangs, *Rod Stewart*. New York: Delilah Books, 1981.

Neil Strauss, "The Man Who Disappeared," *Rolling Stone* (28 December 2006–11 January 2007).

FOLK MUSIC TODAY–RAPTURE
Interview
September 2006

"One of the ancients by now, whom all moderns prize"—so said Bob Dylan on his first *Theme Time Radio Hour*, now running weekly on XM Radio. He was speaking of Muddy Waters, but he could have been talking about the mostly traditional songs remade—from the ground up, from the inside out—on *Shaken by a Low Sound*, the second album by Crooked Still, a four-person Boston combo. Not long ago, the *New York Times* Arts & Leisure section featured one of its patented idiot trend pieces, this one on "Freak Folk," a celebration of the likes of Devendra Banhart, pixie dust, Joanna Newsom, beard-stroking, "the Vermont musical collective Feathers," and hugs. There would have been no way to fit in Crooked Still. People die in their songs. People are dead before the songs begin.

Taking up tunes that were tired clichés even during the folk revival of the 1950s and '60s—"Railroad Bill," "Little Sadie," "Wind

and Rain"—and some that, though just as old, were never so shop-
worn—"New Railroad," "Ain't No Grave," "Lone Pilgrim," and
"Ecstasy"—singer Aoife O'Donovan, cellist Rushad Eggleston,
banjo player Gregory Liszt, and bassist Corey DiMario seem to
trust the songs they've chosen to give up what they've never given
up before. Each song, you can feel, is like a book written at once in
English and an unknown tongue. If you read it you will read what
everyone before you has read. If you speak the words out loud,
you will say what has never been said.

O'Donovan doesn't conform the characters in her songs to her
gender. It's a man who shoots Little Sadie—no reason given, a face,
a hand to a pistol, a finger squeezing the trigger, and it's the in-
comprehensibility of the act, or the obviousness, that's kept the
story alive for so many lifetimes—and so O'Donovan becomes that
man. In a high, thin but commanding voice that at first calls back
Alison Krauss, Sandy Denny, or the less-well-known Anna Domino
of Snakefarm, O'Donovan enters the songs as if through a back-
door visible only to her. Finding herself alone in the rooms of the
songs, she's Goldilocks trying out every bed—reliving, as she lays
herself down, every nightmare and every act of love each bed ever
witnessed. Then she rises. Facing the judge in "Little Sadie," the
gravestone in "Lone Pilgrim," the hangman in "New Railroad," Jesus in "Ain't No Grave," the fields of heaven in "Ecstasy," she
knows exactly what to do.

In "Little Sadie," it's a turn Eggleston makes on his cello—
really, it's as if he's physically turned it, turned its back on you—
that opens the song to a kind of suspense it may never have held
before. You realize, suddenly, that the simple murder 'n' justice tale
the words tell is not what the song is about at all; now it's an opening into something much darker, beyond the reach of any law.
"Ain't No Grave" is a stomp, moving fast, a syncopation built on
the cello that carries everyone off the edge of the world in a spirit
of pure abandon because they know God will be there to catch
them. When Liszt opens up on banjo—playing easily, then picking
up the pace, then playing as if with two instruments and four

hands—you find yourself shaking your head in wonder, no idea how you reached the place Liszt has taken you, and not willing to leave. In the same way, as the band crawls into "Ecstasy," it all but hides itself from the music it's making, because this song, from the 1844 backwoods hymnal *The Sacred Harp,* does not belong to the band. But what they learn, as they play, so slowly the rhythm the song makes is a rhythm of coming as close as you can to a complete stop, is that it never belonged to anyone, and never will.

The songs to which Crooked Still now applies itself were made to capture whole countries of experience, fantasy, forgetting, revenge, guilt, and escape—countries that had already vanished as the songs were made, countries as they were, countries yet to come. The band takes up the songs as if they contain knowledge far beyond any person who might sing them. "Hang me, oh hang me, I'll be dead and gone / It's not the hanging that I mind, it's the laying in the grave so long"—it's not the words that get inside you, because the knowledge isn't in the words. It's in the melodies, and, here, you can hear the melodies giving the singer the knowledge they hold, if she can rise to their challenge—like learning that God is real by reciting a prayer.

Crooked Still, *Shaken by a Low Sound* (Signature Sounds, 2006).

REAL LIFE ROCK TOP 10

THE TRAIL OF DEAD

Interview
November 2006

1) The Drones: *Gala Mill* (ATP/R). I was attracted to this solely because the title of the band's last album, *Wait Long by the River and the Bodies of Your Enemies Will Float By,* echoes two of my favorite

band names: When People Were Shorter and Lived Near the Water and And You Will Know Us by the Trail of Dead. How could *Gala Mill* be anything but great? Sure, dull title, but according to the press release, this Australian four-piece, led by singer-guitarist Gareth Liddiard, recorded on "an isolated 10,000-acre farm" in Tasmania. Eat your heart out, Nick Cave.

None of that—and none of the band's earlier music—is any preparation for what happens here, from the first moment. "Jezebel" is a long, delirious song that seems to suck all the chaos and horror of the present moment into a single human being, who struggles to contain that world inside himself: a world that seemingly takes the shape of the Belsan school massacre of 2004, which in this noise is all but recreated. Especially on the choruses, when a drone comes up, hovers, waits—and it's unnerving, waiting for the sound to break—you can't tell if the singer succeeds or not, or if it would be better if he succeeded or failed. Better for who? You are dragged into this song as if you were a prisoner. The performance is a shocker—and the album, casting off its echoes of Neil Young and Eleventh Dream Day, staking out its own territory in song after song, can hardly recover from it. Not until the final number, a nine-minute reenvisioning of a traditional Australian convicts' ballad—and after that, you really will know this band by their trail of dead.

2) Someone Still Loves You Boris Yeltsin: *Broom* (Polyvinyl). Okay, but they don't do "Are You Lonesome Tonight?"—Boris's favorite song.

3) *Clerks II,* written and directed by Kevin Smith (The Weinstein Company). Last line of the film: "Today is the first day of the rest of our lives." Immediately jettisoned by Soul Asylum's suicidal "Misery."

4) Grates: *Gravity Won't Get You High* (Dew Process). For "Inside Outside"—fast, desperate, cool, absolutely unafraid of how smart it is. "I might live to tell the tale," says singer Patience, "of how young girls once rode a whale."

5) Ellen Barkin: "It's nighttime in the big city . . ." *Theme Time Radio Hour with Bob Dylan* (XM Radio). Every week, before Dylan as disc jockey begins spinning his discs and telling his tales, Barkin, the woman who so long ago in *Diner* couldn't put her husband's records back in the right order, now stands back and lowers the boom. After her opening line, what by now amounts to a poem in progress unfolds: "A woman walks barefoot, her high heels in a handbag . . . A man gets drunk, he shaves off his moustache . . . A cat knocks over a lamp . . . An off-duty cop parks in front of his ex-wife's house." Is he stalking her, or do they still sleep together?

6) Cat Power: Live on KEXP (eMusic exclusives). Four numbers recorded on the air with only guitar and piano, and likely a more complete summation of who this woman is and what she does than can be found anywhere else. It's all so quiet you don't know whether to hold your breath or scream.

7) Robert Plant: *Nine Lives* (Rhino). In 1982 the ex-Led Zeppelin dervish drifted in a sea all his own, a surfer on a wave that never reached shore. That was "Far Post," then a B-side, nearly impossible to find since. It's here. You can play it all day long.

8) Bob Dylan: *Modern Times* (Columbia). Inside the sometimes slack rhythms and the deceptively easy lines, a deep longing. For a trail of dead.

9/10) Peter Stampfel: Karen Dalton, *It's So Hard to Tell Who's Going to Love You the Best* (1969: Koch, 1997) and Holy Modal Rounders, *Alleged in Their Own Time* (Rounder, 1975). On *Gala Mill,* the Drones cover "Are You Leaving for the Country," a song learned from a recording by the '60s Greenwich Village folk-scene jazz singer Karen Dalton ("My favorite singer in the place," Bob Dylan says in *Chronicles of the Café Wha?* in 1961). She had an acrid voice, and she lived an acrid life, caught like a purse-snatcher in Stampfel's song "Sally in the Alley." He uses the lyrics to "Sally" to end his notes to the reissue of Dalton's 1969 album; he recorded it on the Holy Modal Rounders' *Alleged in Their Own Time* nearly twenty years before Dalton died. You'll forget the Drones' version of "Are You Leaving for the Country"; you may forget Dalton's (on her just-reissued 1971 album *In My Own Time*). You won't forget "Sally"—a nursery rhyme about a junkie.

A TRIP TO HIBBING HIGH
Daedalus
Spring 2007*

"As I walked out—" Those are the first words of "Ain't Talkin'," the last song on Bob Dylan's *Modern Times,* released in the fall of 2006. It's a great opening line for anything: a song, a tall tale, a fable, a novel, a soliloquy. The world opens at the feet of that line. How one gets there—to the point where those words can take on their true authority, raise suspense like a curtain, and make anyone want to know what happens next—is what I want to look for.

For me this road opened in the spring of 2005, upstairs in the once-famous, now shut Cody's Books on Telegraph Avenue in Berkeley. I was giving a reading from a book about Bob Dylan's "Like a Rolling Stone." Older guys—people my age—were talking about the Dylan shows they'd seen in 1965: he had played Berkeley on his first tour with a band that December. People were asking questions—or making speeches. The old saw came up: "How does someone like Bob Dylan come out of a place like Hibbing, Minnesota, a worn-out mining town in the middle of nowhere?"

A woman stood up. She was about thirty-five, maybe forty, definitely younger than the people who'd been talking. Her face was dark with indignation. "Have any of you ever *been* to Hibbing?" she said. There was a general shaking of heads and murmuring of no's—from me and everyone else. "You ought to be ashamed of

---

*First given as a talk at the Morgan Library, New York, 16 November 2006 and at the conference Highway 61 Revisited, University of Minnesota, 25 March 2007.

yourselves," the woman said. "You don't know what you're talking about. If you'd been to Hibbing, you'd know why Bob Dylan came from there. There's poetry on the *walls*. Everywhere you look. There are bars where arguments between socialists and the IWW, between Communists and Trotskyists, arguments that started a hundred years ago, are still going on. It's *there*—and it was there when Bob Dylan was there."

"I don't remember the rest of what she said," my wife said when I asked her about that night. "I was already planning our trip."

Along with our younger daughter and her husband, who live in Minneapolis, we arrived in Hibbing a year later, coincidentally during Dylan Days, a now-annual weekend celebration of Bob Dylan's birthday, in this case his sixty-fifth. There was a bus trip, the premiere of a new movie, and a sort of Bob Dylan Idol contest at a restaurant called Zimmy's. But we went straight to the high school. On the bus tour the next day, we went back. And that was the shock: Hibbing High.

In his revelatory 1993 essay "When We Were Good: Class and Culture in the Folk Revival," the historian Robert Cantwell takes you by the hand, guides you back, and reveals the new America that rose up out of World War II. "If you were born between, roughly, 1941 and 1948," he says,

> born, that is, into the new postwar middle class, you grew up in a reality perplexingly divided by the intermingling of an emerging mass society and a decaying industrial culture . . . Obscurely taking shape around you, of a definite order and texture, was an environment of new neighborhoods, new schools, new businesses, new forms of recreation and entertainment, and new technologies that in the course of the 1950s would virtually abolish the world in which your parents had grown up.

That sentence is typical of Cantwell's style: apparently obvious social changes charted into the realm of familiarity, then a hammer coming down: as you are feeling your way into your own world, your parents' world is *abolished*.

Growing up in the certified postwar suburb towns of Palo Alto and Menlo Park in California, I lived some of this life. Though Bob Dylan did not grow up in the suburbs—Hibbing is not close enough to Duluth, or any other city, to be a suburb of anything— he lived some of this life, too.

Cantwell moves on to talk about how the new prosperity of the 1950s was likely paradise to your parents, how their aspirations became your seeming inevitabilities: "Very likely, you saw yourself growing up to be a doctor or a lawyer, scientist or engineer, teacher, nurse, or mother—pictures held up to you at school and at home as pictures of your special destiny." And, Cantwell says,

> You probably attended, too, an overcrowded public school, typically a building built shortly before World War I . . . [you] may have had to share a desk with another student, and in addition to the normal fire and tornado drills had from time to time to crawl under your desk in order to shield yourself from the imagined explosion of an atomic bomb.

So, Cantwell writes, "in this vision of consumer Valhalla there was a lingering note of caution, even of dread"—but let's go back to the schools.

The public schools I attended—Elizabeth Van Auken Elementary School in Palo Alto, and Menlo Atherton High School in Menlo Park—were not built before World War I. They were built after the Second World War, part of the world that was already changing. The past was still there: Miss Van Auken, a beloved former teacher, was always present to celebrate the school's birthday. When our third-grade class read the Little House books, we wrote Laura Ingalls Wilder and she wrote back. But the past was fading as new houses went up all around the school. A few miles away, Menlo-Atherton High was a sleek, modern plant: one story, flat roofs, huge banks of windows in every classroom, lawns everywhere, and three parking lots, one reserved strictly for members of the senior class.

The school produced Olympic swimmers in the early 1960s; a few years later Lindsey Buckingham and Stevie Nicks would graduate and, a few years after that, make Fleetwood Mac the biggest band in the world. The school sparkled with suburban money, rock 'n' roll cool, surfer swagger, and San Francisco ambition—and compared to Hibbing High School it was a shack. "I know Hibbing," Harry Truman said in 1947, when he was introduced to Hibbing's John Galeb, the National Commander of Disabled American Veterans. "That's where the high school has gold door knobs."

Outside of Washington, D.C., it's the most impressive public building I've ever seen. In aerial photographs, it's a colossus: four stories, ninety-three feet high, with wings 180 feet long flying out from a 416 foot front. From the ground it is more than anything a monument to benign authority, a giant hand welcoming the town, all of its generations, into a cave where the treasure is buried, all the knowledge of mankind. It speaks for the community, for its faith in education, not only as a road to success, to wealth and security, reputation and honor, but as a good in itself. This town, the building says, will have the best school in the world.

In the plaza before the building there is a spire, a war memorial. On its four sides, as you turn from one panel to another, are the names of those students from Hibbing who died in the First World War, the Second World War, the Korean and Vietnam Wars—and, on the last panel, with no names, a commemoration of the terrorist attacks of 2001. Past the memorial are steps worthy of a state capitol leading to the entrance of the building. It was late Friday afternoon; there were no students around, but the doors were open.

Hibbing High School was built near the end of the era when Hibbing was known as "the richest village in the world." A crusading mayor, Victor Power, enforced mineral taxes on US Steel, operator of the huge iron-ore pit mines that surrounded the original Hibbing. Elected after a general strike in 1913, he fought off the mine company's allies in the state legislature and the courts in battle after battle. When ore was discovered under Hibbing itself, Power and others forced the company to spend sixteen million dollars to move the whole town—houses, hotels, churches, public buildings—four miles south. The bigger buildings were cut in quarters and reassembled in the new Hibbing like Legos.

Tax revenues had mounted over the years in the old north Hibbing; at one point, the story goes, when a social-improvement society took up donations for poor families, none could be found. But in the new south Hibbing, in a maneuver aimed at building support for lower corporate tax rates in the future, the mining company offered even more money in the form of donations, or bribes: school-board members directed most of it to what became Hibbing High, which Mayor Power had demanded as part of the price of moving the town. With prosperity seemingly assured, the town turned out Power in favor of a mayor closer to the mines. Soon a law was passed limiting public spending to a hundred dollars per capita per year; then the limit was lowered, and lowered again. The tax base of the town began to crumble; with World War II, when the town was not allowed to tax mineral production, and after, when the mines were nearly played out, the tax base all but collapsed. Ultimately, the mines shifted from iron ore to taconite, low-grade pellets that today find a market in China, but Hibbing never recovered. In the 1950s it was a dying town, the school a seventh wonder of a time that had passed, a ziggurat built by a forgotten king. And yet it was still a ziggurat.

When it opened in 1924, Hibbing High School had cost four million dollars, an unimaginable sum for the time. At first it was the ultimate consolidated school, from kindergarten through junior college. There were three gyms, two indoor running tracks, and every kind of shop that in the years to come would be commonplace in American high schools—as well as an electronics shop, an auto shop, a conservatory. There was a full-time doctor, dentist, and nurse. There were extensive programs in music, art, and theater. But more than eight decades later, you didn't have to know any of this to catch the glow of the place.

Climbing the enclosed stairway that followed the expanse of outdoor steps, we saw not a hint of graffiti, not a sign of deteriora-

tion in the intricate colored tile designs on the walls and the ceilings, in the curving woodwork. We gazed up at old-fashioned but
still majestic murals depicting the history of Minnesota, with bold
trappers surrounded by submissive Indians, huge trees and roam-
ing animals, the forest and the emerging towns. It was strange, the
pristine condition of the place. It spoke not for emptiness, for Hibbing High as a version of Pompeii High—though the school, with a
capacity of over two thousand, was down to six hundred students,
up from four hundred only a few years before—and, somehow, you
knew the state of the building didn't speak for discipline. You
could sense self-respect, passed down over the years.

We followed the empty corridors in search of the legendary auditorium. A custodian let us in, and told us the stories. Seating for
eighteen hundred, and stained glass everywhere, even in the form
of blazing candles on the fire box. In large, gilded paintings in the
back, the muses waited; they smiled over the proscenium arch, too,
over a stage that, in imitation of thousands of years of ancestors,
had the weight of immortality hammered into its boards. "No wonder he turned into Bob Dylan," said a visitor the next day, when
the bus tour stopped at the school, speaking of the talent show Dylan played here with his high-school band the Golden Chords.
Anybody on that stage could see kingdoms waiting.

There were huge chandeliers, imported from Czechoslovakia,
four thousand dollars each when they were shipped across the Atlantic in the 1920s, irreplaceable today. We weren't in Hibbing, a
redundant mining town in northern Minnesota; we were in the
opera house in Buenos Aires. Yet we were in Hibbing; there were
high-school Bob Dylan artifacts in a case just down the hall. There
were more in the public library some blocks away, in a small exhibit in the basement. Scattered among commonplace talismans
and oddities were the lyrics to the Golden Chords' "Big Black
Train," from 1958, a rewrite of Elvis's 1954 "Mystery Train," credited to Monte Edwardson, LeRoy Hoikkala, and Bob Zimmerman:

> Well, big black train, coming down the line
> Well, big black train, coming down the line

Well, you got my woman, you bring her back to me
Well, that cute little chick is the girl I want to see

Well, I've been waiting for a long long time
Well, I've been waiting for a long long time
Well, I've been looking for my baby
Searching down the line

Well, here comes the train, yeah it's coming down the line
Well, here comes the train, yeah it's coming down the line
Well, you see my baby is finally coming home

The next day, walking up and down Howard Street, the main street of Hibbing, we looked for the poetry on the walls. "A NEW LIFE," read an ad for an insurance company—was that it? Was there anything in that beer sign that could be twisted into a metaphor? What was the woman in Berkeley talking about? Later we found out that the walls with the poetry were in the high school itself.

In the school library there were busts and chiseled words of wisdom and murals. Murals told the story of the mining industry, all in the style of what Daniel Pinkwater, in his young-adult novel *Young Adults,* called "heroic realism." There were sixteen life-size workers, representing the nationalities that formed Hibbing: native-born Americans, Finns, Swedes, Italians, Norwegians, Croatians, Serbs, Slovenians, Austrians, Germans, Jews, French, Poles, Russians, Armenians, Bulgarians, and more. There was a huge mine on the left, a misty steelworks on the right, and, in the middle, to take the fruit of Hibbing to the corners of the earth, Lake Superior. With art-nouveau dots between each word, the inscription over the mine quoted Tennyson's "Oenone":

LIFTING•THE•HIDDEN•IRON•
THAT•GLIMPSES•IN•LABOURED•
MINES•UNDRAINABLE•OF•ORE

—while over the factory one could read

THEY•FORCE•THE•BURNT•

AND•YET•UNBLOODED•STEEL•

TO•DO•THEIR•WILL

That was the poetry on the walls—but not even this was the real poetry in Hibbing. The real poetry was in the classroom.

After stopping by the auditorium and the library, the tour made its way upstairs to Room 204, where for five years in the 1950s, B. J. Rolfzen taught English at Hibbing High—after that, he taught for twenty-five years at Hibbing Community College. Eighty-three in May of 2006, and slowed down by a stroke, getting around in a motorized wheelchair, Rolfzen sat on the desk in the small, suddenly steamy room, as forty or more people crowded in. There was a small podium in front of him. Presumably we were there to hear his reminiscences about the former Bob Zimmerman—or, as Rolfzen called him, and never anything else, Robert. Rolfzen held up a slate where he'd chalked lines from "Floater," from Dylan's 2001 *"Love and Theft"*: "Gotta sit up near the teacher / If you want to learn anything." Rolfzen pointed to the tour member who was sitting in the seat directly in front of the desk. "I always stood in front of the desk, never behind it," he said. "And that's where Robert always sat." He talked about Dylan's "Not Dark Yet," from his 1997 *Time Out of Mind:* "'I was born here and I'll die here / Against my will.'" "I'm with him. I'll stay right here. I don't care what's on the other side," Rolfzen said, a teacher thrilled to be learning from a student. With that out of the way, he proceeded to teach a class in poetry.

He handed out a photocopied booklet of poems by Wordsworth, Frost, Carver, the Minneapolis poet Colleen Sheehy, and himself; moving back and forth for more than half an hour, he returned again and again to the eight lines of William Carlos Williams's "The Red Wheelbarrow."

so much depends

upon

a red wheel
barrow

glazed with rain
water

beside the white
chickens.

He kept reading it, changing inflections, until the words seemed to dance out of order, shifting their meanings. Each time, a different word seemed to take over the poem. "Rain," he would say, opening up the poem one way; "beside," he'd say, and an entirely different drama seemed under way. Finally he came full circle. "'so much depends / upon a red wheel barrow,'" he said. "*So much depends*. This isn't about *rain*. It's not about *chickens*. So much depends on the decisions we make. My decision to enlist in the Navy in 1941, when I was seventeen. My decision to teach. *So much depends* on the decisions you've made, and will make."

The poem stayed in the air: the loudness of the first line faded into "beside the white chickens," not because they were unimportant, but because from "so much depends," from the decision with which the poem began, the poem, like a life, could have gone anywhere; it was simply that in this case the poem happened to go toward chickens, before it went off the page, to wherever it went next. Rolfzen made the eight lines particular and universal, unlikely and fated; he made them apply to everyone in the room, or rather led each person to apply them to him or herself. This was not the sort of teacher you encounter every day—or even in a lifetime.

"Bits and pieces of the Great Depression still lie about," Rolfzen wrote in *The Spring of My Life,* a memoir of the 1930s he published himself in 2005—but, he said, "The experiences and frightful hopelessness of one day of the Great Depression can never be understood or appreciated except by those who have lived it." Nevertheless, he tried to make whoever might read his book understand. He went back to the village of Melrose, Minnesota, where he was born and grew up. He spoke quietly, flatly, sardonically of a family that was poor beyond poverty: "Life during the Great Depression was not a complex life. It was a simple one. No health insurance needed to be paid, no life insurance, no car insurance, no savings for a college education or any education beyond high school, no savings account, no automobile needed to be purchased, no gas was necessary to buy, no utilities beyond the $3.00 a month my dad paid for six 25 watt bulbs." There were eleven children; B. J.—then Boniface—slept in a bed with three brothers.

His father was an electrical worker and a drunk: the "most frightening day," Rolfzen writes, was payday, when his father would stagger home, then and every day until the money ran out. One day he tried to kill himself by grabbing high-voltage lines; instead he lost both arms just below the elbow, and sent the family onto relief. "I never saw my mother with a coin in her hand," Rolfzen writes; everything they bought they bought on credit against fifty dollars a month. There was a family of four that boarded up the windows of their house to keep out the cold, but the Rolfzens would not advertise their misery, even if the windows sometimes broke and, before they could be replaced, maybe not until winter passed, maybe not for months after that, snow piled up in the room where Rolfzen slept.

All through the book, through its continual memories of privation and idyll—of catching bullheads, playing marbles, picking berries, working on a farm for three months at the age of sixteen for four cents a day, or the toe of a young Boniface's shoe falling off as he walked to school—one can feel Rolfzen holding his rage in check. His rage against his father, against the cold, against the plague that was on the land, against the alcoholism that followed from his father to his brothers, against the Catholic elementary school he was named for, St. Boniface, run by nuns who "enjoyed causing pain," a place where students were threatened with hell for every errant act—where religion "was a senseless, heartless and unforgiving practice. I still bear its scars."

"In times behind, I too / wished I'd lived / in the hungry Thirties," Bob Dylan wrote in 1964 in "Eleven Outlined Epitaphs," his
notes to *The Times They Are A-Changin'*. "Rode freight trains for
kicks / Got beat up for laughs / I was making my own depression,"
he wrote the year before in "My Life in a Stolen Moment"—speaking of leaving Hibbing, leaving the University of Minnesota, traveling west, trying to learn how to live on his own. "I cannot
remember ever having a conversation with my dad about anything," Rolfzen writes—but you can imagine him having conversations about the thirties with Robert. Maybe especially about the
tramp armies that passed through Melrose, starting every day at
ten when the train pulled in, twenty men or more riding on top of
the box cars, jumping from the doors, men who had abandoned
their families, who broke into abandoned buildings and knocked
on the Rolfzens' back door begging for food—"My mother never
refused them," Rolfzen writes. With whatever they could scav-
enge, they headed to a hollow near the tracks, the place called the
Bums' Nest or the Jungle. As a boy, Rolfzen was there, watching
and listening, but he will not allow a moment of romance, freedom,
or escape: "Theirs was a controlled camaraderie with limited
laughter. Each man was alone on these tracks that led to nowhere
. . . And so they left. More would arrive the next day. One gentleman in particular I remember. An old bent man dressed in a long
shabby coat, a tattered hat on his head and a cane in his hand. The
last time I saw him, he was headed west along the railroad tracks,
headed for an empty world."

This is not how the song of the open road goes—and while Bob
Dylan has sung that song as much as anyone, as the road opened it
also forked, even from the start. "At the end of the great English
epic *Paradise Lost*," Rolfzen writes, "Milton observes the departure of Adam and Eve from the Garden, and as he observes their
leaving by the Eastern Gate, he utters these beautiful words: 'The
world was all before them.'" *So much depends*—think of "Bob Dylan's Dream," from *The Freewheelin' Bob Dylan,* in 1963. There he
is, twenty-two, "riding on a train going west," dreaming of his

true friends, his soulmates—and then suddenly he is an old man. He and his friends have long since vanished to each other. Their roads haven't split so much as crumbled, disappeared—"shattered," he sings. How was it that, in 1963, his voice and guitar calling up a smoky, out-of-focus portrait, Bob Dylan was already looking back, from forty, fifty, sixty years later?

"As I walked out . . ." With those first words for "Ain't Talkin'"— not only the longest song on *Modern Times,* and the strongest, but the only performance on the album where you don't hear calculation—Bob Dylan disappears. Someone other than the singer you think you know seems to be singing the song. He doesn't seem to know what effects to use, what they might even be for. It's the only song on the album, really, without an ending—and with those first four words, a cloud is cast. The singer doesn't know what's going to happen—and it's the way he expects that nothing will happen, the way he communicates an innocence you instantly don't trust, that steels you for the story that he's about to tell, or that's about to sweep him up. He walks out into "the mystic garden." He stares at the flowers on the vines. He passes a fountain. Someone hits him from behind.

This is when he finds the world all before him—because he can't go back. There is only one reason to travel this road: revenge.

For the only time on *Modern Times,* the music doesn't orchestrate, doesn't pump, doesn't give itself away with its first note. Led by Tony Garnier's cello and Donnie Herron's viola, the band curls around the singer's voice even as he curls around the band's quiet, retreating, resolute sound, as if the whole song is the opening and closing of a fist, over and over again, the slow rhythm turning lyrics that are pretentious, even precious on the page into a kind of oracular bar talk, the old drunk who's there every night and never speaks finally telling his story. "I practice a faith that's long abandoned," he says, and that might be the most frightening line Bob Dylan has written in years.

The singer moves down his road of patience and blood. You can sense his head turning from side to side as he tells you why his head is bursting: "If I catch my opponents ever sleeping," he says, "I'll just slaughter 'em where they lie." He snaps off the line casually, as if it's hardly worth the time it takes to say, as if he's done it before, like William Munny in *Unforgiven* killing children on his way to wherever he went, but that will be nothing to what the singer does to get wherever it is he's going. God doesn't care: "the gardener," the singer says to a woman he finds in the mystic garden, "is gone."

Now, Bob Dylan didn't need B. J. Rolfzen's tales of the tramp armies that passed through Melrose during the Great Depression to catch a feel for "tracks that led to nowhere." Empathy has always been the genie of his work, of the tones of his voice, his sense of rhythm, his feel for how to fill up a line or leave it half empty, his sense of when to ride a melody and when to bury it, so that it might dissolve all of a listener's defenses—and this is what allowed Dylan, in 1962 at the Gaslight Café in Greenwich Village, at home in that secret community of tradition and mystery, to become not only the pining lover in the old ballad "Handsome Molly," but also Handsome Molly herself.

There's no tracing that quality of empathy to anything—*so much depends*—but if effects like these had causes, then there would be people doing the same on every corner, in any time. On the way to Hibbing, we stopped at an antique store; shoved in among a shelf of children's books was a small, cracked book called *From Lincoln to Coolidge,* published in 1924, a collection of news dispatches, excerpts from congressional hearings, and speeches, among them the speech Woodrow Wilson gave to dedicate Abraham Lincoln's official birthplace in Hodgenville, Kentucky, on 4 September 1916—according to the story a young Bob Dylan was told, just weeks before his one-year-old mother was taken by her parents to see the president campaign in Hibbing from the back of a train. "This is the sacred mystery of democracy," Wilson said that day in Hodgenville, "that its richest fruits spring up out of soils that no man has prepared and in circumstances amidst which they are least expected."

That is the truth, and that is the mystery. In the case of Bob Dylan, as with any person who does things others don't do, the mystery is always there. But from the overwhelming fact of the pure size of Hibbing High School, from the ambition and vision placed in the murals in its entryway, from the poetry on the walls to the poetry in the classroom, perhaps to memories recounted after everyone else had gone—or memories picked up by a student from the way a teacher moved, hesitated over a word, dropped hints he never quite turned into stories—these soils were not unprepared at all.

Robert Cantwell, "When We Were Good: Class and Culture in the Folk Revival," collected in *Transforming Tradition: Folk Music Revivals Examined,* edited by Neil V. Rosenberg. Urbana, IL: University of Illinois, 1993.

———. *When We Were Good: The Folk Revival.* Cambridge: Harvard, 1996.

B. J. Rolfzen, *The Spring of My Life.* Hibbing, MN: Band Printing, 2004. Rolfzen died in 2009 at 86.

Bob Dylan, "11 Outlined Epitaphs," liner notes to *The Times They Are A-Changin'* (Columbia, 1964).

———. "Bob Dylan's Dream," from *The Freewheelin' Bob Dylan* (Columbia, 1963).

———. "Ain't Talkin'," from *Modern Times* (Columbia, 2006).

Woodrow Wilson, "Address of Woodrow Wilson at Lincoln's Birthplace," collected in *From Lincoln to Coolidge,* edited by Alfred E. Logie. Chicago: Lyons and Carnahan, 1925.

See also the booklet *The Hibbing High School,* text by Dan Bergan, photos by Chuck Perry, Hibbing: 2001; Bergan and Larry Ryan's documentary film *The High School of Bob Dylan* (DVD, 2010); and Dave Engle, *Just Like*

Bob Zimmerman's Blues: Dylan in Minnesota, Mesabi, Rudolph, Wisconsin: River City Memoirs, 1997.

REAL LIFE ROCK TOP 10
Interview
June 2007

9/10) Larry Kegan, Howard Rutman, Robert Zimmerman: "Let the Good Times Roll," "Lawdy Miss Clawdy," "Boppin' the Blues," Frankie Lymon and the Teenagers' "I Want You to Be My Girl," "Ready Teddy," and "Confidential," and *Bob Dylan's American Journey, 1956–1966* (Weisman Museum of Art, University of Minnesota). On Christmas Eve, 1956, three boys, two fourteen and one fifteen, pooled their quarters for the record machine at Terline Music in St. Paul, Minnesota. You put in a coin, you got about thirty seconds, so with the fifteen-year-old pounding a piano they rushed to harmonize on whatever they could until the machine cut off and then started up again with another tune. It sounds like a slumber party, kids giddy from staying up past their bedtime, and what's surprising is not that one of these kids turned into Bob Dylan, but that little more than a year later he was—as pictured in a recently discovered photo featured in the Weisman exhibit—singing the same songs in the Golden Chords, commanding a stage with fervor

The Golden Chords (from left, Monte Edwardson, Leroy Hoikkala, Robert Zimmerman) at the Little Theater, Hibbing, Minnesota, Winter Frolic Talent Contest, 14 February 1958.

and confidence, looking pretty much as he looks now: flash coat, dark pants, dark shirt, white tie, hair in a pompadour, eyes like slits.

Interview
May 2007

10) Howard Fishman: "I'm Not There (1956)," from *Howard Fishman Performs Bob Dylan & the Band's "Basement Tapes" Live at Joe's Pub* (Monkey Farm). An interpretation but, for as a long as it plays, an irrefutable translation of a legendary song that seems beyond human ken, and not only because half of its words are missing and you can't quite be sure if the other half are there or not. Soon to be a major motion picture.

I'M NOT THERE

Interview
November 2007
with DVD notes to *I'm Not There*
2008, rewritten 2010

Imagine that, given all the different masks, wardrobes, accents, and gestures Bob Dylan has assumed over the years—the way in which he has seemed to be, moment by moment, almost different people—that he was different people. Each with his own different name, face, motive, passions, way of walking, way of talking—and different destiny. Then the story—of a generation, an era, or merely a single person whose voice other people wanted to hear—could open up in any direction at all. The full range of the imaginative transformation Bob Dylan has for nearly five decades offered the world at large—from Puritan folksinger to drunken Surrealist to born-again Christian to fatalistic traveler, with countless selves in between—could be transferred to an audience, who could then reimagine the story for themselves. Todd Haynes made his film *I'm*

Not There as part of that audience. "You think," he says, "I'm going to give people the Dylan movie and be very rigorous about trying to convey as many aspects of him as I think are true and recurrent"—but a spirit of play, the thrill of improvising on the spot with actors, musicians, designers, cinematographer, makeup artists, carries your rigorous intentions away. The result is a film with a cakewalk of lead actors, none playing a character who is precisely Bob Dylan—and, just as vitally, a film where no one on the screen is precisely not.

Todd Haynes's movies get under your skin or they pass right over it. *Velvet Goldmine* (1998) was seductive from start to finish and I've almost never thought of it since. I could hardly bear *Safe* (1995) and *Far from Heaven* (2002) when they came out, and few weeks have gone by without some blocked gesture, an uncompleted sentence, crawling out of what I had no intention of ever thinking about again. *I'm Not There* is different. It's immediately engaging. It cuts back and forth between different times, stories, protagonists. Music—Dylan's songs in his own voice, in the voices of the actors, in the voices of the singers the actors are miming— flies through the air like a trapeze artist shooting out of the frame on one side of the screen and returning on the other with a different face and different clothes.

The story of one character is not dependent on the story of another. All of the characters pursue their own fate—often with a crowd professing love or hate pursuing them—independently of each other. Each character's story reaches a kind of conclusion in a territory none of the others may have ever visited.

Still, nothing is resolved. Perhaps because no character is killed off (there is a motorcycle accident, the rider is laid out on a table, but since we know Bob Dylan is not dead, the scenes communicate as a device, merely literary), not one story ends, or even merely stops, in a manner that's acceptable, that doesn't leave you hanging, trying to imagine how it could have come out differently. So you leave the theater ready to talk about the movie, buttonholing the person next to you—but even more than that, you want to see the picture again, right away.

It all moves so fast, there are streams of lines and facial expressions and physical stances no one could catch entire the first time through, and walking away, looking back over your shoulder, you find yourself thinking that maybe what you thought happened isn't what happened at all. Maybe the citizens of Riddle rush the bandstand and kick Pat Garrett to death. Maybe Jude Quinn gets away clean. Maybe Pastor John will come back to the world—or lead you to accept Jesus into your heart.

Picture yourself taking a figure from postwar culture and contriving an imaginary biography for that person: John F. Kennedy. Philip Roth. Elvis Presley. Marilyn Monroe. Aretha Franklin. Chuck Berry. Elvis Presley. Martin Luther King, Jr., Frank Sinatra. Now imagine that this person, whoever you choose, will be portrayed by numerous persons unlike each other. Young. Old. White. Black. Male. Female.

Right away, you can tell who contains multitudes—and who doesn't. For some, the idea breaks down in the face of the person it's supposed to realize. For others, you realize you've never had a clue who this person was—and you believe this may be the way to understand, if not who that person actually was, who and what he or she might have been. What the person wanted from his or her time, and what the time wanted from the person.

Who is that person? Throughout the film, there are interludes with Ben Whishaw as a dandy claiming his name is Rimbaud and facing a battery of are-you-now-or-have-you-ever-been-a-poet inquisitors—but the story truly begins in 1959, with Marcus Carl Franklin as an eleven-year-old African-American boy named Woody. He's a hobo guitar-player in love with the dust-bowl ballads of the Great Depression and trying to live them out, a dreamer brought up short when a woman who's taken him in for a decent meal looks him in the eye and tells him to "sing your own time." He runs, hops a freight, is pitched out of a boxcar by old men as the train passes over a bridge and into a river, where like Pip he sees a whale coming right at him: the rest of the story.

Soon we meet Christian Bale as the early sixties protest singer Jack Rollins, his face all angles and anguish. He is an instant legend so potent that a movie actor named Robbie Clark will become world-famous when he stars in a film about the young conscience of his generation. As Robbie Clark is played by Heath Ledger—and Clark's wife is played by Charlotte Gainsbourg as a cross between Bob Dylan's real-life girlfriend Suze Rotolo, his real-life wife Sara Lowndes, Patti Smith, and, as she has built a persona over the years, Gainsbourg herself—they will together act out a version of the romantic life of a real-life Bob Dylan who is now, already, no longer anything like the owner of his own story.

We meet Christian Bale again, now called Pastor John: Jack Rollins twenty years after he fled to an evangelical ministry in the Gateway Fellowship Church. And then, at first slowly, then with an unstoppable momentum—with Cate Blanchett's Jude Quinn, a mid-sixties pop star at war with his own audience, and with the dreamlike vertigo of Richard Gere's Billy the Kid, a hermit living on the outskirts of the dream-town called Riddle—the balance of the film shifts. The play of identities slows, and the pace of characters in trouble, trying to outrun their own fate, takes over.

Blanchett is a marionette in constant motion, an actress scaring her own character as the character, trying to manipulate his own strings, makes history with every fluttering gesture, every errant or loaded word. The sardonic face he tries desperately to keep in place—sometimes hilariously, as he dances before a bigger-than-life statute of Jesus on the cross, crowing "Do your early stuff!" like one of his own angry fans—is turned not forward but backward, as he attempts to keep the flood of the history he has already made and that has made him from sweeping him out of history, his own and anyone else's. That's how *I'm Not There* gets Blanchett's Jude to a Warhol-like gallery party in 1966 where a huge video screen shows the president of the United States quoting Bob Dylan's "Tombstone Blues" just like a college student: where, in his own voice, LBJ all but bursts out of the movie like Pecos Bill to thunder "DEATH TO ALL THOSE WHO WOULD WHIMPER AND CRY" and you can't believe he didn't say exactly that when he had the chance. Jude collapses, vomits; hustled out of the building and into a waiting limousine surrounded by screaming fans pounding on the windows, he looks straight into the eyes of a woman in the crowd looking straight into his, straight through him, as she lights a match and, without blinking, sets her hair on fire. That, the woman seems to be saying to Jude Quinn, is the real song inside the music you're making now—the song you're afraid to sing, the song I'm not afraid of. Over the years, countless people have told Bob Dylan that he said what they felt but couldn't say, that he gave them a voice. This small, irreducible event is that story—an incident which my memory tells me happened then, though my memory won't tell me where, why, who did it and to whom—turned back on the singer.

Gere's performance—and the setting of a small country town where the citizens carry the names of characters in Dylan's crazy-quilt farrago of the mostly still-unreleased songs from the basement tapes—may be the key to the vitality of the film itself.

"The Billy section," Haynes says, "enacts one of Dylan's escapes, one of his retreats from life, from the public glare, which happened throughout his career, and first and most notably in 1967 after his motorcycle crash. And his retreats from public life were also, at times, retreats from modernity, from the urban life"— and so, Haynes says, "you had to have a western." In his retreats from public life, "Dylan was a wanted man, an outlaw—to me, it wasn't a huge departure from the real." But as with the woman setting her hair on fire, it's a departure big enough to allow the people of Riddle to step out of the basement and tell a story the real Dylan's songs never contemplated. Here, everyone goes about in masks, one person with a flag painted over one side of his face, another wearing a woven basket around her head. When, to speak at a public gathering, Gere's Billy puts on a clear plastic mask, it becomes plain that, as in a miniature of the conceit of the film itself, it is only when one can appear as someone else that he or she is free to say what he or she really thinks, to truly use that voice that, here, every character did receive from some now spectral, perhaps altogether mythical figure named Bob Dylan.

The departure from the real is big enough for the reimagining or invention of moments that may go farther into Bob Dylan's real-life career than any writer, filmmaker, poet, or musician—any fan—has gone before. For me, at least, there is a clarity in Haynes's film that actual, documented, all but court-adjudicated events have never given up. There are two incidents in Bob Dylan's career that I've never understood: fans booing him at the Newport Folk Festival when he came onstage with a band and played "Subterranean Homesick Blues," and his conversion to Christianity. But on Haynes's screen they make living sense.

On the West Coast, the reaction of East Coast folkies to Bob Dylan's new rock 'n' roll seemed absurd. Where I lived, where the Beatles and the Rolling Stones were a constant, people wondered not why Dylan had turned his back on folk music, but why it had taken him so long to get on the train. As Haynes restages the Newport crisis, it's an assault: from both sides. The music that is flung out at the crowd is so nerve-smashing, and so loud—loud on the soundtrack, in decibels, but loud in a deeper manner, as if rising out of some internal rhythm—that, in the theater, it's shocking, or even evil. I could imagine myself in the crowd, and I realized I had no idea how I would have responded.

Christian Bale's Pastor John speaks quietly, even blankly—"with a paunch," Haynes says, "and a bad perm"—of his new life with Jesus. He's speaking from a film inside the film: a documentary, made for evangelical TV, with "the first interview with Jack Rollins in more than twenty years!"—and with the unnatural color of its cheap production perfectly validating its reality, taking you right out of the movie you thought you were watching. We sit with the interviewer in Pastor John's little office, and then we move into a commons room. Pastor John takes the stage; behind him are three well-dressed black women, and a band made up of a few men who look like meth addicts rounded up off the street. Before him are twenty or so people seated in folding chairs, with a few children playing in the background. It looks like an AA meeting. "Hi," you can imagine Bale saying. "My name is John, and I'm a folk singer." The people in the audience are human wreckage. But they are not an audience. They are part of the same fellowship that Pastor John is part of. As he begins to preach, and then, with the voice of John Doe, founder in the 1970s of the Los Angeles punk band X, coming out of Christian Bale's mouth, as Father John begins to sing and play "Pressing On," with a straining voice and a sense of mission the song may never have given its composer, you realize that the man on the stage is not giving the people in the chairs anything they have not given him, that he is not telling them anything they have not told him. There is no star, there is no audience, there is no persona, there are no puppet's strings, there is no mask in this place; in this church, everyone is accepted for who he or she wishes to be, a servant of the same god, and in that way, of each other. For the first time, I did understand: Bob Dylan had been offered the kingdom of being recognized as himself, as someone he had all but forgotten, and he had said yes. It was no matter that Todd Haynes made it all up.

The film is confusing only if one demands that a dream explain itself—and if one refuses the implacable logic on which dreams float. When identity is as fluid as it is in *I'm Not There*—and when a person whose public life has been so bound up with the lives of other people wants to break the invisible contract between performer and audience—then the possibility must be present that identity can be cast aside altogether.

The private person must be able to lose himself in the community. The performer must be able to disappear into the audience. He must be able to dissolve into the fantasies of his own songs: once his own fantasies, then the fantasies of whoever heard the songs.

"I'm Not There" remains the most haunting of the basement tapes songs—and, though it has been bootlegged for years, it has never, until now, as Dylan's original recording plays on the soundtrack of *I'm Not There*, been officially made public. Here it is as much of a whirlpool as it ever was, but instead of capsizing a filmmaker's fables with its own supposed authenticity, it fades into the picture, nothing more and nothing less than one more story among all the rest.

The picture holds its shifting shape. In Todd Solondz's *Palindromes* (2004), a slew of people play a single young girl, but the impression you have at the close is that the character required so many actors because she didn't exist; here, by the end, the figure of Bob Dylan is at once more elusive and more interesting than before, and you are still certain neither he nor any of Haynes's characters have told half of what they know. In *What's Love Got to Do with It* (1993), you may be with Angela Bassett's Tina Turner all the way—and then the real Tina Turner appears and the movie dissolves. In the last moments of *I'm Not There*, Bob Dylan appears, playing his way across a Möbius strip of a harmonica solo—and he, the real thing, does not reduce the people whose adventures you have watched in any way. You don't know where the notes Bob Dylan is playing are headed, or even, necessarily, what song they're from; you don't know what really happens in Riddle, or, if Billy does escape, where he could possibly go. And that is why, leaving the theater, you are already on your way back in.

I'm Not There, directed by Todd Haynes, written by Haynes and Oren Moverman (Weinstein Company, 2007).

Bob Dylan, "I'm Not There," from *I'm Not There—Original Soundtrack* (Columbia, 2007).

VISIONS AND VISIONS OF JOHANNA*
2008

The June 1966 issue of the youth-oriented American fashion magazine *Glamour* carried an unusual feature: lyrics from the soon to be released Bob Dylan song "Visions of Johanna," which Dylan had

---

*An introduction to "Great Lyrics," a chapbook published by the *Guardian* (London).

been performing onstage, alone, with an acoustic guitar, since late in the previous fall. "Seems Like a Freeze Out," he'd say to introduce the song before stepping into its slow, languid account of a night of bohemian gloom. Soon the song, recorded in Nashville earlier in the year with the best session players in town, would make a black hole on the first side of Dylan's double album *Blonde on Blonde*.

What was unusual about this was that the lyrics worked on the *Glamour* page as they were presented: bare, without accompaniment, without a singing voice, as poetry. All through Bob Dylan's writing life—beginning before his 1962 debut album *Bob Dylan*, the songs leaping in ambition, sophistication, daring, and style at first year by year and then month by month if not week by week—Dylan had written words meant to come to life when they were played and sung. A clumsy line meant as no more than a way to get from one place to another—the limp "He wasn't really where it's at" between the unflinching "Ain't it hard when you discover that" and the swirling "After he took from you everything that he could steal" in "Like a Rolling Stone"—could fly by all without harm when it was lifted by a melody that was itself shot out of the cannon of a song by the singer increasing the pressure. But on the page a song's words are naked. Line by line, "Blowin' in the Wind" is pious, or falsely innocent—isn't it obvious whoever wrote "Yes, 'n' how many seas must a white dove sail / Before she sleeps in the sand?" already knows the answer, assuming he or anyone can actually bring him or herself to care about such a precious question? But "Visions of Johanna" is asking different sorts of questions. Such as: Where are you? Who are you? What are you doing here? So you want to leave? Think you can find the door?

If you happened to have read "We sit here stranded, though we're all doing our best to deny it" in *Glamour* in 1966, without having ever heard the line in a song, you could feel stranded in the white spaces between the words. People wandering from one corner of a loft to another, doped, drunk, half awake, fast asleep, no point to the next breath, let alone the next step, "sitting on the floor," as the musician Steve Strauss wrote of the song in 1967,

"collecting highs like so many stockbrokers collecting shares before retirement"—as slowly as the song was played in late 1965 (at
the time, the story was that the song had been written during the
great East Coast blackout of 9 November 1965) on the page it was
slower, because as a reader you stopped at every word, trying to
make it give up as much as it promised.

As a set of five verses, "Visions of Johanna" makes a narrative
solely out of atmosphere. That's one reason why it read so slowly
in 1966, and why it can read so slowly today: why the song as
words on a page can silence the song you might carry in your
head, and make you say the song yourself. There is a drama taking
place here, in this dank room—somehow too big, too much space
for too many people, too many shadows, for the person who's
telling the story to get his bearings—even if nothing is happening,
or if whatever does happen, whatever events actually push the air
aside and mark a moment in time the narrator can actually remember, are not really events at all. This is what happens here: "We can
hear the night watchman click his flashlight." Someone says
"Name me someone who's not a parasite and I'll go out and say a
prayer for him." A woman opens her fist to show the drugs she has
and dares anyone to say no. "The country music station plays
soft." And yet the peculiar contours of the fable that is being related immediately make sense. The words seem to meet each other
in perfect balance, and separate with a sense of having said everything there is to say. With poetry having left rhyme behind in the
nineteenth century, rhyming couplets are now almost impossible
for the modern eye to scan; here the gravity of the words, the
dread in the synapses ("But there's nothing, really nothing to turn
off"), erases all awareness that a line that ends with face is followed
by one that ends in place. It's a locked-room mystery and you're in
the room. As you read, you can't imagine wanting to get out, because you haven't yet explored every corner or plumbed the darkness for whoever might be lying in it. You haven't found the
skeleton keys the guy on the other side of the room keeps muttering he's going to play on his harmonica.

As the room is locked, there is a way that for the reader no less than for the characters in the song—Louise, her lover, little boy lost, the D train whores—the walls are made of air. That may be why, over the last months of 1965 and the first months of 1966, Dylan was able to record the song in so many different ways. Always singing solo when he took the song to a crowd, in the studio he always took it to the band he was touring with, the Hawks. In New York in November the song is almost a honky-tonk, with a bouncy rhythm, and then in another take in the same session it's a fury, threatening to shatter anyone who gets too close to the sound; two months later, again in New York, it rises off the ground like a cloud; not long after in Nashville it's low-budget film noir, *Detour* without a road but with the same dead end. Reading the song as it moves across a page, it's hard to hear any of that. The words make their own rhythms, and their rhythms enforce their own quiet.

The other songs collected here—"Desolation Row," "Masters of War," "Blind Willie McTell," "Tangled Up in Blue," "Talking John Birch Paranoid Blues," "Blowin' in the Wind," "The Lonesome Death of Hattie Carroll"—struggle to escape from the recordings the reader brings to them, and sometimes, for moments, they do, but there's no reason why they should; they weren't made to live a life outside of music. Who knows what life "Visions of Johanna" was meant to lead when it was written? The answer is to a different question: this is a song with countless lives, most of them as yet unlived.

Bob Dylan, "Visions of Johanna," on *Blonde on Blonde*, recorded in Nashville, 14 February 1966 (Columbia, 1966). Solo versions can be found in Martin Scorsese's film *No Direction Home* (PBS, Spitfire Pictures DVD, 2005), on *The Bootleg Series Vol. 4: Live 1966—The "Royal Albert Hall" Concert* (Columbia, 1998, recorded Manchester Free Trade Hall, 17 May 1966), and on various bootlegs from that month. The first recordings of "Seems Like a Freeze Out" were made in New York City with the Hawks and Al Kooper. The honky-tonk version, from 30 November 1966, can be found as "Freeze Out (2)" on *Thin Wild Mercury Music* (SP bootleg), with the assaulting recording from the same date included on *No*

Direction Home: The Soundtrack—The Bootleg Series Vol. 7 (Columbia, 2005); a New York version from 21 January 1966 is on *Thin Wild Mercury Music* as "Freeze Out (1)."

Steve Strauss, "A Romance on Either Side of Dada," from *Rock and Roll Will Stand,* edited by GM. Boston: Beacon, 1969.

THE BEGINNING AND THE END
Interview
April 2008

Vince White joined a legendary punk band in late 1983, seven years into the band's life; his *Out of Control: The Last Days of the Clash* is about the end of a story. Suze Rotolo's *A Freewheelin' Time: A Memoir of Greenwich Village in the Sixties* is about the beginning of a story. "I met Bob Dylan in 1961," she writes, "when I was 17 years old and he was 20."

For a time Rotolo and Dylan were a couple; the cover of the book is a version of the photo that in 1963 appeared on the cover of *The Freewheelin' Bob Dylan,* the singer and a glowing Rotolo clinging to each other against the cold of a snow-covered Village street. The image radiated freedom, autonomy, adventure, invulnerability. These two people had their whole future ahead of them—theirs, and, it seemed, that of everyone who bought the album, everyone they stood for.

Telling her own tale more than Dylan's—so rooted to her own ground you can almost feel her feet on the pavement as she walks west on 4th Street across MacDougal—Rotolo writes with the lightest touch. "He was funny, engaging, intense, and he was persistent. Those words completely describe who he was throughout the time we were together, only the order of the words would shift depending on the mood or circumstance." You might read this as a description of Bob Dylan; you might read it for the pleasure of how much is said in so few words. You might read it for the way a whirlpool of connection and separation opens up at the foot of the second sentence. Rotolo's tone creates a drama that is both public and personal, as when she watches Dylan perform the traditional "Dink's Song" at a Philadelphia coffeehouse. "The audience slowed their chattering; he stilled the room. It was as though I had never heard the song before. He stilled my room, for sure."

The book is demure, quiet, level, even through a nervous breakdown. Rotolo tells the story of a shared milieu and of a romance that, in its way, was also shared, but her self-respect is such that it translates into respect for the reader. She never violates her own privacy, and thus she never violates yours. Sex is never mentioned; with drugs, other than marijuana there is only the one awful night someone doses her drink with LSD. And as for the third part of the equation, there is that *Freewheelin'* album: "It was folk music, but it was really rock and roll." She makes her own textures, so that what is left out doesn't feel as if it's missing, and what is left in maps the territory she wants to bring into view.

The great thrill of Vince White's book is that, more than twenty years after the fact, he summons up the frantic state of mind of two years in the Clash as if they were still unfinished.

After Joe Strummer and Paul Simonon kicked guitarist Mick Jones out of the Clash, they held auditions. People showed up, played to backing tapes, weren't told what band they might be joining. Vince White was one of two guitar players hired—as an employee. He was never off probation. In 1985 Strummer tells White he's reforming the original band—he never did—and tells him to get married.

White brought a pure punk mind into the group. After graduating from college, he found himself overwhelmed by a sense of corruption and futility: "Everyone I met seemed to accept all the appearances of reality as truth. Like a giant conspiracy of assumptions that said a bus was a bus. But a bus wasn't a bus. It was an obscene red metal object that moved down the street carrying blank faces that had come from nowhere and were going absolutely nowhere."

That was the sense of the world that went into the first Clash songs, which seemed to batter the city walls in a search for a way out. Now the band is in Los Angeles and Strummer, here portrayed as all but driven mad by his own messiahship, is making radio promos: "'We want you there to take the floor and break it down and get with the *real* sound of *Rebel rock!*'" There wasn't "a trace of irony," White writes. "I was shocked. I didn't recognize him . . . It was insulting and degrading. To people's intelligence. To us and everyone who came to the shows. Surely people weren't that stupid?"

White's book turns its end into a beginning: he goes to work as a cab driver, makes more money than he ever did as a musician, and travels the world as a free person. Rotolo turns her beginning into an ending: her book, it becomes clear, is about the freedom a certain place and time offered those who were willing to grasp it, and as Village memoirists have written for more than a century, that place and time are gone. But unlike most of her countless forebears, from Malcolm Cowley and Edmund Wilson on down, Rotolo doesn't rest with *I was there* (and you weren't): "Though it is a concept now priced out of its physical space, as a state of mind, it will never be out of bounds . . . it doesn't matter whether there is an actual physical neighborhood or not." Both White and Rotolo are seeking truth and freedom, and neither writes as if their reader is any less worthy than they are.

Vince White, *The Last Days of the Clash*. London: Moving Target, 2007.

Suze Rotolo, *A Freewheelin' Time: A Memoir of Greenwich Village in the Sixties*. New York: Broadway Books, 2008.

THE DRAWN BLANK SERIES
London *Times*
7 June 2008

What's this stick-figure fisherman looking over a harbor full of blues and yellows and lots of sunny white? It's one of the 170 *Drawn Blank* gouaches and watercolors that Bob Dylan made last year—going back to a collection of *Drawn Blank* black and white drawings and sketches he'd made between 1989 and 1992, taking transfers of the old work, painting over them, discovering what the old pictures wanted to become.

Like many pictures more—*Amagansett, Vista from a Balcony, Bicycle, Still Life with Peaches, Sunday Afternoon* (which could be called "Sunday Painter")—*Fisherman* is also postcard art. It's the sort of stuff that's sold in tourist towns in the retail equivalent of tea rooms, the stores that call themselves shoppes and charge extra for the cards "By Our Local Artists." An overstylization, which here is a lack of style, presses a banality that often seems to be the ruling principle of the pictures ("Drawn Blank?" Firing blanks? Or a shooter who doesn't even look at what he's shooting at?). Depthless bodies and faces match the dullness of the pleasant scenes, their primitiveness its own kind of pretentiousness, whether it's *Woman Near a Window, Society Lady* (so much less than the Weegees it seems to come from, just as *Reno Balcony* calls up Robert Frank's 1956 view from a hotel room in *Butte, Montana*), portraits of Tom Clark, Paul Karaian, Nick LeBlanc, *Cupid Doll,* or any of the nudes and semi-nudes. You've seen it all before. But others draw you into a dialogue. Where is this place? Have I been there? Is it real?

Here, working through three or four new paintings made from a single old drawing, what's shown no longer fits into its cliché. Houses—*House on Chestnut Street, Front Porch of a House on Hayes Street*—seem almost to burst from some unseen pressure, as if they're rotting from the inside. The heat that comes out of the density in *Freret Street New Orleans* is instantly recognizable if you've ever been there, but you haven't seen it before: unlike the person who painted this, you haven't imagined how it looks. TV sets, found in motel rooms—*Lakeside Cabin, View from Two Windows*—hold more secrets than women. The women pretend to be alive, or the painter is trying to bring them to life; the TV sets acknowledge they're already dead, or the painter has somehow broken them before they were turned on. Looking at these little boxes, you can't imagine that they ever carried pictures of their own.

The work here that sings with invention, play, seriousness—a commitment to the moment the image is making—comes with a few *Twilight Zone*–like variations: like an octopus changing colors before your eyes, in *Corner Flat* the same chair is occupied by four different people, seemingly in an instant, as if it's a single person in disguise against his or her own self.

In *Rose on a Hillside,* there is a rose in the foreground. Behind it, absolutely different scenes—mountains, a small town, a house, the New York skyline from across the Hudson—loom up in turn, as if, if you know how to look at the rose, it will call up whatever you desire. There is *Train Tracks:* a western scene, a track to its vanishing point, mountains in the background, a depot, a telegraph pole. One in blue and green and brown, two in black and white except for a warm brown for the track, three, it's a movie set—and then, with the final version, the whole scene in black and white, save for the sky, blank before, now a quiet explosion of pure gold.

It's a visionary moment, just as the oh-so-contemplative series *Man on a Bridge* is its counterfeit—for those who need to reduce all art to autobiography, pictures which allow the viewer to imagine that the bearded figure there is Bob Dylan himself, at the crossroads of life. Symbolism! But the last *Train Tracks* is not symbolism. It's not reducible. You want to go to this place. You want to see that sky happen. You can't, so you settle for the next best thing. You keep looking at the picture—which after all made up that sky as if it had never been, which maybe it hadn't.

The portrait of Bob Dylan that serves as a frontispiece for the book version of *The Drawn Blank Series* is a 2006 photo by William Claxton—the jazz photographer best known for his intimate, almost preternaturally cool mid-1950s pictures of Art Pepper, Billie Holiday, and most of all Chet Baker. His Dylan picture seems based on the only photo known of the protean Mississippi bluesman Charley Patton, made in about 1929. Dylan's floppy bow tie ties the two together; both communicate a sense of weight, knowledge, experience, fatalism. Those qualities are present here and there in the *Drawn Blank* pictures—not so fully as in the strongest of Dylan's recent music, "Ain't Talkin'" from the 2006 *Modern Times,* but with an unlikelihood to make you realize Dylan's songs don't say all he might want to say.

Bob Dylan, *The Drawn Blank Series.* New York: Prestel USA, 2008.

REAL LIFE ROCK TOP 10
The Believer
September 2008

3) Howard Hampton writes (June 11): "I stumbled on Dylan's endorsement of Obama (*London Times,* June 5: 'Right now America is in a state of upheaval. Poverty is demoralizing. You can't expect

people to have the virtue of purity when they are poor. But we've got this guy out there now who is redefining the nature of politics from the ground up—Barack Obama . . . Am I hopeful? Yes, I'm hopeful that things might change. Some things are going to have to'). Makes sense that there would be that spark of recognition—the thing that amazes me is that the Clintons never seemed to get that they were dealing with someone more formidable than a Howard Dean in blackface. So they wound up looking like Baez and Seeger, the Old Regime, undone by the sound of a greater sense of possibility than they were willing to entertain—hence the whole 'Electability' issue would frame the election as 'No We Can't' (elect a black man) vs. 'Yes We Can' (dream a better country, as MLK or poor tortured RFK did once upon a time)."

TELL TALE SIGNS:
Rare and Unreleased, 1989–2006—
The Bootleg Series Volume 8
(Columbia Legacy)
Barnes and Noble Review
10 October 2008

You can find a map of the transformation Bob Dylan has wrought in American music over the last twenty years—a transformation in the way he has made it, certainly, but perhaps even more deeply in the way that many people now hear it—in the first two tracks of the third CD of *Tell Tale Signs:* a disc available only in the cruelly priced "Expanded Deluxe Edition." ($169.99, as opposed to $22.99 for the two-CD set). I don't mean to one-up; what is here is where it's been placed, and as one person associated with the production put it, "Ultimately it will all be available to everyone; people will just download it." Time will tell.

But here is Bob Dylan in Chicago in 1992, taking up the folk song "Duncan and Brady," just months before moving on to the stripped-down, solo investigations of American commonplace songs—from black, white, and shared traditions—that first came to light later that year with his *Good as I Been to You* and continued in 1993 with *World Gone Wrong*. For those records, Dylan worked in his own home studio, without other musicians, without a producer. He found more of a voice in the melodies, twisted and jumped on his own acoustic guitar, than in the words. But in Chicago, with the concept not yet clear—with the songs yet to tell him how they wanted to be played—Dylan has given himself over to the producer David Bromberg, a musician who, as is said of a pompous rabbi in Philip Roth's *The Plot Against America*, "knows everything. Too bad he doesn't know anything else."

"The ballad gets what the ballad wants," the singer David Thomas is fond of saying—except when someone like Bromberg kidnaps it and holds it for ransom. Here is a tale about a gunman and a bartender that has never, in its more than a century of changing hands, cried out to be done up with bass, drums, two or three guitars, organ, and synthesizer, all played as if the instruments themselves are self-orchestrating robots, with a perfectly congruent disembodied, science-fiction sound. The song doesn't know what to do with all this, and Dylan doesn't either. The mess of the thing ultimately goes back to his own uncertainty about what his music is and what it is for; he was coming out of a long period of contrived writing, fallow orchestration, more than ten years of desperate flailing for a something that not only could be put on the market but demanded to be brought into the world. So he tries gamely to keep up with the big band's hurried clackety-clack, as if to say, moment to moment, *this will all be over in three minutes, two minutes, one minute*—There's no soul in the performance, and no body.

The old songs that sprung to such cryptic life on *Good as I Been to You* and *World Gone Wrong* took a new form in 1997 with *Time Out of Mind*. There the likes of Blind Willie McTell's "Ragged and

Dirty" and the mists-of-time British ballad "Love Henry" shed their skins and grew new ones, turning into "Dirt Road Blues," "Standing in the Doorway," "Not Dark Yet," "Tryin' to Get to Heaven," "Cold Irons Bound." Onstage the songs changed shape yet again, as if they were less made than found, daring their putative composer to keep up with them. On numerous real bootlegs— as opposed to Dylan's own official bootlegs—it was plain that "Cold Irons Bound" grew faster and bigger than anything else, but I have never heard anything like the *Tell Tale Signs* performance, from the Bonnaroo Festival in Manchester, Tennessee, in 2004.

The band is Tony Garnier, bass, Larry Campbell, guitar, Stu Kimble, guitar, George Recile, drums. Over many years on Dylan's stages, Garnier and Campbell have probably accompanied him with a deeper affinity than anyone else, and the result here is that Dylan takes the song with such command it feels as if he's playing every instrument, not merely his own piano and harmonica. How could other hands know what to do? It's all moving so fast, with such coursing strength, the rhythm its own flood, cutting its own banks out of the melody, the singer's out-of-the-ground voice all but laughing at its own power: after all, it was he who blew up the dam in the first place. The piece has the rockabilly flash of Elvis Presley's "Mystery Train," the defiant syncopation of Howlin' Wolf's "How Many More Years," the sly menace of Muddy Waters's "Mannish Boy," the all-hell-is-breaking-loose thrill of Rod Stewart's "Every Picture Tells a Story." At its highest pitch, the singer seems to be trying to top himself, growl against growl, grin against grin, oath against oath, reveling in some otherworldly two-man standup comedy routine that's only a few steps away from the circular firing squad at the end of *Reservoir Dogs*. It moves past so quickly that the music seems to fragment, and you catch echoes of voices from much farther back, from before anyone in this song was born, whispering that they knew the song before the singer did, that they always knew it sounded just like this, and that they're in on the joke: that when you're "cold irons bound" you're on the way to your deathbed.

Both the standard and expanded versions of *Tell Tale Signs* include unusually illuminating, engaging liner notes by Larry "Ratso" Sloman, who wrote a book about Dylan's 1975 Rolling Thunder tour, and has happily survived turning up dead in Kinky Friedman's 1993 mystery *Elvis, Jesus & Coca-Cola;* the deluxe edition packages Sloman's commentary in an illustrated book and adds an art book collecting sleeves from Dylan singles from Columbia outlets far and wide to go with the extra third disc. And though it emerges far more completely across three CDs, the story told is of a piece.

The music Bob Dylan has made since 1992 has been based on a hunch that there is a body of American song, or an American ethos of expression, that is a constant. It's a scattered form that in words and metaphors, riffs and moans, hesitations and shouts, can always be rediscovered, and can rediscover and renew whoever remembers it, as if one can not only speak but listen in tongues. Collecting mostly alternate studio or live versions of material already released ("Ring Them Bells" and "Most of the Time" from the otherwise cramped 1989 *Oh Mercy,* "Ain't Talkin'" from the 2006 *Modern Times*), soundtrack compositions ("Huck's Tune" from *Lucky You,* the endless "'Cross the Green Mountains" from the misbegotten Civil War epic *Gods and Generals*), and abandoned songs now heard for the first time ("Marchin' to the City," "Dreamin' of You," "Red River Shore," all left off of *Time Out of Mind*), the twenty-seven tracks of the standard *Tell Tale Signs,* and the twelve additional numbers in the expanded package, trace Bob Dylan's exploration of this territory. There are blind alleys (the programmatic "Dignity," the ready-made protest song "Everything Is Broken"), and alleys made for muggings ("Tryin' to Get to You," its initial Carter Family shape dissolved on stage in London in 2000 as it's sung by someone who must have looked like Bob Dylan but sounds exactly like the sort of fifties crooner the critic Nik Cohn once described as "white, sleek, nicely spoken, and phony to your toenails"—and it's a tour de force). There are variations that don't expand the possibilities of a song but wear it out (the three *Time*

Out of Mind versions of "Mississippi," which was rerecorded for the 2001 *"Love and Theft"*).

At first it can seem like a pile of footnotes and appendices. But as a fan's compendium of Dylan's thirty-one 1993 live performances of the folk song "Jim Jones" (from *Good as I Been to You*) makes plain—as over nine months on tour the song's melody swallows its words, its words spur a new force in its rhythm, and finally the rhythm turns toward abstraction, and the song's narrator, a prisoner sent from London to the hell-hole of nineteenth-century Australia, becomes a figment of his own imagination, his own landlocked Flying Dutchman—there is no end to what, when the spirit is right, Dylan can do with a song. A performance that at first seems flat reveals layers; a singer missing the cues in his own words turns out to be after something else entirely. The music here won't be heard the first time around.

For just that reason, there is little point in saying that "Red River Shore," despite the tragedy of its story, is as open as the plains, the only limit to what it can say a matter of whether you can see from one end of its Kansas to the other. After a few listenings, it might seem too sweet, not the tragedy it means to be at all. As you listen it might be replaced at the top of this set's chart by "Most of the Time," a song so carefully composed you can imagine that had Dean Martin or Fred Astaire had the chance to record it their versions would have been better than Dylan's—and as Dylan performs it, solo on the first disc, with quiet, retreating accompaniment on the third, it can make you lose track of time, to the point that the fact that *Tell Tale Signs* has dropped its clues over nearly two decades need mean nothing at all.

SAM MCGEE'S "RAILROAD BLUES" AND OTHER VERSIONS OF THE REPUBLIC

Threepenny Review
Winter 2008

In 1964, a man named Sam McGee cut a new version of a tune he'd first recorded in 1934: "Railroad Blues."

In the way that McGee's guitar seemed to have twenty strings and McGee himself four hands, he was a whole orchestra. In the way he shouted as his notes rushed past—shouting "Wah-HOO!" like Harmonica Frank Floyd recording "Rocking Chair Daddy" for Sam Phillips in Memphis in 1951, like Elvis Presley recording "Mystery Train" for Phillips four years later, an entire era later— in the way McGee aimed his voice at the sky, he was standing by himself on top of a mountain, alone in the world, not another sign of human presence as far as his eyes could see.

But whatever image came to mind as McGee's "Railroad Blues" played, you couldn't imagine the man who was spinning the song standing still. As the tune played, the player went from one place to another. And he was no longer merely Sam McGee. From the first move into the tune—an almost unbearably delicious down- ward swoop on a fat bass note, making you feel as if you were be- ing lifted off your feet—from that first gesture, the player was something bigger, more various. He was Daniel Boone with faster feet; Johnny Appleseed with songs for pips; Cooper's Leather- stocking with a sense of humor; Huck Finn as an old man, having long since discovered, in words Edmund Wilson wrote in 1922, "for what drama" his "setting was the setting."

The drama was to make a sound that would prove to all the world that the world remained to be made, or even found. "Went to the depot, looked up on the board," McGee sang for a first verse, taking a commonplace line and throwing it away, out of the way of the story he was telling with his guitar. "Went to the depot, looked up on the board / It read, 'Good times here, but better down the road.'"

Whoever it is who's playing, in an instant you can see him standing on a table in a bar full of drunks, and then in a concert hall, dashing back and forth from one side of the stage to the other as an audience of respectful folk revivalists sits thrilled and confused. You can glimpse a man walking into a barbershop looking for change, filling his hat, then tossing the coins back at the rounders like Levon Helm in the Band's "Up on Cripple Creek," telling the tale of what his Bessie did with her half of their racetrack winnings: "Tore it up and threw it in my face, just for a laugh."

Who is this man—not Sam McGee, but the figure who comes to life as Sam McGee plays?

He is one of many figures who appear in American vernacular music as it was recorded in the 1920s and '30s—who appear with such force, and such charm, such a broad smile or such an implacable scowl as to claim the whole of the country's story as if it were his or hers alone.

It is incontestable, for example, that there is no room for the creature running through "Railroad Blues" in the nation established by Bela Lam and his Greene County Singers, as they recorded in Richmond, Virginia, when OKeh Records held a joint recording session there in 1929—which featured as well the Monarch Jubilee Quartet, the Roanoke Jug Band, the Tubsize Hawaiian Orchestra, the Bubbling Over Five, and eight other acts.

Born around 1870, dead in 1944, Zandervon Orbeliah Lamb was a big man with a big white handlebar moustache. The Greene County Singers were Lam (as OKeh spelled out his name), his wife Rose, their son Alva, and Rose's brother Paul. In 1927, in New York City, they recorded a profoundly peaceful version of "See That My Grave Is Kept Green," an old song about the countless unmarked graves from the Civil War that found its way into Blind Lemon Jefferson's "See That My Grave Is Kept Clean." In 1929 in Richmond, though, the sylvan glade was nowhere in evidence.

Bizarrely atonal banjo and guitar clang unpleasantly into even uglier singing, into nothing that can be called a rhythm or a melody, but rather a translation into music of a conviction so murderously complete, so uninterested in what you think you believe, that suddenly you feel very small—on the outside of a story that is yours whether you like it or not. The story of Jesus Christ, your Savior, come to take you, in the person of the Greene County Singers.

"Tell It Again"—the refrain sounds like "Kill it again"—is people rooted to their ground, certain no merely human force can move them an inch. "If Tonight Should End the World" is a procession of singers stumbling down the street—stumbling because they can't keep time, because their harmonies are as arthritic as their hands must be, if their cracked and quivering voices are any clue to their age. But the music builds on itself, until you, too, are waiting for the end of the world. If tonight should end the world, then—what? They know; you don't.

It isn't that the faithful in "If Tonight Should End the World" would turn away from the man in "Railroad Blues" as a sinner, or that they would turn him away from their church. They don't recognize him. He doesn't exist. They are people who move into the settlement the railroad bluesman has just left, working hard, looking straight ahead, raising the church, building the town, so that when the man blows back into the place in a year or so, he won't even know where he is.

To the Greene County Singers, free in their knowledge that history has already come to an end, free in the embrace of the Lord, the rounder is no more than a prisoner, a prisoner of his own animal appetites, and against people like him, their town has no need for a jail. Bela Lam's banjo picks out "Crown Him" ("Lord above"), and you can feel that they are already in another world, even as they claim this one.

In the same way, it's hard to imagine the free American in "Railroad Blues" countenancing the destroyed individual in Emry Arthur's 1928 "I'm a Man of Constant Sorrow."

It's not, today, an obscure song. Bob Dylan recorded a version of it early in his career. As "The Maid of Constant Sorrow," Judy Collins sang it with pseudo-Elizabethan preciousness at the height of the folk revival. The Stanley Brothers recorded it, and many more. In 2001, in the Coen Brothers's film *O Brother, Where Art Thou?* George Clooney, John Turturro, Tim Blake Nelson, and Chris Thomas King—for the moment the Soggy Bottom Boys, with Dan Tyminski of Alison Krauss's band the voice behind Clooney's dashing mike work—swept the movie's south with it, and you didn't doubt for a minute that everyone there wanted to hear it more than they wanted to hear anything else.

But Emry Arthur, who in 1929 accompanied the banjoist Dock Boggs on guitar, who, Boggs recalled, "had been shot through the hands—he couldn't reach the chords—bullets went through his hands," was the first to record "Man of Constant Sorrow."

Say the first lines: "I am a man of constant sorrow / I've seen trouble all my days." They are instantly, overwhelmingly senti-mental—and unless you completely ignore the lines as you sing, as the Soggy Bottom Boys do, going for speed and flash, they are im-possible not to dramatize. As Dylan and Collins found, the more quietly you sing the lines, the louder they become—and the more of a poseur they reveal you to be.

Arthur bangs on his guitar as if he's been shot through the hands. You can almost see the bones sticking out. Plink, plink, he says, no more musically than Bela Lam. "I am a man of constant sorrow," he says plainly, as if he were saying "I am hungry," or "I am cold," as if he's learned to say such things with dignity. "I have seen trouble all my days." It's that "have," instead of the usual contraction of "I've," that says what the singer is saying is not ob-vious, not common, not something you really want to hear about.

You can imagine the Greene County Singers trying to pull Emry Arthur into their fold. They would recognize him, if only because they speak the same blank language, the Greene County Singers singing as if they don't care if you hear them, Emry Arthur as if he can't believe anyone would listen. But why would the man in "Railroad Blues" even pause? In his thin voice, which imperceptibly moves from bitterness to acceptance, from anger to peace, the figure in "Man of Constant Sorrow" offers a kind of challenge, a rebuke to God's gifts, and it's this that will keep him out of Bela Lam's church.

After a verse or two, the tunelessness of Arthur's performance settles into a hurdy-gurdy beat, and you are no longer afraid of the singer. He has put you at ease, so he can put you on the spot, so he can show you how absolutely you will never know him:

> Oh you can bury me in some deep valley
> For many years there I will lay
> And when you're dreaming, while you're sleeping
> While I am sleeping in the clay

It's the irreducible individualism of the details—details that rarely if ever moved into later versions of the already traditional song, perhaps because they communicate as so specific to a specific person that to appropriate them would be a theft no notion of the folk process could excuse—that seals its bottomless well: the unusual reference to dreaming, the use of clay, not mere ground. The singer goes on, after this verse, not in death but relating more of his travails, but he doesn't need to.

Like the Greene County Singers, he has told a finished story: having done so, he has delivered a finished verdict on, in his words, "the land that I have loved so well." If that nation, as it has composed itself into a republic, of which the singer is a citizen, has cast him out, then the country is a fiction, and there is no home for anyone—or ought not to be.

Born in 1900 in Wayne County, Kentucky, Emry Arthur died in 1966 in Indianapolis. He likely would not have recognized—or, maybe, would not have deigned to recognize—the Bob Dylan who recorded "Man of Constant Sorrow" in the early sixties, but he would have recognized the very old song "When First Unto This Country," as Dylan sang it in 1997. Whether he would have recognized, or accepted, the majesty Dylan brought to a song as bereft as his own I have no idea.

Starting in the mid-1980s, Dylan, playing by himself, with acoustic guitar and harmonica, then later with a band, began working more and more traditional material into his concerts, old songs about knights and damsels, sailors and buffalo skinners, all sung without a trace of irony or doubt, just an awareness of one's own smallness in the face of their enormity. Many were collected on the insanely rigorous nine-CD bootleg *The Genuine Never Ending Tour: Covers Collection 1988–2000*, which presented Dylan's concert performances of songs by others organized into different discs for country, soul, R&B, folk songs, traditional blues, pop, and on, and on, right down to "Alternates and Retakes," more versions of songs already appearing on the other discs—one last, obviously redundant piece of plastic, meant to squeeze another thirty dollars out of whoever was foolish enough to even think about buying the set. And this is where the action was. The first eight CDs make an enormous, colorless lump; in the last one, every genre mixed up, everything is alive. And here you find the version of "When First Unto This Country" that cuts.

"When first unto this country / A stranger I came." You cannot say more; you cannot overdramatize. That is the whole story of the country, as surely as a *TV Guide* summary for the move version of *Moby-Dick* I once saw was the whole story: "A mad captain enlists others in his quest to kill a white whale."

Dylan takes all the drama the song has. An electric guitar finds the hesitation in the melody, in the bass notes, and plays an actual overture. A wash of cymbal noise is like a wave lapping at the side of a ship; a muffled thump from the bass drum lets you feel the singer step ashore. And then everything slows down, as if, before the story has even begun, you must hear the ending—and you do. The theme has been stated, and it is elegant and fine, but beautiful in the way that you can imagine that the ruins of a Greek temple are more beautiful than the untouched temple could ever have been. A second electric guitar turns the melody into a count, and as the singer walks into America, his steps are measured.

He courts Nancy: "Her love I didn't obtain." For reasons he never gives—out of rage, a will to self-destruction, a sense of irredeemable estrangement from the land and the people who already claim to belong—he steals a horse. He is captured, his head shaved, he is beaten, thrown into prison, and forgotten. "I wished I'd never been a thief," he says, tearing the words out, like Stevie Wonder at the end of "Living for the City" in 1973—not like Dylan himself in his sardonic rewrite of the song he'd learned years before he turned it into "Bob Dylan's 115th Dream" in 1965. You can imagine the man finally free, moving from town to town, bar to bar, trying to find someone to listen to him. He repeats the first lines of the song, now with the finished story weighing down on every word: the first lines of the country.

All of these people—the happy man in "Railroad Blues," the saved in "If Tonight Should End the World," the dead man in "Man of Constant Sorrow," the walking dead man in "When First Unto This Country"—are separate from each other, isolatoes, in Melville's word from *Moby-Dick*, miles and miles between the church and this congregation of Ishmaels. "Good times here, but better down the road," the man in "Railroad Blues" says with every note; neither the Emry Arthur in "Man of Constant Sorrow" nor the Bob Dylan in "When First Unto This Country" would hear that man any more than Bela Lam would suffer to listen to him. What these songs, these performances say, is plain: if this is a republic, it is fated to scatter. It was made to guarantee its citizens the freedom that was theirs by right, not to limit it; so everyone understands, and that's the rub. Within the boundaries of that freedom, anything can happen, and everything will. If this is one republic, no one can see it whole; only the bravest can even think about it.

Now, when Sam McGee first recorded "Railroad Blues," in 1934, he was just then stepping out of a hole that had opened up in the story of vernacular American music. Hundreds of people had come forth to begin to tell that story in the 1920s, when early in the decade it became clear to northern record companies that there were paying audiences for the kind of music they already knew, the stuff they could hear on a neighbor's front porch or in the local barrelhouse, for blues, for ballads, for the folk-lyric hybrids of the two, for sounds that carried novelty, for sounds that were already called "old-time music."

From all over the South, from Texas, New Orleans, the Carolinas, Tennessee, Kentucky, the Virginias, from Arkansas and Alabama and Mississippi, an America that had hidden in folktales and the unwritten journals of the wanderings of the first generation of African-Americans to be born out of slavery emerged from the shadows of family memory and solitary meditation. That America took the form of many bodies—prophet, trickster, laborer, gambler, whore, preacher, thief, penitent, killer, dead woman, dead man—but the queer thing was that this country was seen and heard almost exclusively by those who already lived in it. People bought records that reminded them of themselves, that gave them proof of their existence, that raised their existence from the dirt level of subsistence into a heaven of representation.

Then came the Depression, and the music market collapsed; communities that had harbored the stories the nation at large still had no time for collapsed in its wake. Subsistence was no longer the boredom of one indistinguishable day following another, but a real drama, and in this squalid tragedy a father spending the family's only dollar on a phonograph record would have been a horror story. Record companies recalled their scouts, cleared their catalogues, closed their recording facilities.

By 1934 businesses had begun to reorganize, not because the economy had come back to life, but because people looked out at the ruins of their society and realized with a shock that they were not dead. When the recording of black and white folk music— much of it traditional, authorless and commonplace, much of it composed, little of it copyrighted, most of it entering the public domain as if it had been there forever, as if a blues as distinctive as Robert Johnson's "Stones in My Passway" had been passed from hand to hand long before he was born—began again, it was on a much more rational basis than had obtained in the 1920s. Instead of the open auditions where local oddballs and families appeared in their strange clothes with Sears catalogue instruments and their neighbors' or grandparents' songs, professionals were favored; instead of music everybody knew and almost anybody could play, record companies looked for virtuosity, for the music only a few could make.

That is where the first "Railroad Blues" came from. Born in 1894, Sam McGee lived until 1975, when he was killed in a tractor accident. He played and recorded for years with Uncle Dave Macon. He could play anything, and when he recorded "Railroad Blues" in 1934 he sounded as if he were in a cutting contest with himself. It's brilliant, the way an instrumental phrase goes down like a yo-yo and then slips right back up, now you see it now you don't. But there is something missing, something only the version McGee made precisely thirty years later reveals.

The 1934 "Railroad Blues" puts the spotlight on the performer himself, the guy who can kick it like nobody else, the fastest gunslinger in town. But in 1964, something closer to what happened when vernacular music was recorded in the 1920s was taking place. Many of the people who made that music were different from those around them: they had more nerve, were less afraid of the shame of failure, had a deeper belief in themselves, took greater risks—the risk of appearing before a businessman in a suit who more than likely would send you away as no better than anybody else. Robert Christgau writes tellingly of Dock Boggs, Boggs passing an audition in his hometown of Norton, Virginia, in 1927, then traveling to New York to record his scary, damned tunes about death, but "so full of beans" at the chance he's gotten he can barely contain not his rage, his resentment, his sense of exclusion, his fear of embarrassing himself in front of New York sharpies— not that, but "so full of beans" he can barely contain his joy.

You can hear the like of this all through the generic but also unique discs Harry Smith compiled for the anthology he at first flatly called *American Folk Music*. That thrill at the chance to speak, even only as a faraway premise, to speak one's piece to the country, even the world at large (the Sears catalogue not only sold banjos to people like Dock Boggs or Uncle Dave Macon, it made their 78s available in Japan, Turkey, and Tierra del Fuego), had to be at the root of the peculiar spell so many of the folk recordings cast on the present when Smith rereleased them in 1952, and the spell they cast today. When, in the 1960s, folk revivalists sat before such 1920s and '30s heroes as Mississippi John Hurt, Clarence Ashley, Boggs, Buell Kazee, Skip James, or Son House, they might have celebrated them as representatives of a people, of the People, as the folk musicians of the Folk—but as they listened, as they watched, as they were thrilled, they may have been responding less to what made these musicians part of a folk than to what set them apart from their folk: their ambition, their inner drive, their inability to tolerate their fellow human beings.

But the music was nothing if not a mystery, the mystery that occurs when a version of a nation's story has been excluded from the story as it is officially told is suddenly offered to the public. That is what happened in the 1920s, when southern musicians produced their version of America: taken together, they argued for a more contingent life, a less absolute death, an America where nothing was impossible and no settlement was ever final. In this mystery, the radical individualism one can hear in '20s folk music is always questioned, and by the same voice.

One of the most shadowy features of the music, one of the most queer, is an element of anonymity, the way the performer seems to step back from himself or herself, back into the community of which the performer was a part—or, if the performer was not part of a community, or sounded as if he or she could not be, the anonymity of the way the performer seemed to slip back into the oblivion where he or she lived alone, like Paul Muni stepping back from the camera and into darkness at the end of *I Was a Fugitive from a Chain Gang*. "How do you live?" the fugitive is asked. "I steal," he says.

When the tension between the self-presentation of the artist and the anonymous, even seemingly bodiless being behind the artist comes to a verge, the result is something no less exciting, no less unsettling, than the appearance of the radical individual—and this is what I think is happening in Sam McGee's "Railroad Blues" as he recorded it in 1964.

This is no longer the experienced sideman stepping out to claim his own career, to record under his own name, to show off all the tricks in his bag. Something bigger is happening—and a country with more room in it than the country present in the 1934 version comes into view. You are hearing someone who has seen all around the country, its past and its future, and he has made a remarkable discovery: America has never changed and it never will.

In the version of the republic that is enacted in "Railroad Blues" in 1964, nothing matters but movement: how you move. How you carry yourself. The promises you make in your very demeanor, the way you walk, the way your clothes fit, the way your expression fits your face, the way your face somehow changes everything you see. The specter in the music emerges immediately: the pioneer, the wanderer. In his freedom, he threatens those who stay home, working, saving, hoping, frightened—but he also leaves a blessing. Without living his life, you are allowed to know how it feels.

So it is no longer Sam McGee but a kind of abstraction who offers "Railroad Blues" in 1964—or in 2002, twenty-seven years after his death, on a Smithsonian Folkways collection called *Classic Mountain Songs,* which is where I first heard "Railroad Blues."

When McGee recorded in 1934, that signpost was crucial, the kickoff to the record. "Went the depot, looked up on the board / Went to the depot, looked up on the board / It read, 'Good times here, but better down the road.'" In 1934 that was a direct and specific political statement. It had to be said; in 1934, in the ditch of the Depression, it was the last thing anyone could take for granted, if they could believe it at all. The same words are said in 1964, tossed off, but as an event in the music, they have already happened.

That swoop, that astonishing lift, that fat note breaking into a thousand glittering fragments as the strings shake, has already called the train before a word gets out of the performer's mouth. The high notes are no longer a virtuoso's calling card—they have a life of their own. Thinner with every measure, so they can reach farther, their pace quickening, even as a bass note says "not so fast," the notes shoot out into the air and hang there fading, until you're sure they're gone—but the way the next movement picks up off the note you're still trying to hold in your memory tells you that the note was never gone at all.

That's what's uncanny—the sense that the truest tales the country can tell about itself must be incomplete, unfinished, left hanging in the air, so that whoever finds them can take up the story in the middle. And that, finally, is what took place near the beginning of this story, if this story is about a certain historical emergence of certain versions of the American story.

The one piece of music I know that sees every Gothic, pious, drunken, murdering, thieving, loving figure moving through the old American music for who he or she is, and embraces them all, is Richard "Rabbit" Brown's "James Alley Blues," recorded one day in New Orleans in 1927—the only day Brown ever recorded.

Brown lived and died. That he recorded only once is like Melville neglecting to keep Hawthorne's letter about *Moby-Dick*, the letter of which Melville could say "a sense of unspeakable security is in me" because Hawthorne had, in Melville's unbearably direct words, "understood the book."

The smallest, most modest notes creep out of Brown's guitar like tadpoles, swimming in search of their melody, their rhythm. A bass note gongs, shaking the air. Nothing is pressed. An old, ragged voice, now sour, now laughing at its own sourness, begins to tell a story about a marriage. He snaps at his strings to drive a point home, but every time he does, that weird gonging is there, pulling the real story away from the story being told.

When Jerry Leiber and Mike Stoller produced the Drifters' "There Goes My Baby" in 1959, for the first time layering the equivalent of a complete symphony orchestra over a piece of rock 'n' roll, the effect, they said, was like a radio dial stuck between two different stations. You can imagine that Rabbit Brown's "James Alley Blues" could have had a similar effect for those few who heard it—except that it would have been as if the performance existed between different eras, different lives, different ways of understanding the world and, like "There Goes My Baby," made you understand that those differences are meaningless. That was the meaning of that mystical gonging behind the prosaic facts the singer was relating; that was the meaning of the small searching notes that shot out ahead of every theme, blindly seeking a destination that could never be named.

It was those tiny, seeking notes that Sam McGee would seek himself in 1934, but not truly capture until three decades after that. He would from the start cast off the fatalism those notes carried. The thick, fat notes McGee would use to symbolize escape and liberation—that swoop, down and up, up and out, that "If you don't believe I'm leaving you can count the days I'm gone"—the notes that in "James Alley Blues" are filled up by Brown's echoing, flapping gongings, not warnings of what might happen but portents of what will—in McGee's hands, those notes will no longer speak of death.

In "If Tonight Should End the World," "Man of Constant Sorrow," and "When First Unto This Country," the singers value nothing so much as death—and "James Alley Blues" has room for them too. The small notes in "James Alley Blues" move like mice scurrying from one room to the other, never stopping, and the house only gets bigger. The man singing "James Alley Blues"—and you have to imagine him small, wiry, wary, moving carefully, smiling, looking over his shoulder—welcomes them all, and they enter his house, because they sense that he knows more about death than they do.

But that is not all Rabbit Brown knows. "Railroad Blues" is frank about the fact that it is made for pleasure; it is an argument that freedom is more pleasurable than death. "If Tonight Should End the World," "Man of Constant Sorrow," and "When First Unto This Country" are arguments that death is more meaningful than pleasure—arguments that hide their power in passion or the perfection of form, elements of performance that give pleasure because their beauty makes it seem as if their arguments are true.

But Rabbit Brown knows something about pleasure that, it seems, no one else does; he knows how to give pleasure as if it were the gift of a guardian angel. What he leaves behind—the sense of a place that is so big there is room for anyone, a place that is too big for anyone to escape—is exactly a story that can only start in the middle, with whoever might be telling it unsure if he or she should go forward, or go back.

Sam McGee, "Railroad Blues" (Champion, 1934), collected on *Sam McGee: Complete Recorded Works in Chronological Order, 1926–1934* (Document, 1999) and on the anthology *Times Ain't Like They Used to Be, Vol. 5* (Yazoo, 2002).

————. "Railroad Blues" (1964), collected on the anthology *Classic Mountain Songs* (Smithsonian Folkways, 2002). Originally released on McGee Brothers and Arthur Smith, *Old Timers of the Grand Old Opry* (Folkways, 1964).

Bela Lam and His Greene County Singers, "Tell It Again," "If Tonight Should End the World," "Glory Bye and Bye," and "Crown Him" (OKeh, 1929), collected on the anthology *Virginia Roots: The 1929 Richmond Sessions* (Outhouse 2002).

————. "See That My Grave Is Kept Green" (OKeh, 1927), collected on the anthology *Rural String Bands of Virginia* (County, 1993). See also Bela Lam with Rose Lam and a little boy filmed in front of a sharecropper shack performing "Poor Little Benny," on the video anthology *Times Ain't Like They Used to Be: Early Rural & Popular American Music, 1928–1935* (Yazoo DVD, 2000), a performance that can also be found on YouTube.

Emry Arthur, "I'm a Man of Constant Sorrow" (Vocalion, 1928). Collected with "Reuben Oh Reuben," "She Lied to Me" (both 1929) and "Short Life of Trouble" (1931) on the anthology *The Music of Kentucky, Vol. 2* (Yazoo, 1995). See also "I Am a Poor Pilgrim of Sorrow" by the Indian Bottom Association of Defeated Creek Church, Linefork, Kentucky, an Old Regular Baptist version recorded in 1997 by Jeff Todd Titon and collected on *Classic Mountain Songs.*

Bob Dylan, "Man of Constant Sorrow," *Bob Dylan* (Columbia, 1962).

―――. "When First Unto This Country," from "Alternates & Retakes," *The Genuine Never Ending Tour Covers Collection 1988–2000* (Ashes & Sand bootleg). See also the uncanny performance of the related "Sometimes in This Country" by Lee Monroe Presnell of North Carolina, recorded by Ann and Frank Warner in 1951, collected on the anthology *Her Bright Smile Haunts Me Still* (Appleseed, 2000). "We are accustomed to looking at photographs of people born before Washington died," Jeff Davis writes in his notes, "but we are not used to hearing their voices." Presnell was born in 1876; unaccompanied, he sang as if it were 1776. Live versions of "Man of Constant Sorrow" and "When First Unto This Country" from between 1988 and 1992 can be found on the remarkable Dylan bootleg *Golden Vanity* (Wanted Man).

Soggy Bottom Boys, "Man of Constant Sorrow," ghost vocal by Dan Tyminski as George Clooney, John Turturro, Tim Blake Nelson, and Chris Thomas King tear it up on screen, from *Oh Brother, Where Art Thou? Soundtrack* (Mercury, 2000).

Richard "Rabbit" Brown, "James Alley Blues" (Victor, 1927). Collected on *Anthology of American Folk Music* (1952; Smithsonian Folkways, 1997), and on *The Greatest Songsters: Complete Works (1927–1929)* (Document), which also includes Brown's other four recordings: "Never Let the Same Bee Sting You Twice," "I'm Not Jealous," "Mystery of the Dunbar Child" (for the mystery behind that, see Tal McThenia's report "The Ghost of Bobby Dunbar," *This American Life* (14 March 2008, http://www.thisamericanlife.org/Radio_Episode.aspx?episode=352), and the unforgettably gleeful "Sinking of the Titanic."

STORIES OF A BAD SONG
New York/Dublin
2005/2010*

It was six years ago that *Mojo* magazine ranked "Masters of War," Bob Dylan's 1963 song about arms merchants—*"war profiteers,"* Franklin Roosevelt liked to call them, his voice dripping with contempt—number one on a chart of "The 100 Greatest Protest Songs."

It was followed by Pete Seeger's version of "We Shall Overcome," James Brown's 1968 "Say It Loud—I'm Black and I'm Proud," the Sex Pistols' 1977 "God Save the Queen," and Billie Holiday's 1939 "Strange Fruit." Not to mention Lesley Gore's 1963 "You Don't Own Me," one of the first feminist rock 'n' roll hits (written by a man, of course), let alone Eddie Cochran's 1958 "Summertime Blues"—a record about a teenager with a mean boss, mean parents, and a congressman who won't help because the kid's too young to vote.

But really, "Masters of War"—that lumbering old warhorse? Why not Barry McGuire's "Eve of Destruction," which in 1965 was such an obvious jump on the protest-song trend it went past parody and became the thing itself, and which didn't make the chart at all?

Except for "Eve of Destruction," all of these songs were less obvious, less self-deciphering, than "Masters of War"—but for "Masters of War" the lack of subtlety was the point. "Come you masters of war, you that build the big guns," Dylan begins slowly: "You

---

*I gave a first, short version of this talk at Columbia University in 2005, on a panel with Sean Wilentz and Christopher Ricks, who wiped the floor with both of us; that was published in the Winter 2006 number of *Threepenny Review*. I've continued to revise and adapt it, as times changed the song and people continued to try to get the song to change the times. The most recent version was part of Forever Young? Changing Images of America, the European American Studies Association conference held in Dublin 26-29 March 2010.

that build the death planes / You that build the big bombs." He goes on, flattening a somehow mysterious, inviting melody. The masters of war cause death and destruction: that's their bottom line. It's like a cartoon from *The Masses*. You can see the fat businessmen smoking cigars and gorging on huge meals as their feet rest on the necks of honest workers. They're old, evil, and rich: cannibals. "Not even Jesus would forgive what you do," the twenty-two-year-old Bob Dylan sings.

And then he does something that, even for a protest song, was shocking in 1963 and is shocking now: he calls for the death of the people he's singing about. "I hope that you die," he says, directly, without embellishment, like a gunfighter in a western shootout—like Marshal Matt Dillon of *Gunsmoke,* whom Bob Dylan might as likely named himself for as Dylan Thomas, Matt Dillon standing in the middle of main street for a shootout in Dodge City  in the 1955 Hollywood version of Kansas in 1873, Dillon waiting for the bad guy to draw first, Dillon's draw a split-second later, but his nerves cooler, the bad guy's shot going wide, his own true.

> I hope that you die
> And your death will come soon
> I'll follow your casket
> In the pale afternoon
> And I'll watch while you're lowered
> Down to your death bed
> And I'll stand over your grave till I'm sure that you're dead

No matter what Bob Dylan has done in the last forty-seven years, or what he will do for the rest of his life, his obituary has already been written. "Bob Dylan, best known as a protest singer from the

1960s, died yesterday . . ." The media loves a simple idea. No matter how famous you are, how complex you are, how not obvious you are, when you die, you get one idea, and one only.

In 1963, in the world of folk music, the protest song was a speech a lot of people wanted to hear and a language a lot of people wanted to learn. Protest songs were the currency. They said that the world should be changed, even implied that songs could change it, and no one wrote better protest songs—or as many— than Bob Dylan. It was a way of jumping on the train of his own career, he'd say years later. But to the high-school and college students who had begun to listen to Bob Dylan because, they said, he could say what they felt but couldn't express—because he could draw on their own unshaped anger and rage, terror and fear, and make it all real, even, they said, make it poetry—for these people, more with each passing day in the early 1960s, the songs seemed not to contain the cynicism Dylan later proclaimed but to banish it.

They felt like warnings that the world couldn't turn away from, crimes that had to be paid, promises that had to be kept. Bob Dylan wrote songs about the nuclear war that, in 1963, almost everyone was sure would happen sometime, somewhere—and in 1962, with the Cuban Missile Crisis, almost had happened, the war that, Robert McNamara said just a few years ago, in the film *The Fog of War,* holding his thumb and forefinger not a half-inch apart, came closer than even the most paranoid protest singer dared imagine.

Dylan wrote and sang long, detailed songs about racial injustice, from "The Death of Emmett Till" to "The Lonesome Death of Hattie Carroll" to "Only a Pawn in Their Game," called "The Death of Medgar Evers" when Dylan sang it on the steps of the Lincoln Memorial at the March on Washington in 1963. He wrote visionary protest songs, like "A Hard Rain's A-Gonna Fall." He wrote funny protest songs like "Talking World War III Blues," where he dreamed of himself alone in the city after the bomb has fallen: he walks into a Cadillac dealership, gets into a Cadillac, and heads out. "Good car to drive," he says with a smile-when-you-say-that pause: "Good car to drive . . . after a war."

Most of all, Dylan wrote and sang songs that told stories about the wrong inside a nation that believed it was always right: "With God on Our Side," "The Times They Are A-Changin'," "Blowin' in the Wind." These were the songs that brought Bob Dylan into the common imagination of the nation, and those were the songs that fixed him there. "You have to have power and dominion over the spirits," Dylan said in 2004, in *Chronicles,* of what it took to write these songs.

But even in the heyday of the protest song, "Masters of War" seemed like too much. Too sententious, too self-righteous, too full of itself—stilted, as if it was less a matter of someone writing a protest song than the protest song as such spontaneously generating its own copy, or its own cartoon. "You hide in your mansion / While young people's blood/ flows out of their bodies / And into the mud," Dylan sang in "Masters of War"—still, that almost was poetry compared to "You Been Hiding too Long," another Bob Dylan protest song from the same moment.

"Come all you phony super-patriotic—" OK, stop right there, we don't need to hear any more—but there is more, a lot more, no melody, no rhythm, no meter, no heart, no conviction, really no song at all, but press a button and the protest song comes out: "You lie and mislead / You—for your aims and your selfish greed . . . Don't think that I'll ever stand on your side . . ." And on, and on, and on.

This song is so awful it's been erased from Dylan's published song collections. Look through the Archive section on his Web site: it isn't there. Dylan probably never recorded it. He may have only performed it once, at a concert in New York in 1963, when he also sang "Masters of War"—but this self-congratulatory spew is inside "Masters of War" as much as President Eisenhower's 1961 Farewell Address about the military-industrial complex, which Dylan would later claim as his inspiration: "The spirit was in the air," he said in 2001, as if he were quoting himself, "and I picked it up." This song is the deformed spawn of the impulses behind "Masters of War." Even if "You've Been Hiding Too Long" was only performed once, it was once too often: someone had a tape recorder that night, and thirty years later the thing turned up on a bootleg.

Unlike "You've Been Hiding Too Long," "Masters of War" does have a melody—the melody of "Nottamun Town," a British folk song that might go back five hundred years, though it seems older than that, from a time beyond historical ken. In the feeling it carries, it seems to come from the devastation that fell on Arthur's kingdom when Guinevere turned to Lancelot.

It's often described as a nonsense song; that's the last thing it is. Today it communicates as 20th century surrealism in 16th century clothes: "Not a soul would look up, not a soul would look down . . . Come a stark-naked drummer a-beating the drum . . . Ten thousand stood round me, yet I was alone . . . Ten thousand got drownded that never was born." It is a protean song, bottomless: just as Dylan took its melody for "Masters of War," he took its language for "A Hard Rain's A-Gonna Fall," where a man travels the world and returns with a tale to tell: "I heard one hundred drummers whose hands were a-blazing / Heard ten thousand whispering and nobody listening . . . I saw ten thousand talkers whose tongues were all broken." And yet even in "A Hard Rain's A-Gonna Fall," which is a great song, Dylan couldn't find the road that would take him all the way back to the strangeness of "Nottamun Town"—where the world turns upside down, and the curse is that, somehow, nothing has changed. "Ten thousand got drownded that never was born": this is the first protest song; this is the end of the world.

The British song collector Cecil Sharpe found "Nottamun Town" in Kentucky in 1917; the old ballads had held their shape in Appalachia far longer than they had in Britain. Traditional versions of "Nottamun Town" were in a major key; that put a sardonic smile in the music. But at Gerde's Folk City in Greenwich Village, Dylan heard a version in a minor key by the Cambridge folk singer Jackie Washington.

The twist put a chill on the melody. It gave Dylan an opening into the bad dream he was after for "Masters of War": shadowed, doomstruck, the sound of a funeral procession, or a crowd chasing one.

Dylan himself stopped singing the song by 1964. Songs like "Masters of War" were "lies that life is black and white," he sang that year. The protest song was a prison of meaning, or anti-meaning; Dylan's refusal of the protest song was a prison break. Protest songs destroyed the songs that gave them life, ate them. As "Nottamun Town" disappeared into the belly of "Masters of War," you could understand that protest songs were themselves cannibals.

Singing "Masters of War," knowing what lay behind it, Dylan might have flinched at what he had himself created: flinched at how he'd cheated "Nottamun Town" of its own mysteries, cheated it to make a point or outrun his folk-song rivals. He might have stepped back at the recognition that audiences didn't want to be taken to far distant lands that never were, let alone to a world that made no sense—they wanted to be told that the world was exactly what they thought it was. They wanted to be told that the world was divided into two sides, right and wrong, and they wanted to be told that they were right. And that's what he gave them.

It was a sensibility—a way of being the world—that has never gone away. In 1988, Sut Jhally of the University of Massachusetts and Ian Angus of Simon Fraser University in British Columbia published an anthology called *Cultural Politics in Contemporary America*. In their introduction, they attacked Bruce Springsteen for his protest song "Born in the U.S.A." They attacked him because that song—released in 1984, a song about a Vietnam veteran who, a decade after the war ended, still feels like an outcast in his own country—could be heard, and understood, in more than one way. Ronald Reagan could appropriate it for a campaign speech, trumpeting the song as a celebration of shared values—even though someone else might have heard the song as damning the betrayal of those values. But John Lennon protest songs, Jhally and Angus said, were different—such absolutely forgotten work as "Sunday Bloody Sunday," "Attica State," "Angela," for Angela Davis, and "John Sinclair," which FBI agents in an audience for a John Lennon–Yoko Ono concert in Detroit reported "probably will become a million-seller"—even though, the agents wrote in their report, inaugurating the new genre of FBI rock criticism, "Yoko

Ono can't even remain on key" and the song itself "was lacking Lennon's usual standards."

John Lennon "suffered from no such ambiguity" as Bruce Springsteen, Jhally and Angus said, and there was "no possible misunderstanding of his art"—and really, aren't they writing like FBI agents in academic clothes? Forget that when there is no possibility of misunderstanding, there is no art. That is what Bob Dylan remembered when he stopped singing "Masters of War."

Dylan brought "Masters of War" back into his repertoire in the late 1970s. He was playing more than a hundred shows a year, and to fill the nights he brought back everything. It was a crowd-pleaser, the number-one protest song even before anyone bothered to run a poll on the question. Even so many years after the fact, many of Bob Dylan's fans were still uncomfortable with songs that didn't divide the world into right and wrong; they still liked the old protest songs the best. But nothing in the song as Dylan was playing it the second time around hinted at what it would turn into on 21 February 1991, at the Grammy Awards telecast, where Dylan was to receive a Lifetime Achievement Award.

These days Lifetime Achievement Awards at the Grammys are handed out like parking passes; most of the many recipients don't even bother to show up. In 1991 the idea was new; it was a big deal. And that year the Grammy show came square in the middle of the first Iraqi-American war—as television, a break from round-the-clock footage of the bombing of Baghdad.

Just a week or two before, at the unprestigious American Music Awards telecast, Donnie Wahlberg of the pioneering boy-band New Kids on the Block appeared wearing a "WAR SUCKS" T-shirt. It was a brave thing to do. He had a lot to lose, and he may have lost his career—today Donnie Wahlberg is mostly remembered as the older brother of the actor Mark Wahlberg, who in 1991 was still the would-be rap star Marky Mark. The Grammys officials announced that nothing like what Donnie Wahlberg had done would take place on their show.

"Uncle Bobby," Jack Nicholson said, introducing Dylan, as Dylan and his four-piece band came onstage to play one song. In dark suits, with fedoras pulled down over their faces, the musicians looked like small-time hipster gangsters who'd spent the previous ten years in the same bar waiting for the right deal to break and finally said the hell with it; Dylan held himself with authority, as if he were the bartender. He looked terrible, bloated and pig-eyed. He wore a gray hat and there was a white thunderbolt on his red guitar strap.

It was an instantly infamous performance, and one of the greatest of Dylan's career. He sang "Masters of War," but in disguise: a version, the film critic Amy Taubin wrote in 2005, "as abstract as a black hole." At first, you couldn't tell what it was; you couldn't understand a word Dylan was singing, but not because he was mumbling. Whatever Dylan was doing, he was pressing hard. He was all tension, all vehemence.

He slurred the words as if whatever narrative they contained was irrelevant. He was saying that the performance had to communicate as a symbol or not at all. He broke the words down and smashed them up until they worked as pure excitement, until the appearance of a single, whole signifier—"Jesus," "Guns," "Die"—lit up the night like a tracer bullet. The performance was almost unbearably fast, the beat snapping back on itself, then fragmenting as guitar lines shot out of the music as if without human agency—and it might have been a minute, it might have been two, it might have been as long as the performance lasted for the melody to creep out of the noise, for the song to reveal itself for what it was.

Dylan was asked why, on this night of all nights, he chose to sing "Masters of War." "The war going on," he said. Why did he slur the words, he was asked. "I had a cold," he said.

With that night, the song began its second life. Three years later, on 16 February 1994, without his band, Dylan sang "Masters of War" in Hiroshima. On 5 October 2001, in Spokane, Washington, at Dylan's first concert after the terrorist attacks on New York City and Washington, D.C., he played "Masters of War" as some of the crowd shouted "Death to Bin Laden!" A year later, when George

W. Bush made plain his intent to launch a second Iraq war—on 11 November 2002, just after the mid-term elections that Bush had used the specter of war to win—Dylan appeared at Madison Square Garden, and again offered "Masters of War," and again as an answer record to real life. He gathered three musicians in a circle, with himself at the center: playing acoustic guitars and a bass fiddle, seated on chairs, they looked like a coven, and the song sounded like a curse dug out of the ground.

The song began to travel. In May of 2003, with the war under way, the jazz drummer Scott Amendola and the singer Carla Bozulich of Berkeley put a nine-minute version on the Internet. They made a storm; cowering under a harsh, seemingly inexhaustible solo by the saxophonist Eric Crystal, they took the song's rage into the realm of fairy tale, all mist and lightning, a storm so strong there were moments when the sound made it difficult to remember what you were listening to. The hectoring self-satisfaction of speakers at anti-war rallies began to creep into Bozulich's voice— the tone that let you know that the last thing such people want is for the powerful to do good; if that happened, how could they feel superior?—but then came the final verse. The instrumentation dropped to almost nothing, only bare taps and silences, and you could hear someone speaking for herself: a single voice, letting you imagine that this was all that was left, after the war.

More than a year later, in October 2004, with Bush and John Kerry battling for the presidency and Minnesota up for grabs, a Minneapolis record-store owner, Mark Trehaus, working with the St. Paul punk band the Dillinger Four—in the thirties, St. Paul was the gangster John Dillinger's favorite hideout—released their own version of the song. It was credited to Brother Mark Treehouse and the Dylanger Four plus Four.

Except for Arzu D2 of the great St. Paul punk band Selby Tigers, who spoke the words of the song in the flat, plain tones of a young woman accusing her parents of looting her college fund, it was a pure, tuneless rant. But the record was perhaps more about the cover, which pictured Bush, his Secretary of Defense Donald

Rumsfeld, his Attorney General John Ashcroft, and Vice President Dick Cheney—Cheney pointing his finger, but not, like Uncle Sam, looking you in the eye. It wasn't immediately clear what you were looking at; the faces were washed in the reds, whites, and grays of an old 3-D comic book, the kind you needed 3-D glasses to read.

A month after that, on November 2, on election night 2004, in Oshkosh, Wisconsin, with the votes cast but the outcome still unknown, Dylan sang the song once more, again in the middle of a war—a middle, that night, without an end. At first his delivery was clipped, the words rushed and stuttered. As certain lines seemed to draw more from him, the song seemed to rewrite itself. "You put a gun in my hand," Dylan sang to the arms merchants in an old-cowboy voice; it sounded like "You put a gun to my head." An electric guitar came down hard, and the music turned fierce. "I'll stand over your grave till I'm sure that you're dead"—as the words came out of Dylan's mouth his voice was shaking, or he was making it shake. And none of this matched what happened in Boulder, Colorado, at Boulder High School, the very next day.

The day after the election, students staged a sit-in in the school library: "Bush will directly affect our generation's future," one Boulder freshman said, "and we were upset we didn't have a voice in that." The principal refused to have the students removed. Congressman Mark Udall came to the school to speak with the students; so did U.S. senator-elect Ken Salazar. TV crews arrived. And then the stakes were raised.

The annual school talent show was scheduled for November 12; a teacher named Jim Kavanagh helped bring a group of students together as a band. "Your basic juvenile delinquent types," he said later, in plain English, then dropping into teacher's language: "at risk." Fooling around on guitar, someone began playing in D Minor. "That sounds like 'Masters of War,'" one student said. That wasn't what the guitar player thought he was playing, but in a moment it was what the group was playing. The students came up with a name for their group: the Taliband. A singer came forward, a student named Allyse Wojtanek. "Not a singer," Kavanagh said: "a very brave kid." The group went to the audition. "Nobody did anything close to what we did," Kavanagh said—at the start, he and another teacher were in the group—"and we really sucked. I never heard such a horrible sound. We found out the next day that not only did we make the show, we were the last act. And at this point, one of the kids who was doing karaoke stuff went home and said to her mother, 'I didn't make the show, but this other band that wants to kill Bush did.'" Instead of "I hope that you die," the student had heard "Die, Bush, Die"—or so she said.

The mother got on the phone to the local right-wing radio stations—and once again news trucks hit the school. Talk show hosts called for the Taliband to be kicked out of the talent show. And then the Secret Service arrived. They collected the lyrics to "Masters of War" and left. The story went over the AP wire. The principal had to take his phone off the hook.

The band changed its name—to Coalition of the Willing.* They opened negotiations with the school administration over video footage to be projected onto the musicians as they played: they wanted footage of Bush and Iraq. "Does it have to be *Bush?*" the

---

*It was the same name that Andreas Simonyi, the Hungarian ambassador to the United States, had chosen for his own Washington, D.C., band two years before. "When I was listening to rock music" in Hungary, he told the *New York Times,* "I became part of the West. This was my link to the free world." Band members included Lincoln P. Bloomfield, Jr., a former assistant secretary of state for military affairs; Alexander Vershbow, then the U.S. Ambassador to Russia; and, not really as a ringer, Jeff "Skunk" Baxter, best known to the world at large as the lead guitarist for Steely Dan, but, since the Reagan administration, best known in Washington as a tireless advocate of missile defense schemes. In 2005 the Coalition of the Willing played the Walter Reed Army Medical Center; while they did not play "Masters of War," they did lead off with Johnny Rivers's

principal asked. "Why not *lots* of masters of war," a student suggested: Bush, Hitler, and Stalin. "Why do there have to be *any*
faces?" the administration begged. Finally they settled for generic
war footage and the American flag. It was in 1958 that Bob Dylan,
leading the Golden Chords, played his own high school talent
show. The story has always been that a teacher, outraged by the
noise from the likes of "I Want You to Be My Girl" and "Let the
Good Times Roll," brought the curtain down while the band was
still playing. "That never happened," Monte Edwardson, the guitarist in the Golden Chords, recently told a reporter—but the
Coalition of the Willing had to worry that they were setting themselves up for the same fate.

As the talent show began, three gangly boys came on to MC the
show, miming to ZZ Top's "Sharp-Dressed Man." They didn't miss
a step all night.

A twelve-student assemblage did the Eurythmics' "Sweet
Dreams (Are Made of This)." A young woman played a classical
piano piece. Another danced. The crowd gave everyone wild
applause.

As one of the MCs began a joke, an off-stage electric guitar
drowned him out. "I can't work under these conditions!" he
shouted. "I'm going to protest this next act!" "Oh my God," said a
second MC. "You're *protesting* it? Can you do that? This could be
national newsworthy!" Dressed now in a black suit, the third MC
pulled out a video camera and began filming the other two. The

"Secret Agent Man." In 2007, in response to a taunt from the fake right-wing TV
talk show host Stephen Colbert that "Hungarians can't play the guitar," Simonyi
appeared on Colbert's show. Raising an electric guitar with an eagle jutting out
of its body, Simonyi snapped off one hot riff after another before announcing
that Colbert must have confused Hungarians with Finns—who when it came to
the electric guitar, Simonyi said, totally "suck." The jazz drummer Bobby Pre-
vite formed a third Coalition of the Willing in New York in 2006. With Charlie
Hunter on guitar and Steve Bernstein on trumpet, the band became the first under its name with an official release: *Coalition of the Willing* (Ropeadope, 2006),
which came in a Stalinist jacket. A second album, *All's Well That Ends* (download only, 2008), featured both the singer Andrew M. and "Let's Start a War."

three accused each other of planning to burn down the school—
not a casual joke, thirty-five miles from Columbine High School,
just five years before the site of the worst school shooting in the
history of the country. "This next act," said one MC, "is the controversial act you've been waiting for—the Russian Jugglers!"

Aside from Coalition of the Willing, brother and sister Olga and
Vova Galdrenko were the highlight of the show. There were ten
more acts—and then the seven-student Coalition came out, with
Allyse Wojtanek in a black halter. There were video battlefield images of Korea, Vietnam, Iraq then, Iraq now, projected right onto
the musicians.

The sound was big and atonal, with guitar and saxophone on
the top and Wojtanek screaming. When she got to "I hope that you
die" she talked the line, making each word stand alone. When she
hit "SURE THAT YOU'RE DEAD" she all but tore her throat out.

Backstage, students came up to Wojtanek to congratulate her.
"Perspiration had run Allyse's thick black eyeliner into her bright
green eye shadow," wrote Brittany Anas, a reporter for the *Boulder
Daily Camera*. "We were misunderstood," Wojtanek told Anas.
"People thought we were like communists, and that was not it at
all." "We think that the war we are involved in is wrong, and that
people need to come to their senses," said Brian Martens—he had
played guitar. One student announced that she and her friends
were going to get fake IDs so they could vote.

The band and its audience got through the night, and nobody
got hurt. They made their moment. For the moment, the war was
theirs, perhaps waiting for them six months or a year down the
line—and the song was theirs, waiting for them for more than
forty years.

People continue to sing the song. One of the most memorable per-
formances came on 7 November 2007, at the Beacon Theatre in
New York, at a show celebrating the release of Todd Haynes's film
I'm Not There, by the Roots.

The Philadelphia band—never definable, not as hip-hop, not as soul, but closer to rock 'n' roll as the word made sense in 1965 than anything else—was, this night, singer and guitarist Captain Kirk Douglas, drummer Questlove, and Damon "Tuba Gooding Jr." Bryson, playing a sousaphone so enormous he looked as if he had an elephant wrapped around his neck. There was a long military drum roll. Douglas cleared his throat and sang the first two verses of "Masters of War" in the exact cadence of "The Star-Spangled Banner."

Barely strumming his guitar, with Questlove and Bryson waiting silently behind him, Kirk sang in the clearest tone imaginable, filling the room with sound, hitting every note. When he came to that point where, in the National Anthem, the word "free" is shot into the sky—

O'er the land of the *free*

—Kirk held the word "far"—

And you turn and run *far*—

—for a gorgeous, shattering twelve seconds before the tune broke back to its original body and Questlove and Bryson came into the song.

The greatest protest song of all time wasn't even on the *Mojo* poll: Jimi Hendrix's Woodstock version of "The Star-Spangled Banner." As both "A Hard Rain's A-Gonna Fall" and "Masters of War" go back to "Nottamun Town," the Roots' "Masters of War" twice reaches back to Hendrix: for the National Anthem at the beginning, and, for the rest of their performance, to Hendrix's "Machine Gun," from 1970, the year after Woodstock, the year Hendrix died. And it wasn't altogether a new idea. That same year, 1970, the singer-songwriter Leon Russell sang a single verse of "Masters of War" to the tune of "The Star-Spangled Banner," called it "Old Masters," and put it out as the last track of his first solo album. It was just him at a piano, fooling around; within weeks it had disappeared from the record. Because the idea was too controversial? Because it was so obviously a rehearsal, a throw-away? When the album was reissued in 1995, the little song was put back on. Had the Roots ever heard it? "Very much so," Questlove said when I asked. "My dad had that record when I was younger and actually I remember hearing that before I even heard the Dylan version."

Shouldering "Machine Gun," the Roots smashed their way through the song after those first two verses. They were so alive to the theatricality buried in "Masters of War" it came across as an action movie: you could see Jim Brown and Bruce Willis in it. The band pushed a stair-climbing rhythm—Questlove playing ever more quietly, running a parade-ground funeral march through the firefight Douglas was orchestrating with his guitar. With strange, displacing, seemingly endless instrumental breaks thrown in between the last two lines of each verse after the "Star-Spangled" beginning, it went on and on, unpredictably, all the familiarity one might have brought to the song blown away. And those instrumental passages opened up the territory the song claimed. It no longer had any limits. It seemed as if it could speak any language, mark any spot—that it could expand, year after year, into the future, taking in the whole of the country, all of its wars.

As the Roots played, you could feel how the song had outlived its callow adolescence. And it was the Iraq war, five years on that night, with, some were planning as the Roots played, lifetimes of it to come, that let the song walk the land like someone who had lived to see the world, his or her own country, double down on every bad dream.

People are still afraid of the song. Joan Baez could never bring herself to sing the last verse; she couldn't say "I hope that you die." The late historian Howard Zinn's *Artists in Times of War,* from 2003, is a return-with-us-now-to-the-golden-days-of-yesteryear book of left-wing American martyrs that has almost nothing to do with art or artists; still, as an example of great art produced in times of war, Zinn quoted in full the first seven verses of "Masters of War"—and like Joan Baez he omitted the last verse. To have associated his heroes—Thomas Paine, Emma Goldman, Helen Keller, Kurt Vonnegut—with such venom might have robbed them of their saintliness. "I hope that you die"? Howard Zinn wouldn't sing that song either.

But songs play tricks. In 2008, a Boston public television station put on *The People Speak,* in part a series of dramatic readings based on Zinn's best-known book, *A People's History of the United States.* The actor Viggo Mortensen, the heroic killer of David Cronenberg's daunting movies *A History of Violence* and *Eastern Promises,* appeared to sing "Masters of War."

He sang it, probably, as no one ever sang it before. He sang with no accompaniment, the way a murder ballad like "Omie Wise" or "Tom Dooley" would have been sung in the Appalachian mountains a hundred or two hundred years ago. Dressed in a brown suit and an orange T-shirt, he began with a deep, otherworldly hum—a burrowing sound that might have come out of the ground. Sometimes looking into a distance, sometimes turning to face the camera directly, he sang quietly but in a full voice, reading from a lyric sheet as if giving a speech, ringing certain words near the ends of lines: "won," "eyes," "watch." His demeanor was considered, as if he'd thought through what he was saying many times. As the song went on Mortensen seemed to gather authority from the speech he was giving; when he reached "Let me ask you one question," you saw a prosecutor from *Law & Order.* When he came to the beginning of the last verse, and said the words "I hope that you die," he nodded, as if confirming the judgment of a higher court; at the end of the verse, he dragged out the last word, "dead," until the harsh, grating vowels dissolved the word and returned it to the hum with which he'd begun. He sang the song as if it were itself the old folk song that had passed unchanged from then to now, from old England to Kentucky, from there to New York, and now to Boston, one place where the nation began.

Following these stories, it becomes clear that, beyond new wars, what has kept the song alive is its melody, and its vehemence: that final "I hope that you die." It's the elegance of the melody and the extremism of the words that attract people—the way the song does go too far, to the limits of free speech. Those are scary words to sing; you need courage to do it. You can't come to the song as if it's a joke; you can't come away from it pretending you didn't mean what you've just said. That's what people want: a chance to go that far. Because "Masters of War" gives people permission to go that far, the song continues to make meaning, to find new bodies to inhabit, new voices to ride.

"The Mojo 100 Greatest Protest Songs," *Mojo,* May 2004.

Bob Dylan, "Masters of War" and "A Hard Rain's A-Gonna Fall, from *The Freewheelin' Bob Dylan* (Columbia, 1963).

————. "Masters of War," Grammy Awards, 21 February 1991. The performance can be found on YouTube. See Amy Taubin, "From There to Here," *Film Comment,* Nov./Dec. 2005.

————. "You Been Hiding Too Long," Town Hall, New York, 12 April 1963; see *Bob Dylan at Town Hall—The Complete Concert* (bootleg) and *The Genuine Bootleg Series* (bootleg).

————. *Chronicles, Volume One.* New York: Simon and Schuster, 2004, 219.

The Fog of War: Eleven Lessons from the Life of Robert S. McNamara, directed by Errol Morris (Sony Pictures Classics, 2003).

Jackie Washington, "Nottamun Town," on *Jackie Washington* (Vanguard, 1962). The best known traditional version, from which Washington worked, was recorded in 1957 by Jean Ritchie, who, after threatening to sue Dylan over "Masters of War," claimed "Nottamun Town" as "a Ritchie Family song" and attempted to copyright the number along with the likes of "O Love Is Teasin'" and "Lord Randal," on which Dylan based "A Hard Rain's A-Gonna Come." (Cecil Sharpe apparently took down his version of "Nottamun Town" from a Ritchie great-aunt; Ritchie's story is that the song was brought to America by a great-great grandfather, that it would have been lost to history had he not done so and had she not kept it alive, and that it was thus part of her legal patrimony.) For "Nottamun Town" see Ritchie's *Mountain Hearth & Home: Jean Sings the Songs of Her Kentucky Mountain Family* (Elektra Rhino, 2004, recorded 1952–1965); for "Lord Randal" see her *Ballads from her Appalachian family tradition* (Smithsonian Folkways, 2003, recorded 1961).

Cultural Politics in Contemporary America, edited by Sut Jhally and Ian Angus. London and New York: Routledge, 1988.

Jon Wiener, "FBI Rock Criticism," in *Come Together: John Lennon in His Time.* New York: Random House, 1984, xvi.

Scott Amendola and Carla Bozulich, "Masters of War," included on the Scott Amendola Band's *Cry* (Cryptogramaphone, 2003).

Brother Mark Treehouse and the Dylanger Four Plus Four, "Masters of War" (Heart of a Champion/Treehouse Records, 2004).

Roots, "Masters of War," Beacon Theatre, New York, concert for *I'm Not There,* 7 November 2007. The concert recording can be found at Wolfgangsvault.com.

Leon Russell, "Masters of War (Old Masters)" from *Leon Russell* (Shelter, 1970/The Right Stuff, 1995).

Jimi Hendrix, "Star Spangled Banner," from *Live at Woodstock* (MCA, 1999).

———. "Machine Gun," from Band of Gypsies (Capitol, 1970).

Howard Zinn, *Artists in Time of War.* New York: Seven Stories Press, 2003.

Viggo Mortensen's "Masters of War" is not included on the DVD of *The People Speak.* It appeared briefly on YouTube and was taken down.

REAL LIFE ROCK TOP 10
The Believer
March/April 2009

8/9) *Eden,* directed by Declan Recks (Samson Films). In this film about a miserable Irish couple's tenth anniversary, Aidan Kelly's Billy Farrell leaves his wife in a disco for a party, chasing a girl he thinks has eyes for him, though all she sees is an old man. He passes out drunk; in a room behind him, people start singing "House of the Rising Sun." Farrell wakes up, automatically singing along, sees the girl, stumbles to his feet, and as he grabs her, forcing himself on her as she tries to push him away, the song continues, but now the voice you hear belongs to Sinéad O'Connor, an avenging angel who seems to be singing from inside Farrell's heart, which she's turned against him. The song has gone from its commonplace beginnings somewhere in the American south, sometime in the late 19th or early 20th century, to Bob Dylan's first album in 1962 to the Animals' epochal 1964 worldwide hit, to countless versions by street singers and karaoke belters to a party in an Irish town in the early 21st century, where if nothing else it's a song everybody knows, and from there into the spectral hands of a woman who could stare down anyone on the planet—and who's to say where its true home is, who owns it, whose singing most rings true?

The Believer
July 2009

1) Bob Dylan, *Together Through Life* (Columbia). Casual, to the point where the clumsiness comes to the surface—except with "Forgetful Heart," where a shadow passes over the singer's face. But nothing here quite carries the weight of a scene from last season's *In Treatment,* when Mia Wasikowska's smart, sarcastic, suicidal teenage gymnast Sophie turns the tables on Gabriel Bryne's fifty-something psychologist Paul Weston, as if once she was so much older but

she's younger than that now and he's too old to know what she's talking about. "'The times they are a-changing,'" she says as a session is ending. "It's from a Bob Dylan song. My gift to you."

10) Bob Dylan, video for "Beyond Here Lies Nothing" (YouTube). A montage of photos from Bruce Davidson's 1959 series "Brooklyn Gang"—Larry Clark's *Tulsa* made suitable for *Vogue*—with the Jokers getting tattoos, hanging around, taking their shirts off, going to Coney Island, trying to look as if they don't care. Near the end a woman with lank black hair and black eye-makeup comes into the story. She carries experience the boys don't, desires they couldn't fathom, but she has nowhere else to go and so she's here. She's a dead ringer for Amy Winehouse, and you miss her more than ever.

The Believer
February 2010

6/7) Bob Dylan and Dion, United Palace Theater (New York, 17 November 2009). The stage of the Rev. Ike's old stomping grounds was pure House of Blue lights before Dylan came on: deep velvet background, upside down electric candles ringing the top of the stage. In that stetting "Beyond Here Lies Nothing," from *Together Through Life* last spring, was a sultry vamp from a '40s supper club. Clearly the song was still opening itself up to Dylan; he sang with heart, as if looking to find how much it might tell him. "Dedicated to our troops," Dion had said earlier, for "Abraham, Martin and John," and the mood Dylan was creating was already too fine for "Masters of War." Instead he sang the mom-sends-son-off-to-glory-and-then-he-comes-back number "John Brown" (it sounds like an ancient British broadsheet; Dylan copyrighted it in 1963) in a hard-boiled voice, the Continental Op running down the murders in *Red Harvest*. Most striking of all was "Ballad of a Thin Man." In Todd Haynes's film *I'm Not There,* Cate Blanchett, as Dylan in London in 1966, acts out the song standing alone behind a mike stand

like a nightclub singer, no protection of a guitar between performer and audience. It was something Bob Dylan had never done,
but that was precisely the posture he assumed now, as if the movie
had taught him something new about his own song: how to make it
more intimate, more direct, so that it was the audience, not the
singer, that was left more naked, more defenseless.

For all that, Dion stole the show. He began with Buddy Holly's
"Rave On"—and that had be to remind both Dylan and the crowd
of the night in early 1959, just days before Holly died, when a sev-
enteen-year-old Robert Zimmerman sat in the Duluth National
Guard Armory, Holly himself sang "Rave On," and Dion was an
opening act on that show, too. Now he was seventy, and his voice
grew, spread out, gained in suppleness and reach with every song.
One by one, he put the oldies behind him, so that it all came to a
head with "King of the New York Streets," from 1989.

It's a gorgeous, panoramic song: a strutting brag that in the end
turns back on itself, a Bronx match for the Geto Boys' "Mind Playing Tricks on Me." It leads with huge, doomy chords, wide silences
between the notes, creating a sense of wonder and suspension, and
you don't want the moment to break, for the music to take a single
step forward—just as, after the song has gone on and on, you can't
bear the idea that it's going to end. From that almost frozen beginning, the pace seemed to speed up with every verse, but it wasn't
the beat that was doubling; it was the intensity and the drama.
Dion's wails were as fierce as ever, but never so full of wide-open
spaces, the voice itself an undiscovered country, and it was hard to
believe that he had ever sung better.

The Believer
June 2010

2) Alfred: "Like a Rolling Stone," in *Bob Dylan Revisited: 13 Graphic
Interpretations of Bob Dylan's Songs* (Norton). Almost everything
here is destructively literal, to the point that most of the pictures

meant to illustrate the songs are accompanied by matching lyrics that instead illustrate the pictures—or reveal the complete lack of imagination behind them. By contrast—and with the use of shifting color schemes, where each chapter in the story of a woman attempting to escape into a life of her own and continually finding herself imprisoned by the life she was born to is governed by shadings of blue, taupe, yellow, olive green, brown, gray, and finally a bright, light-filled page that is scarier than anything darker—Alfred trusts abstraction. Until the very last of his sixty-seven panels there isn't a word to be seen. The story he tells isn't obvious, isn't clear. It doesn't match Dylan's soaring, heat-seeking-missile crescendos and choruses—it brings them down to earth. It isn't a social allegory; it's one person's odyssey, a lifetime that returns her to precisely the place she first flees. And the Siamese cat isn't a symbol of evil or anything else. It's the woman's conscience, or the one who, all along, has been singing the song that has been playing deep in the farthest back corners of her mind.

The Believer
September 2010

5&6) Matt Diehl interviews Joni Mitchell (*Los Angeles Times,* April 22). "Bob is not authentic at all," Mitchell said. "He's a plagiarist, and his name and voice are fake. Everything about Bob is a deception." Charles Taylor: "In protest, Chelsea Clinton changes her name to Hibbing."

EPILOGUE

I BELIEVE ALL THE POLLS, AND NONE OF THEM

Salon

3 November 2008

I write four days before the election, in Minnesota, where yard signs are everywhere. Here in the modest Uptown part of Minneapolis, it's almost all Obama; in the wealthier sections you can find McCain signs that loom as large as billboards. At a family dinner one night we toasted misery on the next-door neighbors. This is a very patriotic part of the country. People are proud of their convictions.

For weeks, all of the indicators, measurements, polls, and calculations have pointed to an Obama victory, even an overwhelming rout. But while I read the polls many times a day and half believe them—believe them all, the poll that has Obama leading by 15 as much as I believe the poll on the same day that has him leading by 2—I also believe absolutely none of it. My whole life, my upbringing, education, travel, and talk, from working in Congress as an intern at the height of the Civil Rights movement in the mid-1960s to every election in which I've ever voted, makes it all but impossible for me to believe that, on Tuesday, a single state will turn its face toward the face of a black man and name him president of the United States.

Throughout the primary season it was trumpeted again and again that regardless of the outcome of the Democratic contest, the nation would see its first major-party ticket headed by either a woman or a citizen whose skin was not white. But it was not remarked on that, in a world where women have led Israel, India, Great Britain, and Germany, a female president was not unthinkable, but that an African-American president was. "I never expected to see this in my lifetime," the white, left-wing journalist

McCain rally, Concord, South Carolina, 21 October 2008, New York Times.

Larry Bensky, in his sixties, said one day on the radio, bitterly, because while it was a fact, it was not necessarily true: he could not
credit it. He might have been thinking that it was all an illusion, a
trick the country was playing on itself. Could the election be a vast
and horrible twenty-first century version of the now-forgotten
1950s embarrassment Take a Negro to Lunch Day, or the nation remade as its own blackface minstrel show, with the whole thing
over when the sun goes down?

The more likely an Obama victory seems, the more monstrous
the alternative has become. That is partly because McCain has
made himself a monster of hate and lies, homing in on the evil that
lies as a legacy in the heart of every white American: a guilt that
turns into fear, less of a strangely calm, eloquent, dark-skinned
man not yet fifty, but of even symbolic reckoning for four hundred
years of racist crime.

But the specter of a McCain presidency, with Sarah Palin waiting in the wings—a Dominionist, which is to say she believes, and
entered politics to ensure, that her God by right has and by her

hand will enjoy dominion over every aspect of life in the United States—seems monstrous also because it promises, at best, in merely practical terms, to wreck the country, if not to erase it, leaving the Constitution the dead letter Bush and Cheney have worked to make it, acting, throughout their terms, as if it already were. The country that as it has for more than 200 years struggled both to escape and live up to its charter is still recognizable, but there have always been Americans who never recognized that America, and McCain now stands for them.

What sort of president might Barack Obama be ("If," in the thought that crosses so many minds if not so many mouths, "he lives")? The presidency changes people; there is no way of telling. He might be ground down, his gift for speaking of complex things in a complex way that sounds like ordinary talk breaking up into catch-phrases and clichés, as on the campaign trail in its last days, Obama like McCain repeating the same lines hour after hour until even he must be nearly choking over the way a truth can feel like a lie. Or he might, with a carriage and a way with words that makes comparisons with John F. Kennedy seem to flatter Kennedy, not him, again plant seeds of possibility that anyone might harvest.

There are also comparisons to Lincoln, and these map the desert Obama as president would have to cross. "Instead of glory, he once said," the historian Richard Hofstadter wrote of Lincoln, "he found only 'ashes and blood.'" For the moment, for the country, perhaps for Obama too, that would be reward enough.

ELECTION NIGHT
GQ Style March 2009/
Black Clock 2010

"It's been a long time comin', but—" So said Barack Obama in the first moments of his victory speech in Grant Park in Chicago on election night, calling on Sam Cooke along with the other familiars—Abraham Lincoln, Martin Luther King, Jr.—he invisibly but unmistakably gathered to his side. "If you ever hear me sing 'A Change Is Gonna Come,'" Rod Stewart once said of Cooke's song, released in late December 1964, just after Cooke was shot to death outside a motel in Watts, "you'll know my career will be over"—because, Stewart seemed to imply, he would not be able to look an audience in the face after failing to live up to the song. But Obama had more confidence—or, because he was perhaps testifying that, not four years old when "A Change Is Gonna Come" first aired on the radio, he had lived out his life under the shadow of the song, had carried it with him like a manifesto, Obama was asserting that he could not only sing the song, in his own way, in his own cadence, but rewrite it. "But I know, a change gone come," Cooke sang. "Change has come to America," Obama said. *Did* he *really do that? Did* Sam Cooke *really do that?*

I wasn't in Chicago that night. I was in Minneapolis, in Northrop Auditorium at the University of Minnesota, in the audience, as Bob Dylan played for the first time on the campus of his erstwhile alma mater. The second song was "The Times They Are A-Changin'," from the year before "A Change Is Gonna Come," a song I've never liked. It always seemed as if it were written by the times, which is to say it felt like a manifesto written by a committee, or commissioned by one. But on this night so much history was loaded into the song it was impossible not to be sucked into its gravity.

Dylan paced the song with space between the words, the rhythm the steps of someone making his way through an empty mansion with both care and dread. It was as if the song, or the history it carried, was moving in slow motion, carrying—as Obama would say later in the night of a 106-year-old voter named Ann Nixon Cooper, "born just a generation past slavery"—not only the history the song was made to celebrate—"She was there for the buses in Montgomery, the hoses in Birmingham, a bridge in Selma, and a preacher from Atlanta who told a people 'we shall overcome'"—but the history that remained to be made: the history that the song and those present to hear it would witness as it and they had witnessed what had come before.

But it was more than that. As Dylan took all of the triumphalism out of the song, the cheering, the defiance, all of the easy ride the song had promised when it first appeared, he turned it into a kind of dirge. He divided history in two: the time the song had, now, outlasted, and the time that would, now, test it. As a dirge the song became a warning: in the past, the people listening had or had not made the history the song spoke for, but now they would have to make it, or fail the song just as Rod Stewart believed he would fail "A Change Is Gonna Come."

The last song of the night was "Blowin' in the Wind," another song I've never liked, another song that, this night, for me rang a bell it never had before—even if it was, as Sam Cooke himself stated plainly, the song that inspired him to write "A Change Is Gonna Come." "I was born in 1941," Dylan said just before he began the number. "That was the year they bombed Pearl Harbor. I've been living in a world of darkness ever since. But it looks like things are going to change now." I only caught the last line; when the song ended, everyone crowded into the Northrop lobby, under a giant television screen tuned to CNN. It was ten o'clock, just as the polls closed in California, just as the anchorman over our heads announced that Barack Obama had been elected president of the United States. Dylan had not gone a minute past where he knew the show had to end.

What happened then, all over the country, and all over the world—people shouting through their tears—is not unrelated to the way Obama was able to call up "A Change Is Gonna Come" as he spoke that night. It is not unrelated to the sense of authority that has surrounded Obama since. Almost always, when someone is elected president of the United States, whether it is someone you supported or someone you opposed, it takes a long time before the attachment of the word *president* to that person's name begins to sound even remotely real, and with Obama that was not true on election night and it has not been true since. That is, I think, because of the way he speaks—a manner for which the word eloquence is merely pretty, and hollow.

It's the ability to speak of complex things to large numbers of people in a way that neither compromises the complexity of what the speaker means to say nor insults the intelligence of those who are listening—to speak in a manner that itself attunes those who are listening to their own complexity. I am thinking of Obama's speech on race, from March 18 of last year, when controversy over statements and sermons by the Rev. Jeremiah Wright threatened to derail his campaign—a thirty-seven-minute address that gathered listeners as if around a campfire—but I am also thinking of a scene from John Ford's 1939 film *Young Mr. Lincoln* as described in *Short Letter, Long Farewell,* a novel published by Peter Handke in 1972.

The narrator, a young Austrian in America, goes to a theater. Lincoln, played by Henry Fonda, has agreed to defend two brothers accused of murder; a drunken mob arrives at the jail to lynch them, and Lincoln faces it down. He talks; he captures the drunks, the narrator says in wonder and awe, not missing the flicker of an eyelash, the turn of a vowel, "by softly reminding them of themselves, of what they were, what they could be, and what they had forgotten. This scene—Lincoln on the wooden steps of the jailhouse, with his hand on the battering ram—embodied every possibility of human behavior. In the end not only the drunks, but also the actors playing the drunks, were listening intently to Lincoln, and when he had finished they dispersed, changed forever. All around me in the theater I felt the audience breathing differently and coming to life again." That is what eloquence is too weak a word for: speech that is not only about democracy, but that is itself democratic.

In *The Human Stain,* published in 2000, Philip Roth tells the story of Coleman Silk, a seventy-two-year-old man from an African-American family from East Orange, New Jersey, who has passed as a Jew—that is, as a white man—his entire adult life. Reading the novel now, one can hardly avoid imagining Barack Obama into its pages, not because he ever passed or ever could, but because as an African-American he seems to have invented himself as absolutely as does Coleman Silk. "What do we really know about this man?" John McCain asked throughout the fall campaign, and even without the innuendo—was he a Muslim, a communist, somehow a terrorist?—the question hit home because it was about something real. Obama's very ease in his own skin, his apparent immunity from slurs and lies—like Jackie Robinson in his ability to trust in his own gifts and never betray his own rage at the slurs and lies that by election day had at Republican rallies become a torrent of hate, with crowds shouting "Traitor!" and "Kill him!" at the mention of his name—spoke for, as Roth wrote of Coleman Silk, "the democratic invitation to throw your origins overboard if to do so contributes to the pursuit of happiness." Obama seems like his own creation: that is the source of his aura, the sense of self-command that draws people to him, and it is at least partly the sense that he is not quite real, not quite human, that terrifies, or sickens, others. The self-made American embodies America, a nation that was itself made up—"Every day," Roth wrote, "you woke up to be what you had made yourself"—but the self-made American is also a kind of Frankenstein.

The banner headline on the front page of the *New York Times* the day after the election was queer in its affirmation of what the election had been about: RACIAL BARRIER FALLS IN HEAVY TURNOUT. As a self-invented American, one who could claim the history of the Civil Rights movement, as in his litany of place names from Montgomery to Atlanta, without excluding anyone from that history, Obama did not run as someone who had set himself against a racial barrier. A particular individual set himself a goal and achieved it; America was not less racist the day after the election than it was the day before it. But perhaps what was wrong about the headline was that it spoke in terms that were too narrow, too small, too merely functional for what had actually occurred.

The country may not have changed, but its history did. It rewrote itself. For as a friend said, "Blowin' in the Wind," Bob Dylan's last word on election night, was not just "Blowin' in the

Wind." It was also the song Dylan has long said he "took it off," "a spiritual," a song that dates to the Civil War, a song Lincoln might have heard, but not likely ever sang—as, one night in Greenwich Village, in a performance of an empathy so great it might better be called transubstantiation, a Jew in 1962, turning himself into an African-American in 1862, Bob Dylan sang the song: "No More Auction Block."

CODA

ACKNOWLEDGMENTS

This book covers work written over more than forty years, but the conversations behind it go back further than that—to whenever it was that any given person heard Bob Dylan or heard of him, or for that matter first heard or was forced to sing a folk song, or heard a rock 'n' roll record on the radio, or fell in love with the myths of American history even as one suspected that no story could be quite so perfect as America made its story out to be. But sooner or later Bob Dylan was a focal point. He has always been someone who you couldn't not have an opinion about. The people named here— friends, chance acquaintances, colleagues, fellow-travelers, editors, teachers, students—talked, argued, went to concerts and shouted for more or wondered when it would be over, listened to records and traded tapes, wrote and published, cursed and celebrated, told stories and spread rumors, made judgments they lived to regret or in some cases didn't, but in all ways were generous, querulous, open, suspicious, disbelieving that you hadn't yet heard, read, seen, and convincing that you had to hear it, read it, see it, right now. I'm glad our paths crossed, and glad that in so many cases they still do: Nick Amster, Doon Arbus, Gina Arnold, the late Richard Avedon, the late Lester Bangs, the late John Bauldie, Sara Beck, Erik Bernstein, Joel Bernstein, Paula Bernstein, Sara Bernstein, William Bernstein, Gérard Beréby and François Escaig of Editions Allia, Dean Blackwood and Susan Archie of Revenant Records, the late Adam Block, Liz Bordow, Betsey Bowden, Meredith Brody, Bart Bull, Sarah Bures, Robert Cantwell, Bob Carlin, Robert Christgau, Joe Christiano, Pete Ciccione, T. J. Clark, Mary Clemmey, Joshua Clover, Frances Coady and James Meader of Picador USA, John Cohen, Emmanuelle Collas of Galaade Editions, Elvis Costello, Jonathan Cott, Sue D'Alonzo, Mike Daly, the late Sandy Darlington, Don DeLillo, Maddie Deutch, Carola Dibbell, Julia Dorner, Elizabeth

Dunn-Ruiz, Danielle Durbin, Monte and Kathy Edwardson, Steve Erickson, expectingrain.com, Barry Franklin, Hal Foster, Ken Friedman, Simon Frith, David Gans, B. George, Courtney Gildersleeve, the late Charlie Gillett, Evan Glasson, the late Ralph J. Gleason, Tony Glover, Jeff Gold, Joan Goodwin, Mike Gordon, Peter Guralnick, Marybeth Hamilton, Howard Hampton, Clinton Heylin, Niko Hansen and Birgit Polityki of Rogner and Bernhard, Todd Haynes, Bob Hocking and Linda Stroback-Hocking, Amy Horowitz, Jeff Place and Andras Goldinger of Smithsonian Folkways, Glenn Howard, Garth Hudson, Maud Hudson, Rose Idlet of Black Ace Books, the late Norman Jacobson, Michael Jennings, Steve Jepsen, Loyal Jones, Branden Joseph, the late Pauline Kael, the late Ed Kahn, Jim Kavanagh, Kalen Keir, the late Stewart Kessler, Russ Ketter, Brent Kite, Al Kooper, Doug Kroll, Carol Krueger, Tony Lacey of Penguin, Jon Landau, Elliott Landy, Jon Langford, Mark Lilla, Daniel Marcus, Steve Marcus, the late William Marcus, Brice Marden, Dave Marsh, James Marsh, Paula Matthews, Sharyn McCrumb, Paul Metsa, Linda Mevorach, Jim Miller, Bruce Miroff, Toru Mitsui, John Morthland, Colin B. Morton, Paul Muldoon, the late Paul Nelson (at right), Bob Neuwirth, Matthew Noyes, Michael Oliver-Goodwin, Donn Pennebaker, Sherri Phillips, Michael Pisaro, Robert Polito, Beth Puchtel, Scott Puchtel, Kit Rachlis, Kyle Rafferty,  Robert Ray, Kevin Reilly, Christopher Ricks, Jon Riley, Robbie Robertson, John Rockwell, the late Michael Rogin, the late B. J. Rolfzen, Mary Rome, Cynthia Rose, David Ross, Peggy Ross, Luc Sante, Jon Savage, John Schaar, Fritz Schneider, Matthew Schneider-Mayerson, Beth Schwartzapfel, the late Mike Seeger, Joel Selvin, the late Greg Shaw, Christine Sheu, Cameron Siewert, Rani Singh, Alexia Smith, Brett Sparks, Rennie Sparks, Bruce Springsteen, Peter Stampfel, Bob Steiner, Jim Storey, Bill Strachan, Tracy Brown, Jack Macrae and Katy Hope of Henry Holt, Steve Strauss, Sara Stroud, Elisabeth Sussman, Sandy Tait, Marisa Tam, Charles Taylor, Pat Thomas, Caitlin Thompson, Ray Thompson, Greg Tomeoni, Ken Tucker, Gerard van der Leun (who one day in 1968 passed me a basement tapes cassette on a Berkeley street corner as if we were conducting a dope deal), Lin van Heuit, Richard Vaughn, Amy Vecchione, Eric Vigne of Folio, Sarah Vowell, Ed Ward, Lindsay Waters, Lydia Wegman, Janet Weiss, the late Bill Whitehead, Benjamin Wiggins, Sean Wilentz, Hal Willner, Langdon Winner, Lori Ann Woltner, Ian Woodward, Todd Wright, Stephanie Zacharek, and Michael Zilkha.

I thank all those who helped see the work collected here into print: at the *San Francisco Express Times* (later *Good Times*), the late Sandy Darlington, Marvin Garson, and Joyce Mancini; at *Rolling Stone,* over the years from 1968 to the present, Jann Wenner (from before *Self Portrait* and on from there, but especially for his understanding my contribution to the issue on the 2001 mass murders in an instant), John Burks, Ben Fong-Torres, Robert Kingsbury, Barbara Downey Landau, Christine Doudna, Sarah Lazin, David Young, Terry McDonell, Susan Brenneman, Anthony DeCurtis, Robert Love, Joe Levy, Ally Lewis, and Nathan Brackett; at *Creem,* Dave Marsh, the late Barry Kramer, the late Connie Kramer, and Deday LaRene; at the *New York Times,* the late Seymour Peck, John Darnton, Martin Arnold, Olive Evans, and John Rockwell, who found the piece I was trying to hide inside a review of *"Love and Theft";* at *City,* John Burks; at the *Village Voice,* Robert Christgau, Richard Goldstein, and Doug Simmons; at *San Francisco Focus,* Heidi Benson; at *New West* (later *California*), Jon Carroll, Nancy Friedman, Janet Duckworth, Bill Broyles, and B. K. Moran; at *Artforum,* Ingrid Sischy, David Frankel, Robin Cembalest, Ida Panicelli, Jack Bankowsky, Sydney Pokorny, Melissa Harris, and Anthony Korner; at *Threepenny Review,* always a port in a storm, Wendy Lesser; at *Image* (later *San Francisco Examiner Magazine*), Paul Wilner; at *Interview,* Ingrid Sischy, Graham Fuller, and Brad Goldfarb; at *Salon,* Bill Wyman and Gary Kamiya; at the *Los Angeles Times Book Review,* Steve Wasserman and Tom Curwen; at *Nouvelle Revue Française,* Michel Braudeau; at *Granta,* Liz Jobey and Sophie Harrison; at the *East Bay Express,* Michael Covino; at *City*

Pages, Steve Perry, Will Hermes, Terri Sutton, Jim Walsh, Michael Tortorello, and Melissa Maerz; at *Mojo,* Paul Trynka and Andrew Male; at *Black Clock,* Steve Erickson; at *GQ Style,* David Annand.

I thank as well those who gave me the chance to tell many of the stories I found in public: Tom Luddy, Gary Meyer, and Julie Huntsinger of the Telluride Film Festival; Jerome McGann and Eric Lott at the University of Virginia; Akeel Bilgrami at Columbia University; M. Richard Zinman at Michigan State University; Rabbi Alan Berg at Temple Beth El in San Mateo; Mary E. Davis at Case Western in Cleveland, with Warren Zanes and James Henke at the Rock & Roll Hall of Fame; Eric Weisbard, Ann Powers, and Robert Santelli at the Experience Music Project in Seattle; Colleen Sheehy for heroic work at the Weisman Art Museum at the University of Minnesota; John Harris and Thomas Crow at the J. Paul Getty Museum in Los Angeles; Karen Kelly and Evelyn McDonnell at the Dia Center for the Arts in New York; Ben Saunders at Duke University; for the events commemorating the Free Speech Movement in Berkeley, the late Michael Rossman; Ramona Naddaff at the University of California at Berkeley; Robert Batscha at the Museum of Television and Radio in New York; the late Harvey Weinstein and Pamela Johns of the Dorothy and Lillian Gish Foundation in New York; Lawrence Weschler at the New York Institute for the Humanities; Margaret O'Neill of the Walker Art Center in Minneapolis; Zebrock in Paris; Heather O'Donnell at Princeton; Mark Francis at the Centre Pompidou in Paris; Robert Parks at the Morgan Library in New York; Adele Lander Burke at the Skirball Cultural Center in Los Angeles; Steve Weiss of the Southern Folklife Collection at the University of North Carolina in Chapel Hill; Barry Sarchett at Colorado College in Colorado Springs; Grazia Quaroni, Isabelle Guadefroy, Alaín Dominique Perrin, and Sophie Perceval at the Fondation Cartier de l'art contemporain in Paris; James Cushing at Cal Poly in San Luis Obispo; Toby Kamps of the Contemporary Arts Museum in Houston; Andrea Veyaveeran at the Graduate Center for the Humanities in New York; Michael Lesy, Ralph Hexter, and Norman Holland at Hampshire College in Amherst; Jay Bonner of the

Asheville School in Asheville; Liam Kennedy of the Clinton Center for American Studies at University College, Dublin.

I thank those who let me find my themes, and hear so much I would never have thought of myself, in the semipublic of a seminar room or a lecture hall: at the University of California at Berkeley, Kathleen Moran and Carolyn Porter, many times over; at Princeton, Sean Wilentz, Carol Rigolot, Anthony Grafton, and Judith Ferszt; at the University of Minnesota, Ann Waltner, Paula Rabinowitz, David Weissbrodt, Barbara Lhenhoff, and Nicole Tollefson; at the New School in New York, Robert Polito, Laura Cronk, Leah Iannone, Nicholas Nienaber, Luis Jaramillo, and Lori Lynn Turner.

I've been lucky to spend years of hours in record stores and book stores: Record City, where from 1963 to 1965 you could find same-day tickets to Bob Dylan's Berkeley Community Theatre shows, where I bought *Magic Bus—The Who on Tour,* the first record I ever reviewed, and where I came across an album with a dramatic cover called *King of the Delta Blues Singers;* Moe's Books, which for years featured an elegant *Royal Albert Hall* bootleg; Rather Ripped, where the most commonplace item could seem unlikely; Asta's, named for Nick and Nora's dog; Down Home Music, with its vast caverns of obscurity; Amoeba Records, a fan's paradise from the day it opened. The office of Bob Dylan Music has itself been a kind of record store, not only for tickets and records so warmly and generously provided, but for the kind of *I can't believe you haven't heard* talk that goes on in record stores, or ought to; it's a pleasure to thank Debbie Sweeney, Diane Lapson, Robert Bower, April Hayes, Callie Gladman, and Lynn Okin Sheridan—and, for his keen understanding of metaphysics, Jeff Rosen.

As twice before, Clive Priddle of PublicAffairs has been an editor with a sharpening sense of where a book is in a manuscript; working with him is always gratifying, as it is with Susan Weinberg, Melissa Raymond, Tessa Shanks, Jessica Campbell, Robert Kimzey, Christine Marra, Jane Raese, and Gray Cutler. I hope a long relationship with Lee Brackstone at Faber and Faber will only be longer; my thanks there go as well to Helen Francis and Kate

Burton. I have relied on the friendliness, responsiveness, and judgment of Wendy Weil, Emily Forland, and Emma Paterson at the Wendy Weil Agency, of Anthony Goff at the David Higham Agency in London, the late Mary Kling of La nouvelle agence in Paris, and Christian Dittus and Peter Fritz of the Paul and Peter Fritz Agency in Zurich.

Emily and Cecily have been a constant presence in this book almost from the time the first piece in it was written, and Steve Perry, first as an editor, then as a friend, then as a family member, for more than twenty-five years. But Jenny was there from almost before I first heard of Bob Dylan, and as a girl from St. Paul, she already had.

LYRIC AND ILLUSTRATION CREDITS

Lyric and Poetry Credits*

"Don't Ya Tell Henry" copyright © 1971 by Dwarf Music; renewed 1999 by Dwarf Music. All rights reserved. International copyright secured. Used by permission.

"Sign on the Window" copyright © 1970 by Big Sky Music; renewed 1998 by Big Sky Music. All rights reserved. International copyright secured. Used by permission.

"Watching the River Flow" copyright © 1971 by Big Sky Music; renewed 1999 by Big Sky Music. All rights reserved. International copyright secured. Used by permission.

"Buckets of Rain" copyright © 1974 by Ram's Horn Music; renewed 2002 by Ram's Horn Music.
All rights reserved. International copyright secured. Used by permission.

"Idiot Wind" copyright © 1974 by Ram's Horn Music; renewed 2002 by Ram's Horn Music. All rights reserved. International copyright secured. Used by permission.

"You're a Big Girl Now" copyright © 1974 by Ram's Horn Music; renewed 2002 by Ram's Horn Music. All rights reserved. International copyright secured. Used by permission.

"Is Your Love in Vain?" copyright © 1978 by Special Rider Music. All rights reserved. International copyright secured. Used by permission.

"Señor" copyright © 1978 by Special Rider Music. All rights reserved. International copyright secured. Used by permission.

"Precious Angel" copyright © 1979 by Special Rider Music. All rights reserved. International copyright secured. Used by permission.

"Blind Willie McTell" copyright © 1983 by Special Rider Music. All rights reserved. International copyright secured. Used by permission.

"The Times They Are A-Changin'" copyright © 1963, 1964 by Warner Bros. Inc.; renewed 1991, 1992 by Special Rider Music. All rights reserved. International copyright secured. Used by permission.

All songs not otherwise credited by Bob Dylan.

Illustration Credits

INDEX

ABOUT THE AUTHOR

Greil Marcus is the author of *When That Rough God Goes Riding* and *Like a Rolling Stone* (both with PublicAffairs), *The Old Weird America, The Shape of Things to Come, Mystery Train, Dead Elvis, In the Fascist Bathroom*, and other books; a twentieth anniversary edition of his *Lipstick Traces* was published in 2009. With Werner Sollors he is the editor of *A New Literary History of America*, published by Harvard University Press. Since 2000 he has taught at Berkeley, Princeton, Minnesota, and the New School in New York; his column Real Life Rock Top 10 appears regularly in the *Believer*. He lives in Berkeley.

PUBLICAFFAIRS is a publishing house founded in 1997. It is a tribute to the standards, values, and flair of three persons who have served as mentors to countless reporters, writers, editors, and book people of all kinds, including me.

I. F. STONE, proprietor of *I. F. Stone's Weekly,* combined a commitment to the First Amendment with entrepreneurial zeal and reporting skill and became one of the great independent journalists in American history. At the age of eighty, Izzy published *The Trial of Socrates,* which was a national bestseller. He wrote the book after he taught himself ancient Greek.

BENJAMIN C. BRADLEE was for nearly thirty years the charismatic editorial leader of *The Washington Post.* It was Ben who gave the *Post* the range and courage to pursue such historic issues as Watergate. He supported his reporters with a tenacity that made them fearless, and it is no accident that so many became authors of influential, best-selling books.

ROBERT L. BERNSTEIN, the chief executive of Random House for more than a quarter century, guided one of the nation's premier publishing houses. Bob was personally responsible for many books of political dissent and argument that challenged tyranny around the globe. He is also the founder and was the longtime chair of Human Rights Watch, one of the most respected human rights organizations in the world.

.   .   .

For fifty years, the banner of Public Affairs Press was carried by its owner, Morris B. Schnapper, who published Gandhi, Nasser, Toynbee, Truman, and about 1,500 other authors. In 1983 Schnapper was described by *The Washington Post* as "a redoubtable gadfly." His legacy will endure in the books to come.

Peter Osnos, *Founder and Editor-at-Large*